INSIGHT GUIDE

GLASGOW

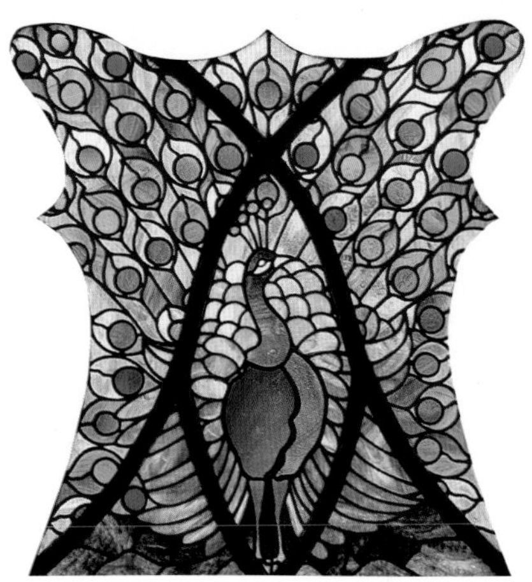

Part of the Langenscheidt Publishing Group

About This Book

Editorial
Project Editor
Brian Bell
Principal Photographer
Douglas Corrance
Updated by
Hugh Taylor and Moira McCrossan

Distribution

UK & Ireland
GeoCenter International Ltd
The Viables Centre, Harrow Way
Basingstoke, Hants RG22 4BJ
Fax: (44) 1256-817988

United States
Langenscheidt Publishers, Inc.
46–35 54th Road, Maspeth, NY 11378
Fax: (1) 718 784-0640

Canada
Thomas Allen & Son Ltd
390 Steelcase Road East
Markham, Ontario L3R 1G2
Fax: (1) 905 475 6747

Australia
Universal Press
1 Waterloo Road
Macquarie Park, NSW 2113
Fax: (61) 2 9888 9074

New Zealand
Hema Maps New Zealand Ltd (HNZ)
Unit D, 24 Ra ORA Drive
East Tamaki, Auckland
Fax: (64) 9 273 6479

Worldwide
Apa Publications GmbH & Co. Verlag KG (Singapore branch)
38 Joo Koon Road, Singapore 628990
Tel: (65) 865-1600. Fax: (65) 861-6438

Printing

Insight Print Services (Pte) Ltd
38 Joo Koon Road, Singapore 628990
Tel: (65) 865-1600. Fax: (65) 861-6438

First Edition 1990
Third Edition 2001

CONTACTING THE EDITORS

We would appreciate it if readers would alert us to errors or outdated information by writing to:
Insight Guides, P.O. Box 7910, London SE1 1WE, England.
Fax: (44) 20 7403-0290.
insight@apaguide.demon.co.uk

www.insightguides.com

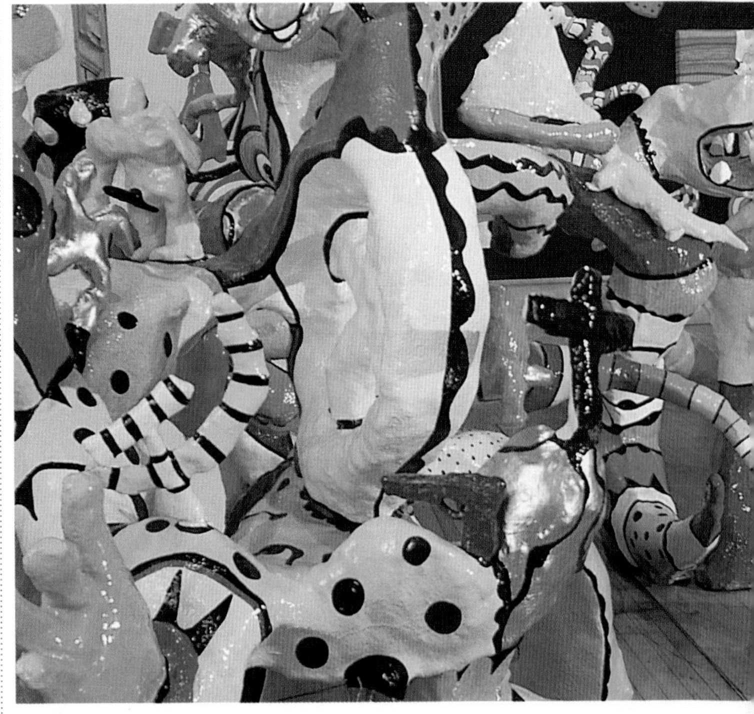

This guidebook combines the interests and enthusiasms of two of the world's best known information providers: Insight Guides, whose range of titles has set the standard for visual travel guides since 1970, and Discovery Channel, the world's premier source of nonfiction television programming.

The editors of Insight Guides provide both practical advice and general understanding about a destination's history, culture, institutions and people. Discovery Channel and its celebrated Web site, www.discovery.com, help millions of viewers to explore their world from the comfort of their own home and encourage them to explore it first hand.

How to use this book

This fully updated edition of *Insight Guide: Glasgow* is structured to convey an understanding of the city and its culture as well as to guide readers through its sights and activities:

- ◆ The **Features** section covers the history and culture of the city in a series of lively essays by local experts.
- ◆ The main **Places** section gives a detailed guide to all the sights and areas worth visiting. Places of special interest are coordinated by number with the maps.

Above: viewing the McLellan Galleries

◆ The **Travel Tips** listings section provides a convenient reference section filled with information on travel, hotels, restaurants, shops and more. Information may be located quickly by using the index printed on the back cover flap – while the flaps themselves are designed to act as convenient bookmarks.

The contributors

This new edition of *Insight Guide: Glasgow* was thoroughly updated by **Hugh Taylor** and **Moira McCrossan**, two Scottish-based travel writers who work regularly for a variety of newspapers, magazines and the BBC. They have written several guidebooks, including two about Scotland, and have contributed to many others. Taylor also contributed two new features, on folk music and on the literary scene, plus two one-page panels, on shopping and Alexander "Greek" Thomson.

The updaters built on the solid foundations of earlier editions. These were laid principally by **Marcus Brooke**, who wrote the entire Places section, as well as the chapters on "Glaswegians All" and the performing arts, and panels on Glasgow's reinvention, the "patter", Charles Rennie Mackintosh, the Citizens' Theatre, and golf. Having lived in various parts of the world, Brooke, a regular contributor to Insight Guides, has now returned to his native Glasgow, and he provided some new photography for this edition.

The introductory chapter on "The Glasgow Character" was written by **Brian Bell**, Insight Guides' editorial director, and the chapters tracing the city's turbulent history by **Julie Davidson**, a leading Scottish journalist.

Naomi May, a Glasgow-born writer and artist, wrote "The Visual Arts", an area in which Glasgow is especially strong, and local journalist **Jack McLean** demonstrated his knowledge of "Pub Culture" as well as writing the panels on tenement living and comedian Billy Connolly.

Glasgow's *Herald* has long been staffed by expert newspapermen and one of them, **Ian Paul**, wrote on another of the city's eternal obsessions, football. Another, **Anne Simpson**, summed up "Glasgow Chic".

Dominating the book's visual style is top Scottish photographer **Douglas Corrance**, whose many books include *The Eye in the Sky*, a photographic record of Glasgow from the air.

Elizabeth Cook compiled the index.

Map Legend

– – – –	County Boundary
●	National Park/Reserve
Ⓜ	Underground
✈ ✈	Airport: International/ Regional
🚌	Bus Station
ℹ	Tourist Information
✉	Post Office
† †	Church/Ruins
†	Monastery
☪	Mosque
✡	Synagogue
♜	Castle/Ruins
🏛	Mansion/Stately home
∴	Archaeological Site
Ω	Cave
𝐈	Statue/Monument
★	Place of Interest

The main places of interest in the Places section are coordinated by number with a full-colour map (e.g. ❶), and a symbol at the top of every right-hand page tells you where to find the map.

CONTENTS

Maps

Introduction

History

Features

Kelvingrove Art Gallery

Information panels

Travel Tips

♦ **Full Travel Tips index is on page 257**

Places

BASSOON CLARINET MASTER BANDON VIOLIN

to open
to open
to open
to open

'IF YOU'VE GOT IT...'

Glasgow has always refused to be knocked down and, as its industrial heyday recedes, it is busy reinventing itself

The Scottish Lowlands is divided into west and east almost as rigorously by character as by geography. Easterners regard themselves as people of taste and refinement, appropriately reflected in the ordered glory of Georgian Edinburgh. They approve of the city's sobriquet "Athens of the North". Just 40 miles (64 km) away, the westerners of industrial Glasgow consider themselves warm-hearted, less pretentious and more realistic than the scions of the Scottish capital. It has often been remarked that Glasgow's ambience is closer to that of an American city than any other metropolis in Britain ("If you've got it, flaunt it!").

Like most long-cherished generalities, such comparisons do contain a grain of truth. There is something austere in Edinburgh's beauty and this, at times, is reflected in the restrained nature of its citizens. Glaswegians, by contrast, are ebullient and demonstrative, with a black, sardonic humour nurtured by the hard times that arrived as the city's industrial base, which helped power the British Empire, weakened in the 20th century.

Culturally, Edinburgh flaunts its annual arts festival, the world's biggest. But Glaswegians point out that they don't need this annual binge – *their* culture is vibrant for 12 months of the year.

Until recently that vibrancy was enjoyed chiefly by locals, and Glaswegians are still getting used to the idea of visitors from abroad actually wanting to come and see their city. Its reputation as a dour, violent slum persisted for so long that there is almost a measure of gratitude in the welcome for outsiders who appreciate it. The defining moment in Glasgow's recent past was its selection in 1990 as European City of Culture, an accolade that came right on the heels of the enormously successful Garden Festival in 1988. There was a certain economic and social drift throughout the 1990s, but winning the title of UK City of Architecture and Design in 1999 provided a fresh impetus as people planned for a new millennium.

As well as the architectural heritage bestowed by such giants as Charles Rennie Mackintosh and Alexander "Greek" Thomson, Glasgow can offer the visitor a remarkable range of art – the Kelvingrove Art Gallery and Museum, the Burrell Collection and the Hunterian Art Gallery are just three world-class venues. Scottish Opera is also world-class, and the Citizens' Theatre is renowned for its inconoclastic drama. There are more than 70 parks and, when it rains, the shopping opportunities are legendary. It's not hard to feel as enthusiastic about the city as Glaswegians themselves do. ❑

PRECEDING PAGES: an Orange Order band; antiques shop in the city's West End; a night out at the Scottish Exhibition and Conference Centre; young Glasgow at play.
LEFT: a big day in Blythswood Square.

UP YER KILT
WHERE ELSE

THE GLASGOW CHARACTER

"They can have life-long friendships in which the only time a civil word is spoken is at funerals – which, incidentally, they enjoy hugely too"

"There's a lightness about the town, without heavy industry," said the Glasgow-born comedian Billy Connolly. "It's as if they've discovered how to work the sun-roof, or something."

Connolly's attitude conjures up the true spirit of Glaswegian resilience. Yesterday, soap-box orators raged against the hardships brought about by the closure of so many factories; today, they celebrate new opportunities, spicing their pronouncements with a characteristic dash of the surreal. The title of an academic study of Glasgow's regeneration hit the right melodramatic note: *The City That Refused To Die*.

Glasgow, in its industrial heyday, was known as the second city of the British Empire. Yet, paradoxically, it has also been called the least British of British cities. It has great vitality, but not a refined vitality. It is warm and vibrant, but not subtle. It likes to show itself off. It is in every sense Scottish and in no sense English. Because of its brashness, its nose for new trends and its willingness to experiment, it reminds many of an American city.

It is, for some, an acquired taste. One rather reserved visitor from the south of England, taken aback by the nosiness and apparent aggression of Glaswegians, suggested that, if the city were searching for a soul-mate overseas with which it might conclude a twinning arrangement, it need look no further than Tel Aviv.

Family feud

Self-assertion, of course, is often the flip-side of insecurity, a feeling fostered by many years of toffee-nosed sniping from its equally self-regarding sibling, Edinburgh – the "Athens of the North", just 40 miles (64 km) away to the east. The European Community unwittingly enflamed this interminable family feud by naming Glasgow as European City of Culture for 1990. The only people more surprised than the citizens of Edinburgh were the citizens of Glasgow.

LEFT: making music in Buchanan Street.
RIGHT: enjoying a beer in Princes Square.

However, they lost no time in celebrating their Cinderella dream come true – so much so that the poet and biographer Alan Bold likened their reaction to a wave of religious hysteria sweeping all before it. Obliterating its image as "razor city", Glasgow suddenly became God, rather as Liverpool in the 1960s had been declared by

Allen Ginsberg to be "the centre of the universe". It was a concept, said Bold, no more meaningful than the notion that Elvis Lives.

In fact, Glaswegians were simply demonstrating once more that their creed is not that of English understatement, much less that of Edinburgh hauteur, but an echo of the self-made American's maxim: "If you've got it, flaunt it."

For centuries, the ebullience of Glaswegians has either delighted or appalled visitors. In 1767, David Boswell described the city as "a place which I shall ever hold in contempt as being filled with a set of unmannerly, low-bred, narrow-minded wretches; the place itself, however, is really pretty, and were the present inhabitants taken out and drowned in the ocean, and others with generous souls put in their stead, it would be an honour to Scotland."

In 1934 George Blake painted a fairer picture in *The Heart of Scotland.* "This fantastic mixture of racial strains, this collection of survivors from one of the most exacting of social processes, is a dynamo of confident, ruthless, literal energy," he wrote. "The Glasgow man is downright, unpolished, direct, and immediate... He hates pretence, ceremonial, form – and is at the same time capable of the most abysmal sentimentality. He is grave – and one of the world's most devastating humorists."

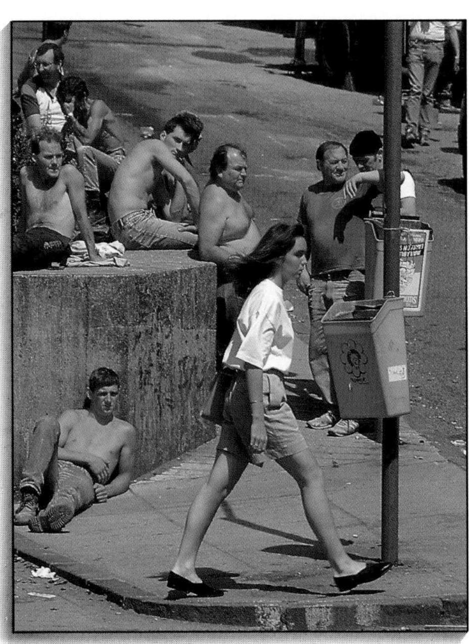

He also seems, to the outsider, to be exceedingly disputatious. In reality, this simply means that he enjoys a good argument. "Glaswegians are naturally scathing about each other and do not take their quarelling seriously," says columnist Jack McLean, a contributor to this book. "They can have life-long friendships in which the only time a civil word is spoken is at funerals – which, incidentally, they enjoy hugely too."

American echoes

But it is to America that most commentators have turned in search of apt comparisons. "Glasgow plays the part of Chicago to Edinburgh's Boston," wrote the inveterate traveller H.V. Morton. "Glasgow is a city of the glad hand and the smack on the back; Edinburgh is a city of silence until birth or brains open the social circle. In Glasgow a man is innocent until he is found guilty; in Edinburgh a man is guilty until he is found innocent. Glasgow is willing to believe the best of an unknown quantity; Edinburgh, the worst."

The grid-like layout of so many city streets also recalls America, and with good reason. For Glasgow, like so many US cities, expanded rapidly, driven in its case by the engine of the Industrial Revolution. "The Clyde made Glasgow and Glasgow made the Clyde" is the saying that best sums up the role played by the river in the city's impulsive development as a port and one of the world's great shipbuilding centres.

And the speed at which it acquired wealth helped determine its character, too. "In its combination of riches and tastelessness upper-class Glasgow is very like the United States," wrote Edwin Muir in *Scottish Journey* in 1935.

But one man's tastelessness is another's zest. For that reason, Glasgow attracts film makers – and not just local boys like Bill Forsyth (*Gregory's Girl*, *Local Hero*). They view the place, as do its natives, as a character in its own right – a star, even.

And yet the iconoclasm in the Glaswegian character can't be suppressed. Although Glaswegians won't hear a word against their city from a foreigner (especially a foreigner from England or Edinburgh), they can be extremely critical of well-meaning attempts to "improve" it. This tendency to denigrate sends tourism officials into an apoplectic rage.

But then perhaps the tourism officials have been set on making the place seem too respectable, too dull. The latest headline proclaiming an influx of foreign visitors will never seem as interesting as the story that begins: "Vandals set fire to drums of anti-vandal chemicals in a storage shed at Bilsland Drive, Glasgow, yesterday."

THE LONG GOODBYE

"At funerals, four rounds of whisky were considered due to wounded affection and departed worth, and respect was shown to the dead by the intoxication of the living."
– Rev. Charles Rogers, 1884

Inferiority complex

The Earl of Glasgow, by profession a television producer and director, said that Glaswegians distrust the word "culture" because of its middle-class associations. "But it is a paradox that a people who had at one time an exaggerated reputation for violent drunkenness on Saturday night can really be so warm, generous and genuinely concerned for strangers as well as for each other. At the same time, they have a pronounced inferiority complex, particularly towards the English, and a humour that is self-deprecating, so that their best jokes are usually against themselves. Glaswegians are very quick and funny, when you can understand what they are saying."

But who cares about image, anyway? Glasgow's attitude towards the judgements of the outside world is summed up in a tale told by Edinburgh journalist George Rosie. Having taken a train to Glasgow at a time when the European City of Culture hype was reaching a crescendo, Rosie was leaving Queen Street Station by taxi when he noticed the archetypal Glaswegian drunk, bottle in hand, throwing up violently into a waste bin.

"What's all that about?" Rosie asked the taxi driver. "I thought you fellows were supposed to be all cultured now."

"Oh we are, we are," replied the cabbie, quick as a flash. "See that coming up there? That's Beaujolais Nouveau." ❑

FAR LEFT: sacred thoughts in Kelvingrove.
LEFT: secular thoughts in the city centre.
ABOVE: stall holder in Paddy's Market.

SPENCER & C°

Decisive Dates

AD 80: The Roman general Agricola builds a line of forts between the Firths of Forth and Clyde. The Clyde valley is occupied by a Celtic tribe, the Damnonii, who begin trading with the Romans.
AD 142: The Romans build the defensive Antonine Wall along the Forth-Clyde line.
AD 211: As the Romans retreat behind Hadrian's Wall, the Damnonii are absorbed into the larger unit of the Britons of Strathclyde.
AD 525: According to popular legend, the infant St Mungo is set adrift with his mother on a boat in the Forth. Raised in a Christian community in Fife, he then goes on to "found" Glasgow by building its first church by the side of the Molendinar Burn.

1015: The old kingdom of Strathclyde becomes part of Scotland under King Malcolm II.
1114–18: Bishop John Achaius begins building Glasgow Cathedral. (It is consecrated in 1136.)
1297: Bishop Wishart of Glasgow organises a brief rebellion against the English King Edward I.
1451: King James II accords the town a "grant of regality" and founds the University of Glasgow – the fourth oldest university in Great Britain.
1560: The Reformation is rubber-stamped by the Scots Parliament. Scotland is now Protestant.
1568: Mary Queen of Scots and her husband, the Earl of Bothwell, are defeated at the Battle of Langside, just outside Glasgow.
1605: Glasgow begins to develop two unique institutions: the Merchants' House, which looked after indigent merchants' families, and the Trades House, which did the same for craftsmen.
1636: Glasgow becomes a royal burgh.
1645: The Marquis of Montrose, harrying Scots Covenanters, enters Glasgow. He attempts to restrain his Highland army from looting by hanging some of the ringleaders.
1652: A fire destroys one-third of the city's housing stock, leaving more than 1,000 families homeless.
1662: The years of the "Killing Time" of the Covenanting Wars begin, and siignificant numbers of Covenanters are executed in Glasgow.
1674: The first recorded cargo of tobacco is imported into the city from Virginia.
1707: The Union of the Parliaments gives Scotland access to the English colonies, and Glasgow's trade with America and the West Indies begins to make the city's fortune.
1715: Progress towards prosperity is briefly interrupted by the Jacobite uprising.
1740: Gentlemen's clubs begin to play a big part in the social lives of the "tobacco lords".
1745: Glasgow remains resolutely anti-Jacobite during the rising under Charles Edward Stuart. The Prince enters the city on his retreat from Derby.
1775: First attempts to improve the navigability of the Clyde are made when the river is deepened up to the Broomielaw quay, in the heart of the city.
1783: Glasgow establishes a "Chamber of Commerce and Manufacturers".
1786: Cotton manufacturer and city benefactor David Dale opens the New Lanark mills and, with the coming of mechanised weaving, the Industrial Revolution gets under way.
1787: Handloom weavers in Calton maintain a four-month strike after manufacturers cut wage rates. Six weavers are killed and many wounded when the military fire on a demonstration.
1812: Henry Bell, a Glasgow engineer, becomes the first man to fit a steam engine to a boat and the *Comet* is launched on the Clyde.
1831: The Glasgow and Garnkirk Railway opens – the first passenger-carrying line in Scotland.
1840: The dredging and enlargement of the Clyde to its present dimensions is completed. Glasgow's role as a major port is assured.
1840s: Glasgow's population is swelled by thousands of Irish immigrants escaping the effects of the potato famine in Ireland.

1848: The Bread Riots, violent confrontations between hungry demonstrators and the military, are one expression of working-class radicalism.
1832 and 1848: Outbreaks of cholera in the city expose the despair and deficiency of Glasgow's slums to outraged social reformers.
1860: The opening of the Loch Katrine reservoir introduces a clean water supply to the city.
1868: Organised football begins with the forming of Queen's Park in 1867, and their first arranged match is played the following year.
1870: The university moves to its present site on Gilmorehill.
1872: Horse-drawn trams are licensed.
1872: The first home international football match between Scotland and England.
1887: Entertainer Harry Lauder makes his first appearance in Glasgow, at the Scotia theatre.
1888: Glasgow's status as "Second City of the Empire" is consolidated by the International Exhibition, visited by Queen Victoria.
1896: The opening of Glasgow District Subway, later to be dubbed "the Clockwork Orange".
1898: The opening of the People's Palace, a museum and cultural centre for the working-class population of the East End.
1899: The opening of Glasgow School of Art building, designed by Charles Rennie Mackintosh.
1901: A second International Exhibition is even more successful than the first.
1914: Suffragettes arm themselves with Indian clubs to resist the arrest of Mrs Pankhurst, who is speaking at St Andrew's Halls. Many are injured.
1915: Independent Labour Party (ILP) leaders make the city the focus of pacifist agitation. Jimmy Maxton and John Wheatley organise a strike of Clyde shipbuilders.
1916: Jimmy Maxton imprisoned after making an anti-war speech on Glasgow Green.
1919: Police and striking shipyard workers clash violently in George Square.
1922: In the General Election, Glasgow returns 10 Independent Labour Party MPs out of 15 seats. The "Red Clydesiders" leave for Westminster.
1931: Work on the *Queen Mary* is suspended, confirming that Glasgow and the Clyde Valley are gripped by the Depression.
1935: Two influential Glasgow novels are published: *The Shipbuilders* and *No Mean City*.

PRECEDING PAGES: *Panoramic View of Glasgow* by James Anderson, dating from around 1835.
LEFT AND RIGHT: two views of the city's crest.

1938: The Empire Exhibition at Bellahouston Park is overshadowed by the prospect of war.
1939: The *Athenia*, sailing from Glasgow to Canada, is torpedoed by a German submarine and becomes the first shipping casualty of the war.
1941: Greenock and Clydebank become the targets of German saturation bombing.
1942: The founding of the Citizens' Theatre.
1946: The Clyde Valley plan prescribes massive slum clearance.
1971: The opening of the Kingston Bridge marks Glasgow's transformation into the "motorway city".
1972: Jimmy Reid leads the "sit-in" at Upper Clyde Shipbuilders' Govan yard.

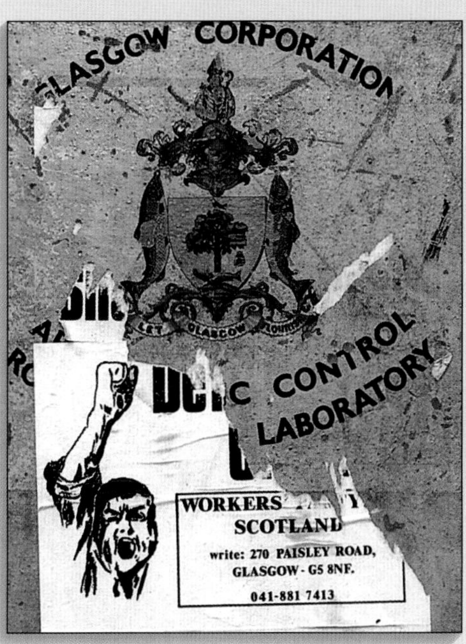

1975: Glasgow becomes part of Strathclyde Region under local government reorganisation.
1976: Glasgow Eastern Area Renewal (GEAR) is an early milestone on the route to renaissance.
1982: Pope John Paul II draws crowd of 250,000.
1983: The founding of the annual Mayfest arts festival points to a new cultural confidence.
1988: The International Garden Festival is held.
1990: Glasgow, somewhat to its citizens' surprise, becomes European City of Culture.
1999: Having won the coveted UK City of Architecture and Design award, Glasgow sets about refurbishing many of its old buildings.
2000: The city's re-birth continues with a series of innovative projects such as the Science Park. ❑

BEGINNINGS

By the 12th century Glasgow had a cathedral, and in the 15th century it underlined its importance by acquiring a university

Glaswegians take much pride in telling you that their city's name means "dear green place", from the Celtic *glas* (green) and *cu* (dear). This incongruous rebuttal of the old, grim industrial image tickles their sense of mischief. But, in fact, there's as much dispute about the genesis of the name as there is about the origins of Glasgow's patron saint, Kentigern or Mungo. This bastard princeling of the Celts was expelled with his dishonoured mother from the Lothians and drifted in an open boat across the Forth to Fife, where he found refuge with an early Christian called St Serf.

The St Mungo legend

The holy man became so fond of the boy that he changed his name from Kentigern to Mungo, "dear one", and sent him forth to convert the barbarians of Strathclyde. (Glaswegians are less inclined to recall that their cheery patron was an East Coast man.) His journey to a rudimentary settlement to the north of the River Clyde was magically effected by two wild bulls yoked to a cart. This, at any rate, is the most straightforward version of the St Mungo legend and places his death at the beginning of the 7th century, conveniently ignoring the fact that St Serf (or Servanus) postdates this period by 200 years.

Further lore concerning Mungo's spiritual talent explains the robin, the tree, the salmon and the ring on Glasgow's coat of arms *(pictured on page 22)*. Each of them is associated with a somewhat homely miracle. He is credited, for example, with raising St Serf's pet robin from the dead after it had been killed by some young thugs; and in a tale of dubious morality St Mungo instructs a salmon to rescue the ring from the Clyde to spare the embarrassment of an adulterous Strathclyde queen.

But few dare challenge the central event of his story: Mungo it was who first established a monastery on the banks of the Molendinar Burn, the modest tributary of the Clyde which the Victorians turned into an underground sewer. And Mungo it was who delivered the sermon which gave Glasgow its early motto: "Let Glasgow flourish by the preaching of the word." These sentiments take an abbreviated form today: "Let Glasgow flourish". This brisk piece of editing, transforming Glasgow's aspirations from the spiritual to the secular, was performed in 1866 by the lawyer who designed the coat of arms, clearly taking his brief from the entrepreneurial spirit of the city's thrusting Victorians.

Although St Mungo gets the credit, Christianity had come to Strathclyde before the Lothian missionary arrived in his bull-cart. It's likely that St Columba's influence on the Scots and northern Picts had extended into Strathclyde by the end of the 6th century, and that the influence of St Ninian, Scotland's first saint, had spread northwards from his Wigtonshire

LEFT: Virginia Colley's painting, *The Legends of St Mungo*, celebrating Glasgow's patron saint.
RIGHT: a 15th-century depiction of St Ninian.

heartland at an even earlier date. It has been argued, in fact, that the story of St Mungo has been confused with the better-documented story of St Ninian, who is said to have founded a cemetery on the site where Glasgow Cathedral later rose – the same site where Mungo built a wooden church.

These vague histories, whether fact or myth, are unlikely to have supplied the only impetus to the construction of the cathedral around 1124 and the consecration of Bishop John Achaius to the see of Glasgow. By then, the community must have had some substance, perhaps even the status of a market town.

Although its original centre was established over half a mile to the north of a salmon-fishing village on the Clyde, the presence of that great waterway and the configuration of its valley gave Glasgow all the natural advantages which seem obvious today.

Another interpretation of the origins of its name suggests *glas cau*, meaning green hollows (according to one scholar, "the correct pronunciation, *Glesca*, is heard daily on the lips of Glaswegians") and the vast bowl of hills which contains the modern city was attractive territory to its earliest settlers: first Stone-Age hunters and fishers, whose relics have been found on the Clyde, then the agriculturalists who began clearing the forests of the valley, and then the first identifiable tribe, the Celtic Damnonii.

By this time the Romans had reached the Clyde, seeking a northern frontier for their province of Britannia. In AD 80 the provincial governor, the general Agricola, built a line of forts between the estuaries of Forth and Clyde as a temporary defence against the wild northern tribes whom the Romans called Caledonians. But before he could pursue his ambition to bring them to heel and occupy the rest of Scotland he was recalled to Rome leaving his fort at Castledykes, near what is now the town of Lanark, to develop trading links with the Druidical Damnonii of the Clyde valley.

Agricola's efforts were followed by the Emperor Hadrian, who had a more modest plan. He decided to write off the northern half of Britannia by building a restraining barrier between the estuaries of the Tyne and Solway, and Hadrian's Wall was raised between AD 122 and 128. Despite its massive stone fortifications, it wasn't strong enough to limit the activities of the tribes to the north and some 20 years later, when Antoninus Pius was emperor, the old Forth-Clyde line of forts was reinforced by a rampart of turf on stone foundations. Today, there are chunks of the Antonine Wall *(see page 231)* to be found at the bottom of the gardens of bungalows in Bearsden, the Glasgow suburb which is a by-word for propriety.

After the Romans

The history of the Clyde valley then disappears into the Dark Ages, although it's known that the Damnonii were absorbed by the tribe of Britons who established the kingdom of Strathclyde, with Dumbarton, on the north bank of the Firth, as their capital. Shafts of light appear with the coming of Christianity and the St Mungo legend, and when that tangle of peoples called Britons, Scots and Picts finally coalesced under King Malcolm II in 1015. About this time something approximating the kingdom of Scotland came into being, with a south-east boundary marked by the River Tweed; and about this time Cleschu, Glasgu' or Glasgow became part of it.

It was not to be conspicuous by its presence for several centuries. Between building its cathedral in the 12th century and opening up trade with the Americas in the 17th, Glasgow's imprint on the military, political, social and commercial history of Scotland was sketchy. Except for a few incidents occuring now and then, it was pretty well by-passed by the bitter internecine conflicts of pre-Reformation Scotland and the running battles with the English. Most of Scotland's early trade, too, was conducted with the Low Countries from the East Coast ports, so its position near the Clyde estuary held no great advantage until British commerce began to look to the west.

It was even protected from the excesses of the sea empire of the Vikings, which was commanded from their base in Orkney. These Norsemen were not just the maurauders of legend. Between the 10th and 13th centuries they attacked and colonised the western and northern seaboards of Scotland, but don't seem to have sailed their longboats up the Clyde as far as Glasgow presumably because the river was too shallow. But the city did have a minor role in Scotland's Wars of Independence. In 1297, when King Edward I of England, the "Hammer of the Scots", began his persistent attempts to impose English rule on Scotland, it was a Glasgow cleric, Bishop Wishart, who organised an early if brief resistance.

WALLACE'S WARS

William Wallace triumphed over an over-confident English force at Stirling Bridge in 1297. But in 1298 England's archers and cavalry easily defeated his spearmen.

William Wallace, the first and arguably the greatest patriot of the Wars of Independence, was born near Glasgow, in Renfrewshire, and in 1305 was betrayed to the English near Glasgow, at Robroyston. Two centuries later an enigmatic balladeer called Blind Harry chronicled his adventures in verse, describing various heroic acts performed in and around Glasgow. But Blind Harry's idea of history is reckoned to owe as much to folklore and his own imagination as it does to authentic record. The same can be said of Mel Gibson's portrayal of Wallace in the 1995 movie *Braveheart*.

LEFT: Hadrian, a Roman ruler with a wall named after him, remembered at the Hunterian Museum. **ABOVE:** David I (left) and Malcolm IV depicted on an 1159 charter.

Glasgow Fair

Despite these interruptions Glasgow prospered steadily during the Middle Ages. The timber cathedral built by Bishop Achaius was consecrated in 1136, and when it was burnt down and destroyed some 50 years later a new cathedral was constructed and re-consecrated by Bishop Jocelin, the influential cleric who also secured a burgh charter from King William the Lion, rubber-stamping Glasgow's status as market town. By 1172 it was significant enough to be called *civitas*, city, in a papal bull and in 1190 the Glasgow Fair became an annual July holiday, making the expanded "Fair Fortnight" holiday of today one of the oldest fixtures in any local calendar.

Medieval Glasgow, like all cathedral towns, developed in the precincts of its church. Only a fragment remains (Provand's Lordship, the 15th-century manse of the Laird of Provan) but the pattern of streets round the cathedral follows much the same ground plan, and eventually it put out feelers towards the Clyde and

brought the salmon-fishing village on its banks into the burgh. Scotland, like England, was very much an agricultural country until the late Middle Ages, and the interface between town and country was less well defined than it is today. All the Scottish burghs were given grants of land along with their charters, and a series of strips of arable land can still be traced in the city's foundations.

It was the function of the burghs to export the produce of coast and country – wool, hides, herring and salmon – and import manufactured goods and other commodities. The salmon-fishing village thus became important to Glasgow, along with the sea lochs of the Firth of Clyde and a considerable acreage of arable lands, commons and crofts. By the 15th century – and whatever the origins of its name – Glasgow was indeed the "dear green place", with commercial rivalry brewing between it and the neighbouring burghs of Rutherglen, Renfrew and Dumbarton, "fort of the Britons", the ancient capital of Strathclyde. The 15th century, however, also ushered in an event which was to guarantee the eclipse of these neighbours. Few could compete with a town which had both cathedral and university.

A university town

Another Glasgow cleric ambitious for his city was Bishop William Turnbull, who persuaded King James II to solicit a papal Bull authorising the founding of the University of Glasgow. In 1451, consequently, a new building rose among the thatched cottages and timbered houses round the cathedral (unlike Edinburgh, Glasgow didn't start building tenements for another four centuries), occupying a site on Rottenrow. Today, this wonderfully named street is sentimentally associated with its eponymous maternity hospital – "going into Rottenrow" has been a key experience for generations of Glasgow mothers – but the origins of the name are more majestic. It derives from the Gaelic *Rat-an-righ*, which means: "road of the king".

The university later moved to the High Street, and was rehoused again in 1870 on Gilmorehill, where the silhouette of the Victorian building now dominates the western skyline. It's the second oldest university in Scotland, pre-dated only by St Andrews, situated on the east coast of Fife, and the two towns rapidly became ecclesiastical as well as academic rivals.

When St Andrews was raised to an archbishopric in 1472, Glasgow set off in pursuit, and with the support of James IV and the Scots parliament won the necessary promotion from the Pope in 1492. This elevation "furthered the good repute and attraction of the western city", even if it "exaggerated the already top-heavy form of the ecclesiastical establishment of Scotland". And Glasgow's future importance – still two centuries away in commercial terms – was assured. ❑

LEFT: St Vincent, a Dominican friar, at work.
RIGHT: James IV (1473–1513) at prayer, from the *Vienna Book of Hours*.

In my
defens

D·G· SCOTIÆ REGINA, GALLIÆ DOTARIA, MAII 17·1568· AVXILII AB ELISABE
SI SPE ET OPINIONE DESCENDIT IN ANGLIAM· VBI CONTRA IVS GEN
IS IVRATI FIDEM, ANNOS VNDEVIGINTI RETENTA, TANDEM HOS
ETHÆ PARRICIDIO CHRISTI MARTYRIBVS ADDITA, SANGV
ITER EFFVSI TESTI- MONIO DEI LEGITIMVM
CLESIÆ ROMANÆ FIDEM PROFESSA, CO
T IN CŒLIS, ILLIS TRIBVS ILLVSTRIOR
VSVM VIOLENTER AMISIT IN TERRIS
EBRVAR 158

DYNASTIC STRUGGLES

While the rest of Scotland reeled from the Reformation's lethal mix of religion and politics, Glasgow's merchants and craftsmen put their trust in trade

Glasgow's quiet consolidation of its status as cathedral city, university town and thriving burgh was not seriously disrupted by the turbulent events of the 16th century, when the Reformation reached Scotland from Europe and a power struggle followed the return of Mary Stuart from France. As a leading ecclesiastical centre, it managed to escape the worst of the violence associated with the religious upheaval, most of which took place in the east. But in 1538, two young preachers of the reformed religion were brought to trial before the Archbishop of Glasgow, Gavin Dunbar.

Dunbar had no appetite for persecution. All over Scotland the accepted sentence for "heretics" was death at the stake. "I think it is better to spare these men, than to put them to death," he said. There is irony here. Today, the heartland of sectarian bigotry in Scotland is Glasgow – a misfortune which didn't befall the city until its social and religious fabric became entangled with that of Ireland in later centuries. But in the 16th century, it seems, Glasgow was a more tolerant place. Dunbar's clemency, however, was overturned by agents of the powerful and sanguinary Archbishop Beaton of St Andrews, who insisted that the preachers be burned.

Criminal offence

Eight years later Beaton himself was murdered and by 1560 Scotland's conversion to the Protestant religion was complete, ratified by Acts of Parliament which abolished the authority of the Pope and made the celebration of Mass a criminal offence. In England, the powers wrested from the Roman Catholic Church passed to the Crown, but in Scotland (more democratically) they became the province of the General Assembly, which was composed of lay and religious members. This meant that the Reformation was never popular with Scottish monarchs, and – with a young Roman Catholic queen poised to reclaim her throne from her regents – the stage was set for a drama which still haunts the Scottish imagination to this day.

It's a drama which has also provided novelists and film-makers with one of their favourite characters: the tragic Queen of Scots, who lost her heart, her throne and her head. And the penultimate act of that drama took place in what is now the respectable inner suburb of Langside, on the south side of Glasgow. Mary's story never fails to recall her beauty, courage and romantic spirit, but often neglects her performance as monarch, which was plain incompetent. She couldn't control her unruly nobles, she failed to reach a rapprochement with the leaders of the new religion (including the implacable John Knox) and her choice of consort was unreliable. When she and her third husband, the disreputable Earl of Bothwell, were accused of the mysterious murder of Bothwell's predecessor, Lord Darnley, the Scottish throne began to slip away from her.

LEFT: Mary Queen of Scots (1542–87).
RIGHT: Samuel Sidley's 19th-century portrait of the Protestant leader John Knox confronting Mary.

Although Glasgow's citizens had been little involved in the power struggle which saw Mary imprisoned by her half-brother, the Earl of Moray, they were present in their thousands at her last-ditch attempt to recover her crown. When Mary escaped from Loch Leven Castle, rallied her forces and headed for Dumbarton Castle, which was one of her strongholds, she was intercepted by Regent Moray and his army on the hill of Langside. Many of the Regent's forces were Glaswegians, and they held the high ground. The Queen's army was routed and Mary and Bothwell fled – him to madness and death in a Danish jail, her to the "mercy" of her cousin Elizabeth, Queen of England, which meant long years of imprisonment and eventual execution at Fotheringay in Northamptonshire in 1587.

There is a certain inevitability about Mary's story. No Roman Catholic monarch could ever sit comfortably on a throne whose authority was so powerfully challenged by the Protestant Church. The repercussions of the Reformation were to harass both Scotland and England for another two centuries – until, in fact, the final routing of the Stuart dynasty at Culloden in 1746. Nor did the hostilities between Scotland and England end with the Union of the Crowns in 1606, when Mary's son James became the first king of

the two united nations, although increasingly, thereafter, alliances were made and challenged along sectarian, rather than national, lines.

Religion as well as politics underpinned the wars of the 17th century: the Civil War in England and the bitter conflicts between hardline Presbyterian "Covenanters" and Episcopalian Royalists in Scotland. Despite some interventions by their bishops and city fathers, Glaswegians were largely spared any heavy involvement in these troubles, and continued to improve the standing of their city as a centre of entrepreneurial excellence. By the early 17th century the guilds of their merchants and craftsmen were celebrated for their skill and enter-

JOHN KNOX

John Knox (*c.*1513–72), one of the Reformation's most influential religious leaders in Scotland, was educated at Glasgow University, after which he became a church lawyer. When George Wishart, the man who converted him to the ideas of reform, was burnt at the stake for his views, Knox began to champion the Protestant cause by means of his powerful and uncompromising preaching.

He spent much time in England, and married an English woman, Marjory Bowes. A stay in Geneva exposed him directly to John Calvin's teachings, which he integrated into the forms and institutions of Scottish Presbyterianism. In 1559 he became Minister of Edinburgh.

prise, and the town's population nudged 8,000.

In 1643 England's civil war spilled over into Scotland. The English Parliamentarians, led by Oliver Cromwell, sought help from Scots Presbyterians in ousting the inadequate Charles I, another hapless Stuart king, and the minutes of Glasgow Town Council record the recruitment of men who took part in Cromwell's victory at Marston Moor. Within a year or two, however, Glasgow was making nervous overtures to the Royalist Marquis of Montrose, who had just trounced Covenanting forces in a battle near the city. Montrose occupied Glasgow peacefully enough, although he couldn't prevent his Highlanders doing a spot of looting in the prosperous Saltmarket and Gallowgate. What's more, he is still in debt to the town council – to the tune of 50,000 Scottish pounds, borrowed and never repaid.

Glasgow was also required to entertain Oliver Cromwell after his invasion of Scotland. The Protector, as the general called himself, was treated to a hostile sermon in the Barony Church, but got his revenge by inviting the minister to supper and holding a prayer meeting which lasted until 3am. The city also had some serious domestic worries. In 1647 there was an outbreak of plague which was so severe it drove the university population from its lodgings to the coastal town of Irvine, and five years later more than 1,000 families were made homeless in a fire which destroyed one-third of Glasgow's housing stock.

LEFT: David Rizzio, murdered in front of Mary in 1566 (painting by John Opie).
ABOVE: a group of Covenanters pledging to protect their threatened Presbyterian heritage.

Burgeoning trade

One of the best assessments of Glasgow's economic potential at this time came from an agent of Cromwell, Thomas Tucker, who predicted a golden future "were she not checqued and kept under by the shallowness of her river." The sandbanks which had protected Glasgow from the Vikings were now hampering her growth, yet she ranked with Montrose and Kirkcaldy as sea ports second only to the flourishing Leith. The 12 vessels owned by the city and many smaller boats ferried coal to Ireland and returned with "hoopes, ringes, barrell-staves, meale, oates, and butter", took cloth, coal and herring to France in exchange for salt, pepper, raisins and prunes, fetched timber from Norway and plied the harbours of Scotland's west coast and islands.

Tucker noticed something even more significant. "Here hath likewise been some who have adventured as far as Barbadoes." It was the first intimation that Glasgow was beginning to look across the Atlantic. But as the city took steps to improve the prospects for its sea-going trade by building the first quay at the Broomielaw and then opening a harbour at what is now Port Glasgow, nearly 20 miles (32 km) down river, there were more bloody interruptions: the restoration of the monarchy was followed by the brutal Covenanting wars, when another Stuart king, Charles II, tried to impose an episcopalian structure on the increasingly zealous ministry of the Presbyterian church.

For all the tension in its dealings with Cromwell, Glasgow was essentially a Puritan city. When, in 1662, the restored monarch appointed an Archbishop of Glasgow with hefty civil powers, his authority was ignored by ministers, and these dissenters were banished from their churches and manses.

The spectre of the "killing time" stalked central and southern Scotland, with the Covenanters hunted like vermin. Many were executed in Glasgow in 1666, and again in 1684, with their heads publicly displayed, and the Tolbooth was packed with prisoners.

This savagery was not the monopoly of the king's side. When the Covenanters gained a temporary advantage over their most successful enemy, Graham of Claverhouse, and chased his troops out of Glasgow, they performed some frightful atrocities at the home of the Bishop of Argyll. They disinterred the Bishop's two recently dead children from their graves in the chapel and ran their swords through their corpses.

With the so-called "bloodless revolution" of 1688 (it wasn't bloodless in Ireland) and the displacement of the Stuart dynasty by the Protestant William and Mary of Orange, Glasgow was able to pursue its austere religious impulses in peace. The town council mounted a campaign against debauchery, forbidding citizens or visitors from drinking in taverns after 10 o'clock at night on weekdays "or in tyme of sermon, or thereafter, on the Sabbath dayes." (The "10 o'clock bell" persisted in Scotland until the reform of the licensing laws in the 1970s.)

And godliness was accompanied by cleanliness. An ordinance of 1696 prohibited the casting "out att the windows be day or night, wither on fore or back streets, or in lanes, or closses, any excrement, dirt, or urine, or other filth, or water foul or clean." The high-living people of Edinburgh, meanwhile, continued to hurl the contents of their chamberpots out of their tenement windows for another few decades.

Last barrier

As the 18th century got under way, there came the moment which set the seal on Glasgow's economic future. Although the English Navigation Acts prevented other countries, including Scotland, from trading with English colonies, Glasgow ships had sometimes managed to circumnavigate the rule book. In 1674, the city's records note the first cargo of tobacco from Virginia. These 40 hogsheads of weed were the harbingers of a trade which was to make Glasgow's fortune, and in 1707 the last impediment to this trade was removed by the Act of Union, which gave Scotland access to England's colonies.

In Glasgow, as elsewhere, the people rioted against the forfeit of Scotland's sovereignty to Westminster, and the city's Member of Parliament voted against the union of the two parliaments. But it guaranteed the prosperity which was to carry Glasgow through the 18th century to an economic base able to exploit the Industrial Revolution and turn the town on the Clyde into the Second City of the Empire. ❑

LEFT: intimations of Glasgow's future as a major port.
RIGHT: memorial to the Covenanters' persecution.

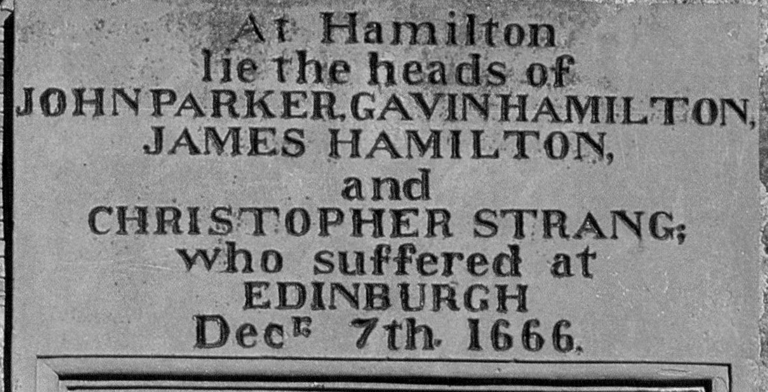
At Hamilton
lie the heads of
JOHN PARKER, GAVIN HAMILTON,
JAMES HAMILTON,
and
CHRISTOPHER STRANG;
who suffered at
EDINBURGH
Decr 7th. 1666.

Stay, passenger take notice
what thou reads!
At Edinburgh lie our bodies,
here our heads;
Our right hands stood at Lanark
these we want.
Because with them we sware
the Covenant.
Renewed

THE INDUSTRIAL REVOLUTION

Tobacco provided the first fortunes, then cotton, followed by engineering and shipbuilding. But not everyone shared in the prosperity

The most quoted writer on Glasgow in the 18th century is Daniel Defoe. His celebrated judgement – "'tis the cleanest and beautifulness, and best built city in Britain, London excepted" – was to be recalled wistfully by mid-20th century writers observing its industrial grime and material decline. The author of *Robinson Crusoe* (who found the prototype for his castaway, Alexander Selkirk, in the Fife fishing village of Lower Largo) was sent to Scotland by the English Government to consolidate support for the Union of the Parliaments.

This generally sympathetic spy made another four trips between 1724 and 1726 before publishing the third volume of his *Tour Thro' the Whole Island of Great Britain*; and during this period he updated his notes on Glasgow.

Trade with America

He was already an enthusiast for the city, and now found it charged with economic vigour. The trading boom with the Colonies was well under way. "I am ass'red that they send nearly fifty sail to Virginia, New England, and other English colonies in America, and are every year increasing…" Glasgow was importing not only tobacco but sugar, which Defoe called the "home trade of the city", and its two handsome sugar-baking houses were kept fully employed.

From the molasses a large distillery produced spirits "which they call'd Glasgow brandy". Other important industries were curing herring and manufacturing cloth, including fine muslins and linen.

But tobacco was pre-eminent in the city's fortunes. Geography gave Glasgow's ships an advantage. They could make the Atlantic crossing more quickly than vessels from ports in the south, and importers were able to undercut all their English competitors when they re-exported the weed to France and other parts of Europe. They also developed the custom of sailing up rivers to plantation landings and trading goods for tobacco on the spot, which encouraged the resentful merchants of Whitehaven, Lancaster, Liverpool and Bristol to accuse them of evading custom duties. In 1721, however, an official inquiry cleared Glasgow's traders of this charge, and remarked that it had been brought in a "spirit of envy".

LEFT: *First Steamboat on the Clyde*, by John Knox.
RIGHT: the much quoted Daniel Defoe (*c.*1660–1733).

The "tobacco lords" became a class of their own. Their warehouses and mansions have mostly gone, swept away by the Victorians who raised the massive fabric of a new "Merchant City" in that eastern enclave of the city centre which has been resuscitated by restoration and property development to become the aspirants' symbol of the New Glasgow.

But their influence still remains. By redeploying their capital, they laid the foundation for the growth of banking in the west of Scotland, founding several banks. They also used their profits to buy country estates and send their sons on the Grand Tour of Europe.

Edinburgh, what's more, was not the only

Scottish city to suffer from deference to the English ruling class. Some of the more pretentious merchants deserted the Presbyterian Church for the Scottish Episcopal Church and despatched their sons to England to be tutored by Anglican clerics.

Their fief was centred on the Trongate. These upwardly mobile merchants, in the process of transforming themselves from middle-class to landed gentry, claimed exclusive rights to patrol the Trongate's pavements. Their daily perambulations, in all the finery of satin suits, powdered wigs and gold-topped canes, took them to the Tontine Coffee House at noon to drink their "meridian" – claret or whisky – and read the newspapers, freshly arrived from Edinburgh and London by stage-coach. Lesser Glaswegians were unimpressed by their display. It's said that the coffee room waiter distributed the newspapers by throwing a bundle in the air and letting the wealthy worthies scramble for them.

The even tenor of Glasgow's prosperous progress was interrupted only twice by external events in the 18th century: once by the outbreak of the American War of Independence, when tobacco imports slumped between 1775 and 1777, only to recover in 1778, although not to their pre-war volume; and earlier in 1745, when the city had a brush with Bonnie Prince Charlie and his army of Jacobites. Glasgow, like much of the Lowlands, was hostile to the adventure of the Pretender to the throne, which had passed securely to the Hanover family. But the Roman Catholic Highlands were still sympathetic to the ambitions of the old Stuart dynasty and by September 1745, after their victory over the Hanoverian troops of Sir John Cope at Prestonpans, the Jacobites had control of Edinburgh.

Glasgow's allegiance hadn't changed since the earlier Jacobite Rebellion of 1715, when it contributed 500 men to the Hanoverian forces of the Duke of Argyll. But, with the popular prince in the capital, the city was required to donate £5,000 and £500 in goods to his cause.

Two months later, fatally retreating from England, Charles and his army occupied Glasgow itself and the prince proclaimed himself Regent at the Cross. He took up residence at Shawfield Mansion and extracted "6,000 short cloath coats, 12,000 linen shirts, 6,000 pairs of shoes, and the like number of pairs of tartan hose" from the city by way of penalty for its Hanoverian sympathies. Despite some ceremonial wooing and all the prince's charm, support for the cause was dismal, and Charles could find only 60 Glaswegians willing to join his army.

He left the city early in the New Year, taking two magistrates as hostages for the goods still missing from his inventory, but by April he was on his "flight through the heather" after defeat at Culloden – the last pitched battle fought on mainland Britain. He was bitter about Glasgow. "Nowhere," he said, "have I found so few friends as in Glasgow."

The Glasgow of the the prince's time was still very much the dear green place, and it remained so until the end of the century. An 18th-century local historian, John M'Ure, described the city streets as "surrounded with corn-fields, kitchen and flower gardens and beautiful orchyards, abounding with fruits of all sorts", and many of the tobacco merchants' new mansions had their own large gardens and orchards.

Then there was Glasgow Green. This great pasture beside the Clyde had been the common grazing ground of the medieval town, and was acquired by the burgh in 1662. Prosperous Glaswegians sent their servants to do the laundry at the wash-house there, and to this day Glasgow women have the right to dry their washing on the Green.

THE VITAL WATERWAY

The first attempts to improve the navigability of the Clyde were made in 1775 when the river was deepened up to the Broomielaw quay, in the heart of the city.

Unlike Edinburgh, which had piped water by the end of the 18th century, the city still drew its supplies from the Clyde and public wells. Sewage was collected from back courts by horse and cart, although the first sewer (for the benefit of gentlefolk) was laid in 1790 between the new squares of St George and St Enoch, where sheep still grazed. As the century advanced, the diet of Glaswegians became more elaborate (and possibly less wholesome) as their simple breakfasts of porridge and herring and suppers of broth, salt beef, boiled fowl or Clyde salmon were supplanted by fancier fare.

LEFT: the 19th-century tobacco lord, John Glassford, at home. **ABOVE:** a Glasgow shopkeeper in the 1790s, portrayed by an unknown artist.

The demon drink

With the new prosperity came Glasgow's (and Scotland's) reputation for heavy drinking. While the humble took to the proliferating taverns the affluent drank in their homes – claret or punch, rather than whisky – and in some households a servant was dedicated to the task of loosening cravats after dinner, so that guests who had drunk themselves insensible wouldn't choke.

Towards the end of the 1700s, social life for

gentlemen centred more and more on clubs and coffee houses, while the ladies, as ever, stayed in the drawing room. The lowly had to be content with their taverns or drinking shops – little grocery-shops, often run by women, where it was customary to tipple wine and spirits in a back room. Otherwise, they turned for entertainment to such free pastimes as stone-throwing competitions, or inexpensive ones like the New Year's Day tradition in Govan of cock shooting, which cost a penny a shot for the sport of shooting a cock tied to a stake.

But there was change in the air. The city of merchants and professional men was soon to be transformed. In the last quarter of the century its population almost doubled as immigrants arrived from the Highlands to find work in a new industry. Cotton was replacing tobacco as Glasgow's heftiest economic plank, and by 1792 one commentator was able to observe: "The traveller approaching this city beholds before him nothing but spires, buildings and smoke." The Industrial Revolution was under way.

The greatest name associated with Glasgow's cotton industry is David Dale, who was also one of the city's major benefactors, supporting the building of the Royal Infirmary in 1792. This likeable, far-sighted manufacturer brought mechanised weaving to the Clyde valley and in 1786 founded the New Lanark cotton mills, which not only prospered but – although they employed men, women and children – became a model for industrial and social organisation. Dale's daughter married the innovative social engineer Robert Owen, who used New Lanark as the laboratory for his ideas.

ROBERT OWEN

Although born in Wales, Robert Owen (1771–1858), a pioneer of socialism, developed many of the ideas that led to the founding of the cooperative movement when in 1800 he became one of the owners of the New Lanark Mills, founded by his father-in-law.

A master weaver by trade, he was appalled by the poor working conditions, inadequate housing and lack of good education that were a consequence of the Industrial Revolution. Character was created by environment, he told the clergy, and they should condemn capitalism rather than their sinning flocks. His model community in Lanark was imitated in the US and elsewhere in England.

But the infant cotton industry had its troubles. In 1787 the handloom weavers of the Glasgow suburb of Calton went on strike for four months when their employers cut their rates of pay by 25 percent. This organised withdrawal of labour was an early example of the radicalism which was to become a tradition on the

Clyde, but the strike was brutally put down when magistrates called in the military. A confrontation near the Drygate bridge ended when three weavers died in a hail of bullets and many more were wounded. The soldiers were rewarded with free shoes and stockings.

At the turn of the century the city's population was 47,000, and from then on it exploded in a manner which has caused Glasgow to be called an "instant city". By 1830 it had quadrupled to 200,000 and by 1870 it was half a million. In that time, the Industrial Revolution took Glasgow from cotton-weaving town to "Workhorse of the World" as all the ingredients for its future in heavy engineering and shipbuilding came together with the arrival of the steam engine, invented by a Scot, James Watt.

A NEW SLUMP

In 1776, when the Americans decided they had had their fill of colonialism, the tobacco industry on which Glasgow was founded virtually disappeared overnight.

The Clyde had been made navigable to the heart of the city at the Broomielaw (a process begun in the 1780s) and the building of Port Dundas, at the west end of the Forth-Clyde canal, linked Glasgow to the shipping lanes of Europe. The coalfields of Lanarkshire fuelled the ironworks of the Clyde valley; and there was a ready supply of cheap labour in crofters cleared from the land by the "improving" estate owners of the Highlands and hungry Irish immigrants driven across the sea by the potato famine of the 1840s.

The new century saw, too, the beginnings of a "leisure industry" whose remnants remain today in excursions on the Clyde, although its repercussions were far more fundamental to the city's economy. The launch of the *Comet*, the first of generations of steamboats which were to ferry Glaswegians "doon the watter", is described by a chronicler who credits a local man with the birth of steam navigation: "At that period (1812) Mr Henry Bell, an ingenious, untutored engineer, and Citizen of Glasgow, fitted up, or it may be said, without the hazard of impropriety, that he invented the steam-propelling system and applied it to his boat, the *Comet*… After various experiments, the *Comet* was at length propelled on the Clyde by an engine of three horse power."

The early 1800s also saw the planning of the new merchant city to the east of George Square. Surviving buildings such as the Trades Hall in Glassford Street and Hutcheson's Hospital

LEFT: the Gorbals before they became a slum.
ABOVE: John Knox's *Trongate of Glasgow*.

followed the classical forms which influenced Georgian architecture, although much of it was to be overwhelmed by later Victorian building. But the century also produced an architecture destined to become notoriously synonymous with Glasgow: the lofty tenement, which soon came under pressure from the swell of population.

Living conditions

The social consequences were terrible, and bred a reputation which was to dog Glasgow, justly and unjustly, into the second half of the 20th century. In 1839 a Parliamentary report on housing in Great Britain made this contribution: "I have seen human degradation in some of the worst places, both in England and abroad, but I did not believe until I had visited the wynds of Glasgow that so large an amount of filth, crime, misery and disease existed in one spot in any civilised country." In 1842 Edwin Chadwick, documenting the *Sanitary Condition of the Labouring Population of Great Britain*, called the city "possibly the filthiest and unhealthiest of all the British towns of this period… in the courts of Argyle Street there were no privies or drains, and the dung heaps received all the filth which the swarms of wretched inhabitants could give."

Despite the new building, despite the vigour of its entrepreneurial class, the dear green place, "the beautifulness city" was becoming an urban Hades. (Housing problems were to haunt Glasgow for another century: in 1924 a Member of Parliament for the city called his home town "earth's nearest suburb to hell".) Until a clean water supply was provided with the opening of the Loch Katrine reservoir in 1859, typhus and cholera were endemic.

Smallpox was also commonplace and the infant mortality rate one of the worst in Europe. In 1850 one half of all children born in Glasgow died before their fifth birthday, and a report on the city's mortality bills for 1851 moved its author to make this heartwringing plea: "The want of care on the part of the mother, called to toil beyond her home, which is left filthy and neglected, the want thereby of nature's nutriment to her child, who, when crying to others for food, is too often only soothed by opiates, or when assailed by disease, is permitted to die without the aid of medical skill or nutritious appliances, are all elements in this frightful waste of life. Can nothing be suggested to meet this cruel calamity?"

Mothers were called to toil beyond the home by necessity. But if poverty and squalor bred disease and drunkenness (the easy availability of whisky was a solace which only compounded these problems) they also provided fertile ground for radical politics. Glasgow's contribution to the Chartist movement which, throughout the middle of the 19th century, agitated for universal male suffrage, was energetic. Trade unions became more and more assertive.

In 1848, provoked by hunger and unemployment and encouraged by the political climate (in February of that year the Communist Manifesto was issued), a mass of demonstrators assembled on Glasgow Green in a series of protests which became known as the Bread Riots. They marched through the streets looting shops, and the crisis came to a head when the military fired on the crowd, killing six and wounding others, including blameless by-standers.

As the century advanced, however, and piecemeal progress towards male suffrage was made, the Glasgow Chartists entered municipal politics as civic reformers. The Victorian conscience was at last being roused and improvements in the city's services got under way. In 1863 the first medical officer of health was appointed, and in 1875 the Public Health Act brought pollution from industrial chimneys under some kind of control. The slums and their entrenched problems remained, and many of their ills spread from the city centre to the east and its suburbs, where more and more of Glasgow's escalating population were finding labour in the ironworks and coalfields of Lanarkshire.

The city was expanding fast. Development to the south of the Clyde had taken place between 1800 and 1830 in Gorbals and Laurieston (Gorbals fleetingly enjoyed a life as an affluent suburb before its decline) but prosperous Victorians were now moving west to Charing Cross, and beyond to Hillhead and the environs of the Botanic Gardens, which were laid out in 1842.

LEFT: Andrew Shanks's *The Saltmarket in 1849.*
ABOVE: David Small's *Broomielaw.*

Rich rewards

Despite the Stygian picture painted by social reformers of the period, the city was moving handsomely towards the apotheosis of its economic and civic achievements. By the second half of the century, it was well on course for its destiny as Second City of the Empire.

The Victorians embarked on that proud and prolonged exercise in aspirational building which dominates the city's character today. Churches, hospitals, theatres, banks, public buildings, shipping offices, shops and veritable temples of commerce were raised by architects who also turned the humble tenement into Glasgow's most distinctive domestic building. In the suburbs to the west and north, in the flourishing shipbuilding communities of Govan and Partick and Clydebank, streets of confident dignity were planned for both bourgeois and working-class families, their tenement flats differing only in capacity and decorative detail. New city parks were a central part of the Victorian vision, and today there are more than 70 – "more green space per head of population than any other city in Europe," according to pub statisticians.

With engineering and shipbuilding now its main industries, Glasgow logically took an aggressive interest in transport systems. Railway companies were founded and promptly did bat-

tle for status as well as custom, vying with each other to build the most magnificent stations and hotels. Railway bridges were raised over the Clyde and, in the 1880s, suburban railway networks and a tramway system were developed.

In 1896 one of the earliest underground railways in the country was opened. Glasgow District Subway, now running in the livery which has given it the sobriquet "the Clockwork Orange", is the only British system which, American-style, calls itself "the Subway".

Rapid expansion, too, was taking place in Glasgow's earliest transport system. By 1872 the docks and wharves and maritime life of the Clyde had become a tourist attraction. *Tweed's Guide* of the year urges the visitor to Glasgow not to ignore them, or "he'll miss one of its greatest marvels if he neglects to spend a few hours strolling along the quays of the harbour. He may have seen much of shipping in his travels... but he has probably never witnessed a greater triumph of human industry, enterprise, and sagacity than Glasgow Harbour."

From these quays the products of the city's engineering works – the massive locomotives which pulled the British Empire's trains and the boilers and machinery which powered its ships – were dispatched all over the world; and from the Clyde's shipyards the ships themselves set forth. Glasgow's industrial status was internationally confirmed, while the city's cultural life had both local energy and universal appeal.

In the last two decades of the century the "Glasgow Boys", a school of painters despised by the Scottish artistic establishment, were invited to exhibit in major galleries in Europe and America; and in 1899 the new School of Art was opened – designed by Charles Rennie Mackintosh, who was to become a hero of the Modern Movement. Popular culture, as elsewhere, centred on the music hall. In 1887 Harry Lauder made his first appearance in the city at the Scotia theatre, to be told by its manageress: "Gang hame and practice, Harry, I'll gie ye a week's engagement when the winter comes round."

The great exhibitions

Two exhibitions marked the zenith of Glasgow's confidence. The International Exhibition of 1888 was held in Kelvingrove Park and splendidly visited by Queen Victoria, who was also in town "to perform the ceremony of opening the new Municipal Buildings lately erected in George-square for the City Corporation"; and in 1901 an even more successful International Exhibition was attended by Tsar Nicholas II.

As the century turned on that high note, the development of the steam-turbine engine on the Clyde seemed to guarantee limitless labour for its engineers and workforce, and an even more golden future for the Second City. The most pessimistic Glaswegian could not have predicted that within three decades it would be afflicted with decline and gripped by despair. ❑

LEFT: Sir John Lavery's portrait of Queen Victoria at the Glasgow Exhibition of 1888. **RIGHT:** the other side of the story – High Street slums in 1868.

BOOMS AND SLUMPS

The rapidly acquired prosperity vanished even more rapidly, and Glasgow began to be perceived as a city of slums and gang violence

"It was in a sense a procession that he witnessed, the high, tragic pageant of the Clyde. Yard after yard passed by, the berths empty, the grass growing about the sinking keel-blocks. He remembered how, in the brave days, there would be scores of ships ready for the launching along this reach, their sterns hanging over the tide, and how the men at work on them on high stagings would turn from the job and tug off their caps and cheer the new ship setting out to sea. And now only the gaunt, dumb poles and groups of men, workless, watching in silence…"

George Blake's novel *The Shipbuilders*, published in 1935, is a work of fiction which has helped cement in folk memory the image of the "high, tragic pageant of the Clyde" which persists to this day. Writing in an eloquent essay which challenged the more destructive aspects of its "debilitating nostalgia", Alf Young, Scotland's leading economic and industrial journalist, confessed: "I, too, can walk round that room in the Museum of Transport and feel my heart ache, measuring case after case of hand-crafted Clyde-built ship models against the silent dereliction that grips much of the river today."

Haunting images

The Shipbuilders wasn't the only novel to come out of Glasgow in 1935. Even more potent, in its impact on public perceptions of Glasgow, was *No Mean City*, by Alexander McArthur and H. Kingsley Long, which was notoriously successful and still sells well *(see page 92)*. This "terrible story of drink, poverty, moral corruption and brutality" introduced the razor gangs of Calton, Bridgeton and the Gorbals to a wider public and confirmed the city's reputation for violence. Although today Glasgow is no more violent than any other comparable city – and less so than some – the slur has stuck.

The ghostly Clyde and the spectre of violence: the two images which have haunted Glasgow were not invented by works of fiction. There is reality in them both, and indeed many (male) Glaswegians have come to relish their city's primacy as a town of "wee hard men". When the visions of the Second City began to dissipate after World War I the huge unemployed workforce contained the ingredients of a potentially explosive social mix: the historical combativeness of the Scot and the constitutional recklessness of the Irish. Nor was Glasgow's industrial diversity to save it from the worst effects of the Great Depression in the 1930s.

LEFT: Glasgow goes high-rise in the 20th century.
RIGHT: an Agnes Raeburn poster from 1897.

Secret of success

How did the confident economic infrastructure of the Victorian city crumble so swiftly? The first decade of the 20th century was entered on a high tide of contracts for the Clyde, where the volume of shipbuilding had grown from about 100,000 tons in the early 1860s to 750,000 tons by 1913. In 1915, when more than 60,000 men were employed in Clyde shipyards and marine engineering works, the Town Clerk was able to point with pride to a variety of other industries: the continuing prominence of textiles, as well as pottery and glass-making, distilleries, breweries, tan-works, dye-works and paper manufacture. "Accordingly," he added, with premature complacency, "Glasgow does not feel any of those universal depressions which so frequently occur in places limited to one or two branches of manufacture or commerce."

Glasgow's economy was also able to provide all the basic services for its citizens out of the municipal purse – a fact which astonished an American professor of civic administration who

ANCHOR LINE
PASSENGER AND FREIGHT SERVICES BETWEEN
GLASGOW & NEW YORK
...
GLASGOW LIVERPOOL GIBRALTAR SUEZ PORT SAID & BOMBAY
...

visited the city in 1905. "Enthusiasm and interest, devotion and pride – these are the characteristics of Glasgow citizenship," he wrote. "I have talked with the heads of the city departments, with a score of town councillors, with police and fire officials, with clerks, bath-house custodians and conductors on the tram-cars – with all sorts of men, Tories and Liberals, Radicals and Socialists, from the Lord Provost down to the cab-driver. And this is the only citizenship I have been able to find."

This solid spirit of unity was to be challenged by World War I, which not only falsely inflated the shipbuilding boom but inflamed the radical instinct which had been just below the surface of Glasgow's political consciousness since the start of the Industrial Revolution.

This was the period when the Independent Labour Party, inspired by the magnetic Jimmy Maxton and his colleague John Wheatley, made Glasgow a focus of pacifist agitation. In 1915 they organised an all-out strike on the Clyde and in 1916 Maxton was imprisoned for the speech he made at an anti-war demonstration on Glasgow Green on May Day.

Woman power

Suffragettes, too, were active in the city (supported by many members of the ILP) and

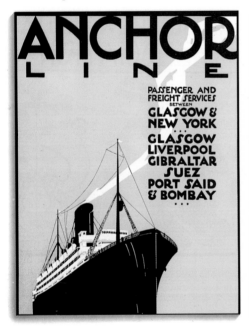

armed themselves with Indian clubs to help resist the arrest of the movement's leader, Mrs Pankhurst, when she visited Glasgow in 1914. Witnesses reported that they were brutally treated by the police force, who charged the platform at St Andrew's Halls where the Suffragette leader was speaking. (Similar charges were made against the Glasgow police when they broke up a demonstration of strikers in George Square five years later.)

The fires kindled by the ILP were further fuelled when the war ended and the first intimations of decline produced a wave of unemployment. There was a reduction in the demand for new ships – partly because confiscated German ships were being re-sold – and the yards began a programme of "rationalisation". Glasgow's locomotive engineering works, almost as important as shipbuilding to the city, were also affected when the control of Scotland's railways moved south after a series of company mergers.

> **AMERICA'S GLASGOW**
>
> In 1902 the mayor of Chicago, which had borrowed engineers from Glasgow, wrote to the Lord Provost: "Here in Chicago we are building the Glasgow of America."

By 1922 the unemployment figures had reached 80,000, and the city's famed diversity was being undermined, too. The great conurbation of the Clyde Valley was almost entirely dependent on heavy industry, and when the decline of the 1920s was followed by the Depression of the 1930s Glasgow's service and consumer industries were severely affected by the miseries of the Clyde Valley population, as well as its own.

In the General Election of 1922, 10 out of Glasgow's 15 seats were won by the ILP. The "Red Clydesiders" were off to Westminster, cheered onto the night train by thousands of supporters gathered at St Enoch Station. But their noble manifesto, dedicated "to the reconciliation and unity of the nations of the world and the development and happiness of the people of these islands", was soon to come under pressure from the inevitable compromises of practising politics. John Wheatley became a minister in the Labour Government of 1924, and was the architect of the far-reaching Housing Act which allowed the building of 74,000 local authority houses in Scotland; but conflict was growing between the Labour Party and the ILP, who were soon to lose two of their Glasgow MPs, Emmanuel Shinwell and Tom Johnston (a future and most distinguished Secretary of State for Scotland) to the larger party.

The significance of the ILP dwindled in the 1930s, but the totems bequeathed by the Red Clydesiders have never quite disappeared from the political landscape of Glasgow and its river valley; while Jimmy Maxton, the purist of their idealists, remains the greatest folk-hero of the Scottish Left. Their spirit was reinvoked most memorably in 1972, when four of the five remaining yards on the Upper Clyde were threatened with closure and shop steward Jimmy Reid organised the Govan "sit-in". Such was the success of this orderly and prolonged

FAR LEFT: an early 20th-century poster.
LEFT: a male view of local suffragettes.
ABOVE: traffic jam on Jamaica Bridge as early as 1924.

occupation of the Upper Clyde Shipbuilders' yard that the government put up the money for the formation of an amalgamated Govan Shipbuilders and only a few hundred jobs were lost. Today, Govan Shipbuilders survive – under Norwegian ownership.

Sense of humour

Throughout the first half of the century, despite the chronic poverty of many of its citizens and the periodic hardships of its workforce, Glasgow never lost the capacity to enjoy itself. Apart from its flourishing street, pub and football cultures, it became the centre of Scotland's music hall industry (even today, as writer Jack House has said, "most Scotch comics either belong to Glasgow or pretend that they do") and it was an early enthusiast for the cinema. By 1917 there were 100 picture houses in the city, more than any per head of population in the country, and in 1929 the "talkies" came to Glasgow with *The Singing Fool*.

At a higher level, the "second Scottish Enlightenment", which the city enjoyed in the early part of the century, found a permanent monument in the Citizens' Theatre, which was founded in 1942 by the playwright James Bridie and Dr Tom Honeyman, director of Glasgow Art Gallery. Wartime servicemen stationed in Glasgow also discovered a city devoted to ballroom dancing, with its palatial dance halls not at all discouraged by blackout restrictions.

The years of World War II – despite the devastating saturation bombing of the shipbuilding towns of Greenock and Clydebank – were vigorous ones for the Clyde, which had an early taste of disaster when a Glasgow ship, the passenger liner *Athenia*, became the first shipping casualty of the war: it was sunk en route to Canada by a German submarine on 3 September 1939. The yards were busy again and Glasgow, like Liverpool, became a major port for merchant shipping into wartime Britain, as the southern ports were exposed to greater bombing risks. The city centre was left relatively unscathed by the Luftwaffe, but after the spring raids of 1941 only seven houses were still standing in Clydebank and nearly 1,500 people had been killed.

Although the shipyards were kept active into the 1950s with replacement orders, the writing was again on the wall for the Clyde's greatest industry. The war had already seen off the last of Glasgow's regular transatlantic passenger and cargo services, and sea traffic was declining everywhere as air travel developed. In the 1930s the great Cunard liners *Queen Mary* and *Queen Elizabeth* had been built and launched on the

Clyde, and an echo of those days was recalled when Cunard commissioned the *QE2*. But her launch in 1967 was to mark the passing of the majestic line ship (now given over to cruising) on the Clyde.

The river's vitality got a boost in the 1970s when the opening up of the North Sea oil fields brought new work on supply vessels and oil platforms. By this time, however, Glasgow was no longer looking to the Clyde for its salvation. Glasgow had other problems, many of them self-inflicted.

CONSERVING THE OLD

During the 1980s, there was a revulsion against tearing down old temements. Also, warehouses and office blocks from the 1790s to the 1930s were turned into flats.

council homes in Green Belt estates such as Easterhouse and Castlemilk. In all, 85,000 tenement houses were demolished and a network of urban motorways changed the face of the city centre and swept away whole communities. A new multi-storey Gorbals rose from the rubble of the old.

In 20 years the city had transformed itself into something modern, rational and unlikeable. There was a price to pay. The population had declined from more than a million in 1951 to less than 900,000 in 1971, but many of those

In the post-war years the city's priority was housing. The malaise of the slums persisted, and they had to be cleared. The Clyde Valley plan of 1946 prescribed systematic depopulation, "overspill" New Towns, and massive peripheral estates. With hindsight there was much that was wrong with this vision, but the planners believed they had the best interests of the city and its people at heart. Throughout the 1950s and 1960s thousands of Glaswegians were rehoused in the New Towns of East Kilbride, Cumbernauld and Irvine and thousands more were given brave new

LEFT: Clyde shipbuilding became a dying industry.
ABOVE: the high-rise solution to housing problems.

who moved to the New Towns were young and vigorous wage-earners. The urban motorways also encouraged the middle class to flee the city in increasing numbers to new private estates in the suburbs, and the old working-class districts which – however rotten their fabric or legion their problems – had given Glasgow a coherent social character, were now being dismantled.

The new high-rises of the Gorbals and the isolated sprawl of Easterhouse were creating as many problems as they solved. The city had already lost much of its heart, and it was now in danger of losing its soul. "The problem is," said the late Geoffrey Shaw, who was housing convenor when Glasgow became part of Strathclyde

Region under local government reorganisation in 1975, "that while people could live with violence and poverty, we've never quite learned to live with concrete."

Then, in 1976, came the imaginative stroke which was to redefine planning policy and become one of the milestones on the route to renaissance. GEAR was launched. The regeneration of 4,000 acres (1,600 hectares) of the East End – Glasgow Eastern Area Renewal – has been the most ambitious scheme of its kind in Western Europe, and it started a momentum which produced a whole series of initiatives. Glasgow finally realised that many of its tenement buildings were not only sound but handsome. Rehabilitation and stone-cleaning replaced demolition. Whole communities, including the people of the East End, were more closely involved in planning decisions and the design of local authority housing. And, recognising that it had what the advertising industry call an "image problem", the city began to look to its public relations.

A new confidence

There followed the dynamic "Glasgow's Miles Better" campaign; new co-operation between local authority and private enterprise to revitalise the old "Merchant City" of derelict warehouses and gap sites and bring people back to live there; the cleaning and display of the Victorian city with its splendid buildings; the opening of an adventurous new museum in Pollok Country Park to house the eclectic and long-neglected Burrell Collection; and, in 1988, the prodigious International Garden Festival which, along with the Scottish Exhibition Centre opened in 1985, successfully converted some of the wasteland of empty docks and weedy wharves on the banks of the Clyde from an area of barren stillness to one of fertile activity.

Glasgow is still a city in transition. While its morale is high and its looks have improved the residue of decades of unemployment, bad housing and social debilitation remains. But over the past 20 years it has revived its own spirit in a manner which is startling. If its elevation to European City of Culture in 1990 marked the apogee of its renaissance, there are many who still believe its economic base is unsound. However, in its progress from dear green place to post-industrial metropolis, the city has shown a capacity to re-invent itself over and over again. The will to do so remains. Whatever its future, Glasgow will always have one. ❑

ABOVE: concert on Glasgow Green by local pop group Wet Wet Wet, who achieved international success.

The City That Reinvented Itself

At the start of the 1980s Glasgow was down, if not out. In the 1970s it had made national headlines when workers took over the Upper Clyde Shipyard. Much of the world then decided that the waters of the Clyde flowed red and investors returned their money, if not to their sporrans, at least to their banks. Then, during the 1980s, Glasgow, for some of its inhabitants at any rate, proved that there is life after death – or, at least, after moribundity. How was it done?

To kick-start economic regeneration, McKinsey and Company, the consultants, suggested a fourfold attack: put life back into the inner city; expand the retail sector; attract large companies to relocate in Glasgow; and develop tourism. Such proposals were standard medicine for industrial cities on the skids, but for Glasgow the prescription worked.

One feature which, for centuries, has set Glasgow apart from other comparable cities is that it has always enjoyed a strong partnership between its industrialists and the City Fathers – who, frequently, have been one and the same. In this respect Glasgow is more like a village than a metropolis. Then again, no city has a middle class so conscious of its contribution to high culture.

In 1983, the then Lord Provost, Michael Kelly, approached John Struthers of the advertising company of that name and so was born the city's remarkably successful "Glasgow's Miles Better" campaign. At first it was directed solely at Glaswegians and its aim was to make them "walk tall", but nine months after Mr Happy, the smirking sunburst emblem of the campaign, had lit up the city, it was used to attract businessmen and even tourists. The cost was well under £1 million.

Coincidentally, the Burrell Collection, which had been sitting for decades in basements until the terms of Sir William Burrell's legacy could be fulfilled, finally found its home *(see page 218)*, and the art world – which also includes much of the money world – was abuzz with anticipation.

It was because of the successful "Miles Better" campaign that Glasgow was chosen as the Garden Festival city for 1988 and its handling of that six-month extravaganza brought much kudos. And so, to the amazement of one and all – Glasgow was chosen to be the European City of Culture in 1990. Surely it could not be that bad a place after all? Investors and multinationals, eternally flexible, abandoned their image of the "Red Clyde".

After 1990, however, many began to feel that Glasgow was again drifting into lethargy and inertia, that the impressive achievements had been either brushed aside or even forgotten in what was continuing to be a difficult economic climate. Nevertheless, the definitive spirit of Glasgow lived doggedly on, and its fighting edge has, against all the obstacles and barriers which have been put in its way, helped maintain the pride and strength that the city has always exhibited.

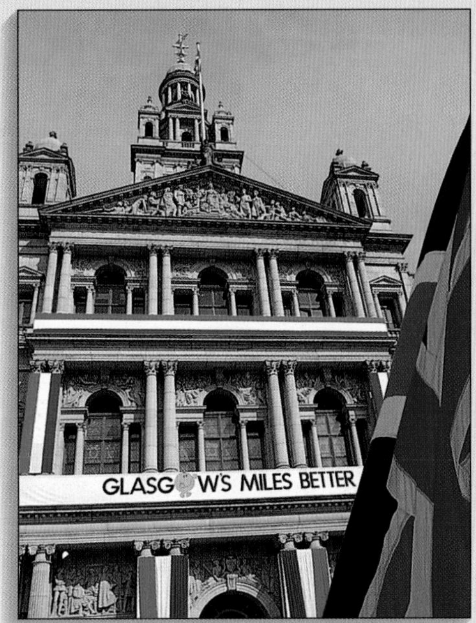

RIGHT: self-confident sloganeering.

Such values, it seems, paid off once again – in 1996 Glasgow hosted its very own Festival of Visual Arts, and in 1999 became the title-holder of the prestigious "UK City of Architecture and Design" award. Old buildings were given facelifts, and new buildings were commissioned as the city went flat out to show its unique architectural heritage to the world. Tourism flourished, and has continued to do so in the years following these high-profile events.

Glasgow may no longer be "second city of the Empire" but it is generally accepted as the number two shopping experience after London and, in an image-conscious age, is fast becoming one of the coolest destinations in the United Kingdom. ❑

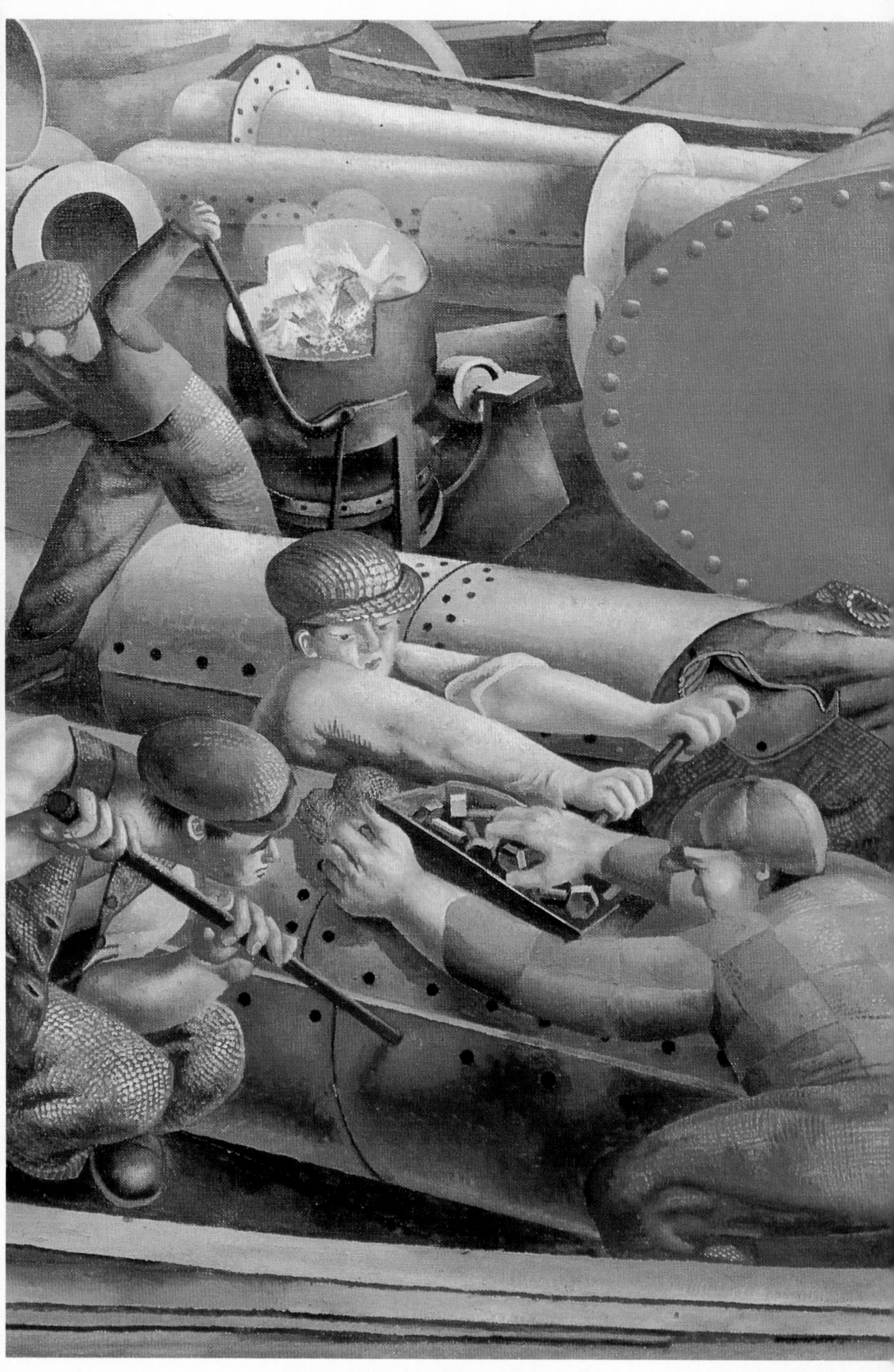

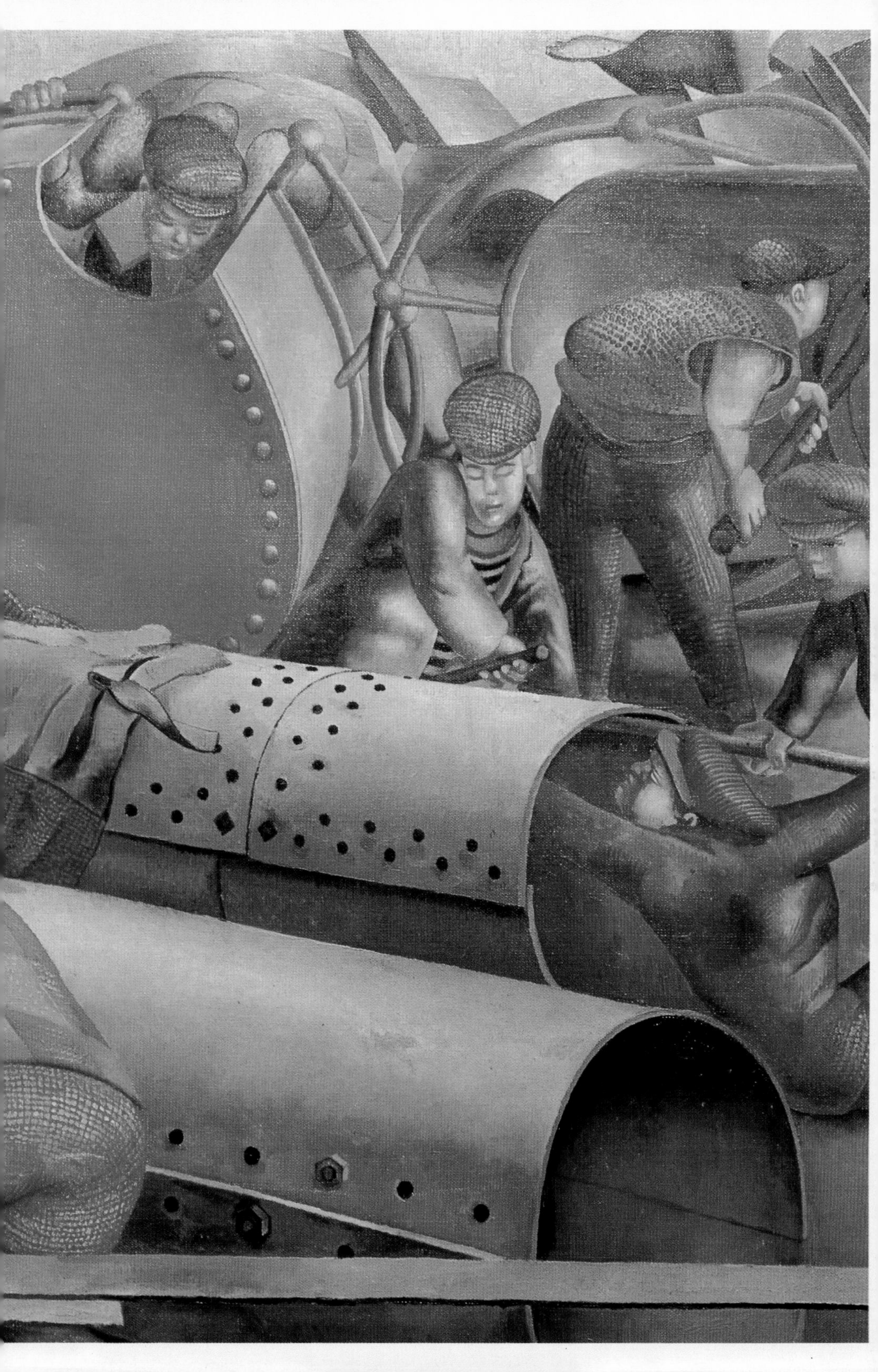

PEOPLE AND CULTURE

What makes Glaswegians tick? We unravel the perplexing tangle of aggressiveness and generosity, cynicism and sentimentality

Glaswegians have a way with words, even if visitors can have difficulty understanding them, and their fast, snappy retorts cement Glasgow's reputation as having something of the feel of an American city. The film director Bill Forsyth has put this down to Glasgow's history of emigration: "Citizens of the city are quite simply the descendants of those who neglected to get on the boat. So we lived a vicarious fantasy life as Americans-who-might-have-been. We embraced the America of the movies warmly."

They also embraced the other arts, so enthusiastically that the city supports 17 important museums, a couple of dozen art galleries, including some of the UK's best civic and private collections, and a range of theatre and music festivals. It's the home of the Scottish Ballet, Scottish Opera and the Scottish National Orchestra, and has produced a string of internationally successful pop groups as well as a clutch of well-known novelists.

Far from implying elitism, the word "culture" in Glasgow, as the following chapters show, is an inclusive concept – that's why a playhouse is called the Citizens' Theatre and a cultural centre is called the People's Palace. As the theatre director Robert Palmer put it: "Glasgow's culture is in its humour, its street songs, its distinctive patter and its football teams. It's in the dance halls and hairdressing salons, at bus-stops, on its buses, and in its pubs. Of course it's also in its opera, ballet, classical music, painting, literature and film. But it's not confined to those things."

Nor is the argumentativeness often associated with Glaswegians confined to vulgar abuse. Jimmy Reid, the militant shipyard shop steward who turned writer and broadcaster, recalled "a punter outside a pub, holding another by the lapels and stoating his heid aff the wa' (which means repeatedly and rhythmically bouncing his head on the side of a building) while intoning, 'I'm telling you there are 49 islands in the Japanese archipelagos'."

Sociologists would argue that the city's celebrated patter, made famous by comedians such as Billy Connolly, is a mix of native sharpness, Highland feyness, Jewish morbidity, and Irish *craic* (witty story-telling). Much of Glasgow's story has been harsh, and raising a laugh could be an antidote to adversity. Despite the new mood of cultural confidence, a cloud of economic uncertainty still hangs over Glasgow's future – which means, at least, that the silver lining of dark humour will not readily fade away. ❑

PRECEDING PAGES: a detail from Sir Stanley Spencer's *Shipbuilding on the Clyde – Riveters*; winning the race for racial equality.
LEFT: something to think about at the Burrell Collection.

P.S.

GLASWEGIANS ALL

Industrial expansion attracted immigrants of all colours and creeds. How did they fare in a city where Protestants and Catholics were at loggerheads?

Highlanders and Irish, Italians and Jews, Chinese and Ghanaians, Poles and Greeks and many different peoples from the Indian sub-continent all make their home in Glasgow. Some have been assimilated, others have not. Some claim racial intolerance, others are more satisfied with their lot.

For many, Glasgow has proved a successful melting-pot. As early as 1905, Michael Simons, a Jew, was Deputy Lieutenant of the County of the City of Glasgow. In recent years the city has had a Jewish Lord Provost, or Mayor (who, incidentally, became the Deputy Speaker of the House of Commons), a Roman Catholic Chief of Police (until a few years ago, the number on the force who "kicked with the left foot" was negligible), and a Director of Education who was a second-generation Italian.

But the path to racial peace has not been smooth. "Dirty, lazy, untrustworthy, thieving" are just some of the adjectives which were uttered and recorded in a Glasgow council meeting in the 18th century. These words did not describe immigrants from foreign lands but referred to the Highlanders who had come south to live in Glasgow. A century later, the same adjectives were used to describe Irish immigrants.

Integrated at last

Glasgow, therefore, has had a long experience, a long history, of racial intolerance. Yet those Highlanders and the Irish who originally formed a sub-group based on religion and language were ultimately integrated, as were in the 20th century the Jews and the Italians and other European minorities.

Even those from the Indian sub-continent who are not yet integrated (and some of whom are racially harassed) consider Glasgow as their home rather than looking backwards and eastwards to India as do their brethren in, for example, the city of Bradford. Second-generation Chinese refer to themselves as "Chinks" in broad Glasgow accents and have taken on board that colourful Glasgow speech which the visitor might assume to be derogatory but which is in reality affectionate and which Glaswegians even apply to their own kith and kin. "Aye, he's a wee keelie" (Yes, he is a small rascal). Or "Away doon to the Tally and buy yerself an ice-cream" (Go down to the Italians and buy an ice-cream.)

LEFT AND RIGHT: aspects of Glasgow's melting pot.

Racial prejudice does exist in Glasgow. However, Glasgow would be, if not at the bottom, then very close to the bottom of any harassment league table which included cities in the United States, France and Germany, or in the rest of Britain. While the Glasgow Hindi claims racial harassment by the natives, he is turning his face and moving southwards because of bedevilment by fellow countrymen from the Indian sub-continent: the Pakistanis.

On the other hand, those antagonisms which are common in the homeland tend to disappear among immigrants: divided they fall, united they stand. And so, whereas in Kashmir the Indian and Pakistani may be at loggerheads, in Glasgow they are all Kashmiris and business partnerships are formed between Indians and Pakistanis. (Incidentally, when they use the word "black" to refer to themselves it naturally has a political and not a pejorative meaning and does not denote skin colour.)

Enquire of a Chinese whether he is Hakka or Cantonese and he looks uncomprehendingly; in Glasgow all Chinese are... Chinese. Many of the city's Iranians and Iraquis, most of whom are students, are firm friends and would like to make Glasgow their home.

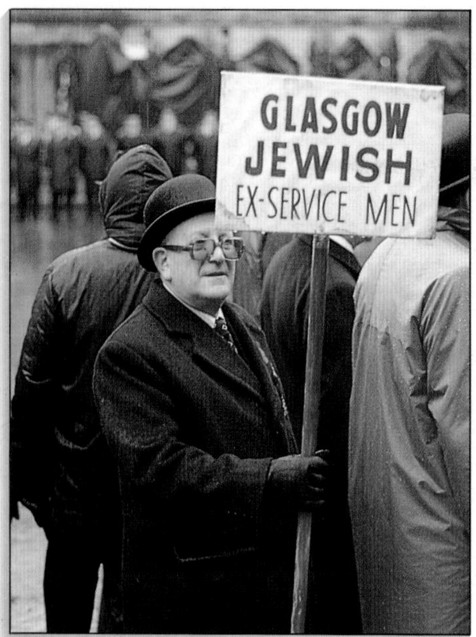

The first major influx of Chinese and Indians in the early 1950s was the result of direct invitations by the City Fathers, who needed people to work both on the buses and in the hospitals. Labourers were not required nor invited. Although the Indians had been born in villages, they were well-educated and the jobs they took were way below their educational achievements. Gradually, they abandoned their original jobs; nowadays they are no longer on the buses but rather have established their own businesses.

The acceptance of these immigrants and those who preceded them might be due, at least in part, to the fact that they, like most Glaswegians, place a great value on education. The Chinese, the Indians and the Jews would top any poll to determine which peoples are most enthralled by education.

It is difficult to assess the number of people from the Indian sub-continent who live in Greater Glasgow but the figure is in the region of 50,000. Pakistanis outnumber Indians by about two to one; there is also a substantial Bangladeshi community and some who, irrespective of their religion, classify themselves as Kashmiris.

Most Indians are from the Punjab and they dominate the Race Councils while the Pakistanis dominate the political scene and vote Labour. Hindus are found in business and law while all groups from the Indian sub-continent appear to be involved in the restaurant business or the running of small general stores.

The small general store of Mr Bashirman, a Pakistani Glaswegian who is now a millionaire Justice of the Peace, grew and grew by concentrating on the sale of that which is dear to so many of his fellow citizens: whisky. In many fields, it is noticeable how closely the Pakistanis have followed in the paths the Jews trod a century ago.

Desirable residences

Ghetto life as such is unknown but there are large enclaves of blacks in the Pollokshields and Govan districts in the south of the city and Woodlands in the west. Those who have made it move to Bishopbriggs and Bearsden, the latter outside even Greater Glasgow – although only 6 miles (10 km) from the city centre.

The community does not believe in parochial schools but language is not lost. Some city secondary schools offer Hindi as a language, for both blacks and whites, and primary schools have black teachers assigned to work alongside the white teachers. The Glasgow Mosque and Islamic Centre is a city landmark. The Sikhs have three temples. There is a Hindu Temple and an Asia-Christian Fellowship.

In Dilip Deb, the community boasts Scotland's only black lawyer and in Gurneet Mattu they have the country's only black playwright. One black bookshop exists – the Crosshill Asian Bookshop – but, surprisingly for a land which produced Tagore, it is run by a Scot, Martin Watson. Black clubs and societies abound, including the Alien Arts Theatre

Group and the Asian Artistes Association.

The vast majority of Greater Glasgow's Chinese community, which numbers between 8,000 and 10,000 – nobody is certain of the precise number – are Cantonese or Hakkas from the Hong Kong New Territories or are first-generation descendants of immigrants, most of whom arrived in Glasgow in the 1950s. They left their country for the same reason that the Highlanders had abandoned their native heath 200 years before and that the Irish had said goodbye to Erin 100 years later: because of the collapse of agriculture and fishing in their own land. A few members of the community are from Malaysia, Singapore and the Republic of China.

Glasgow does not have a Chinatown and the Chinese live throughout the city. Most have homes near the Art School which, coincidentally, is situated close to the casinos. Those who have "made it" reside out of town in Bearsden. Two Chinese schools, one of which accepts students until the age of 12 and the other until the age of 18, hold Chinese language and culture classes on Saturdays. Instruction for the 400 students is in Cantonese, although older students are sometimes taught in Mandarin.

THE ITALO-SCOTS

In the 1880s, immigrants arrived from Italian villages such as Barga and Picinisco. Many made a living from catering. Not settling in any one area, they were assimilated.

Nearly all the Chinese work in the catering industry and greater Glasgow has dozens of Chinese restaurants. Only a few of the younger generation are professional persons, though when this is translated into percentage terms the figure might even be above the Glasgow average. Many are Catholics but Confucianism still reigns in the home and these are the principles – and, in some few instances, those of the triads – to which the Glasgow Chinese kowtow.

LEFT: the city has a strong Jewish tradition.
ABOVE: Asian shopkeepers stay open until late.

Avoiding the riots

In the 1980s Glasgow escaped the race riots which plagued English cities of a comparable size. It is usually claimed that this is because the city, apart from a small number of Ghanaians, does not have an Afro-Caribbean population and because of the political passiveness of its blacks. However, most authorities suggest that the reason was that the breeding grounds which fomented these riots in Birmingham and Liverpool did not exist in Glasgow, whose inner city slums had largely been replaced by peripheral housing estates where few blacks lived.

That Catholic-Protestant intolerance which was formerly such an integral part of the Glasgow scene has, if not disappeared, then greatly diminished. Nowadays, the large annual Orange Day (Protestant) parade is peaceful and the great battles at Ibrox and Parkhead between the Blue and the Green (Rangers and Celtic) supporters are noisy and the air filled with taunting words rather than with weapons: much bark but little bite. The end of religious intolerance on the football field was signalled in the summer of 1989 when Protestant Rangers signed Mo Johnson, a renowned Catholic player. All forecast riots when the two rivals met: nothing actually happened.

Many Chinese and the blacks are convinced that cessation of hostilities between the Catholics and the Protestants has resulted in both these groups seeking alternative outlets for their intolerance – namely, in *their* harassment. When tolerance against one group is removed, must it be replaced with intolerance against another group? Does centuries of intolerance result in an immutable genotype?

Italians form an especially cohesive group. They began arriving in Glasgow in the late 19th century and today they number about 20,000. Most came from the region between Rome and Naples or from Lucca, a province of Tuscany. (Practically every member of the not inconsiderable Italian populace of Greenock and Gourock, which were formerly ports, is from La Spezia in Liguria, which had a maritime civilization before the Roman era.) On arrival, they sought work which nobody else did and at which they, with lack of language and absence of capital, could succeed and so they opened fish-and-chip shops and then ice-cream shops and finally restaurants.

Today they are found in all the professions and in retail and wholesale business, but not in politics. The community is integrated yet maintains its identity with Italian Associations where both culture and language are taught. It has an Italian chaplain.

The Jewish experience

Jews have had a more chequered history. Tom Honeyman, who was director of the Glasgow Art Galleries and co-founder of the Citizens' Theatre, once said: "The trouble with Glasgow Jews is that there are not enough of them." And today, more than half a century after Honeyman made this remark, the outstanding role which Glasgow Jewry plays in the city's art scene, mainly through patronage, belies their numbers. The city has a community of about 9,000 Jews, although with intermarriage this figure is constantly being eroded.

One factor which might have made Glasgow tolerant of its Jewish minority is that some of those Highlanders who arrived in the big city in the 18th century bore Christian names such as Isaac and Abraham and came to regard the Jews as aboriginal Presbyterians. Indeed, some Glaswegians who came from the Highlands firmly believe that they belong to one of the 10 Lost Tribes. To balance this, there are Glasgow Jews with the name Campbell. And has any other city in the world a Jewish bagpipe band?

Yet, even today, bigotry exists: some of Glasgow's private golf clubs refuse to accept Jewish members. The Jewish community resolved this slight by the simple expedient of forming their own club, which is open to all Glaswegians, irrespective of race, colour or religion. ❑

LEFT: musical integration.

Keeping Pace With "The Patter"

If, when in Glasgow, you hear a *wee bachle* (a small, often somewhat misshapen person) calling "Hey Jimmie", do not ignore him: the chances are that, whether your name is Gilbert, Rufus or Lord McClan, he is addressing *you*. Lady McClan, Genevieve or Elspeth are likely to be simply addressed as *Mrs Wummin*.

The visitor does not need to know the patter in order to survive, but a knowledge of it will add considerably to the pleasure of a stay. The patter is especially strong in abuse – which is more often affectionate than it is aggressive and, ever conscious to changes, especially in the social conditions of the city, it is constantly evolving.

Glaswegians are hospitable and the visitor might well be invited for "a refreshment" – a popular euphemism for an alcoholic drink. En route to the pub your host might say: "*Ah'll hiv tae go tae the hole in the wa' afore we hit the boozer.*" ("I must stop at the bank's cash dispenser before we reach the public house.")

Once in the pub, Jimmie may meet some of his pals and invite them for a drink. *S'ma bell: whit'r ye fur?* means, to use another vernacular, "My Shout". Responses might include *C'n ah git a wee nippy sweetie?* ("May I have a small glass of whisky?"); *Jist geeza voddy* ("I shall merely have a vodka"), or the classical *Ah'll hiv a hauf and hauf.* The last named is a half a pint of beer and a half-measure of whisky. One Jimmie more coy – in Glasgow? – than his pals might say: "*Wouldny say eeichie or ochie*" ("I wouldn't say yes or no").

Naturally, the talk will get around to previous blow-outs. *That wis a rare wee sesh last Setterday: Jimmie wis fu' as a wulk.* (That was a splendid drinking evening last Saturday: Jimmie was drunk as a whelk). Other Jimmies would have been *steamin', stotious, oot of their brains* or *wellied.* (The neophyte must take care not to confuse *wellies* and *wallies*; the former are gumboots while the latter are dentures.)

As he *stoated oot* the pub, Jimmie said to his pals: *See yeez the morra then.* ("See you tomorrow".) *Yeez* is the plural of *ye* (you) while *yeez yins* means "those others" or "those persons". Thus, standing at a bus stop one is almost certain to hear the *wummen* talking: *Yeez yins wid fair scunner ye* ("Those people really irritate you") or *Awa ye go ya mug ye,* which translates as "Get lost", with the use of the double *ye* increasing the vehemence.

Donnert is but one of a host of words is used to describe the sanity of one's neighbours. They include *gommy, bampot, nutter, tumshie* and *eejit* or, somewhat more politely, *awa' wi the fairies.* Not quite questioning sanity but suggesting a dreamy person or someone not quite at grips with matters is the phrase *fair glaikit.*

Young love, of course, has its own patter. *Wis that Mary I seed ye with last nicht? I canna stand the sicht o' hir: she's so peely-wally and her hair is like straw hingin oot a midden. Yon lassie's a richt wee brammer; ye'll never get aff w' her.* ("That girl is quite stunning: you will never make it with her.") Or, *have ye seen that burd Jimmie's guan wi noo? She's a wee stoater.* ("Have you seen the girl that Jimmy is presently going out with? She is stunning.")

The girls also have their say. *You mibby think he's somethin, but ah think he's hacket* ("You might think he is attractive but I think he is ugly") or *Ah mind him: whit a nyaff: he's a wee keelie*: ("I remember him: an irritating person: a small nothing.") *Keelie* is a common term for Glaswegians which can be either insulting or affectionate. However, the visitor best not attempt to use it until he is expert with the patter; basically, it means a hooligan. ❑

RIGHT: street trader in the Barras.

J.Y.W.
WINES
LACHIE

PUB CULTURE

They're often referred to as "shops" but Glasgow pubs also serve as offices, community centres and debating chambers. And, of course, drinking dens

The toughest Glasgow pubs, the sports writer Hugh McIlvanney once declared, could be taken by the Red Army in three days – or a day and a half if tactical nuclear weapons were used. This, like all aphorisms about Glasgow, is part-myth and part-fact – and a bit less fact now than it used to be. For Glasgow's pubs, like Glasgow's everything, are changing.

Take the legendary Saracen's Head, for instance – still known everywhere as "The Sarry Heid". Situated in the Gallowgate area of Glasgow's east end, this establishment was at one stage perhaps the most notorious public house in the city. Originally dating back to the 18th century, it was once a haven for tramps, thieves, hawkers, writers, poets and artists who would come here regularly to spend their hours fervently discussing the hopes and dilemmas of the outside world, playing fisticuffs with one another, or peacefully resting their merry heads, snoozing away the drowsy effects of just one to many whiskies. Today, this image has been cast aside and now, after recently being subjected to some extensive refurbishment, the pub is geared to a more younger, "fashionable" clientele.

The linguistics of whisky

In Glasgow, drinking is a passion. The west of Scotland has more pubs per head of population than anywhere else in Europe, and more drinkers too. The Irish/Highland mix has meant that drinking is a serious pursuit in the city and teetotallism is regarded with contempt. As Scots comedian Will Fyffe once put it: "When you're teetotal, ach, when you're teetotal, you have a nasty feeling that everybody's your boss".

The ubiquitous "wee hauf" – Glaswegian dialect for "half" – is a small whisky. When you add a chaser of a half-pint of beer, you get the famed request from the Glaswegian toper for a "hauf and a hauf".

At one time the normal measure of whisky was a half-gill. Today the measure is a quarter-gill, though probably most Scottish pubs sell a fifth-of-a-gill measure. A sixth-gill – the normal volume in England – is regarded with derision, and all whisky drinkers try to take their ease in pubs which sell quarter-gills – "quarter-gill shops".

Visitors can easily be confused by much of this terminology. The normal request for a whisky in Glasgow is "a half". You might hear a drinker ask for "a dram". If you happen to hear someone ask for "a nip", you can rest assure that the fellow is from Edinburgh, or somewhere in the east of Scotland. And if you're offered "a glass" of whisky, expect a double – sometimes known as a "gentleman's measure".

LEFT: the traditional Horseshoe pub, Drury Lane.
RIGHT: a bar sign celebrating the Scottish pint.

Other euphemisms for the amber fluid are: "a wee toddy", "a nippy sweetie", or sometimes in Glaswegians of Irish origin "a ball of malt". It doesn't really matter what you call it, however, Glasgow is a great whisky-drinking city.

After some years when the white spirits such as gin, vodka, or Bacardi were clearly gaining ground among Glaswegian drinkers, whisky has made a comeback, even among the young. This is not due to the fashion for single malts which has become prevalent in England, for Scottish bars have always carried a considerable number of fine single malts. Indeed, one pub – The Pot Still in Hope Street – devotes itself to the purveying nearly every whisky you can think of.

Most whisky drinkers, however, still order a blended whisky, to which they also add a little water or sometimes lemonade. Few Scots take soda water. It is a myth that Scotsmen drink their liquor neat: whisky improves in aroma and taste with a little water in it. The English dilute whisky with soda because their tap water is so vile; Glasgow's tap water is clear and pure, straight from the lovely Loch Katrine. But, water or not, you will be astonished at the sheer range of whiskies, and indeed other spirits, which even a modest pub carries.

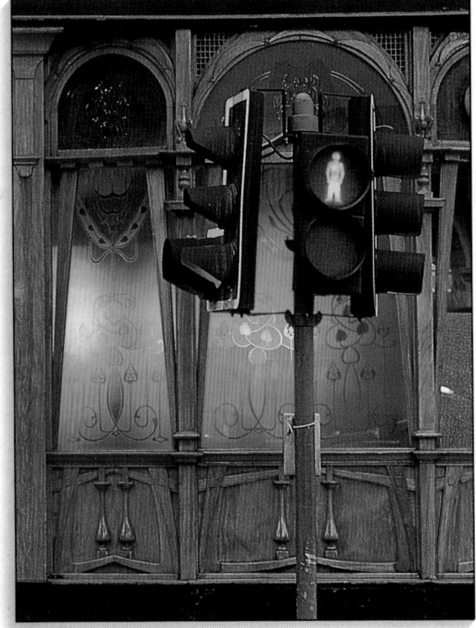

Beer is drunk in plenty too, and not only as a half-pint chaser. A number of pubs have imported English beers, in the form of real ale, but the normal beer sold is called "heavy" instead of "bitter". Scottish beers are stronger and usually sweeter than English ales and the visitor should treat them with respect. Lager is widely drunk, especially by the young, and every bar stocks a large variety of expensive German and continental lagers and pils, both on draught and in bottle. There are several wine bars in the city but they too mainly trade in beers and spirits.

The wine bar began making an appearance in Glasgow a few years ago, and at that time there was a certain resistance because of an old and contemptuous nomenclature in which certain very low dives were known as "wine shops". Such places sold, not table wines, but dessert wines, and very cheap ones at that. The wines were often mixed with whisky to provide a potent brew. They were mixed, too, with methylated spirits by the less well-off denizens, a mixture known, poetically, as "electric soup".

"It's a well-run shop," you will hear natives declaring, or of a publican that "he keeps a clean wee shop". But then pubs are, after all, exactly that: shops. Another term, sometimes used to denote a rough establishment, is *howff*, meaning a somewhat squalid house – in this case, a public one.

Pub etiquette

But all this is academic. What matters is that you enjoy drinking in Glasgow's pubs; to ensure that you do, you need to know some basic rules of etiquette. First, a warning: do not be alarmed by the high level of energy used by Glaswegians in pub arguments. Glaswegians are not temperate in drink or discussion and they go to pubs to argue. They are naturally disputatious and enjoy arguments hugely.

Arguments almost never lead to violence: you will find that Glasgow pubs, no matter how vibrant, enjoy a high level of personal conduct, mainly because such offences would lead to being "barred", a truly dreadful fate to anyone living in a culture so dependant on the pub as a social focus. Any dispute likely to lead to fisticuffs would be conducted outside and round the corner, and it would be bad form to involve anybody else other than the protagonists.

Visitors and strangers, especially from foreign parts, are welcomed in Glasgow bars and you will find a natural curiosity on the part of bar staff and customers. It is best to wait for them to initiate a conversation, though an idle observation on your part to a lone drinker may be permitted. Do not try to enter a strange company, as you will be rebuffed. Glaswegians will think you to be the constabulary, in plain clothes, looking for information. Now we come to a vital point. If you should be invited into company, you will have joined the "round". Each member in the round takes it in turn to buy drinks for all the others, and a failure to meet this obligation will be met with quite ferocious contumely. Even if the last bell goes, signalling the approach of closing time, you must try and squeeze in your round of drinks before the final shutters of the bar come down for the night.

WHY SCOTCH IS UNIQUE

Even the most modern Japanese technology has failed to reproduce the authentic taste of Scotch. The combination of damp climate and soft water flowing through peat cannot be replicated elsewhere.

Do not be surprised either at the local habit of ordering another set of refreshments long before the first drink is finished. It is not uncommon to find a Glaswegian with four whiskies set in front of him. And the English practice of using the same glass all night is not followed in Scotland: it is illegal, in fact.

A home from home

Glasgow pubs are not unlike those of Dublin in that they are used as more than drinking places. Some fulfill the role of public telephone booths, with many a citizen using his local as an office, as extensions to universities and colleges – it is not unusual to find professors conducting informal tutorials in a West End pub – and even as public lavatories, for publicans recognise the city's lack of public conveniences. As the old spit-and-sawdust establishments have died out (much to the regret of many citizens), all the bars in the city possess ladies' toilets now.

Naturally, there are couple of exceptions. One is the famous Heraghty's Bar on Glasgow's southside. Once gloriously ramshackle, it is now revamped into one of the most lovely pubs in the UK but, true to tradition, still does not have a ladies' toilet and the womenfolk simply use the lavatory in the pub next door. Nobody seems to find anything odd about this arrangement.

You will find that Glasgow pubs are invariably rather noisy, but not, blessedly, because of muzak – although there are disco-type pubs for the young, most pubs eschew background music – but because Glaswegians are noisy people generally, drunk or sober. You will find them friendly in the pubs – perhaps too friendly on occasion – and all they will ask of you is that you are friendly back. ❑

LEFT: stained glass in the Griffin pub.
ABOVE: pubs mix strong drink and strong opinions.

The Famous 'Gers
PREMIER LEAGUE CHAMPIONS 1988 89
RANGERS
THE PRIDE OF IBROX

FOOTBALL MANIA

Only a game? Not to the traditional supports of Rangers and Celtic, who replayed the old sectarian battles from across the Irish Sea

There is a very old Glasgow joke about the Rangers supporter whose wife, in the middle of a family agrument, accuses him of loving Rangers more than her. "Rangers?" he booms, "I love *Celtic* more than you."

If the joke does nothing to alleviate the reputation the Glaswegian male has acquired for a particularly virile brand of chauvinism, it does offer a glimpse of the manic obsession the city possesses for the people's game. The notoriety of the contests between Rangers and Celtic has gone around the world and back again, yet there is much more to the Glaswegians' love of football than the abhorrent bigotries which masquerade under religious banners.

It is also interesting to note that this enormous working-class obsession was started in 1867 by middle-class Highlanders. Football in the city was to become the symbol of the labouring class of the 20th century, but it owes its roots to a collection of young Highland tradesmen and embryo businessmen who formed that living bastion to amateurism, Queen's Park.

The birth of Queen's Park

The gentlemen who were to found Queen's, the oldest Scottish football club, had come down from the north where the Highland clearances had scattered the populace towards the Central Belt. The Glasgow in which they chose to settle had also been invaded by Irishmen fleeing famine and destitution, but the mature young men who watched some YMCA lads playing football on Queen's Park Recreation Ground had come to town with the intention of improving their trading prospects.

Perhaps some of them could be termed the Yuppies of their day, but at any rate they liked what they saw, decided to form their club and, by a margin of one vote, chose to call it Queen's Park, which was to become the world's most famous amateur club.

Two Hampden Parks were utilised before they settled on the current site, which has also become the home of the Scottish national team. So successful was the amateur team that it was eight years before it lost a game. Its success can be measured less dramatically nowadays but the fact that it survives at all in a business that is the epitome of professionalism is remarkable enough in itself.

LEFT: you can guess which team he supports.
RIGHT: Celtic and Rangers chase the ball.

If the old stadium, outdated and uncomfortable, is the subject of much criticism today, any visitor with a sporting soul who ventures out to Mount Florida on a match day will surely see and hear and sense the great world stars, the huge crowds, the swell of excitment.

Working-class heroes

Why the working (and non-working) men chose this game as their escape from drudgery, poverty and the bleakness of the overcrowded slums in the "ghetto" sections of the city is not difficult to guess. Football, unlike other activities, costs nothing – apart from a ball of sorts, often one made of cloth. Position a couple of jackets as goal-posts, station a sentry at each end of the street to look out for the "polis" (the police), and the game was on.

Maybe more accurately than any other picture, the image of the raggedy child kicking a ball along a street lit by bleak gas lamps captures the meaning of what sport meant to the Glaswegian. It was the vision of senior football as an escape route to relative wealth, not to mention a rather comfortable and untaxing lifestyle, which fired the teenagers from the slums of the Gorbals before World War II and the great sprawling housing schemes dating from the 1940s and 1950s.

Yet the two teams towards which they mostly gravitated, spiritually and materially, were spawned in humble enough circumstances. Rangers was founded because some lads who enjoyed rowing down the Clyde fancied the idea of playing this new ball game on Glasgow Green. The oarsmen got together in 1873 and "borrowed" the name of an English rugby club, to become Rangers Football Club. Brothers by the name of McNeill were instrumental in founding the club, although one of them, William, was allowed to make his contribution only after he threatened to take away the ball, his personal property.

From those tender beginnings in 1873, Rangers hustled around a few different grounds until it reached Ibrox 14 years later. It is fascinating to recall that the mighty club which was to become a candidate as the most powerful in Britain, as well as one of the richest, was treated with some disdain by Queen's Park in those formative years. Queen's, as the élite of the game, was not disposed to play a team without a proper ground.

Today the amateurs from the south side battle away gallantly in the lower reaches of Scottish football while Rangers, in its magnificient custom-built stadium at Ibrox, enjoys the trappings that go with a multi-million pound business.

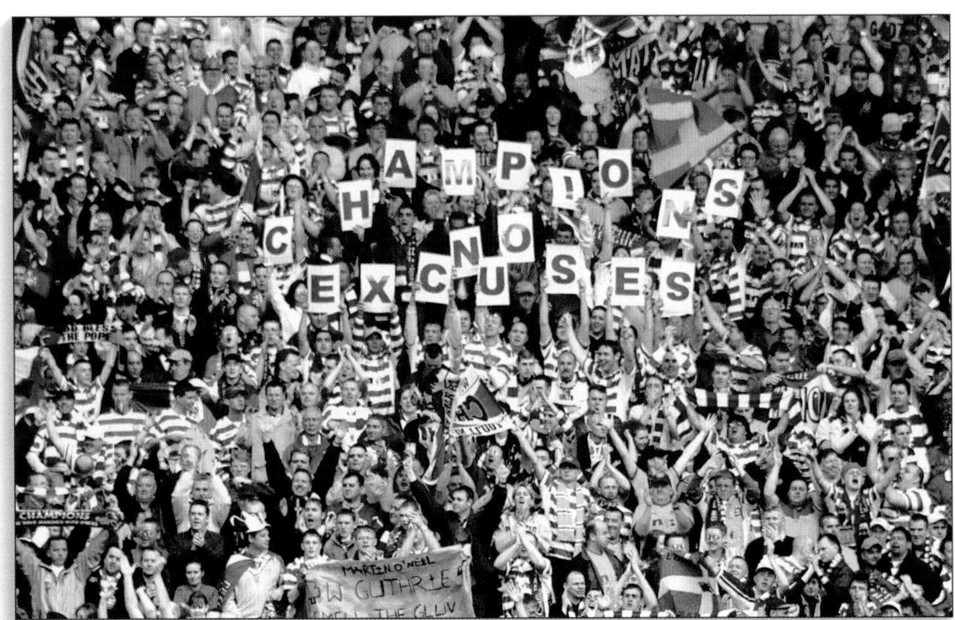

Although it was a long distance short of that eminence by the time Celtic came into being, Rangers had been around long enough to have established a sound base. It was in 1888 that Celtic was given birth, fathered by Irish immigrants for predominantly charitable reasons. The Catholics who had settled mainly in the east end of Glasgow had endured severe poverty for decades and many a parish priest had attempted to start a football team in the hope of raising badly-needed funds for the poor.

None succeeded until a group of prominent

ABOVE: Celtic supporters cheer on their team.

men among the Irish community, motivated particularly by a businessman, John Glass, realised the dream of the West Scotland immigrants by launching Celtic. They played their first game on 28 May 1888, beating Rangers 5 to 2, and thus began the series of derbies which has grown to such notoriety. Yet in those early years there was none of the deep hostility that has proved such an embarrassment to the city. In fact, nearly all the matches they played were friendlies in the true sense of the word.

Religious divide

Gradually, however, the polarisation of the two sets of supporters produced an intense, unhealthy rivalry. Its foundations lay in a number of sociological causes, among them the Presbyterian resentment not only of the Irish Catholic expansion in their city but also of the immigrants' willingness to accept lower rates of pay, and the importation of the Belfast religious divides whose manifestations unhappily continue across the Irish Sea.

The rift between the clubs grew wider as the crowds grew bigger and no less bitter. Rangers' adherence to an unwritten but firmly applied "No Catholics" rule did nothing to reduce the feelings of persecution among the minority, imagined or otherwise.

Today there is hope that the bad – or at least the worst – days are past. Rangers' highly publicised signing of a prominent Catholic player in 1989 demonstrated clearly enough the changing times. And the broadening of the game's frontiers, especially the ever expanding European commitments, has helped to reduce the insularity of clubs and supporters. For a long time, in any case, the great majority of the Glasgow populace has rejected and fumed at the match-day restoration of the ancient hatreds and bigotries.

The other teams

The Glaswegians' genuine love of football has tended to be sunk in the sea of publicity that has carried news of the Old Firm supporters' antics to every corner of the world. But it is there in an extraordinary devotion that is greater than any commitment to a single team. Less passionate, of course, but heart-felt, the city's love affair with the sport in general is best illustrated by the fact that for most of the past century it has supported six senior teams.

Even today five remain: Celtic, Rangers, Queen's Park, Partick Thistle and Clyde. One other, Third Lanark, was mismanaged into liquidation in 1967, but Thistle and Clyde soldier on gallantly in the shadow of the big two.

Army of sympathisers

Thistle, from Partick, close to the heart of the city, were established in 1876 and ever since has been the alternative team for many with leanings to either Celtic or Rangers. Likewise Clyde, from the southern side, which, having been forced to leave its own ground for reasons of economy, shared Thistle's ground, Firhill, and then Cumbernauld's. Each of them has a loyal, if tiny, band of genuine fans, augmented by an army of sympathisers throughout the city. They are alive and have survived testing times only because of this deep attachment to football.

But nothing, even devotion, can be guaranteed forever and the challenge of the 21st century awaits the people's game within the Glasgow boundaries. As yet, football is still attracting booming crowds and still discovering new talents. But perhaps there are signs that things could be different in future. For the moment, however, it is still the game. Or, to use the Glasgow vernacular, *ra gemme*. ❑

A Game of Market Forces

However distasteful the violence over the years at Old Firm matches between Celtic and Rangers, the fact is that the sharpness of the clubs' rivalry probably hoisted the standard of football in the country to a level it might otherwise never have reached. The demands at either end of the city to succeed inevitably meant keeping up with the other lot and, showing a neat appreciation of the *mores* of capitalist competition, the finest exponents of the workers' game responded to market forces, even if their supporters stuck to the same old sectarian slogans.

There have been riots, on and off the field, and, considering the genetic combinations that spawned the supporters of both clubs, that can hardly come as a surprise. There is no prevalence of passive resistance in the Irish or Scottish antecedents but a corollary of the rivalry has been a remarkable domination of football in their country. At the time of writing, Rangers has won the league championship significantly more often than Celtic, but Celtic is ahead on wins in the Scottish Cup.

THE VISUAL ARTS

Scottish painters wanted artistic success and Glasgow's industrialists wanted respectability. The result: art and capital made a remarkable marriage

That such a commercial, philistine city as "dear, dirty Glasgow" should have had the nerve to turn itself into a cultural mecca seems, at first glance, like typical civic cheek. Yet it's the same aggressive dynamism that once built great ships which is now promoting the lavish public galleries and bustling sale rooms and propelling its young native painters towards the glittering prizes of New York recognition. Civic pride, as ever, is unbounded. Where else would taxi drivers regale the visitor with the glories of *our* Burrell Collection or *our* Charles Rennie Mackintosh?

More than 100 years ago, in the 1890s, Francis Newbery, principal of Glasgow School of Art, prophesied that his city would one day emulate the cultural prestige of Venice, Paris and Amsterdam. At the time this seemed an absurd boast – typically Glaswegian. For the place was then run by dour, hard-headed businessmen, while its intellectuals directed their energy to useful pursuits such as medicine, engineering and the law.

The artist was of little account, a mere idler who frittered away his substance on sensory delights disapproved of by the kirk (church). Besides, the arts were the concern of genteel Edinburgh, which Glasgow, second city of the British Empire, had long surpassed. Practical achievements, linked to sound finance, were what mattered. "Edinburgh may *be* the capital," the saying went, "but we *have* the capital."

Given the austerity of the kirk, which frowned on "outer show", it's strange that Scotland should be the only British region with a distinctive school of painting. This originated in 18th-century Edinburgh, where there was a sudden flowering of intellectual activity. In addition to scientists, philosophers and men of letters, the "Athens of the North" also produced Alan Ramsay, court painter to George III, Henry Raeburn, knighted by George IV, the genre painter David Wilkie, and in architecture the brothers Adam whose aerial neo-classicism became the craze of Europe.

Glasgow was still a minor town. Not until the 19th century did it become a great industrial centre, much richer than Edinburgh and jealous of its cultural edge. Ever since, as in Italy during the Renaissance, inter-city rivalry has helped foster the arts. Glasgow opened Scotland's first museum, the Hunterian, in 1807; its now famous School of Art in 1840; then a permanent civic collection, the McLellan Galleries; and an exhibition centre, the Glasgow Institute of Fine Arts. As early as 1867, the Glasgow Art Club was formed, conferring "respectability" on that doubtful creature, the practising artist.

Snobbery, too, played its part. In an era of new money, acquiring fine paintings gave tone to the self-made man. But unworthy cravings for status were balanced by Presbyterian virtue, which insisted that social debts be repaid. Before 1900, Glasgow's public collections were built up almost entirely through private donations from men who had made good: Dr William Hunter (of the Hunterian), who rose to fame as a pioneer of obstetrics; Archibald McLellan, who grew rich more prosaically as a coach builder; and later, the most munificent of all, shipowner William Burrell.

The Glasgow Boys

Initially, the pictorial style of Scottish art was controlled by the Edinburgh establishment. But in the 1870s a rebellion was mounted by a group of young painters, dubbed derisively the Glasgow Boys. Their leader was James Guthrie; others included Arthur Melville, George Henry, John Lavery, Edward Hornel and Joseph Crawhall.

Rejecting the polished technique and grandiose, often moralising subjects of the academic "Gluepots", they broke with convention by abandoning their studios to paint in the open air, choosing scenes from peasant life: a goose girl, a cabbage patch, munching cattle. Inspired by Whistler and the Dutch and French Realists, their sketchy brushwork, luscious colours and, above all, their proletarian themes offended both the prim and the newly genteel. So they fled, disgusted, to Paris.

Years later, when they were acclaimed in Europe's capitals and in distant New York, Glasgow pride was tickled – after all, who from Edinburgh could compete? – and their pictures became highly prized (as well as priced). In

PRECEDING PAGES: painting a local theatre backdrop.
LEFT: the Hunterian Gallery.
ABOVE: Sir John Lavery's *Mrs Stewart-Clark* and J.D. Fergusson's *Voiles Indiennes*.

contrast to the rarefied dabblings emanating from Edinburgh, their honest, earthy vigour were seen as being essentially Glaswegian.

But suspicion and prejudice were still directed at their great contemporary, Charles Rennie Mackintosh, creator of the Glasgow Style. Mocked as a drunken "tea-room designer" and abandoning his architectural dreams in favour of small but exquisite watercolours, "Toshie" died prematurely and in exile *(see page 112)*.

Having gained wealth and respectability, many of the Glasgow Boys lost their freshness. Hornel retreated into orientalism, Lavery painted modish society portraits in Edwardian London, and Guthrie became a conservative president of the Royal Scottish Academy he had once scorned.

Their success, however, gave younger artists the courage to experiment, and the next generation (this time mainly from Edinburgh) produced a second generation of rebels, the Scottish Colourists: J.D. Fergusson, Leslie Hunter, S.J. Peploe and F.C.B. Cadell. Oppressed by what they saw as Scotland's mean-spirited philistinism, they too fled to Paris to join the *avant garde*.

Flouting tradition in the manner of Matisse and the Fauves (wild beasts), the Colourists painted vibrant, joyful pictures in which tonal shading was replaced by pure colour and perspective flattened into a dancing, linear rhythm. In 1914, when the outbreak of World War I forced them to return, they startled the wary Scots by portraying them and their grey landscape bathed in Gallic sunshine.

Once again, a pattern was repeated. The war over, they continued to exhibit in Paris, and success abroad made them (belatedly) so popular at home that Fergusson, who spent his last 20 years in Glasgow, was given a major retrospective, at the city's expense, and an honorary degree from its university.

Surprisingly sensuous

From then on, the status of the artist, once marginal, was assured. Despite a gloomy climate and religious puritanism, Scottish art has at all times been surprisingly buoyant, sensuous and, on the whole, considerably lacking in angst. Influenced by Post-Impressionism and their own Colourists, painters in the 1930s found a ready market for the bright landscapes, fruit, flowers and fishing boats, which they rendered with uninhibited gusto. (Glasgow-trained James Cowie was unusual in his formal restraint.)

But such cheerful preoccupation with the local scene led to parochialism, and the loss of contact with the European mainstream frustrated younger artists. After World War II, many of Glasgow's most talented painters – such as the romantic neo-cubists Robert Colquhoun and Robert MacBryde, iconoclast Bruce MacLean and abstract expressionist Alan Gouk – all bolted to London. Among the gifted few who worked on in isolation was Cowie's pupil Joan Eardley, whose ragged street kids are a poignant record of the Glasgow slums.

After 1945, heavy industry, the basis of Glasgow's wealth, plunged into decline and the city seemed moribund. In the circumstances, it seemed to many a scandal that Tom Honeyman, director of the Kelvingrove Art Gallery and Museum, should squander £8,200 on a Salvador Dalí *Crucifixion*. Yet his dynamic leadership was the first hint of the improbable form in which Glasgow would be resurrected: from grim steelworks and shipyards to European City of Culture.

As the economic crisis deepened, Glaswegians were slow to realise their cultural assets. Years passed before Pollok House, with its fine Spanish paintings, quietly opened its doors. The Hunterian then expanded to show (among other works redeemed from the shadows) a collection of Whistlers rivalled only by the Freer in Washington DC; these had been bequeathed in gratitude because, in 1891, Glasgow Boy E.A. Walton had persuaded the City Fathers to buy a portrait of the Scots philosopher Thomas Carlyle – Whistler's first public sale.

But these treasures slumbered. It was not until 1983 that the world's aesthetes began to buy air tickets for Glasgow and costly art tours added the city to their brochures, alongside Florence, Athens and St Petersburg. The reason was the opening of the Burrell Collection, after 40 shameful years in storage. The 4 million

LEFT: taking a close interest in an exhibit at the Gallery of Modern Art.

ABOVE: music meets painting at the City Arts Centre.

THE BURRELL PHENOMENON

The Queen's opening of the Burrell Collection in Pollok Country Park in 1983 was an early milestone in Glasgow's artistic renaissance. The unveiling of the airy new building was accompanied by relentless hype, provoking critics into pointing out that, although it contained some fine paintings, such as works by Degas and Cézanne, there was also a fair amount of junk, such as some carpets which betrayed the prolonged attention of moths.

The problem was that the shipbuilding magnate Sir William Burrell had insisted in his bequest that his erratic collection of treasures should be shown as a complete exhibit. Achieving that aim took four decades.

people who visited the Burrell in its first three years became aware that the city held further delights; now Kelvingrove is an even greater tourist attraction.

Another factor contributing to Glasgow's cultural prestige was a new curiosity about the art produced by the Scots themselves. From the late 1960s, the London Fine Art Society had been promoting the long-forgotten Glasgow Boys, slowly at first but with increasing success, and in time they included the Colourists. Scottish art is now valued so highly that, when Peploe's *Girl in White* was sold in 1988, it was the most expensive picture to come under the auctioneer's hammer that year, fetching more than £500,000. What's more, it was sold not in London but in Glasgow.

Media fever has spurred the great art auctioneers Sotheby's, Christie's and Phillips to cash in with all the attendant hype and razzmatazz and to despatch their agents to scour Scotland for neglected talent. As a result, even minor artists, who painted bright lochs and glens between the wars, have captured a public which prefers their "parochialism" to the ugliness, gloom or sheer gimmickry of the latest international fashion. In Glasgow's salerooms, foreign dealers – including Japanese on the look-out for orientalist Hornels – jostle alongside Glaswegians proudly investing in "their own".

In 1970, there was only one commercial gallery; now there are more than 30. In addition, the building McLellan gifted to the city with his collection (now in Kelvingrove) has been refurbished for major exhibitions of contemporary art. Big business sponsors, too, have been attracted..

The young ones

Another factor in the "Glasgow phenomenon" is the vitality of its young painters, whose vast canvases take up space in major galleries throughout the UK and in the US. It all started with the critical stir caused by the 1982 degree show of three graduating students: Steven Campbell, Adrian Wiszniewski and Ken Currie. As Wiszniewski put it: "You get one Glasgow artist and he's a freak, two and they're a movement."

Bored with the abstraction and tricksy effects admired by the modern art elite, the students aimed to create an imagery for the troubled world they saw around them and, through political or literary allusion, to express "the confused spirit of the age". Scottish hedonism and the *belle peinture* practised in Edinburgh were also rejected in favour of figurative painting, muscular and hard-edged, on a monumental scale.

Instead of flighty Paris, they looked to German Expressionism and the doom-laden visions of an uncharacteristically tormented Scot, John Bellany. Currie, obsessed with the old industrial Glasgow and the militant trade unions on the Clyde, describes his work as "epic socialist humanism". The more lyrical Wiszniewski, son of Polish immigrants, has adapted Slavic folk art to convey nostalgia for the past, disillusion with the present.

But, although their themes are sober, the execution is flamboyant, rather jolly. The most effervescent of the three, Steven Campbell, draws inspiration from the writers P.G. Wodehouse and Bram Stoker (author of *Dracula*) to cock a snook

at the art boffins with titles like *Nasal and Facial Hair, Reactions to Various Disasters*.

Overnight, Campbell's exuberant fantasies became the rage of New York, whose dealers raced to Glasgow to compete for other new "finds". The city's students were quick to spot a bandwagon, and the School of Art's midsummer degree show became such a lively event that, in 1985, the police had to close surrounding roads to traffic on the opening night.

In the same year, the Third Eye Centre, now the Glasgow Centre for Contemporary Arts, mounted its first exhibition, *New Image Glasgow*, which featured, with the now famous trio, rugged "realists" Stephen Barclay and Peter Howson and the more romantic Italian-Scot Mario Rossi. Although their styles varied, what the "Glasgow Pups" had in common was an extrovert and macho brutalism, often lightened (however glum the subject) by a jokey irreverence reminiscent of Glasgow pantomime.

The new wave of painting: a Steven Campbell (**LEFT**) and Ken Currie's *The Self-Taught Man* (**ABOVE**).

Behind the scenes

Crucial to this youthful boom is the role of the Glasgow School of Art, where academic discipline was never "liberalised", as in England. The tradition of sound technique was reinforced when Jack Knox took over the Fine Art Department in 1981. "Clyde-taught," he said, "should mean Clyde-built."

Drilled with Presbyterian thoroughness, his students would emerge as accomplished draughtsmen and, when taking a trip south to the London galleries, these young Glaswegians – never short on confidence – would decide that their work was not only as good as that of the resented English but *better*.

Exploiting the glamour of a building designed by Mackintosh, the School also organises its own enterprises such as guided tours and a shop. All exhibits are on sale at the annual degree show; in 1986 all of Stephen Conroy's paintings were sold before they were even hung.

Conroys now grace New York's Museum of Metropolitan Art, which has a student and teacher exchange scheme with Glasgow. Among transatlantic visitors was a former School of Art student, Steven Campbell, who had settled in the US but returned to Glasgow to lecture on "How to paint a picture the New York critics will like".

A visual feast

Finally, Glasgow again claimed its much-deserved stake in the arts world in 1996 by hosting its very own Festival of Visual Arts, a feast of exhibitions, art and design events. It was the largest cultural event the city had enjoyed since all the activities of 1990, when Glasgow was the proud wearer of the coveted European City of Culture crown. A major feature of the Festival was the opening of the Gallery of Modern Art, Glasgow's first-ever monument to the aesthetics of the avant-garde. ❑

THE PERFORMING ARTS

The streets aren't broad enough to showcase the extrovert character of Glaswegians, but luckily there are plenty of stages for aspiring entertainers

A major part of Glasgow's renaissance is a flourishing of the performing arts. This covers the entire gamut from grand opera to rock and from classical ballet to Indian dance. In the 1980s the city inaugurated a Mayfest, a Folk Festival, a Jazz Festival and Street Biz, some of which continue as well-established annual events.

Mayfest, that month-long extravaganza of the arts, continued for a number of years and then died. But another musical and cultural festival, Celtic Connections, now runs for several weeks in January. "It will never work," said the Doomsayers. "Who will come to Glasgow in January?" As it happens, they were wrong: the people did come, not just from far-flung reaches of the world but from Glasgow and Scotland as well, and the series of concerts, ceilidhs, lectures and exhibitions devoted to all things Celtic provided a welcome relief in the dark days of midwinter.

Jazz musicians come into their own during the Annual Jazz Festival in June when such luminaries as Stéphane Grappelli and Oscar Peterson have brightened the scene. The one-week International Folk Festival in July attracts traditional music and dance groups from all over the world, while in August Street Biz keeps the pot boiling by bringing mimes, magicians and musicians to the city. And, as if that isn't enough, August is the month of the big blow when the city hosts the World Pipe Band Championships.

Peculiar entertainment

Glasgow has a long tradition of theatre and, as early as the 18th century, the city abounded with such places of entertainment. The vast majority of these were not venues for serious thespians but music halls which spawned a long line of comedians, including Harry Lauder, Will Fyffe and Tommy Lorne, whose fame spread far beyond Glasgow. And then, the city was for long the premier place in all Britain for that peculiar Christmas theatrical entertainment known as pantomime: indeed, the pantomime season at the Princess Theatre, which is now occupied by the internationally renowned Citizens' Theatre, lasted for more than eight months.

Today, commercial theatre, if not quite dead, is almost moribund. The Royal (home of Scottish Opera), the King's and the Pavilion are the only venues which mount purely commercial shows. In addition, a number of venues are available which professional and amateur companies can rent. These include the tiny 90-seat Glasgow Centre for Contemporary Arts auditorium which opened in 1993, the cavernous Tramway which has hosted such unusual productions as Peter Brook's *Carmen* and *Mahabaharata*, and the Mitchell and Royal Scottish Academy of Music and Drama theatres.

Four well-established Glasgow-based groups mount occasional productions. Best known is the Citizens'; it has its own theatre, which is available

LEFT: the Theatre Royal, home of Scottish Opera.
RIGHT: a Scottish Opera production of *Das Rheingold.*

to other companies in its rather long off-season (roughly May–September). Then there is the Tron and the 7:84, each of whose theatres are also available to other companies. Finally there is the Wildcat, which is just that – a splinter group formed by, among others, breakaway 7:84 founders. Both 7:84 and Wildcat, although loathe to admit it, have their roots in the theatre of James Bridie, who had attempted to establish a wholly Scottish theatre in the mid-1940s.

The Tron was founded in 1978 to fill the gap caused by the burning down of the Close in 1973, and by 1981 was a theatre club occupying its present premises. Although the bar is

still popular, it is no longer a club. Plays presented here tend to have political overtones and a Scottish flavour, although the then artistic director, Michael Body, would not admit to the latter. Foreign works, some performed by companies from overseas, are not neglected, possibly because Body worked in theatre in Russia.

Both the 7:84 and the Wildcat are madly Glaswegian and very socialist. Theatre to them is meaningless without social content, which is a cry one also hears from many young Glasgwegians in the other arts. The popular entertainer Billy Connolly said of them: "Political theatre is fine, but so is theatre without politics. In fact, it's better. I'm bored with middle-class boys telling me about socialism." Incidentally, Connolly is not too popular with the Glasgow theatrical fraternity: although a Scottish comic in the line of Harry Lauder, Will Fyffe and Tommy Lorne, he stands accused of having sold out to the establishment, hobnobbing with royalty and society and having forgotten his roots in Partick.

When John McGrath, the founder of the 7:84, was its artistic director, the plays the company presented were out-and-out Marxist. Now their productions are populist rather than agitprop and have included those two Glasgow classics, *No Mean City* and the *Gorbals Story*.

Cocking a snook

The Wildcat, which beats the socialist drum with musical accompaniments, was formed by John McGrath's brother-in-law, writer-director David McLellan, and his sister. Two of their great successes, which it is doubtful if the non-Glaswegian will understand, are *The Steamie* and *The Celtic Story.* The desire to be ethnic and Scottish and cock a snook at the establishment was seen when Michael Tremblay produced a play, *The Guid Sisters*, in broad Glasgow patois which had been translated from Québécois, the patois of the French Canadians of Quebec.

The Cits Theatre, on the other hand, wants its actors to be understood by all and to speak, if not Oxford, at least the Queen's English. Its productions are flamboyant, deviant, biting and anti-establishment, yet not with a specific left-wing content.

Glasgow has a prolific group of playwrights, several of whom are involved in other arts, and nearly all of whom are ethnic and fail to see the point in writing a play unless it has social content. They, like many other Glaswegians, do not look kindly on the establishment, whether it be in Edinburgh or in London, and are constantly worried about whether they should cast their votes for the Scottish Nationalists or for the Labour Party. Recent election results clearly show their decision to favour Labour.

It was in the 1970s that John Byrne, who still paints and designs sets, stirred the public with his *Slab Boys*, the first part of a trilogy. Hector McMillan and Liz Lochhead, the latter a poet and left-wing feminist as well as a dramatist, are both noted for their Scottish ethnicity, while the plays of John McGrath are both Marxist and populist. Tom McGrath (no relation of John) is a poet, musician and dramatist with a strong interest in the Scottish scene. Ian Heggie's fame has spread far beyond the bounds of Scotland with such ethnic plays as *A Wholly Healthy Glasgow* and *American Bagpipes*.

BILL FORSYTH'S FILMS

Born in Glasgow in 1947, Forsyth made his first feature film, *That Sinking Feeling*, in 1979. His gentle humour was evident in *Gregory's Girl*. A 1999 sequel, *Gregory's Two Girls*, was less successful.

Glasgow, which once had more cinemas *per capita* than any other country in Europe, has a small, inchoate, respected film industry. It was at its strongest in the 1950s when John Grierson, the father of the documentary film, impressed all with his *The Drifters*, *Coal Face*, *Night Mail* and then *This Wonderful World*.

Most studios today consist of two men and a dog – and one of the men is probably moonlighting for other companies. Lack of capital means that small-screen productions and commercials are produced rather than large-screen feature films. The best-known feature films are Bill Forsyth's *Gregory's Girl* (1981), which he followed with *Local Hero* and *Comfort and Joy*. All have backgrounds which are familiar to any who come from Glasgow. Forsyth, although now spending much time in the US, is probably still the best-known Glasgow film name.

LEFT: training for the Scottish Ballet.
ABOVE: tomorrow's musicians at the City Arts Centre.

Maybe it's the influence of the waters of the River Clyde, but Glasgow is awash with music. The city is home to half a dozen major classical groups, an active pop scene, several first-class choral groups, a vibrant jazz scene and Scottish Opera. True, the shame of Glasgow for a quarter of a century was that, after the burning down of St Andrew's Halls, the city lacked a decent concert hall and classical music was performed in the acoustically excellent but somewhat parochial City Halls. That, however, was rectified with the opening in 1990 of a purpose-built 2,500-seat International Concert Hall.

Another relatively new venue is the Royal Scottish Academy of Music and Drama. Kelvingrove Art Gallery and Museum is a superb venue for large choral works which involve an organ, while Kelvin Hall and the Scottish Exhibition and Conference Centre readily await the masses who wish to applaud at Promenade or pop concerts respectively. Chamber music and choral ensembles enjoy performing in the Sir Henry Wood Concert Hall.

The city is home to the Royal Scottish

National Orchestra (RSNO) the Scottish BBC Symphony Orchestra, the Scottish Youth Orchestra and Scottish Opera. Both the Scottish BBC Symphony and the RSNO put on regular concerts which can be enjoyed during the evening. An all-too-brief Promenade season by the RSNO enlivens summer nights.

The rock phenomenon

Glasgow has, in the past, given birth to a number of rock bands that have managed to make it big, not just throughout the country, but also throughout Europe and the United States. Probably the best example of this is Simple Minds, a rock group hailing from Bearsden, a suburb of North Glasgow, who have enjoyed many hit singles and albums, and to this day still succeed in effortlessly filling up concert halls and football parks with thousands of enthusiastic followers. Other Glasgow-based groups that have enjoyed similar success over recent years include Wet Wet Wet, Hue and Cry, The Blue Nile, Deacon Blue, The Silencers, The River Detectives and Texas.

Nowadays, Glasgow is still fashionable for music which is aimed at the younger generation – popular music, both dance and rock/independent (universally known as "indie") music, continues to thrive and appeal to the tastes of a whole mass of pub and club goers. Dance music in particular has, over the past few years, consistently played a prominent part in the redefining of popular youth culture and can commonly be heard pumping its powerful rhythms in many of Glasgow's dynamic nightspots. Similarly, rock and indie music are also a strong musical feature of the city. There are a great many unknown bands in Glasgow, the members of which trying desperately hard to establish a keen following of fans, and perpetually longing for that special day when they catch the gleaming eye of an influential talent scout or a record company representative on the lookout for fresh, upcoming bands.

But why, all things considered, have there been relatively more successful bands from Glasgow than from other UK cities of comparable size? Is it because tenements bring youths together and lead to them forming musical groups when in former years they might have formed street gangs? Will this enthusiasm last, or will it have fizzled out by the end of the decade? Fashion looms less large for jazz enthusiasts; they are catered for at half a dozen venues throughout the city.

Scottish Opera, which is based in Glasgow, began its life in 1962 with one week of performances and since then has become, apart from one rather bad hiccup due to financial problems in the late 1970s, a force to be reckoned with internationally. If Scottish Opera can be said to have an ethos which differentiates it from other international companies, it is a desire to employ theatrical-style directors; in this, they take the lead in Britain, together with the English National Opera with whom they occasionally mount co-productions. Yet, as one director said: "We don't do everything wacky." Strange, then, that they have not become more involved with the Citizens', whose directors have been invited to mount operas for several international companies.

OPERA FOR ALL

Scottish Opera for All was created in 1971 and runs Expressive Arts classes for children as young as three. One project allows older children to rehearse and perform a mini-opera in a single day.

A local fieldmouse

Even before the present company was formed under the leadership of dynamic Sir Alexander Gibson and Peter Hemmings opera was not unknown to Glasgow. In the 1930s, the then second city in the empire premiered *The Trojans*. Undoubtedly, the highlight of Scottish opera until now has been the 1982 production of *Das Rheingold*, with its minimal startling blue-and-gold set, as the first part of Wagner's *Ring Cycle*. A huge success, this production attracted audiences from all over Europe and the United States.

Notable among more recent productions is *Die Fledermaus*, directed by Simon Callow and set in contemporary Glasgow.

John Mauceri, Scottish Opera's former music director and artistic chief, justified his mounting of serious musicals – if such justification is necessary – by stating that "popular is not the opposite of serious." Bernstein's *Candide* won for Scottish Opera the SWET (Society of West End Theatre) award for best musical. Mauceri's successor, Richard Armstrong, was named UK Conductor of the Year in 1997.

The average Glaswegian's attitude to opera was revealed when, in the very early days of the company, an unemployed working man was interviewed in a "Man on the Street" television programme. Not a viewer was even remotely surprised when his response to the question of whether or not the city council should subsidise opera was No. However, he went on to add: "Educate the bairns in the

---

LEFT: a jazz concert in the Royal Concert Hall.
ABOVE: a pantomime in the King's Theatre.

school and they'll flock to see opera and to pay for it and there'll be nae need for subsidies". His knowledge of the economics of opera may have been somewhat shaky, but his attitude was admirable.

In 1971, Scottish Opera for Youth was formed as the educational branch of Scottish Opera and offers an unusual programme of music-drama for schoolchildren who are not a passive audience but who are involved in the productions many of which are rock operas. A third group, Opera-Go-Round, tours the hamlets and islands of the country and performs operas with a small cast and a pianist. The programme is not only *La Bohème* and *Tosca* but includes Janacek.

Vocal exercise

Glasgow, much to the outsider's surprise, is home to a substantial number of choirs. One of the most famous is the Phoenix which arose from the ashes of the Orpheus, a Glasgow choir renowned throughout Britain but which died with its founder and conductor Sir Hugh Robertson in the 1960s.

The John Currie Singers is a chamber choir which performs baroque, classical and modern works and also commissions new works on a regular basis. The Cappella Nova specialises in unaccompanied choral music, while the Scottish National Chorus and the New Glasgow Singers continue to be leaders in their field.

When the current Scottish Ballet was formed in 1969 and located in Glasgow, it soon attracted a committed audience. Peter Darrell, its founder, believed in earthy and believable productions. Nobody dies of a broken heart in his ballets: rather they commit suicide. In his *Swan Lake* the hero does not conventionally wander off into the woods and encounter swans in a pond: he has an opium-induced dream.

Darrell also believed in productions which provoked their viewers. Before coming to Glasgow, his *Out of Darkness* both shocked and galvanised London audiences. Since Darrell's death in 1982, the company has had an international commitment, in terms of both dancers and choreographers, and delights in employing younger choreographers and directors. Hands are stretched both eastwards and westwards and a long-term commitment with the Kirov and its director Oleg Vinogradov began with Vinogradov creating for Scottish Ballet his first-ever, and highly successful, non-traditional *Petrushka*. For the younger generation, the company has a strong school commitment. ❑

ABOVE: the Scottish Ballet, formed in 1969.

Billy Connolly and Glaswegian Humour

If English comics invariably died a Friday-night death in the Glasgow Empire, Scottish clowns could never make the transfer south of the border – except for Sir Harry Lauder, who was more of an icon than a comedian. Until, that is, Billy Connolly. The "Big Yin" (literally the Big One) was taken to the English breast early on, and has now an impressive international following. Scottish comics have tended to be parochial, but Connolly's canvas was wider and there was a sharp point to his patter.

Into his fifties now, Billy Connolly has been a star for nearly 30 years. Hailing from Partick, an insignificant district of Glasgow, and then being brought up in the Drumchapel housing estate – which he once described as "a desert wi' windows" – Connolly went on to serve his apprenticeship in the Govan shipyards. It was an ideal university for a professional funnyman.

In fact, he launched his career not as a clown but as a musician. Glasgow in the early 1960s was abuzz with folk clubs and folk musicians. It was where the action was. Connolly found himself sitting in with musicians, students, teachers, lawyers, and the Glasgow intelligentsia in pubs like the Marland Bar in the city's George Street. It was then that he discovered literature and ideas, and above all, music and style – his own style.

His wizard's beard (long gone) dated from that time, as did the banjo. Connolly chose this difficult instrument because there were too many superb guitarists around, and because Bluegrass folk music was especially popular in the Glasgow folk scene of the early 1960s. He also became known as "a patter merchant". Glasgow, rich in such individuals, came to recognise Billy as a master. And it was his patter, rather than his banjo-playing, that the folkies came to admire.

He founded The Humblebums with his pal, Tam Harvey, but Tam, tired of the pressure of constant gigging, soon left, to be replaced by the talented singer-songwriter Gerry Rafferty. Humblebums Two became increasingly a vehicle for Rafferty's haunting songs and Billy came to speak more. His incidental soliloquies got longer and longer and, when Rafferty got the offer to move into the pop world's big time, Connolly transformed himself into a comedian.He was, in this role, an almost instant success. His jokes developed into long, rambling, monologues which were scatological, even eschatological, and very robust indeed. He once described his appearance as back-up to Elton John on a US tour: "I went down like a fart in a space suit." And what an eye and an ear for observation. Talking of a favourite subject, the wee Glasgow housewife, he noted that she had "corn-beef legs through sitting too close to the electric fire." The packed audiences loved it. They cheered like football crowds at every fresh insight that interpreted their own loves and experiences.

Soon Connolly proved he could repeat his success with audiences outside Scotland. He began to spend more time in London, then divorced his wife to marry the fashionable comedienne Pamela Stephenson. But many Scots resented this success; they felt somehow betrayed. They felt further aggrieved when Connolly started hob-nobbing with chat-show hosts and royalty, tried to break into American television, and espoused vegetarianism. Even more astonishingly, he gave up drinking.

He turned next to acting, scoring a success in the 1997 film *Mrs Brown*, playing the Highland ghillie John Brown to Judi Dench's Queen Victoria. He lives in Los Angeles and in a Highland Castle near Braemar, but he has been known to appear, unannounced, at some small Scottish folk festival where he still enjoys the *craic* with local musicians. ❑

RIGHT: Billy Connolly in his hairy heyday in the 1970s.

THE FOLK REVIVAL

Local boy Lonnie Donegan made skiffle a national craze. Then two Glasgow schoolteachers helped folk music to stage a major comeback

In 1950s Britain, Lonnie Donegan, a Glaswegian, was the undisputed king of skiffle. Since all it took to start a skiffle band was a secondhand guitar and a few chords, an old washboard and a bass constructed from a tea chest, broom handle and piece of string, formal training was no longer a prerequisite for making music. Even the Beatles claimed to have been influenced by Donegan.

He in turn was heavily influenced by American blues singer Leadbelly, who, with other black American musicians, became the source of many more songs for the young Glaswegians. They would adapt the songs to fit the events of their own time and place, but would deliver them in a pseudo-American accent. As skiffle declined, rock 'n' roll and the folk song revival took its place and the work of two Glasgow schoolteachers influenced the direction of the folk revival throughout Britain.

Morris Blytheman, a teacher at the well-known Alan Glen's school, started the first folk club in Scotland. He announced to his French class that anyone who was interested should turn up at the end of the day to try singing some folk songs. The entire class attended and hungrily copied down the words of the songs that he sang to them. Eventually he took his students to sing to groups all over the city, to "anybody who would listen". Blytheman and his wife, Marion, held regular open house ceilidhs, where his pupils were able to sing and learn songs from visiting singers and musicians.

Many of the students went on to fame and some even to a wee bit of fortune. One of them, Robin Hall, teamed up with art student Jimmie Macgregor as a successful duo with countless television appearances and a host of albums.

Blytheman, who was heavily into political and protest songs, produced *The Rebel Ceilidh Song Book*. "The Scottish literary tradition is quite clear," he said, "It is a people's tradition, a radical tradition."

The wee red book

Like Morris, Norman Buchan also started a club at the school where he taught, Rutherglen Academy. The comedian Billy Connolly regarded Buchan's "wee red book", the *101 Scottish Songs*, as his bible: "It was a powerhouse of a wee book and the best wee red book on earth and it'll never be disparaged like Chairman Mao's." Buchan went on to collaborate with the collector and singer Peter Hall to produce a second volume called the *Scottish Folksinger*, which is still in print. He also got a group together, based on the American protest song group, the Weavers, called them the Reivers and persuaded Scottish Television to include them in a long-running show, *Jigtime*.

He and his wife believed Glasgow needed a folk club open to the public and the hunt was on for a venue. Some of the singers recall that they almost needed to pawn their shirts to cover the £5 rent on a eaterie called The Corner House in the Trongate. The first night was almost a sell-out. The club moved to premises in Montrose Street and was renamed The Glasgow Folk

Centre. By the late 1960s and early '70s there were so many folk clubs in and around Glasgow that it was possible to go to one every night of the week to hear duos like the Humblebums, with Billy Connolly and Tam Harvey, later replaced by Gerry Rafferty of Baker Street fame, groups like the Laggan fronted by the powerful voice of Arthur Johnstone, and a host of visiting artists from England and the US.

The music expanded into informal settings in a selection of the city's pubs – although it was still illegal to have music in Glasgow pubs. Some were thrown out of establishments for "persistent singing" but eventually found a welcome home in one of the traditional Irish bars where the landlord interpreted regulations with a fine flexibility.

Places like the Scotia Bar in Stockwell Street became a magnet for locals and visiting musicians alike. The wee back room where the singers used to congregate became so popular that the police were convinced something more illegal than singing was going on. They thought it had to be a dope dealers' den, put pressure on the owners and had the back room closed. Despite demonstrations and a picket, it remained closed, and the music moved across the street to the Victoria Bar. But things have a tendency to move full circle and today the folkies are back in the Scotia, although you'll also find them in the Victoria Bar and the Clutha Vaults on the next corner.

Trends come and go but for the moment the latest revival is of Celtic Music. Purists may argue that big business getting involved with their tradition will destroy it, but this new popularity is encouraging young people attending the big concerts to return to the pubs and folk clubs seeking more of the same. The hugely successful Celtic Connection series of concerts, sessions, workshops and lectures draws people to Glasgow from around the globe every January and provides an excuse for local musicians and singers to get together and party.

In the early days of the folk revival, there were no guitar tutors, song books were scarce, and getting folk records meant persuading someone in America to send them across. Nowadays several Glasgow labels specialise in folk music, and there's a bewildering selection of books, tutors and videos. The new Centre for Political Song at Glasgow's Caledonian University is the world's only central research source for political song, its website (http://polsong.gcal.ac.uk/) has a fully searchable database. ❑

LEFT: Lonnie Donegan, influential king of skiffle.
ABOVE: pubs are among the best folk music venues.

LITERARY GLASGOW

Many local writers have provoked controversy, not least because of their powerful portrayal of working-class life and its expletives-undeleted language

Politics, religion and urban deprivation are themes that run through Glasgow literature like the writing on a stick of rock. In Glasgow there was a working-class culture that valued education as the way forward and politics as a means of change. This was firmly rooted in the great radical traditions of the weavers, the oral culture of the Celtic immigrants from Ireland and the Scottish Highlands, and the levelling beliefs of Scottish Presbyterianism. This explosive mixture also fuelled the religious tensions, which lie just below the surface in Glasgow even today.

The tensions of the class system were another focus for Glasgow writers. George Blake in his 1935 novel, *The Shipbuilders*, highlights the tensions between a riveter and the shipyard owner's son. On a similar theme, James Barke, the communist writer best remembered for his fictional work on the life of Robert Burns, explored the conflicts between a businessman and a worker in *Major Operation* in 1936. Dot Allan was a prolific Glasgow novelist whose *Deepening River* (1932) was a historical novel set in the early days of the Clyde shipyards. Her *Hunger March* (1934) dealt with just one day in the Glasgow of the Depression.

The first novel in which Glasgow characters spoke with anything approaching their native accent was Sarah Tytler's *St Mungo's City* in 1885, but it was not until well into the 20th century that Glasgow writers began to produce fiction about Glasgow.

Among the first, in 1920, was Catherine Carswell's *Open the Door*, based on her own life and escape from the confines of a Glasgow, West End, middle-class, Calvinistic family. Her first marriage had been annulled after her husband tried to kill her and the novel was radical in its treatment of women's sexuality and independence. Her reputation was established as literary critic for the *Glasgow Herald* but she was fired after writing a review of D. H. Lawrence's *The Rainbow* against her editor's wishes. Lawrence, whom she met in London, encouraged her to complete *Open the Door* and she attracted more controversy by writing his biography.

No Mean City

One novel from the early 20th century came to be indelibly linked in the public mind with Glasgow. *No Mean City* is an example of the potential power of the novel, even a badly written one. To the world, Glasgow became a city of gangs roaming the streets, of pitched battles in public places and dance halls, and ruled over by a succession of hard men and razor kings. Written by Alexander McArthur, an unschooled and unemployed man from the Gorbals who eventually committed suicide, the original manuscript was so poor that it had to be reworked by an English ghost writer. It caused an outrage locally, but undeniably captured the desperate lives of Glasgow slum dwellers between the wars. Many think the material could have been crafted into a great novel.

Glasgow's past and its people have been a rich source for late 20th century writers like Margaret Thomson Davies and Meg Henderson. Thomson Davies could be described as a writer of historical romances but there is an edge to her work and more than a dash of autobiographical content. Her characters are based on people she has met at writers' groups, in pubs, the hairdressers or the shops. *Hold Me Forever*, for example, is a tale of sexual repression, centred on the conflict between Sophie, a buttoned-up religious fanatic, and her daughter Andrina, who, forced into an unsuitable marriage, has a torrid sexual affair with a younger man.

Meg Henderson uses a similar method of research in her books, the first of which was the heartbreaking *Search for Peggy*, a realistic look at the religious and class tensions of 1950s Glasgow. *Holy City* is an accurate and moving account of the days of the Clydebank Blitz, and *Bloody Mary* exposed the shameful secret of how Glasgow's illegitimate and unwanted children were "boarded out" to a life of virtual slavery in the Western Isles, through a superbly crafted tale of a Glasgow merchant dynasty.

Alistair Gray's classic *Lanark* also takes a vividly realistic look at life in Glasgow just after World War II, but then moves to a nightmarish Glasgow of the future that is beyond recognition. The book is a strange and complicated work of science fiction, that has attained cult status with its interweaving of Glasgow past, present and future through the eyes of its protagonist, Duncan Thaw.

Modern writers

Glasgow also has its fair share of straight novels. Alistair MacLean, the best-selling author of countless adventure stories, was a Rutherglen teacher, who started his literary career by submitting short stories to *Blackwood's* magazine. After winning a *Glasgow Herald* competition, he was asked by the then Glasgow-based publisher Collins to attempt a novel; 10 weeks later he presented *HMS Ulysses*. Six months after publication it had sold 250,000 copies in hardback and MacLean was established, going on to write bestsellers including *The Guns of Navarone*, *Ice Station Zebra* and *The Satan Bug*, and screenplays such as *Where Eagles Dare*.

It was another schoolteacher turned writer who created the gritty Glasgow detective, Laidlaw. William McIlvanney had achieved literary success with his first two works set in his native Ayrshire. But it was quitting teaching for the life of a full time writer that was to generate success. His Whitbread prizewinning 1975 novel, *Docherty*, a hard-hitting story about a tough miner, is a novel of social realism. As well as painting a vivid picture of parts of Glasgow you don't want to visit, Laidlaw uses the language and dialect of the Glaswegian to full effect.

But it was the controversial writer James Kelman who moved Glasgow language to a new dimension, drawing heavily on his own background and upbringing in the city and the various jobs he had had over the years. In *The Bus Conductor Hines* the language is coarse but wonderfully realistic. This realism sparked a row over his novel *How Late it Was, How Late*, whose use of expletives annoyed politicians. Kelman has been vilified by certain sections of the press as a "primitive writer", although there is nothing primitive about his style, which uses to full effect the everyday speech of the working-class people living in the giant housing schemes and deprived areas of the city. Not for the first time, the approach is not to the taste of the literary establishment or the city fathers. Perhaps wisely, he set his next novel, *Translated Accounts*, in an unnamed country apparently under military rule. ❑

LEFT: Alistair MacLean, best-selling thriller writer.
RIGHT: James Kelman, master of everyday speech.

PLACES

A detailed guide to the entire city, with principal sites clearly cross-referenced by number to the maps

Glasgow is a city of superlatives – the first, the best, the highest, the most. The surprise is that many of these claims are not the rantings of chauvinists but are based on fact. During its heyday, in the second half of the 19th century, Glasgow was the "Second City of the Empire" and a major centre for industry and the arts. With the prosperity generated by manufacturing and trade, Glaswegians built scores of magnificent buildings, many of which have recently been renovated, and elegant squares. They also created more than 70 public parks – many laid out by the Victorians to provide green lungs for their then smoky city. Physically, Glasgow's top attraction is itself.

Culturally, Glasgow torpedoes its lowbrow stereotyping. It can rival most European cities with its array of galleries and museums, many containing collections of international importance. And nowhere else in Scotland will you find so much entertainment and culture, from street theatre to opera, plus an ever increasing range of restaurants, bistros, cafés and bars.

Because Glasgow is a relatively compact city, the best way to see it is on foot. The best way to gain an overall view is to climb one of the 36 drumlins (hills) that surround it.

For those whose appetite for exercise is not satisfied by climbing the drumlins, the city has many public tennis courts, bowling greens, indoor swimming pools, ice-rinks and sports centres. There are also 50 golf courses within the city limits and 90 courses within 20 miles (32 km) of the city centre. Spread the net a wee bit wider and within 30 miles (48 km) there are about 150 courses.

Glasgow is easy to get out of and, within 30 minutes, the visitor can be at Loch Lomond or, in twice that time, in the Trossachs or Burns Country. Also, it's only 50 minutes by rail or road to Edinburgh, Scotland's capital and one of Europe's most elegant cities. Not that anyone in Glasgow, of course, could imagine why you would conceivably want to visit Edinburgh.

Those who, failing to follow the directions on the following pages, find themselves lost should take care, for this is one of the friendliest cities on the planet. The danger of asking Glaswegians for directions is that you are liable to find yourself listening to their entire life history before you are taken by the arm and led to your destination, possibly by way of a pub. ❑

PRECEDING PAGES: Glasgow's green lungs; the suspension bridge at Carlton Place; serious shopping at Princes Square.
LEFT: George Square at dusk.

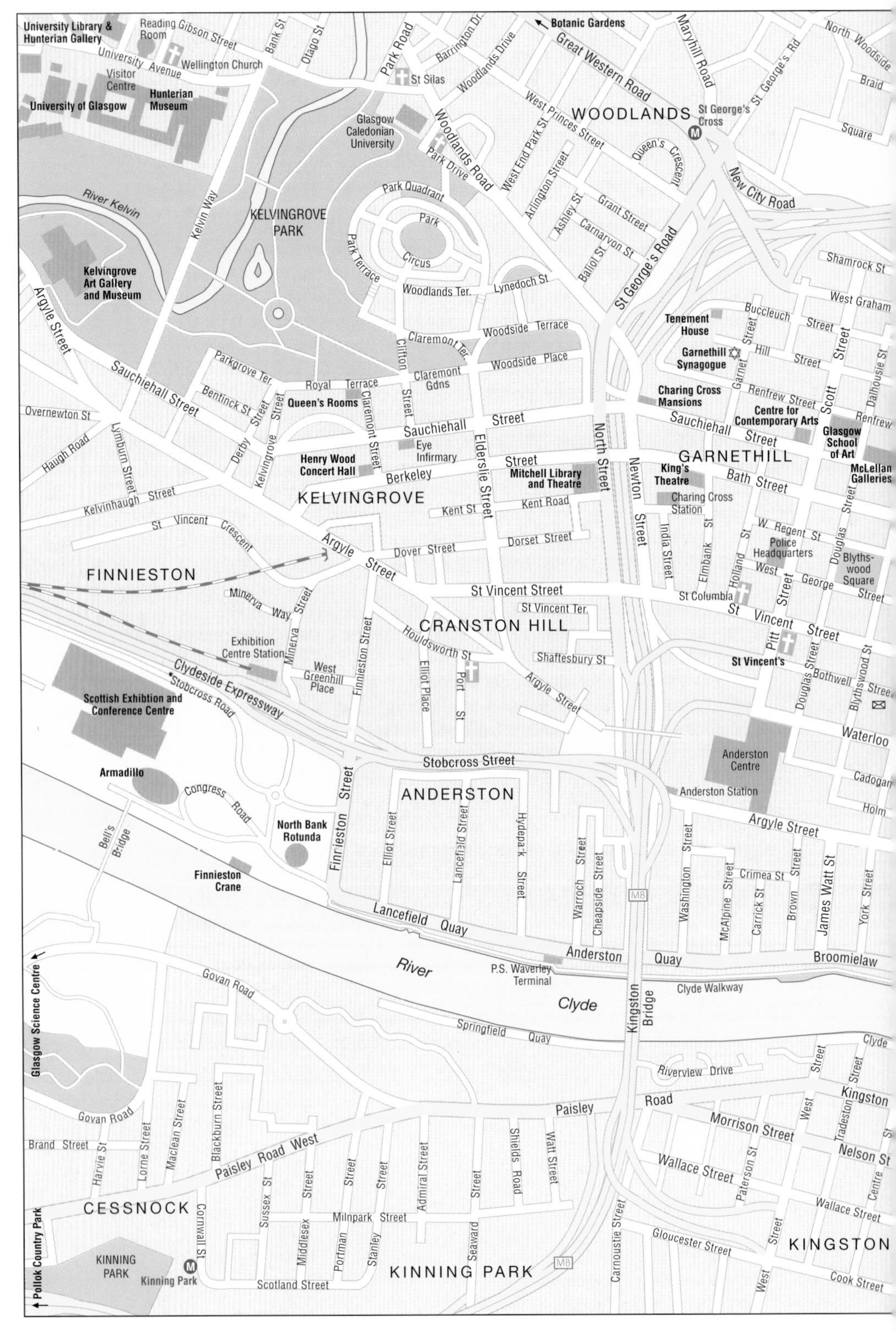

University Library & Hunterian Gallery
Reading Room
Gibson Street
Bank St
Otago St
Park Road
Barrington Dr.
Woodlands Drive
Botanic Gardens
Great Western Road
Maryhill Road
North Woodside
Braid
Square
University Avenue
Wellington Church
Visitor Centre
University of Glasgow
Hunterian Museum
St Silas
Glasgow Caledonian University
Woodlands Road
Park Drive
West Princes Street
West End Park St
WOODLANDS
St George's Cross
St George's Rd
Queen's Crescent
New City Road
Arlington Street
Park Quadrant
Park
Circus
Park Terrace
Ashley St
Grant Street
Carnarvon St
Balliol St
St George's Road
River Kelvin
Kelvin Way
KELVINGROVE PARK
Kelvingrove Art Gallery and Museum
Woodlands Ter.
Lynedoch St
Shamrock St
West Graham
Argyle Street
Claremont Ter.
Woodside Terrace
Woodside Place
Clifton
Claremont Gdns
Tenement House
Buccleuch
Street
Garnet Street
Hill
Street
Garnethill Synagogue
Parkgrove Ter.
Sauchiehall Street
Royal Terrace
Queen's Rooms
Charing Cross Mansions
Renfrew Street
Scott Street
Dalhousie St
Overnewton St
Bentinck St
Street
Street
Claremont Street
Street
Sauchiehall Street
Sauchiehall Street
Centre for Contemporary Arts
Renfrew
Glasgow School of Art
Haugh Road
Lymburn Street
Derby
Kelvingrove
Eye Infirmary
Elderslie Street
North Street
Newton Street
GARNETHILL
Henry Wood Concert Hall
Berkeley Street
Mitchell Library and Theatre
King's Theatre
Bath Street
McLellan Galleries
Kelvinhaugh Street
KELVINGROVE
Kent St
Kent Road
Charing Cross Station
St Vincent Crescent
India Street
Elmbank St
W. Regent St
Douglas
Street
Argyle Street
Dover Street
Dorset Street
Police Headquarters
Blythswood Square
FINNIESTON
Holland St
West George Street
Minerva Way
Street
St Vincent Street
St Columbia
St Vincent Street
St Vincent Ter.
Pitt Street
CRANSTON HILL
Exhibition Centre Station
Minerva
Houldsworth St
Shaftesbury St
St Vincent's
Douglas Street
Bothwell Street
Blythswood St
Clydeside Expressway
Stobcross Road
West Greenhill Place
Finnieston Street
Elliot Place
Port St
Argyle Street
Scottish Exhibition and Conference Centre
Waterloo
Anderston Centre
Cadogan
Stobcross Street
Armadillo
Congress Road
ANDERSTON
Anderston Station
Holm
Finnieston Street
Argyle Street
North Bank Rotunda
Bell's Bridge
Elliot Street
Lancefield Street
Hydepark Street
Warroch Street
Cheapside Street
Washington Street
McAlpine Street
Crimea St
Carrick St
Brown Street
James Watt St
York Street
Finnieston Crane
M8
Lancefield Quay
Anderston Quay
Broomielaw
River
P.S. Waverley Terminal
Clyde
Clyde Walkway
Govan Road
Kingston Bridge
Springfield Quay
Clyde
Glasgow Science Centre
Street
Street
Riverview Drive
Kingston
Govan Road
Paisley Road
Tradeston
West
Morrison Street
Brand Street
Blackburn Street
Maclean Street
Lorne Street
Harvie St
Paisley Road West
Admiral Street
Shields Road
Watt Street
Street
Street
Street
Street
Wallace Street
Paterson St
Nelson St
Centre
Wallace Street
CESSNOCK
Cornwall St
Sussex St
Milnpark Street
Carnoustie Street
Gloucester Street
Street
Pollok Country Park
KINNING PARK
Kinning Park
Middlesex
Portman
Stanley
Seaward
KINNING PARK
M8
KINGSTON
Scotland Street
West
Cook Street

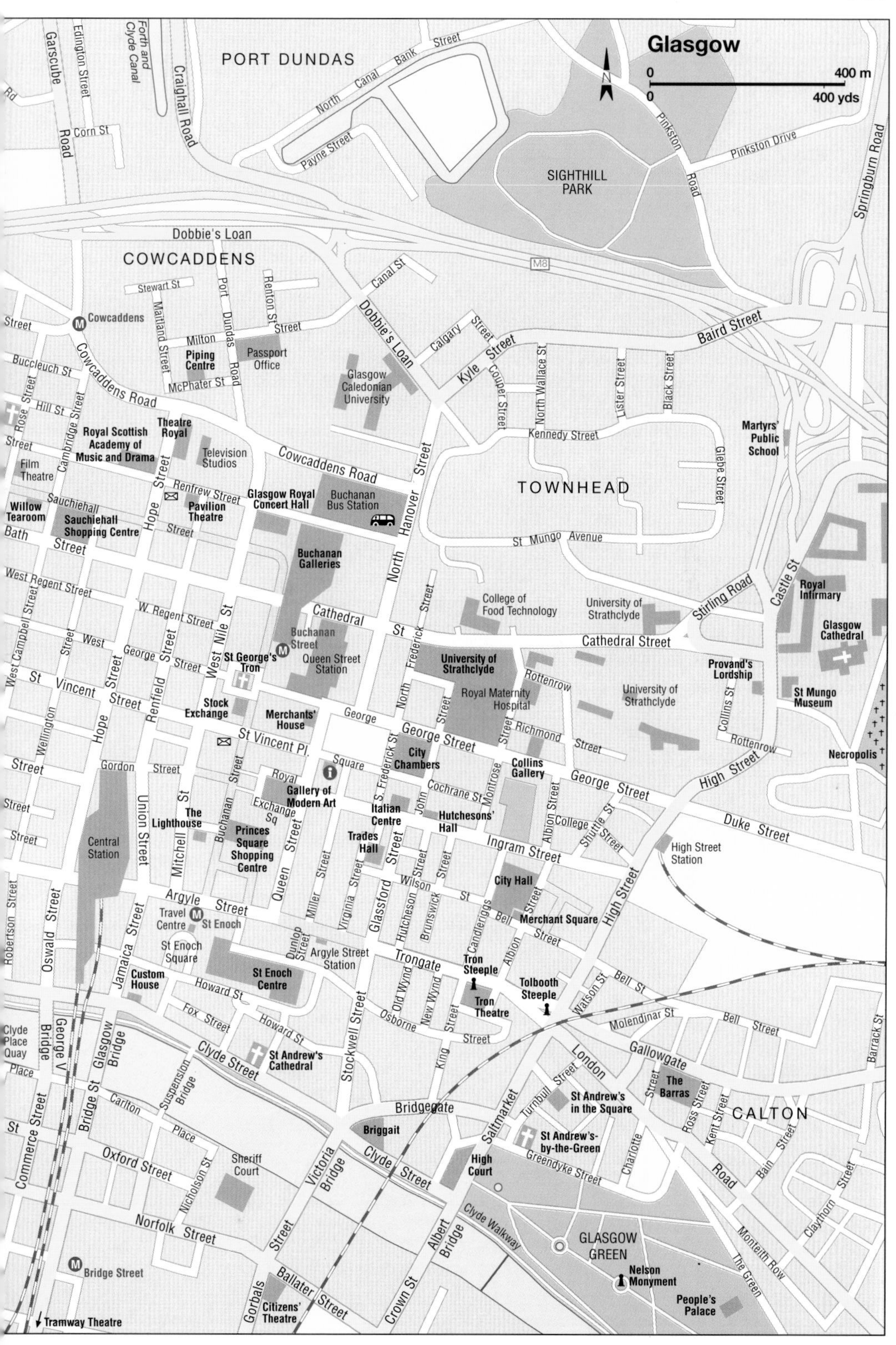
Glasgow
0 400 m
0 400 yds
PORT DUNDAS
COWCADDENS
TOWNHEAD
CALTON
SIGHTHILL PARK
GLASGOW GREEN
Royal Scottish Academy of Music and Drama
Theatre Royal
Television Studios
Film Theatre
Willow Tearoom
Sauchiehall Shopping Centre
Pavilion Theatre
Glasgow Royal Concert Hall
Buchanan Bus Station
Buchanan Galleries
Piping Centre
Passport Office
Glasgow Caledonian University
College of Food Technology
University of Strathclyde
Royal Infirmary
Glasgow Cathedral
Provand's Lordship
St Mungo Museum
Necropolis
Martyrs' Public School
Royal Maternity Hospital
Queen Street Station
St George's Tron
Stock Exchange
Merchants' House
City Chambers
Collins Gallery
Gallery of Modern Art
Italian Centre
Hutchesons' Hall
Trades Hall
The Lighthouse
Princes Square Shopping Centre
Central Station
City Hall
Merchant Square
High Street Station
Travel Centre
St Enoch
St Enoch Square
Argyle Street Station
St Enoch Centre
Custom House
Tron Steeple
Tron Theatre
Tolbooth Steeple
St Andrew's Cathedral
St Andrew's in the Square
The Barras
St Andrew's-by-the-Green
Briggait
High Court
Sheriff Court
Nelson Monyment
People's Palace
Citizens' Theatre
Tramway Theatre
Bridge Street
Cowcaddens
Buchanan Street

Map on page 106

THE CITY CENTRE

Shopping on an ambitious scale dominates here, but there is also fine work by two of Glasgow's greatest architects, Charles Rennie Mackintosh and Alexander "Greek" Thomson

This is where most visitors will start their exploration of the city. Once the heart of commercial Glasgow, the area is enjoying a renaissance as old buildings are renovated and recycled to new uses while brand new offices and hotels rise up around them. It's also the centre of some of the classiest shopping in Europe, in broad pedestrianised, shopping streets, fascinating side alleys and large new malls. In typical Glasgow style, renowned names such as Christie's, Sotheby's, Burberry and Mappin & Webb can be found close to tatty gift shops and second-hand junk. An affluent society has spawned some streets rich in picture framers and galleries, others in bookshops and brasseries.

This, too, is the area with most of the surviving theatres and cinemas and with more Charles Rennie Mackintosh and Alexander "Greek" Thomson buildings than can be seen anywhere else in the world. Glasgow is internationally renowned for its architecture but, to appreciate it properly, visitors should remember to raise their eyes occasionally from the plate-glass frontages at ground level. Some of the finest statues, balustrades, coloured patterns and stone carvings in the city are high on the buildings.

St Enoch Centre

The first of the new shopping centres to be built was the vast glass-covered **St Enoch Centre** ❶ in the square of that name. Occupying the site of a former railway terminal, this was Europe's largest glassed-in area when it opened in 1989. (The name St Enoch is derived from Thennach or Thenew, mother of St Mungo.) The pretty, turreted, red sandstone building in the middle of the square, looking for all the world like a French château in miniature, is the **Travel Centre** ❷, providing information on all public transport within the greater Glasgow area.

LEFT: St Enoch Centre, a lofty glasshouse. **RIGHT:** Princes Square.

From St Enoch's, enter Glasgow's premier shopping street, Buchanan Street, with its grand array of Victorian facades. **Argyll Arcade** ❸, on the east side of the street, is a delightful early 19th-century complex, glassed-in and L-shaped. It was Glasgow's answer to Milan's renowned Galleria and, in the same way that the latter links the Piazza Duomo and the Piazza Scala, so the Argyll Arcade joins Argyle Street and Buchanan Street. The arcade, which is lined mainly by jewellers, is about 160 yards long and has a right-angle turn at its mid-point. Among the jewellers and other shops is Sloan's restaurant (0141-221 8917), claimed to be Glasgow's oldest restaurant, with wooden booths round a circular bar in old-fashioned style.

A little further along Buchanan Street is **Princes Square** ❹, marked by glorious Art Nouveau style decorations and doors. Formerly an open loading area, it has been converted with great élan into a centre that even non-shoppers might like. The tiered balconies, café tables, select shops and the light make this the perfect place to sit and watch the world go by.

At the end of the street are the new **Buchanan Galleries** ❺, built in 1997–99, more than twice the size of the St Enoch Centre, and much more up-market. This is Glasgow's premier shopping experience where, it is rumoured, shopaholics have been known to vanish without trace.

Traces of Mackintosh

Still standing are two buildings with which Rennie Mackintosh's name is associated. Each was once occupied by a major Glasgow newspaper. The **Glasgow Herald Building** on Mitchell Street was constructed in 1893–95 when Mackintosh was a draughtsman rather than an architect but authorities claim that the fenestration, the positioning of the octagonal corner tower and the carved stone and wrought-iron ornamentation all announce his distinctive combination of art nouveau and Scottish baronial styles. (*The Herald*, established in 1783, claims to be the oldest daily paper in the English-speaking world.)

The building was converted during the Year of Architecture in 1999 and opened as **The Lighthouse** ❻ (0141-221 6362, www.the lighthouse.co.uk), a visitor centre aiming to illuminate Glasgow's architectural heritage. As well as temporary displays, there's a permanent Mackintosh exhibition, which puts his work in perspective. This is the essential first stop for anyone intending to visit his buildings.

The nearby former **Daily Record Building** (1901) on Renfield Lane also has many Mackintosh hallmarks, including glazed green-and-white brickwork patterned with a triangular tree motif and a row of steeply battered dormer windows. Admiring these and other delightful touches incurs a stiff neck on account of the narrowness of Renfield Lane.

Stop to admire the **Ca'd'Oro** ❼ (corner

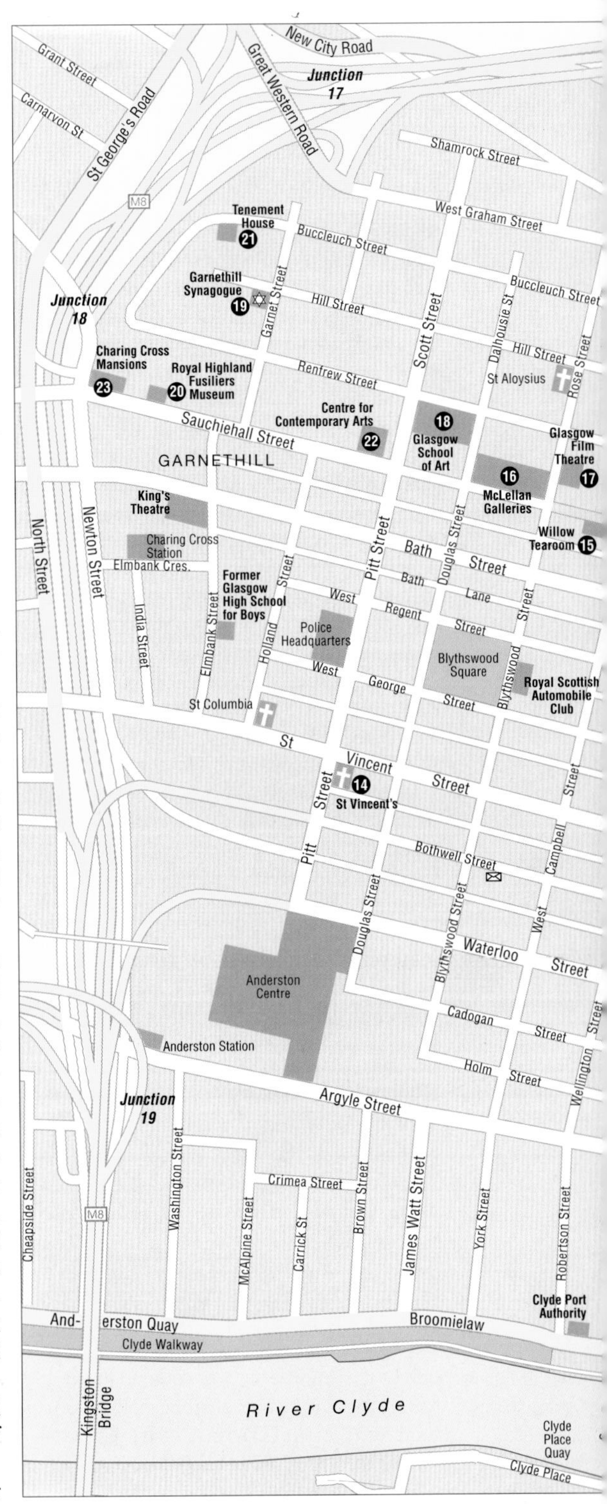

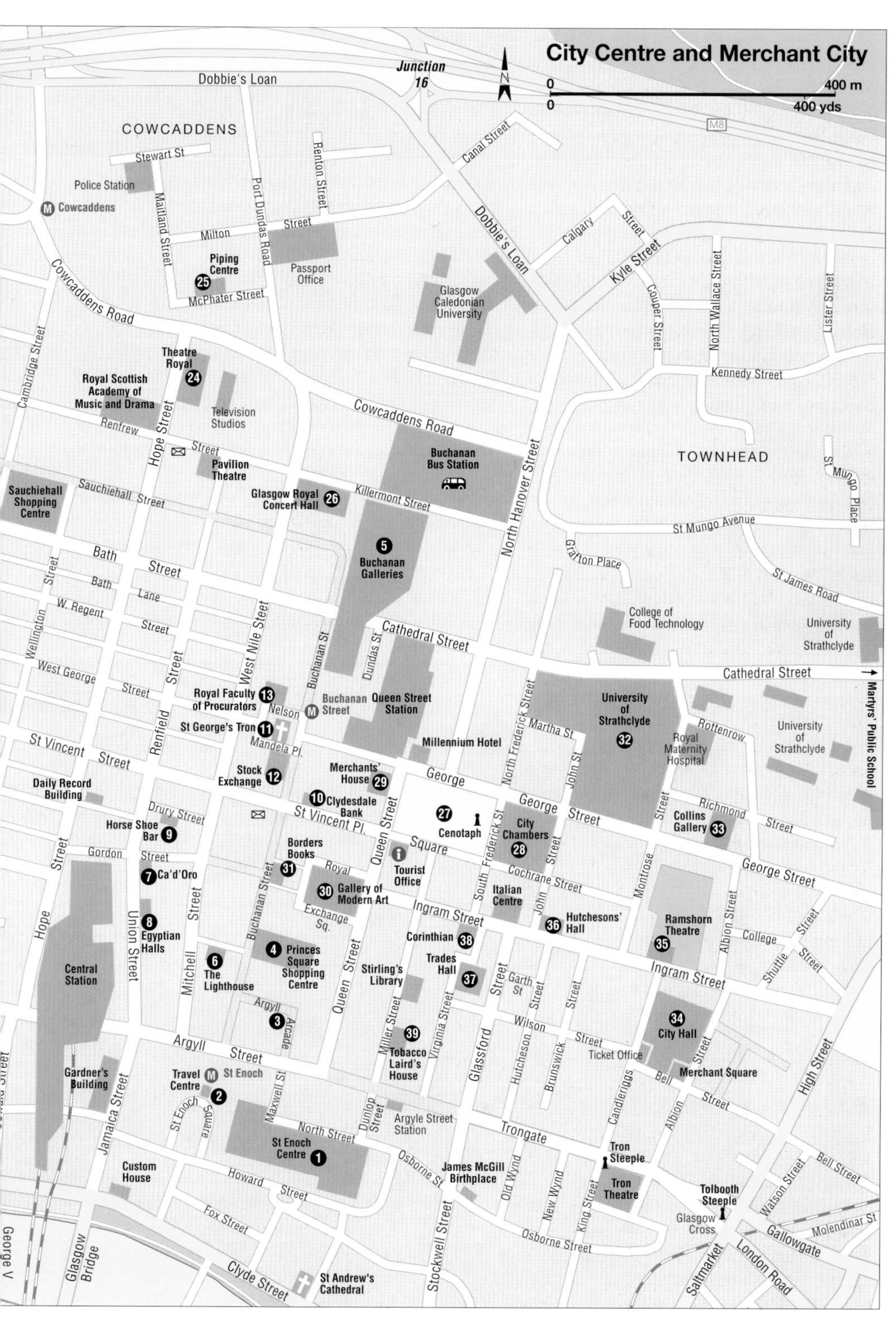
City Centre and Merchant City
0
400 m
0
400 yds
Junction 16
Dobbie's Loan
M8
COWCADDENS
TOWNHEAD
Cowcaddens
Police Station
Stewart St
Maitland Street
Milton Street
Renton Street
Port Dundas Road
Passport Office
Piping Centre 25
McPhater Street
Canal Street
Dobbie's Loan
Calgary Street
Kyle Street
Couper Street
North Wallace Street
Lister Street
Glasgow Caledonian University
Cowcaddens Road
Cambridge Street
Theatre Royal 24
Royal Scottish Academy of Music and Drama
Television Studios
Renfrew Street
Hope Street
Pavilion Theatre
Buchanan Bus Station
North Hanover Street
Kennedy Street
St Mungo Place
St Mungo Avenue
Sauchiehall Shopping Centre
Sauchiehall Street
Glasgow Royal Concert Hall 26
Killermont Street
5 Buchanan Galleries
Bath Street
Bath Lane
W. Regent Street
Wellington Street
West George Street
Renfield Street
West Nile Street
Buchanan St
Dundas St
Cathedral Street
Grafton Place
St James Road
College of Food Technology
University of Strathclyde
Cathedral Street
Martyrs' Public School
Royal Faculty of Procurators 13
Nelson Mandela Pl.
Buchanan Street
Queen Street Station
St George's Tron 11
Millennium Hotel
North Frederick Street
Martha St
John St
University of Strathclyde 32
Royal Maternity Hospital
Rottenrow
University of Strathclyde
St Vincent Street
Stock Exchange 12
Merchants' House 29
Daily Record Building
Drury Street
10 Clydesdale Bank
St Vincent Pl.
27 Cenotaph
George Square
George Street
South Frederick St
City Chambers 28
Montrose Street
Richmond Street
Collins Gallery 33
Horse Shoe Bar 9
Gordon Street
Borders Books
Queen Street
Tourist Office
7 Ca'd'Oro
31
Royal Exchange Sq.
30 Gallery of Modern Art
Cochrane Street
Italian Centre
George Street
Albion Street
Ramshorn Theatre 35
College Street
Shuttle Street
8 Egyptian Halls
Union Street
Mitchell Street
Ingram Street
John Street
36 Hutchesons' Hall
Corinthian 38
Central Station
6 The Lighthouse
4 Princes Square Shopping Centre
Stirling's Library
Trades Hall 37
Garth St
Hutcheson Street
Brunswick Street
Ingram Street
34 City Hall
High Street
Argyll Arcade 3
Argyll Street
Miller Street
Virginia Street
39 Tobacco Laird's House
Glassford Street
Wilson Street
Ticket Office
Candleriggs
Merchant Square
Bell Street
Gardner's Building
Travel Centre
St Enoch
2
St Enoch Square
Jamaica Street
Maxwell St
North Street
St Enoch Centre 1
Dunlop Street
Argyle Street Station
Trongate
Tron Steeple
Tron Theatre
Albion Street
Bell Street
Watson Street
Custom House
Howard Street
Osborne St
James McGill Birthplace
Old Wynd
New Wynd
King Street
Tolbooth Steeple
Glasgow Cross
Molendinar St
Gallowgate
Fox Street
Osborne Street
George V
Glasgow Bridge
Clyde Street
St Andrew's Cathedral
Stockwell Street
Saltmarket
London Road

of Gordon and Union Streets), another glorious building with a facade of glass and cast-iron, which is Glasgow's answer to Venice's 15th-century Golden House. Giant Romanesque masonry arches sitting on top of Doric pilasters enclose vast expanses of glass and above this is a row of circular attic windows. Here is a rare example of shops not detracting from the beauty of the building.

Almost next to the Ca'd'Oro on Union Street is another, less obvious, cast-iron framed building. The **Egyptian Halls** ❽ are from the drawing-board of Alexander "Greek" Thomson. Especially unusual in this linear building are the dumpy, Egyptian-style columns on the upper floor; they practically form a colonnade or an eaves gallery. Unfortunately, this magnificent building lies empty and abandoned, awaiting a buyer with the imagination to renovate it and return it to use.

On the way back to Buchanan Street, if there is time for a "refreshment", enter the **Horse Shoe Bar** ❾ at 17 Drury Street, which has the second longest continuous bar in Britain. Three hundred yards to the east of here is St Vincent's Place, which is nothing more than a widening, on the south side, of the street of that name. Magnificent Victorian Renaissance buildings, mostly banks and insurance companies, line both sides of the Place, with the vista to the east being closed by the City Chambers.

One of the finest examples is the **Clydesdale Bank** ❿ at numbers 30–40. The modest foyer scarcely prepares the visitor for what is beyond the next glass doors. The black, gold and russet banking hall is arcaded in the Venetian manner and topped by an elliptical cupola. Fanciful wrought-iron designs fill the coffers (not the tills but the lacunae in the ceiling) and permit light to enter the hall, which is decorated with black engaged columns with pseudo-Ionic capitals decorated with laurel leaves. Around the top of the walls are the heads of 30 Roman emperors and empresses.

A little further up Buchanan Street is

BELOW: the former ticket office for St Enoch station, now a tourist centre.

Nelson Mandela Place. Formerly, this was St George's Place but in 1986 the city council changed the name to support Mandela's stand against apartheid in South Africa. He had already been given the freedom of the city in 1981 while still in prison, but after his release he came personally to accept the award in the City Chambers. Coincidentally, the South African Consulate was located in St George's Place.

Dominating the centre of the square and evocative of Sir Christopher Wren is **St George's Tron Church** ⓫ (1807) with a tower topped by an obelisk thrusting heavenwards. The four obelisks at the level of the clocks are poor substitutes for the four evangelists.

Echoes of Venice

The **Stock Exchange** ⓬, that glorious icing cake at the southeast corner of the square, positively shrieks Venice. On the walls of the building are carvings symbolising Building, Engineering and Mining (Nelson Mandela Place side) and Science and Art (Buchanan Street side). The building has been renovated and is to become the Scottish base of yet another large international retailer.

Diagonally opposite is the lavish, two-storey **Royal Faculty of Procurators** ⓭ (1854), modelled on St Mark's Library in Venice. The handsome keystones above the decorated windows represent the great and the good of the legal profession of a by-gone age. Of the intricately detailed carving, the frieze of lions sitting among foliage and the Palladian ensemble on the West Nile Street side are especially attractive. The adjacent building with figures of Purcell (music), Flaxman (sculpture), Wren (architecture) and Reynolds (painting) standing on a ledge supported by four Ionic columns was constructed in 1886 as the Athenaeum and then became the College of Dramatic Art. It has had a spell as a hotel but went back on the market as a "retail opportunity".

Six hundred yards west of Nelson Mandela Place, on the crest of a drumlin on St

BELOW: the Stock Exchange.
RIGHT: St Vincent's Free Church of Scotland.

Vincent Street, stands **St Vincent's Church** ⓮, whose frontage would make a perfect stage for a performance of *Aida*. This quintessential "Greek" Thomson building has eclectic antecedents, as do so many of his buildings.

The site, on a steep hillside, is particularly awkward, but Thomson *(see page 209)* overcame this by designing an enormous podium with Egyptian-like doors leading in to the lower part of the church. On top stands the main church hall, fronted by an Ionic portico; its sides, however, are more Egyptian than Greek and its tower would not have been out of place in India during the Raj. Inside, the colours and designs recall classical Egypt and a delightful anthemion frieze echoes a frieze on the exterior of the building.

A perfect square

From St Vincent's church, it's just a short steep climb to **Blythswood Square** (1823–29), which is possibly the most perfect square in the city: it occupies a flat piece of ground on top of a drumlin, is perfectly square and is planted with grass and flowers. The late classical, three-storey, grey buildings on all four sides, each with three Ionic porches and lintels above the windows of the middle range, were residences but are now clubs, restaurants and offices. The immaculate Royal Scottish Automobile Club building occupies all of the eastern side.

The magnet here for Mackintosh lovers is the doorway at No. 5 on the north side which he designed for the former occupants, the Glasgow Society of Lady Artists. No. 7, next door, was the home of Madeleine Smith, the defendant in one of Scotland's most notorious murder trials. In 1857, she was accused of poisoning her lover. The jury, to rapturous applause, brought in a verdict of "not proven", which in Scots law can be construed to mean "we think you did it but we can't prove it".

Leave the northern side of the square, stroll the 100 yards to **Sauchiehall Street** and turn right for morning coffee or after-

LEFT: Glaswegians love to shop. **BELOW:** to locate the Willow Tearoom, look for a jeweller's.

Map on page 106

noon tea at the readily recognisable, light-coloured, light-hearted, small building bearing the sign Henderson's the Jewellers. The ground floor of this store does sell jewellery but venture upstairs to the **Willow Tearoom** ⓯ (Sauchiehall is Scots for the Meadow of Willow Trees) and be delighted, for this is an exact reconstruction of one of the four tearooms which his patron, Kate Cranston, employed Mackintosh to decorate *(see page 112)*. What's more, it is the only one of the four for which Mackintosh was both architect and interior decorator.

Mackintosh believed in total design and the furniture (reproduction), the cutlery, menu-cards and fittings – leaded mirror glass doors and similarly treated windows – are all Mackintosh designs or the work of his wife, Margaret MacDonald. Note how the windows in this, the Room de Luxe of the original tearoom, arch across the facade, allowing waves of diffused daylight to flicker in and around the furnishings. You will probably have to queue to get in here but it is more than worth it.

If it is raining on leaving the tearoom, then those carrying their macintosh should give thanks to Glasgow. Another MacIntosh from Glasgow, who was also christened Charles but who lived 100 years before the artist, was the inventor of the process which permitted the making of waterproof clothing.

The bust of a young Queen Victoria occupies an alcove below the Glasgow coat of arms above the entrance to the **McLellan Galleries** ⓰ building (immediately to the West of the Willow Tearooms at the corner of Sauchiehall and Rose streets). Archibald McLellan, a coach-maker, was an art lover who bequeathed to the city his not inconsiderable collection, which was especially strong in 16th and 17th-century Italian masters, and the building in which it was housed.

Unfortunately, as with the Burrell Collection *(see page 218)*, there were problems with the legacy and it was only after McLellan's numerous debtors had been

BELOW: inside the Willow Tearoom, designed by Charles Rennie Mackintosh.

Charles Rennie Mackintosh

Charles Rennie Mackintosh (1868–1928), Glasgow born and educated, was the toast of avant-garde architects and designers in Europe, yet in his own country he was a prophet ignored. Budapest, Munich, Dresden, Turin, Venice and Moscow toasted: "To our master Mackintosh, the greatest since the Gothic" – but in Glasgow the vast majority scoffed.

How could such frivolity be taken seriously? The reactions from "the saner seven-eighths of mankind", especially to his School of Art and to Miss Cranston's tearooms, were hilarity, bewilderment and revulsion. Only with the re-awakening of interest in art nouveau in the 1950s did his furniture and architecture begin influence British designers and, to a lesser extent, architects. Today, Mackintosh is a cult figure of international renown, with a reputation built on a remarkably small opus, executed over scarcely more than 20 years.

Although neither his parents nor his 10 siblings showed much interest in the arts, he became an architect, finding his inspiration, as did so many others, in the vernacular buildings of the countryside. This is evident in his *magnum opus*, the Glasgow School of Art. His simple geometrical manipulation of space based on combinations of straight line and gentle curves, with the former predominating, was a harbinger of later purist work. His was an eclectic mixture, part utilitarian and modernistic, part artistic and traditional.

Contemporary with Mackintosh at art school were several talented designers, artists and craft-workers who constituted a group which created the Glasgow Style. Mackintosh insisted that he was not part of that school and never its leader. Yet, in many respects, the Chinese and Cloister rooms which he designed for Miss Cranston's Ingram Street tea-rooms are the ultimate statement of the Glasgow Style.

At art school, Mackintosh and his friend Herbert McNair met the women whom they would marry: the artist sisters Margaret and Frances Macdonald. "The Four", influenced by both Pre-Raphaelitism and Aestheticism, were dedicated to the search for a distinctive modern style and collaborated on designs for furniture, metalwork and illustration. But-Mackintosh's concept of the total integration of architecture and interior design and his insistence on complete control of every detail made commissions few and far between.

He was fortunate to find an ideal client in Kate Cranston. Not only was she an astute businesswoman but she also shared his vision of bringing art into every aspect of daily life and within everyone's reach.

By 1913, with his talent eroded by both a drinking problem and a lack of confidence, he and Margaret abandoned "philistine" Glasgow and went to live in Suffolk where he intended to take up painting seriously. A year later they moved to Chelsea where he attempted to resume his work as an architect and designer. However, by 1923, Mackintosh had abandoned all hope and emigrated to the south of France to devote himself to water-colour painting. In 1928 he died in London, in a Hampstead nursing home, from cancer of the tongue. ❑

LEFT: Mackintosh, a designer who couldn't bear to compromise.

satisfied that Glasgow was able to receive the bequest, which became the basis for the collection in the Kelvingrove Art Gallery. This classical, three-storey building, with a dome at its corner and windows topped by triangular or curved pediments or lintels supported by brackets, was beautifully restored in 1990 after a fire and now houses one of the galleries in the city. For the two years when Kelvingrove Art Gallery is closed for a major refurbishment (late 2002–2004) the core of Glasgow's art collection will return here to its original home.

The Cosmo Cinema or the **Glasgow Film Theatre** ⓱, in nearby Rose Street, a 1930s building in Modern Scandinavian style, is an "art cinema". It continues to show more obscure, foreign-language and classic films, often with talks or discussions to complement them.

Mackintosh's monument

And so to Renfrew Street and a steep climb of 100 yards to that building in Glasgow which attracts most visitors: the **Glasgow School of Art** ⓲. (To determine visiting times, telephone 0141-353 4526.) Built in 1897–99 and with a wing added in 1907–09, this is Charles Rennie Mackintosh's magnum opus, a work which was the harbinger of a new movement in Europe and one which would influence the Continent rather than the homeland. Mention must be made of Francis ("Fra") Newbery, who was the director of the school at the time of the competition for a new building and who insisted that Mackintosh's entry should win.

The design of the building was a challenge, not only because of the paucity of funds available (that is why it was constructed in two parts) but because it is built between two of the steepest hills in the city.

The entrance on Renfrew Street is startlingly asymmetrical and the gentle curvature of the stone stairway contrasts with the linearity of this facade, which is dominated by enormous windows. These, some of which are embellished with fanciful

BELOW AND RIGHT: the Art School, outside and inside.

wrought-iron, permit north light to enter the studios. Although the great proportion of glass to stone in this facade reversed the trend in Victorian buildings, it was not without precedent in Glasgow – compare Gardener's building *(see page 120)* and the Ca'd'oro *(see page 142)*. The east wall is more evocative of an ancient Scottish castle, rough and powerful, and it has been suggested that the Governors accepted this startling design with its lack of ornamentation only because it would be inexpensive to build. (The windows at the northern end of this facade were later additions through which live animals from an adjacent circus were brought in for life classes.)

On the west facade, grille-covered oriel windows soar upwards for three storeys, forming an irregular pattern, which is at its most magnificent when illuminated by the setting sun. The back of the building, which looks down on Sauchiehall Street and is difficult to see, is a powerful mass of Scottish baronial details.

The interior, with its magnificent use of timber, has been described as a "warren of discovery", which was the result, at least in part, of the building being constructed in two stages.

The most celebrated and the most exciting room is the two-storey galleried library. Mackintosh's use of solid dark wood, delicate curves of wrought iron, splashes of primary colours and light is evident everywhere, as surprising windows spill light across the dark solidity of the wood, sculpting the shapes against the airy lightness of the spaces. So, too, is the great attention, which he paid to detail not only for the convenience, but also for the delight, of those who would work in the building. Students still study here, sitting at the priceless Mackintosh chairs and desks. A collection of architectural drawings, watercolours and furniture from several of Mackintosh's other commissions can be found in the Mackintosh Room and the Furniture Gallery.

Continue westwards along Renfrew Street for about 300 yards to **Garnethill Synagogue** ⓳, the principal and oldest Jewish house of worship in Glasgow. Just beyond this, Renfrew Street ends in a modest belvedere from where remarkably splendid views of the towers of the Park Conservation scheme and of the University of Glasgow can be savoured.

War and peace

Two quite different small museums can be reached from here. Descend the steep drumlin to the north to reach the Tenement House at 145 Buccleuch Street or descend the equally steep drumlin to the south to the **Royal Highland Fusiliers Museum** ⓴ at 518 Sauchiehall Street. The latter contains 300 years of military memorabilia of the regiment whose name it bears and which has the greatest number of battle honours of any British regiment.

Time is frozen in the fully furnished **Tenement House** ㉑ (Mar–Oct daily 2–5pm) which is fascinating not because it was so special but because it was so typical. Built in 1892 and unaltered since, it gives an insight into life in Glasgow between 1911 and 1965 when Miss Agnes Toward, who could not bear to throw

LEFT: Art School students are sought after.

Map on page 106

away a scrap of paper, lived here. When she died, she left the tickets, bills and receipts of a lifetime tied up in neat bundles. This ephemera which most people throw away provided a unique record of an ordinary life in a tenement. Most Glaswegians lived in tenement houses, some few grander than this, most not so grand. Enter the flat and enter a time capsule of the gas-lit era with a coal bunker and the yellow glow of gas mantles over the black-leaded cooking range. Miss Toward's jam is still in jars on the kitchen shelves, her cooking pots and utensils are on the range and the table in the front room is laid for afternoon tea with her china tea service.

Still on Sauchiehall Street, a few yards to the east of the Military Museum are the **Grecian Chambers**. This work by "Greek" Thomson has marked similarities, especially in the free-standing row of squat columns which form an eaves gallery, to the Egyptian Halls in Union Street *(see page 144)*.

The **Centre for Contemporary Arts** (CCA) ㉒, which occupies one of the ground-floor shops here, was opened in the mid-1980s as the **Third Eye**, Glasgow's first contemporary arts centre. It has successfully kept up with the times and now boasts a studio-style theatre, two exhibition galleries, a wholefood cafeteria and bar and an arts bookshop.

A grand tenement

A few steps to the west of the Military Museum is the spectacular curve of the five-storey, red sandstone **Charing Cross Mansions** ㉓. This chateau-like building, reminiscent of the 16th-century Hôtel de Ville in Paris, is a Glasgow tenement – not of the kind formerly found in the Gorbals, but nevertheless, a tenement. The oriel windows, steep attic roof and three-bay centre-piece with a clock and galleried cupola are altogether a truly splendid sight to behold.

Across the road from here, on the east side of Elmbank Street, stands a hand-

BELOW: the Tenement House Museum.

some Victorian classical building with statues atop four columns, which flank the entrance. It is now occupied by the city council but was formerly the home of the **Glasgow High School for Boys**, which was founded even before Glasgow University (1451) and which might be the oldest school in Britain.

Theatreland

Three of the oldest and largest theatres in the city can be found in this part of town. The **King's** at Charing Cross, with a rich red-and-gold Edwardian interior, stages musicals and the occasional play from London's West End; although grand and large, it is also rented out at modest sums to amateur groups. Then, close to the junction of Renfield and Sauchiehall streets is the **Pavilion**, a music hall whose boards have been trod by many of Scotland's great comedians and which now presents rock and pop concerts as well as shows for the family.

Nearby is the **Theatre Royal** ㉔, undoubtedly Scotland's most prestigious theatre, the home of Scottish Opera, where opera and ballet usually occupy the stage. Across the road is the relatively new modern brick building of the Royal Scottish Academy of Music and Drama.

Nearby is the **Piping Centre** ㉕, a museum devoted to bagpipes of all kinds and descriptions. The former St Stephen's church building has a Greek-style portico and an Italianate tower performance hall with regular concerts and an excellent brasserie, the **Pipers' Tryst** (0141-353 0220) serving outstanding Scottish fare. Furthermore it's a grand place to stay and has a few bedrooms to let.

To the east of here, opposite Buchanan Street Bus Station, is the **Glasgow Royal Concert Hall** ㉖ (0141-353 8000), purpose-built in 1990; its main auditorium seats 2,500. This is Glasgow's premier venue, hosting every kind of music from classical to rock, and is home of the phenomenally successful three-week Celtic Connections festival in January. ❑

Map on page 106

LEFT: the King's Theatre.
BELOW: the Centre for Contemporary Arts.

Shopping

Serious shoppers will feel no pain after a day's shopping in Glasgow, except aching feet and severely battered credit cards. The city has the largest shopping centre in the UK after London, glorying in a wealth of exclusive shops, designer labels and variety of retail outlets. The prosperous Merchant City intersperses classy wine bars, abundant restaurants and stockbrokers with exclusive clothes shops such as the Italian Centre, stocking rare designer labels for serious dressers.

Further east at Gallowgate, the Barras market may just provide something cheap, cheerful and unexpected to lift designer dressing to pizzazz and style. Alternatively, you can take the underground railway – the Clockwork Orange – out west to the quirky shops lining Great Western Road. From ethnic crafts and silk saris to wholefoods and pottery, there's always something just a little bit different, reflecting the cosmopolitan nature of the area.

In the city centre, the chain stores and specialist shops continue to multiply in Glasgow's "Golden Z", the three famous shopping streets of Argyle Street, Buchanan Street and Sauchiehall Street. The Argyle Arcade, built in 1827 and one of the oldest covered shopping arcades in the UK, is always strewn with young lovers, noses stuck to the windows of the 32 jewellers' shops.

Just along Buchanan Street from the Argyle Arcade is the elegant Princes Square, a historic square dating from 1841, now covered and renovated. Lacoste and Calvin Klein rub shoulders with exclusive leather and jewellery designers, while the style-conscious Glaswegians sip cappuccino or cool white wine at pavement cafés. For those with style aspirations beyond their budgets, The Address – Designer Exchange, tucked in behind Royal Exchange Square, has all the designer labels, as new, at a fraction of original prices.

The Buchanan Galleries shopping centre at the top of Buchanan Street has all the usual chain stores as well as the John Lewis department store and Ottokar's bookshop with its comfy sofas and unhurried coffee shop. A crèche and shopmobility make it user-friendly for disabled and child-laden shoppers. Just opposite is the UK's largest Virgin Megastore. A few steps away is Graham Tiso Ltd, one of the largest outdoor shops in the UK. But for a unique outdoor shopping expedition, continue north beyond the "Golden Z", beyond the Royal Concert Hall and the Bus Station to "Tiso – Glasgow Outdoor Experience" on Couper Street with its 50-ft (15-metre) rock pinnacle, real ice wall and waterfall allowing you to try before you buy its wide range of outdoor equipment.

The chain stores continue along Sauchiehall Street, but hidden away behind it in West Regent Street and Bath Street is a selection of fine art and antiques shops. In Renfrew Street, to the north of Sauchiehall Street, is Glasgow School of Art Enterprises, with a range of contemporary design by Art School students, past and present.

Almost at the end of the Golden Z is Henderson's the Jewellers, incorporating Mackintosh's Willow Tearoom, designed for Miss Kate Cranston. Her success is evidence that the ladies of Victorian Glasgow shopped till they dropped too. ❑

RIGHT: Princes Square, a temple for shoppers.

Map on page 106

THE MERCHANT CITY

In the area bounded by Argyle Street, Cathedral Street, Buchanan Street and High Street are the imposing civic buildings that trumpeted Glasgow's trading triumphs in the 18th and 19th centuries

This was Glasgow's first major expansion. The Act of Union in 1707 opened the lucrative markets of the American colonies to the Scots merchants and Glasgow became a major centre for trade in sugar, cotton and tobacco. As the city prospered, it spread west from the High Street, occupying the relatively flat area lying between what is now Argyle Street in the south to George Street in the north. Here the tobacco lords built their huge warehouses and mansion houses.

In time, they moved from the centre to new homes in the suburbs further west, and their mansions were converted to warehouses and banks as this part of Glasgow became the commercial heart of the city. The American War of Independence badly affected the trade in sugar, cotton and tobacco but Glasgow recovered, becoming a centre of heavy industry during the Industrial Revolution and the "Second City of the Empire".

A return to elegance

At about this time, that part of the city between Trongate and George Street was described as being "occupied by a succession of beautiful streets intersecting each other at right angles… Wilson Street, Great Glassford Street, Miller Street, Queen Street, Buchanan Street, and Ingram Street. Besides these are Cochrane Street, John Street, Glassford Street, George Square, Gordon Street, and Camperdown Place [now West George Street]: in all of which the buildings vie with each other in the expensive and elegant manner in which they have been executed." After a long descent into dilapidated neglect, these streets, cleaned and polished and renovated for new purposes, are beginning once again to merit that Victorian approbation.

After World War II, the steep and almost terminal decline of heavy industry in Glasgow and the Clyde was reflected in the Merchant City. Since about 1980, however, there has been a rejuvenation and a recycling of buildings. Old hotels have been given a facelift, the former grand buildings of major banks are now night clubs, restaurants and pubs and everywhere old warehouses are being converted into apartments, while new modern blocks, designed to blend in with the existing architecture, are springing up in gap sites throughout the area.

In the opening years of the 21st century the Merchant City has come full circle and is now *the* place to stay, with exclusive, three-bedroom penthouse flats in the former Post Office building on George Square selling for half a million pounds.

PRECEDING PAGES: jam session outside the City Chambers. **LEFT:** reflections on the Stock Exchange. **RIGHT:** a city officer on guard.

Nearly every month sees the opening of another new restaurant, a brasserie, a wine bar or an upmarket pub. There's a buzz in the air as the young and trendy go about the daily business of work, rest and play while at the same time, city councillors and soberly dressed business people can be found in the dark comfortable recesses of older establishments. Meanwhile, in traditional and still shabby bars in quiet back streets, cloth-capped Glasgow punters cherish the Glasgow of yesteryear in lengthy discourse with anyone who cares to join in.

Purists may argue over the exact boundaries of the Merchant City, but for the purpose of this guide we'll take it as the area contained within Argyle Street and the Trongate to the south, Cathedral Street to the north, Buchanan Street to the west and High Street to the east.

George Square

Start at **George Square** ㉗, which is the city centre, built in 1787 on a piece of marshland. Sheep grazed in the square until well into the 19th century and were prevented from straying by a 4-ft (1-metre) high railing. Later, the square became the main hotel centre of the city and then, in the 19th century, the Municipal Chambers and the General Post Office were moved to here from Glasgow Cross and the Briggait respectively. One of the old hotels, much changed, still occupies part of the north side of the Square. Previously the Copthorne, it has recently emerged from a massive renovation programme as the **Millennium** and the former Post Office building on the south side is being converted for residential use.

Scattered about the Square are statues of 11 persons who appear to have been selected as the result of a lottery. In the centre, looking down on all, with his plaid, as was his wont, thrown over his left, rather than right, shoulder, is Sir Walter Scott standing atop an 80-ft (24-metre) slender Doric column. This was the first memorial in the land to be erected in honour of Scott, an Edinburgh man, whose connec-

BELOW: the City Chambers.

Map on page 106

tions with Glasgow are at best tenuous. Who said Glaswegians are parochial?

George III, after whom the square was named when it was laid out in 1781, should occupy the spot where Scott stands, but losing the American colonies cost the Glasgow tobacco lords dearly and cost George III, if not his head, at least his position in Glasgow's George Square. However, royalty is represented by statues of Queen Victoria and of Prince Albert.

Robert Burns and James Watt, whose statues stand in the southwest corner of the Square, will be known to all, as will William Gladstone and Robert Peel, but who on earth was Thomas Campbell? He was the most famous of Glasgow's men-of-letters, at least in his time (1777–1844), and was three times elected Lord Rector of the University of Glasgow, on one occasion defeating Scott who now towers over him. Gladstone and Peel also held this title. The other statues are of Sir John Moore, hero of the Battle of Corunna; Lord Clyde (Colin Campbell), a field marshal who crushed the Indian mutiny (does Glasgow's not inconsiderable Indian community know he stands here?); Thomas Graham, the "father of colloid chemistry"; and James Oswald, a minor parliamentarian – Glaswegians all. Finally, dominating the east side of the Square is the **Cenotaph**, a powerful memorial to Glasgow's dead in the two world wars.

The City Chambers

Behind the cenotaph, the entire east side of the square is occupied by the massive **City Chambers** ㉘ (0141-287 4018, www.glasgow.gov.uk/guidedtours Mon–Fri 10.30am and 2.30pm, free). Queen Victoria, who, in her only other visit 39 years previously, had not liked the city and said that she would prefer not to return, opened the City Chambers in 1888.

The style, typical of the time, is Italian Renaissance, although the 216-ft (65-metre) tower, capped by a domed cupola, owes little to the Mediterranean. Each corner carries a domed cupola.

BELOW: the interior of the City Chambers has served as a film set.

The facade is covered with innumerable bas-relief tableaux and sculptural groups. The tableau in the main pediment commemorates the Jubilee Year of Queen Victoria, who sits on her throne atop a flight of steps with the lion at her feet and figures representing England, Scotland, Ireland and Wales supporting her. At the side of these are other figures representing the then many British colonies. The figures, 8 ft high (more than 2 metres), are larger than those in the Elgin Marbles and appear life-sized when viewed from the street.

In a smaller pediment above the entrance, which contains symbolic figures depicting Religion, Virtue and Knowledge, is the city's motto "Let Glasgow Flourish". This is an abbreviated version of the text written on the bell of the Tron Church, cast in 1631, which reads: "Lord, let Glasgow flourish through the preaching of Thy word and praising Thy name".

Although still the seat of local government in Glasgow, the Chambers also enjoys a secondary career as a film set and is in great demand by movie-makers. The richly decorated, ornate interiors have featured as everything from a palace to a High Court, while the exterior has made an appearance as the Kremlin. The triumphal announcement, loud and clear, is of success, wealth and confidence.

The Glasgow City fathers had a "guid conceit" of themselves and the building of the city chambers was a means to show the world that at that time Glasgow was Scotland's premier city, if not its capital, and outside of London the largest and most important city of the far-flung British Empire.

Rich red coupled columns – which look like marble but which are actually cut from Peterhead granite and which are said to be the most beautiful pieces of granite ever quarried in Scotland – stand on grey slabs of Aberdeen granite and are topped by dark green Italian marble capitals. The vaulted ceiling and dome dazzle with brilliant Venetian mosaics while other mosaics cover the floor. Going through

BELOW: Victorian ornateness in the City Chambers.

the front door is like entering an Italian basilica, then from the entrance hall crossing into an Italian Renaissance palace.

Two stairways lead to the upper floors. One can do no better than quote William Young, the architect: "the view from the first landing is really magnificent. Tier upon tier of pillars, arches and cornices, the whole height of the stair, three lofty storeys in various coloured marbles – purple Brescia, veined Carrara and red transparent alabaster surmounted by a vast conical ceiling in richly ornamental plasterwork and a cupola filled with tinted glass."

Visit, among other rooms, the Council Hall, the "Municipal Drawing Room", the Octagonal Room, the Mahogany Salon and the Banqueting Hall. The craftsmanship is first-class, the attention to detail meticulous; but remember that not all the artisans were Scots – some were from France and Italy. The superbly carved Spanish mahogany in the Council Hall evokes memories of skilled medieval artisans. Above the wood is a frieze of wheat-coloured Tynecastle tapestry, a mixture of leather and papier-mâché.

Dining out

However, the *pièce de résistance* is the huge Banqueting Hall – 110 ft (33 metres) long, 48 ft (14 metres) wide and 52 ft (16 metres) high – with its glorious arched ceiling, leaded glass windows and paintings depicting scenes from the history of the city. The south wall is covered by three large murals, which are the work of members of the Glasgow Boys (*see page 77*).

Alexander Roche's painting is of the incident when a ring was found in a salmon caught in the Clyde. The king of Strathclyde believed that Languoreth, his queen, was having an affair with one of his knights and, indeed, she had given the fellow her ring. And so, when the knight was asleep the king stole this ring, hurled it into the Clyde, and ordered the queen to wear it that evening. Languoreth appealed to St Mungo, who dispatched a monk to fish in the river and to bring to him the first fish, which he caught. The salmon had the ring in its mouth. Honour was saved and that is why the fish appears on the Glasgow coat of arms.

Edward Walton's mural is of the "Glasgow Fair" on Glasgow Green *circa* 1500. Walton used a rare technique, at least among British artists, of mixing his paints with sand, resulting in a dramatic almost 3-D effect. The third mural which shows the busy River Clyde towards the middle of the 19th century is by Sir John Lavery. The three large gracious chandeliers in this room are the originals for, even although the Chambers were built in 1885, they were illuminated by electricity.

Directly opposite the City Chambers at the northern corner of the west side of the square is the **Merchants' House** ㉙ (Mon–Thur 9am–12.30pm) whose original members were relatively wealthy wholesalers, exporters and importers. The exterior is remarkable, among other details, for its corner oriel windows supported by corbels in the shape of Amazons. Atop the domed tower is a sailing ship similar to the one atop the Briggait

RIGHT: the Merchants' House.

Steeple. Notable in the Banqueting Hall with its Corinthian engaged columns and pilasters are the mortification boards commemorating bequests made by wealthy members of the House. The Directors' room is also richly furbished and its walls are lined with Tynecastle silk.

One of the occupants of the building is the Glasgow Chamber of Commerce, the oldest such chamber in Britain.

Gallery of Modern Art

Exiting from George Square at its southwest corner leads to **Queen Street** and, after a few steps to **Royal Exchange Square**. The heart of the square is occupied by the **Royal Exchange Building**, which started life in 1780 as the most imposing tobacco lord's mansion in the city. It belonged to William Cunninghame who made an enormous fortune at the time of the American War of Independence by buying up all stocks of Virginia tobacco held by nervous merchants and reselling it later at a 700 percent profit. In 1827, Cunninghame's home became the Royal Exchange and David Hamilton added the impressive portico of 12 giant fluted columns atop a modest pedestal.

The sides of the building are pilastered with, towards their western end, colonnades while the rear of the building has considerably smaller engaged columns and pilasters. All are of the Corinthian order. Hamilton also added the lantern, a handsome affair whose upper part is supported by more Corinthian elements.

It is now the **Gallery of Modern Art** 30 (0141-229 1996, www.glasgow.gov.uk, Mon–Thur and Sat 10am–5pm, Fri and Sun 11am– 5pm, free), and one of the most popular attractions in the city. The placing of this fascinating modern collection within the magnificent Corinthian columns of the Royal Exchange Building has proved to be inspired. The primary colours and mirror mosaic work on the pediment of its classical frontage is startling and immediately thought-provoking. Essentially confident artistic statements of modern times such as

BELOW: on the roof of the Merchants' House.

Map on page 106

pictures by Beryl Cook and Avril Paton, machine sculptures and computer-generated images, are housed within a confident architectural statement of an earlier time.

Inside, the display space is divided on four floors to represent the four elements of fire, water, air and earth, with exhibits as diverse as the amazing kinetic sculpture by the Russian artist Eduard Bersudsky, reminiscent of the work of Heath Robinson, and a scurrilous papier-mâché statue of Her Majesty the Queen as a Glasgow housewife complete with hair net and curlers, dressing gown and old-fashioned slippers. She has a milk bottle in one hand, *Sporting Life* under her arm, and a cigarette dangling from her lip.

Equally irreverent is the treatment of the magnificent equestrian statue of Wellington, which stands before the entrance to the gallery. It was obvious that something was missing until one night some revellers hit the answer and climbed the horse to place an orange traffic cone on the Iron Duke's head. On Monday council workmen were dispatched to remove it, but it was back again the following weekend and is now more or less a permanent fixture, appearing on postcards and posters worldwide. The people of Glasgow had decided and when the cone was removed for a photo shoot there was an outcry.

The **Royal Bank of Scotland** building, to the rear of the library, is now home to **Borders Books** ㉛, fronted by an impressive raised Ionic hexastyle portico atop a flight of steps. Two handsome arches flanked by coupled Ionic columns provide passage between Royal Exchange Square and Buchanan Street.

University of Strathclyde

The **University of Strathclyde** ㉜, which now occupies most of the buildings between George Street and Cathedral Street from North Frederick Street as far east as the High Street, has expanded over the years and now has a splendid new Campus Village, almost at the Cathedral, with architecture drawn from the traditional Glasgow tenement and themes from Charles Rennie Mackintosh. In 1989 the University took over the former Barony Parish Church, which is now the ceremonial Barony Hall.

The University of Strathclyde began life in 1796 as the Andersonian Institution, a technical school which was the brain-child of "Jolly Jack Phosphorus" Anderson, an irascible professor at the University of Glasgow who was "the enemy of lucre-loving professors". In 1912 it became the Royal Technical College and, later, the Royal College of Science and Technology or, to all Glaswegians, simply the "Tech". In 1964 university status was obtained and Strathclyde became the first of Scotland's post-World War II universities. Today it's Scotland's third largest university.

Over the past quarter of a century the university has grown and grown and grown but its heart remains the large red Italianate building on George Street which was built at the beginning of the 20th century. Behind this, on Richmond Street, is the **Collins Gallery** ㉝ where excellent art exhibitions are mounted.

About 1 mile (1.5 km) south from here

RIGHT: Sean Reed statue at the Gallery of Modern Art.

is **Candleriggs** and the **City Hall** ❸❹, which, after a fire in St Andrew's Hall in 1962 and until the opening of the Glasgow Royal Concert Hall in 1990, was the city's principal concert hall. Scarcely a beautiful building – this is partly due to its cramped quarters – the hall has excellent accoustics.

The entire region was once thronged with hawkers, when the city's fruit and vegetable market occupied the basement and rear of the building, now refurbished as an indoor shopping area called **Merchant Square** (0141-552 5908). The old cobbled floor has been retained and contains a selection of trendy, gaily painted barrows, while round the perimeter you'll find speciality shops and restaurants.

Mungo's miracle

Closing the vista at the northern end of Candleriggs (they did make candles here until the 17th century) is the **Ramshorn** ❸❺ or **St Paul's and St David's Parish Church**, which derives its name from the legend that here St Mungo performed the miracle of turning a stolen ram's head into stone. Nowadays, spectators must suspend their disbelief not for miracles but for stories enacted by thespians rather than by theologians, the church having been converted into a theatre for the University of Strathclyde.

The initials R.F. and A.F. inscribed on the pavement to the right of the church entrance mark the graves of the Foulis brothers. They were famous University of Glasgow printers and founders of Glasgow's first School of Art.

Two hundred yards further along **Ingram Street** is a delicate, white square building from 1805 with a clock face steeple. The figures in the two alcoves at the front of **Hutchesons' Hall** ❸❻ (0141-552 8391, www.nts.org.uk, daily 10am–5pm, free) were made in 1649 and occupied a previous building of the same name. They are of the philanthropists George and Thomas Hutcheson, who donated the building as an institutional headquarters

LEFT: Hutchesons' Hall.
BELOW: the philanthropist George Hutcheson.

Map on page 106

and meeting hall. The original building was a hospice built by George in 1639 to take care of "aged decrepit men of the age above 50 years" and then, with a bequest from Thomas, "to also attend to the needs of eleven orphan boys". By the 1870s the orphans had become the nucleus of a new school in the Hutchesontown district of the Gorbals. This school would become Hutchesons' Grammar School, now a co-educational fee-paying school in a south side suburb and one of the most renowned schools in Glasgow.

One of the portraits in the hall is of Sir William Smith who, in Glasgow in 1883, long before Lord Baden Powell had dreamt up the Boy Scouts, founded the **Boys' Brigade**, an organisation with a religious framework and one which has branches in several Commonwealth countries, the United States and Scandinavia. Hutchesons' Hall is now occupied by the West Regional offices of the National Trust for Scotland.

A shop occupies the ground floor and an elegant, richly decorated hall with handsome pedimented doorways is upstairs. It's worth a visit if only to view the video *Glasgow Style*, which is shown in the upstairs hall. The shop on the ground floor sells a unique collection of gifts by Glasgow designers.

The back of a massive neo-classical building, originally the County Chambers and later the Sheriff Court, stands empty directly opposite Hutchesons' Hall in what is sometimes erroneously referred to as Ingram Square.

At the front of the building, a hexastyle Ionic colonnade stands atop a giant plinth on which is carved a rather tired relief frieze showing the course and the functions of justice. Then, in the middle of the west flank – the building grew like Topsy, being altered five times in the first 50 years after it was built in 1842 – a hexastyle Corinthian colonnade flanked on either side by a pair of Corinthian pilasters rises from a balustrade and supports a massive corbel table on which stand giant urns.

Various plans have emerged for this building and it may yet emerge as a hotel, nightclub or apartments, but at the time of writing it is still on the market.

The Trades Hall

Look westwards from the colonnade along **Garth Street** and the view is of the **Trades Hall** ㊲ (open to the public by appointment only, 0141-552 5071). which is the home of the 14 Glasgow trade guilds.

Erected in 1794, this building from the drawing board of the great Scottish architect Robert Adam, is the second oldest in the city still serving its original function (the oldest is the Cathedral). A rusticated ground floor supports a heavily pedimented first floor while the upper floor is topped by a balustrade with a central frieze, above which sits Brittania flanking the Glasgow coat of arms. Behind this is a modest, green dome.

Those who cannot list the guilds – Hammermen, Tailors, Cordiners, Maltmen, Weavers, Bakers and the like – when they enter the building will certainly be able to do so on leaving. Stained-glass windows,

RIGHT: the Trades Hall, designed by Robert Adam.

chairs, the cupola of the dome and walls all carry the coats of arms of the individual guilds as well as the Glasgow coat of arms – but with one subtle difference. Although the familiar bell, fish and bird are all here, the words "Let Glasgow Flourish" are replaced by "Union is Strength".

A 30-ft (9-metre) oak bench, divided into seven sections by heavily carved arms with figure tops, stands on the right of the entrance hall. The coats of arms of the 14 guilds, of various Scottish towns and of various Belgian cities are embossed on the bench, which was carved by Belgian wood carvers who were refugees in Glasgow during the 1914–18 war.

From here a double flight of steps – Adam lovers should not look for anything comparable to the exceptional staircases of Culzean or Mellerstain – ascends to the first floor and a magnificent banqueting hall whose carved wooden ceiling and cupola are especially attractive. A wide, fawn-coloured, silk frieze around the walls pays tribute to the workers of all the trades and mahogany mortification panels tell of bequests.

Next door is the Saloon, with more craft crests and more mahogany mortification panels. Since its inception, one of the objectives of the Trades Hall is to provide hospitals for the sick, pensions for the elderly and to succour the needy. Worthy of a glance is the Almshouse Bell of 1635.

Proceed up **Glassford Street** and immediately turn left back into Ingram Street. Here is Lanarkshire House whose three storeys are topped by a massive corbel table below which stand six figures which are, from left to right, Britannia, Wealth, Justice, Peace, Industry and Glasgow. Built originally as the Union Bank, it is now the **Corinthian** ㊳ (www.corinthian.co.uk), one of the most ornate of Glasgow's new watering holes. The interior, restored to its 19th-century glory, contains a labyrinth of bars, a restaurant and a nightclub. It won the regeneration of Scotland Award in 2000 as well as New Restaurant of the Year.

BELOW: insignia at the Trades Hall

Map on page 106

Walk through Virginia Place at the side of this building to the rear and you will find **Virginia Street**, which has several buildings worth a look, particularly as this area is soon to be renovated. At number 51 is Virginia Court where the tobacco lords worked from 1817. Much later it was the home of Jacobean Corsetry and, although that has gone, the sign remains.

Further along, at numbers 31–35, was the Tobacco Exchange, which has had several incarnations since then, including a spell as the Sugar Exchange. It is now being converted into apartments.

Early architecture

Miller Street, a relatively quiet street, is situated to the west of and parallel to Virginia Street. It was first developed in 1761 when Mr Miller, a Maltman and Glasgow Bailie, decided to extend "a street of Gentleman's Houses" through the garden behind his house.

Number 42, **The Tobacco Laird's House** ㊴, was built in 1775 and is the earliest house to be found in the Merchant City. Recently restored, it still exhibits the strict requirements which Miller laid down for the development of houses on this street: "each house to consist of a half sunk and two square storeys, no gables, chimney or *corbie steps* facing the street and to be entered by a front door and flight of steps projected on the intended pavement". It is now the home of several organisations devoted to the preservation of architectural heritage.

Along from here at numbers 48–56 is Stirling's library on the site of William Stirling's House. Stirling was a merchant who left his collection of books for public use in 1791. It has had a number of homes in its long history, including the building it now occupies, which was previously the Mitchell Library. At its peak, it was housed in the Royal Exchange but was moved back here when that building was earmarked for the Gallery of Modern Art. The library occupies the ground floor. The rest of the building is being renovated. ❑

BELOW: relaxing after work.

Adm R. et Doctissimus
D. D. Leonardus Jansen
Pastor in Vet Weis Vigilan-
tissimus hanc donavit
fenestrā amp: D. Decano
Cap. Tolp: Anno 1681

Map on page 136

OLD GLASGOW

Here are Glasgow's beginnings. As well as a remarkable cathedral and many ancient buildings, there's the Necropolis, commemorating the dead, and the People's Palace, commemorating some very odd things

Glasgow's history begins here on the banks of the Molendinar burn when, sometime during the 4th century, St Ninian stopped long enough on his travels to consecrate a Christian cemetery. Later in the mid-6th century, St Kentigern, travelling west from Culross, encountered a dying holy man called Fergus, attended to his final needs and then transported the corpse in an ox cart until it stopped at Glasgow where he buried Fergus in St Ninian's cemetery. Kentigern then founded his early church near the spot.

He died here in 603 and was buried in his own church. Glasgow people are fond of giving people nicknames and so they called Kentigern, Mungo the "Dear One", which is why Glasgow sometimes appears to have two patron saints, St Kentigern and St Mungo.

Historically, the next 600 years are a void. But then, on 7 July 1136, Bishop John Achaius consecrated a church in the presence of King David I and from there Glasgow started to spread.

Back in fashion

By the end of the 18th century the wealthy were moving west, to magnificent new houses around the new city centre at George Square, leaving their former homes to the less well-off. Gradually the old part of town deteriorated into slums. However, in the closing years of the 20th century, it underwent considerable restoration and is now a lively, bustling area full of tourists and hordes of students from the nearby University of Strathclyde. History has gone full circle and people are now moving from the west to the east where properties are less expensive. The area is becoming fashionable and has been described in one estate agent's literature as "East Merchant City".

The area at the top of the High Street now rejoices in the new name of Cathedral Precinct, a civic space completed in 1990 as the result of an international competition. As you walk across the cobbled courtyard look up at the lamps designed in the shape of the Glasgow Coat of Arms.

At its heart is the awesome medieval **Cathedral ❶** of Glasgow, built on the site of St Mungo's first church. It's Scotland's most important 13th-century building and the only mainland cathedral to have survived intact the Protestant Reformation at the start of the 16th century.

Legend tells of the Glasgow craftsmen rallying to the defence of the cathedral when the Reformers proposed razing it. The fact that the last Catholic Archbishop of Glasgow, James Beaton, had departed for France taking with him the records,

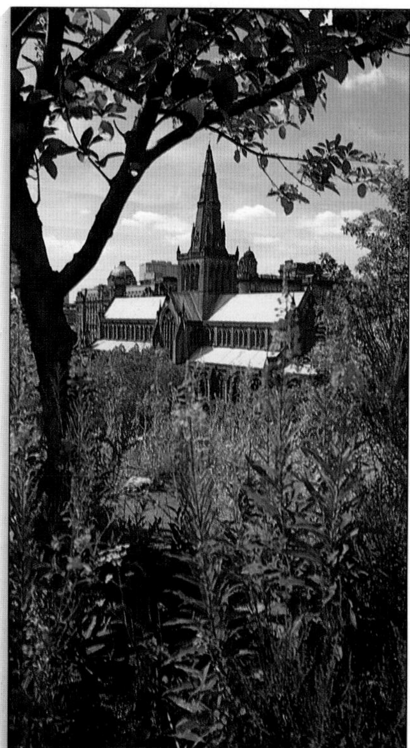

PRECEDING PAGES: Queen Victoria looks over Glasgow Cathedral.
LEFT: window at Provand's Lordship.
RIGHT: Glasgow Cathedral.

jewels and treasures of the cathedral, leaving little of value to plunder, may have been a better reason to leave the building alone. But it is more likely that it survived because it was converted to house three parishes, the Barony congregation in the lower church, the Outer High in the nave, which was walled off from the choir, and the High Kirk in the remainder of the building.

In the late 18th century the Barony congregation moved to a new church nearby and bizarrely filled the space they had vacated with soil and used it as a burying ground until 1844. In 1835 the Outer High departed, leaving only the High Kirk. Increasing awareness of the history of the building led to moves towards restoration.

The exterior of the building, awkwardly placed on a slope above the Molendinar Burn (now culverted) and with almost non-existent transepts, belies the beauty of the interior. The magnificent nave is separated from the aisles by two rows of massive clustered columns. The loftiness and the narrowness of the aisles, the stained-glass windows and the soaring columns form a subdued medieval vista.

Window display

A desire to beautify the cathedral in the middle of the 19th century badly misfired when the church elders, in the belief that no local artisans could produce stained-glass windows to match the glories of their cathedral, placed an order for 123 windows with Old Testament scenes with the Royal Bavarian Stained Glass Establishment in Munich. Less than 100 years elapsed before these windows had to be removed and replaced by the work of local artisans, which, it is hoped, will last rather longer.

The choir, which is about the same length but somewhat higher than the nave, is almost shut off from it by a superbly carved rood screen, on the corbels of which are carved the Seven Deadly Sins. The choir is a beautiful example of early Gothic and is separated from the aisles by clustered columns with flowered capitals. Beyond the choir is the exquisite Lady Chapel with rich, light columns topped by florid capitals supporting a groined roof and lancet windows.

From the nave, a flight of steps descends to the Lower Church, which occupies most of the crypt. (Although the word crypt conjures up visions of a dark underground chamber, it is, as seen here, not necessarily so.) This Lower Church is one of the glories of Scottish medieval architecture and is especially renowned for its fan vaulting which springs from a forest of columns. Four of these surround the tomb of St Mungo, patron saint of Glasgow, who was buried here in 603. In medieval times, tens of thousands of pilgrims came to this spot and, in 451, the Pope decreed that it should be esteemed as meritorious to make a pilgrimage to Glasgow Cathedral as to Rome itself.

On a wall behind the tomb is the handsome St Kentigern Tapestry. It was in this Lower Church, then the Barony Church, that Sir Walter Scott set one of the many Glasgow scenes in his 1817 novel *Rob Roy*.

The Blacader Aisle in a corner of the Lower Church is said to occupy the site of a cemetery consecrated at the start of

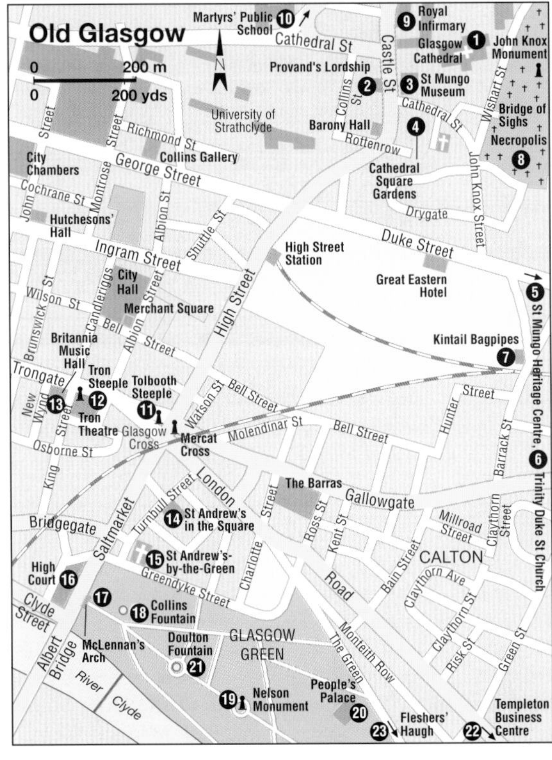

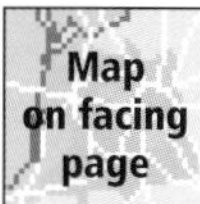

the 5th century by St Ninian. Now it stands as it was built during the primacy of Archbishop Blacader. Especially interesting are the late medieval carved bosses.

Glasgow's oldest house

Opposite the Cathedral on the other side of High Street stands **Provand's Lordship** ❷, the oldest house in Glasgow, built in 1471 (0141-553 2557, Mon–Thur & Sat 10am–5pm, Fri & Sun 11am–5pm, free). It was built for the priest in charge of St Nicholas Hospital. It later became the town house of the Canon of Barlanark, whose rectory was designated the Lordship of Provan. Because King James II and James IV were Canons of Glasgow, it is possible that either or both may have stayed here.

More certain, yet not positive, is a visit in 1567 of Mary Queen of Scots, who spent several days here arranging for Darnley, her husband, who was suffering from "a great fever of the pox" to be transferred to Edinburgh. Others claim that the purpose of Mary's visit was to plan the murder of Darnley and present as evidence the infamous Casket Letters, which were apparently written in Glasgow in January 1567.

During the 19th century and the early part of the 20th, the building had many occupants and at different times was an alehouse, a sweetshop and a cabinet-maker's establishment. Now, it is a museum with furniture and domestic articles. Especially interesting is the reconstruction of an early 16th-century pre-Reformation room occupied by Cuthbert Simon, the clerk to the Cathedral and a notary public.

To the rear of the house is the St Nicholas Gardens, created in 1995 to reflect the changes which took place between the medieval and renaissance periods when there was a gradual shift in the use of herbs from the medicinal and culinary to decorative and formal. Flanked with benches, this is a small haven of tranquillity and a grand place to have a picnic lunch.

Immediately opposite Provand's Lordship is the **St Mungo Museum of Religious Life and Art** ❸ (0141-553 2557,

BELOW: Provand's Lordship, the oldest house in the city.

daily 10am–5pm, Fri & Sun 11am), which opened in 1993 and is the first of its kind in the world, representing all the major religions under one roof – appropriate enough for such a multi-faithed city.

The museum contains Salvador Dalí's *Christ of St John of the Cross*, bought for the city amidst great controversy in 1952 for £8,200 and still causing controversy in the 21st century. Richard DeMarco, Professor of European Cultural Studies at Kingston University, London, has suggested that Glasgow sell the painting to provide funding to run its extensive museum and gallery collections. Needless to say, the suggestion has been dismissed.

To the rear of the museum is another tranquil corner in the Zen Garden, designed by Yasutaro Tanaka.

Joy in worship

Religion is not abandoned on leaving the museum. The two Barony churches, one on either side of the road, stand a couple of hundred yards down High Street. To the left, and back from the road, is the beautiful white **Barony North Church** (1878) in rich Italianate style, with the four evangelists standing atop the balustrade. Once a United Presbyterian kirk, this is now the Glasgow Evangelical Church. The red sandstone Barony Church (1886–90) on the right is now the main ceremonial hall of the University of Strathclyde.

Cathedral Square Gardens ❹, between the two churches, is guarded by an equestrian statue of William III (1650–1702) dressed as a Roman. It's perhaps not immediately obvious to visitors who this is but any passer-by will tell you that this is King Billy, a Dutchman, still revered by Protestant zealots throughout Scotland and Northern Ireland. The statue was erected in 1735 but a 20th-century plinth on the front commemorates the tercentenary of the Glorious Revolution of 1688–89, referring to the removal of the Catholic King James II and his replacement with the Protestant William of Orange. There's a section in the St Mungo Museum dealing

LEFT AND RIGHT: St Mungo Museum of Religious Life and Art.

with religious sectarianism, something regrettably still evident in Glasgow.

King Billy used to be sited on the Trongate but rude things happened to him at Hogmanay and in 1989 the Grand Black Chapter of the Orange Order had it moved to its present location. If it's windy, look closely to see if the horse's tail moves. It is reputed to have a ball and socket joint.

According to Blind Harry, who chronicled the battle many years after the event, the battle of the Bell o' the Brae was fought around here in 1300 between the English, led by Earl Percy, and the Scots, led by William Wallace. The Scots were victorious in the short and bloody conflict. The name of the battle was supposedly derived from a bell rung by an old woman when funeral processions passed on their way to the adjacent Necropolis.

Continue down **High Street**, passing, at the intersection with Duke Street, handsome, red sandstone tenements with attractive baronial touches, which were built in 1905. Near here was the second site of Glasgow University after it moved from Rottenrow in 1470 and here it remained until moving to Gilmorehill in 1870.

Take a detour along **Duke Street**, stopping to have a look at the **Great Eastern Hotel**, one of the city's most imposing 19th-century buildings. But don't be tempted to try and book a room. Despite the name, this former cotton mill has, since 1907, been a hostel for homeless men.

Touring a brewery

Continue to number 161 and the **St Mungo Heritage Centre** ❺ (0141-552 6522, Mon–Thur 2.30–5pm & 7–9.30pm, admission charge), which is within the ancient 200-year-old vaults of the **Tennant Caledonian Wellpark Brewery** (established 1556), where lager was first brewed in Britain. It's worth a visit to see the brewing equipment and pub memorabilia of yesteryear and sample some of the current produce in the centre bar.

Across the road from here at the junction with Sydney Street is an example of more

BELOW: Barony Hall.

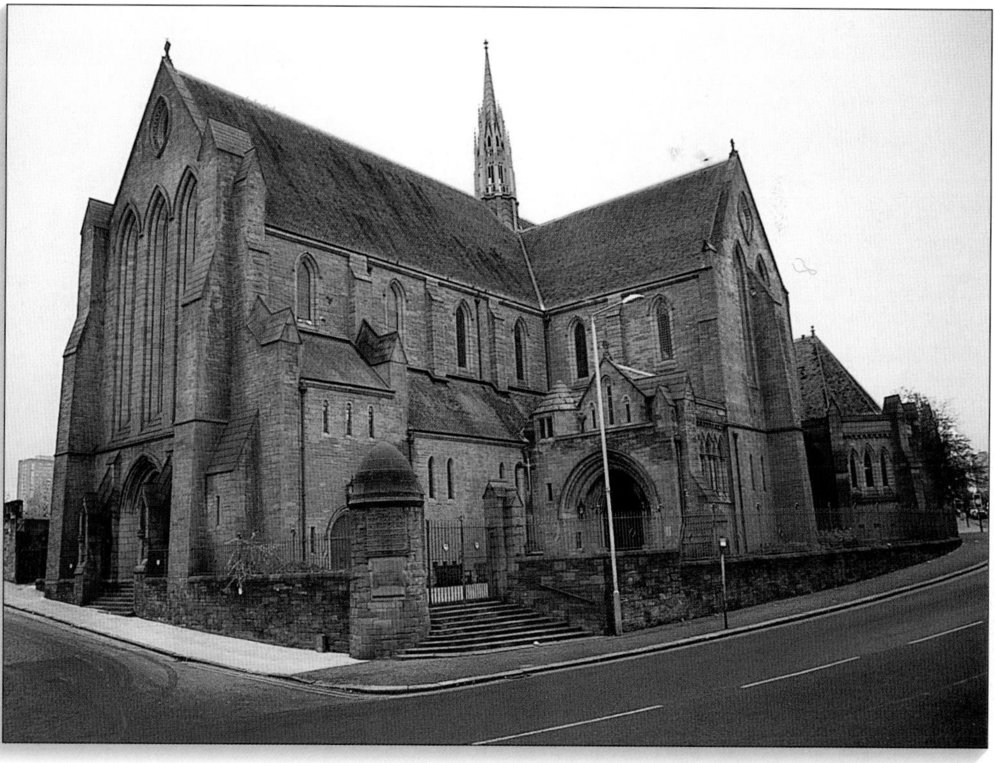

lottery money magic being worked as gentrification continues its push east. The former **Trinity Duke Street Church** ❻ (www.wellpark.co.uk/kirkhaven.html) with its massive Greek façade and fluted Corinthian columns is being restored to provide an extension to the **Wellpark Enterprise Centre**.

The distant strains of bagpipe music may draw you down Barrack Street to number 113, home of **Kintail Bagpipes** ❼ (0141 553 0902, www.kintail.co.uk). This is one of Scotland's top manufacturers of the great Highland bagpipe but the shop also sells full Highland regalia – kilts (made to measure), sporrans, Jacobite shirts and shoes – as well as a great selection of Celtic music on CD and tape.

The Necropolis

From here, head back along Duke Street, turn right into John Knox Street, continue along Cathedral Street and enter the **Necropolis** ❽, one of Europe's great 19th-century cemeteries. It is reached by crossing the **Bridge of Sighs**, under which flows the now culverted Molendinar Burn. The Necropolis is often compared to the celebrated Père Lachaise cemetery in Paris, and many of the tombs are of spectacular proportions and distinguished design. There are Doric temples, Egyptian vaults, neo-Gothic towers and Moorish kiosks designed by the major architects of the day, including Alexander "Greek" Thomson and Charles Rennie Mackintosh. The McCall monument, designed by Mackintosh, is a simple Celtic cross, but the distinctive lettering marks it out. At the extreme northwest corner of the Necropolis a column marks the entrance to the "Jews' Enclosure": outside this enclosure are the tombs of Jews who married Gentiles.

Towering 290 ft (88 metres) above the level of the Clyde on the summit of the hill, the **statue of John Knox** glowers from a soaring Doric column towards the Cathedral, which he would have so loved to have seen destroyed on account of its affiliation

BELOW: a stony stare in the Necropolis.

Map on page 136

to Rome at that time. Superb views of the eastern part of the city can be enjoyed from the summit of the Necropolis and there are also excellent views of the eastern suburbs and the hills to the south.

The black foreboding building in the foreground, which tends to overshadow the Cathedral is the **Royal Infirmary** ❾. Here in 1865 – in a previous building demolished in the 1920s – Joseph Lister introduced the antiseptic system which revolutionised modern surgery and which caused a United States ambassador to Britain to say: "My Lord, it is not a profession, it is not a nation, it is humanity itself which, with uncovered head, salutes you."

Across the pedestrian bridge in front of the Infirmary is the **Martyrs' Public School** ❿ (0141-287 8955, daily 1–4pm, free, wheelchair access), one of the first designs of Charles Rennie Mackintosh. It's a traditional school design and very different from his later imaginative work in Scotland Street. However, his developing style is evident in the fluid ornamentation around the entrances and the open timber roof trusses.

The Tolbooth

From here, head back down the High Street for 1,000 yards (1 km) to Glasgow Cross, which is dominated by the steeple of the **Tolbooth** ⓫. This stark, severe, seven-storey tower topped by a crown now stands amidst swirling traffic at an intersection of five roads. The 126-ft (38-metre) high tower, built in 1636, is all that remains of the original Tolbooth Building which extended to the west and the north and which was used as offices by the town council until 1814.

The jail mentioned by Sir Walter Scott in his tale of Rob Roy was also in this building, which came to be called the Tontine rather than the Tolbooth Building on account of the Tontine Hotel and coffee house which was built adjoining it in 1781. This was Glasgow's most renowned hotel and the terminus for stagecoaches going to and from Edinburgh and London. It also served as Glasgow's Exchange and here, on the Plainstanes, a stretch of paving fronting the hotel, the tobacco lords, dressed in scarlet coats, cocked hats and full-bottomed wigs would stroll, to the contempt of well-established old-money, and flick their gold headed canes at any riff-raff who dared to tread on their territory.

Glasgow Cross continued to thrive as the heart of the city until 1846 when the iron road came to George Square (the first rail connection with Edinburgh was made in 1842; with London in 1846), which then became the city centre. Here, too, stands the **Mercat Cross**, a 1929 replica of the original, which was removed in 1659 and which marked the site of the first Glasgow market dating back to the 12th century. It consists of an octagonal base with a balustraded roof on which stands a slender column supporting a heraldic unicorn. This used to be the site of Glasgow's gallows.

The **Tron Steeple** ⓬ dominates the first part of Trongate, which is that road running west from Glasgow Cross. This squat, four-stage steeple was part of a church, which was built between the end of the

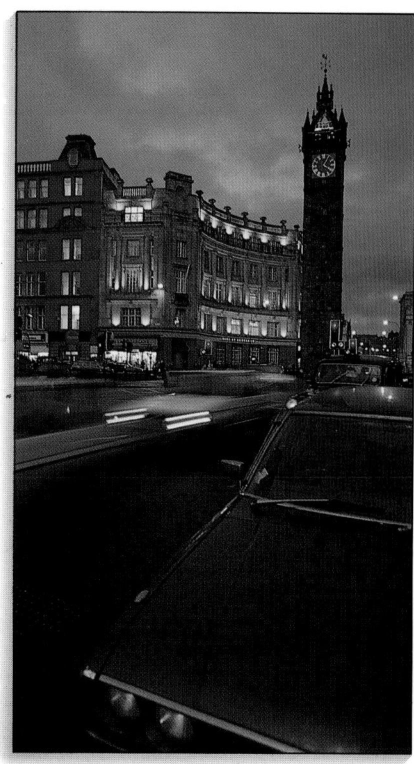

RIGHT: the Tollbooth by night.

16th and the beginning of the 17th century. (The arches in the steeple are 19th-century additions.) The church was destroyed in a spectacular fire in 1793, which was started by hooligan elements of the Hell-Fire Club who, while warming themselves by the watchman's fire, stoked it too high in order to prove their immunity to the heat in Hell. Only the steeple survived and a new church, designed by John Adam, was constructed. The clock faces on the dial were illuminated by gas reflectors in the winter of 1821, the first steeple in Britain to be so lit. Then, when the Trongate was widened in 1825, the open Tudor-style arched vault was carved into the steeple base. Since 1980 the church has been the home of the **Tron Theatre** and a lively restaurant and café bar.

It's worth taking a short stroll along the Trongate from here to see the former **Britannia Music Hall** ⓭ building. Look above the amusement arcade at numbers 109–115. This is the last of Glasgow's surviving music halls and its main auditorium is intact, hardly touched since it closed for good in 1938. Laurel and Hardy are amongst the big names of stage and screen to have performed here and there are plans to restore it to its former glory. The Britannia Panopticon Music Hall Trust (113–117 Trongate, 0141-553 0840) is responsible and until restoration begins it may still be possible to look round the dusty interior. Just telephone and ask.

Serious drinking

Returning to Glasgow Cross, the **Tolbooth Bar** at the southeast corner of the Cross, established in 1906, is Glasgow's oldest Irish pub. It was here, allegedly, that one of Glasgow's greatest contributions to modern civilisation – the hauf an' hauf – was introduced. This is a half-measure of whisky washed down by a half-pint of draft beer. Having downed the whisky, upturn the glass over the beer and knock hard on the bottom of the glass to be sure that "ne'er a drap is lost". Inside, the bar has remained unaltered for years

BELOW: a break for tea.

Map on page 136

and retains the atmosphere of Old Glasgow as well as having regular live Celtic music sessions.

South of the Tolbooth Bar down the Saltmarket, in the 19th century, in an area of about 300 sq. yards (250 sq. metres), were some 150 shebeens (illicit stills) and 200 brothels. Indeed, the Laigh Kirk Close at 59 Trongate contained 20 brothels and three shebeens. Into this section crowded the Irish, who had left their native land for Glasgow during the time of the great potato famine of the 1840s. It was said of the Irish of those days that if they had any money they emigrated to America; if they had only a little they went to Liverpool; and if they had none at all they came to Glasgow.

Turn left into **St Andrew's Square**, dominated by a church of that name; it was the official place of worship for the City Fathers as testified to by the Glasgow coat of arms being sculpted in the tympanum of the pediment. The former **St Andrew's Parish Church** (1739–56) is reminiscent of London's St-Martin-in-the-Fields, although the steeple is somewhat slimmer. The soaring hexastyle Corinthian portico created such a stir that, after the centring was removed, Naismith, the mason, slept beneath it to demonstrate his faith that it wouldn't collapse. The Baroque interior is an ostentatious display of the wealth of the tobacco lords who worshipped here. Now, as **St Andrew's in the Square** ⓮ (0141-548 6020), it's a centre for Scottish traditional music, song and dance with regular concerts and ceilidhs. In the basement you'll find the Café Source, a smart new café-bar and another venue for live music sessions.

Exit from the south side of St Andrew's Square and reach, after 100 yards, on the edge of Glasgow Green, **St-Andrew's-by-the-Green** ⓯, a plain box of classic Georgian architecture (1750–51). This, the fourth oldest building in Glasgow, was the first Episcopalian church in Scotland. When built, just four years after the Battle of Culloden, no love was lost between the Glasgow Presbyterians with their Covenanter traditions and the Episcopalians, or

BELOW: traffic clogs the Trongate. **RIGHT:** glad rags at St Andrew's Church.

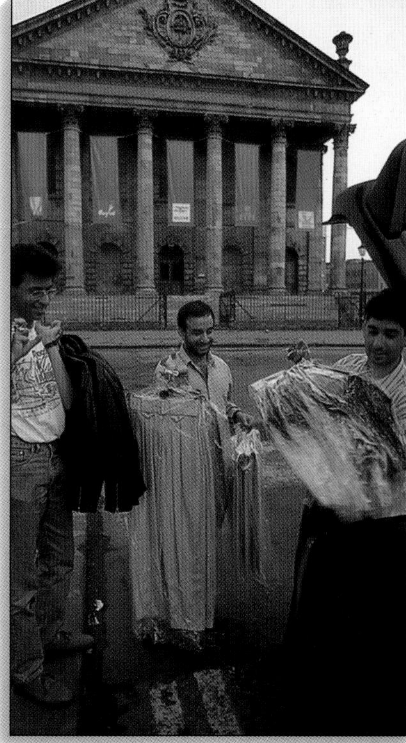

"Piskies", with their Jacobite sympathies. To make matters worse, the "English Chapel", as it was dubbed, was the garrison church of the scarcely popular Regiment of Foot, which was stationed nearby and – can it be believed? – there were cushions on the seats, "stuffed and covered with green cloth" and the organ was played. The dour Presbyterians dubbed it the "Whistling Kirkie" for its licentious luxury.

As the congregation dwindled and the church fell into disuse, it was on the verge of being demolished. Then it was renovated to become the offices of the West of Scotland Housing Association.

The ancient stones in the little graveyard to the east of the building include that of the unfortunate Captain Wemyss Erskine Sutherland and his wife Sarah, who were drowned in the Clyde when the *Comet* steam-boat was run down by the Ayr in 1825. Another remembers the fate that befell Jane Eliza Madden in 1871 when she was "run over by an omnibus" and exhorts: "All little Children that survey The emblem'd Wheel that crush'd me down, Be cautious, as you carelessly play. For shafts of death fly thick around."

Drunkards and vagabonds

Six hundred yards further, on the right, stands the imposing Doric facade of the **High Court** ⓰, the scene on 28 July 1865 of the last public hanging in the city. On that day, no fewer than 30,000 persons made their way to the judiciary buildings to attend upon one Dr Pritchard, an English practitioner who had settled in Glasgow. As a doctor, he was not much more than a quack, but he shone as a ladies' man and a lecturer. The vast crowd, described as "drunkards, thieves, and vagabonds", had not come to hear Dr Pritchard, however; they wanted to see him hanged for poisoning his wife and his mother-in-law.

Facing the High Court is the entrance to **Glasgow Green**, the oldest public park in Britain, adopted by the city in 1662. But before that it had been a village green or

BELOW: rehearsing for a church play.

Map on page 136

common land as far back as 1178. Glasgow people regard it as their own and over the centuries have fought hard to prevent any development that would remove or reduce their rights to enjoy it.

Towards the end of the 19th century a suggestion that the council should mine coal there to provide the funds for a new west end park was met with considerable opposition and the suggestion made that the shaft be sunk in George Square or amongst the crescents where the rich of the city lived. Over the years the Green has been used for sporting and leisure purposes and has been at the centre of political strife and agitation, particularly hosting large Chartist demonstrations before the 1832 Reform Act.

Here, too, was held the annual Glasgow Fair, dating from the 13th century, originally a horse fair and market but later attracting fairs, amusements and drinking tents. The annual Fair is still held on the second Monday in July but nowadays Glasgow empties as its citizens jet to the beaches of Spain for two weeks. The Green has enjoyed a renaissance as Glasgow City Council undertook a £10 million programme of works involving the creation of new sporting and leisure facilities, renovation of the major monuments and the relocation of others.

The entrance to the park is through **McLennan's Arch** ⓱, the work of Robert Adam and once part of the Athenaeum in Ingram Street. It was moved to the Green when that building was demolished. The **Collins Fountain** ⓲, which stands at this entrance to the Green, was erected by temperance supporters in memory of Sir William Collins (1789–1853), of Collins Publishing House (now part of Harper Collins) which had its origins in Glasgow and which had prospered by printing bibles and religious literature. Sir William was a great temperance man and indeed, under his leadership, the European temperance movement began in Glasgow. Great were the meetings in favour of temperance which took place on Glasgow Green.

BELOW: handy advice at Glasgow Fair.

The **Nelson Monument** 19, a 146-ft (44-metre) soaring column, was the first monument in Britain to celebrate the admiral's victory at Trafalgar and was paid for by public subscription.

A large boulder, the **James Watt Memorial Stone**, lies immediately to the south of the Monument. The inscription reads "Near this spot in 1765 James Watt conceived the idea of the separate condenser for the steam engine; patented in 1769". To quote James Watt, "I had gone to take a walk... I had entered the Green... I was thinking upon the engine at the time... when the idea came into my mind that, as steam was an elastic body, it would rush into a vacuum, and if a communication were made between the cylinder and an exhausted vessel, it would rush into it and might be condensed without cooling the cylinder."

That part of the Green between the Collins Fountain and the Nelson Monument was to Glasgow what Speakers' Corner in Hyde Park is to London. Here, in traditional Scottish fashion, the Catholics thundered against the Protestants while "Unitarians, Trinitarians, Good Templars, Good Tipplers, Quack Doctors all gave tongue". This is where so many of Scotland's battles for political freedom have been fought – for one man, one vote; for one woman, one vote; against the demon drink; for the right to work; against social injustice – the Green has seen them all.

The People's Palace

Over at the northeast of the Green stand two large impressive, yet disparate, buildings, constructed towards the end of the 19th century. The solid, red sandstone, renaissance-style **People's Palace** 20 (0141-554 0223, www.glasgow.gov.uk, Mon–Thur & Sat 10am–5pm, Fri & Sun 11am–5pm) is dedicated to the social history of the people of Glasgow. This is the best couple of hours anybody can spend in Glasgow and it's free. After a massive refurbishment, regulars were delighted to learn that the old favourites like Billy Connolly's big Banana Boots, the arte-

Ceramic Celtic Player probably
made by Britannia Pottery, Townhead
Glasgow c1900

BELOW: ceramic models at the People's Palace show how Celtic players used to dress.

Map on page 136

facts of the rich merchants and the "single end", a reproduction of a one-room Glasgow tenement flat, were still there.

The major changes have seen the introduction of thematic displays. The Patter looks at the Glasgow vernacular from children's songs and street rhymes to the utterances of Billy Connolly, Stanley Baxter and Rab C. Nesbit. "The Steamie", a tableau of one of the city's now vanished public washing houses, is a great hit, as is the amusing look at the consumption of alcohol in Glasgow in "The Bevy".

Look particularly for the reconstructed Buttercup Dairy, complete with original fittings. Buttercup Dairies were once to be found all over Scotland, now all are gone. "Glasgow at War" looks at the fortunes of working-class Glaswegians during World War I through the eyes of Private James Riley. There's a particularly poignant letter from his wife informing him of the death of their child.

And of course there's much more, incuding "Dancing at the Barrowland", "Doon the Watter" and "Crime and Punishment" which has an original door from Duke Street jail as well as the bell that was rung to herald executions. An integral part of the building, at the rear, is a large glass conservatory. The **Winter Gardens**, the Kibble Palace of the East End, a "treasure house of the beautiful in shrub and flower", is a sanctuary of dappled green on a grey winter's day and a delightful spot on any day.

In front of the People's Palace stands the **Doulton Fountain** ㉑, a terracotta fountain topped by a statue of Queen Victoria, which glorifies the British Empire. It's the most important fountain of this type in the world and was created by Doulton for the 1888 Empire Exhibition at Kelvingrove Park before being located permanently on the Green.

Just along from the People's Palace is the **Templeton Business Centre** ㉒. When James Templeton, its owner, discovered a new weaving technique, he founded the largest carpet weaving busi-

LEFT: the People's Palace. **RIGHT:** banner on display at the Palace.

ness in the British Commonwealth. This was the factory he built. Architect William Leiper's façade included a representation of the Venetian Doge's palace, using a colourful mixture of glazed and unglazed bricks, sandstone and terracotta, reminiscent of the designs and patterns of the carpets produced in the standard mill within the extravagant shell.

Football history

Back on the Green, that part to the east is the **Fleshers' Haugh** ㉓, where football has been played since 1873. Groups of rowers came ashore here to play football. They called themselves Rangers and the name stuck. All their games were played here until 1875. Then in 1888 Celtic Football Club, which had been formed in the nearby St Mary's Church Hall in Calton, played their first game here. New changing facilites and improved pitches means that this area is still a popular place for games of football.

Great gatherings have been held on this part of the Green. In 1746 Bonnie Prince Charlie, much to the annoyance of most of the populace, set up camp for his 10,000 troops here and, after receiving "6,000 short cloath coats, 12,000 linen shirts, 6,000 pairs of shoes, and the like number of pairs of tartan hose and blue bonnets" from the city, reviewed these troops. (Glasgow craftsmen, accustomed to supplying large quantities of shoes and clothing to America, met the order within three weeks.) More recently, the Fleshers' Haugh has had much larger crowds for pop concerts by such local groups as Wet Wet Wet.

Sporting activities have always been a feature of the Green. Glasgow's first golf course, an eight-hole affair, was laid out in 1730 on this flat sward of grass. In Victorian times, by far the most popular activity was swimming in the River Clyde, whose waters were much purer than today, evidenced by the salmon catch. Bathing boxes lined the river-bank to allow modest Victorian ladies to change into their modest Victorian bathing dresses. ❑

Map on page 136

BELOW: Templeton's, once a carpet factory, now a business centre.

Tenement Life

One in five Glasgwegians lives in a tenement and such flats are much sought after. Basically, a tenement is a three- or four-storey building of red or grey sandstone with a number of apartments on each level. Tenements are not free-standing but are joined together: the largest stretch for 600 yards, although more usually they are about 100 yards long.

The only major difference between a superior tenement flat and a posh apartment is that the latter has an elegant entrance, carpeted lobbies and elevators. Some, even in poor areas, were designed by distinguished architects such as "Greek" Thomson. Some have bow windows, others have cornices, and still others are embellished with falderals. The best flats can have five, six, even 10 large rooms with exquisitely moulded high ceilings.

To view some of these elegant tenements, board the train at Central Station for a 10-minute journey to Maxwell Park. Then one can see why middle-class Glaswegians still scoff at their English counterparts who live in "little boxes" with a small plot of land.

A tenement is entered through a close which, at its worst, is little more than a hole in the front wall which penetrates through the building to the back court. The street entrance to the close is the "close mouth" while the rear part, beyond the stairway, is the "back close". (Correctly, the close refers to the court at the rear of the building but has come to mean the building's entrance.)

A stairway rises from the middle of the close to the two or three levels of the building, each with two or three flats. At its best, the close stands at the top of a flight of stairs, is fronted by a portico and is entered through a door and the stairway is illuminated by painted glass windows with light also entering through a handsome skylight.

Aesthetically, many handsome Glasgow tenements are degraded by their closes. Glasgow is damp; Glasgow can be windy; and so, moisture condenses on the walls and rubbish gathers in the close. Further diminishing the salubriousness is the fact that many tenements have shops on the ground floor with a side entrance in the close. When, after World War II, closes were improved by the simple expedient of placing a door at both the front and the back, some tenements were enormously improved.

So why all the talk of Gorbals slums? These were tenements whose flats had only one or two rooms and which were devoid of any plumbing. Shared toilets, if not in the back green, would be on the landing at the top of each flight of stairs.

More than a dozen people lived in one room and those fortunate enough to have two rooms would take in lodgers. In the 1880s, a quarter of Glaswegians lived in one apartment; lodgers were taken in by 14 percent of those dwelling in one-room flats and by 27 percent of those with two-room houses.

Emmanuel "Manny" Shinwell, a renowned Red Clydesider who became a veteran Member of Parliament, once recalled his early days: "Later my father took me to Glasgow. We lived in the Gorbals. It was terrible, one lavatory to three families and no such thing as a bath... Drunkenness? People were floating across the streets." ❑

RIGHT: the elegant face of tenement life.

ALONG THE RIVER

Once the Clyde was the main artery of Glasgow's Industrial Revolution. Now the emphasis is on leisure rather than work, a trend symbolised by the "Armadillo" exhibition centre

"The Clyde made Glasgow, Glasgow made the Clyde" and the river lies at the very heart of Glasgow literally, historically and, for Glaswegians, psychologically. The days of the great Clyde-built liners and the shipyards that lined the river are long gone, but the decline and desolation of the Clyde, which followed their demise, is now being reversed.

The river is re-emerging as Glasgow's main artery. The **Paddle Steamer *Waverley***, the **Armadillo**, the **SS *Glenlee*** and, across the water, the new **Science Centre** are a "string of pearls" along the banks of the river, about to be joined by new housing, shopping and office developments.

Long-distance walkway

From Glasgow Green, the **Clyde Walkway** west along the bank of the river is part of a long-distance walking route from New Lanark. The **Briggait** ❶ on Clyde Street was Glasgow's fish market until 1977, when it moved to a new site at Blochairn. The great galleried hall of cast iron and glass was converted in 1986 to a shopping centre similar to Covent Garden in London but it closed within 18 months and is still empty. The frontage is French classical in style with twin, arched gateways flanked by massive pillars. Look for the medallions above them with the winged sea horses flanking a very young Queen Victoria and the Glasgow coats of arms.

Behind the Briggait peeks the 164-ft (50-metre) **Merchants' Steeple** ❷ (the **Briggait Steeple**), which is all that remains of the old Dutch style Merchants' House which occupied this site around 1659. Tradition has it that the merchants used this steeple to see if their ships were approaching along the Clyde. The emblem of the house, a sailing ship, still tops the steeple. A similar ship can be seen on top of the Merchants' House in George Square where the merchants eventually ended up.

A more successful market is invariably in progress in Shipbank Lane behind the Briggait. At **Paddy's Market** ❸ you'll find all manner of goods in the railway arches and on piles on the cobbles of the lanes for this is Glasgow's legendary flea market, which has been in operation since the 19th century and at this location since 1935. It was started by immigrant Irish, who sold secondhand clothes to the poverty-stricken local population. Pretty it is not, but if you want to see a slice of ungentrified Glasgow character then this is where to find it.

Go through Shipbank Lane into the Bridgegate and left to Stockwell Street where the **Scotia Bar** ❹, dating from 1792, is one of several pubs which claim to be the oldest in the city. It is a great

PRECEDING PAGES: George V Bridge.
LEFT: Clydeside elegance.
RIGHT: sales pitch at Paddy's Market.

writers' and musicians' pub with regular folk music and poetry sessions where you may come across a prize-winning novelist or a well-known entertainer. You will certainly be engaged in conversation by a host of Glasgow characters. At the corner of the Bridgegate, the **Victoria Bar** is another old favourite and, round the corner where Stockwell Street joins Clyde Place, the **Clutha Vaults** is the last in a trio of good old-fashioned Glasgow boozers. From here, cross Clyde Place back to the Walkway and continue along the Clyde.

Look out on the right for the relatively small **St Andrew's Cathedral** ❺, amongst the first Gothic Revival buildings in Glasgow consecrated as a chapel in 1816, marking the advance into public life of Glasgow's expanding Catholic community. It became the Cathedral in 1889.

Memories of Franco

A little further along the walkway is a black statue on a tall pedestal. This a tribute by the British labour movement and the City of Glasgow to the men and women who fought with the International Brigade against Franco's Fascists during the Spanish Civil War (1936–39). Of the 2,100 volunteers who went from Britain, some 534 were killed, 65 of them from Glasgow. The statue of a woman standing with her outstretched arms above her head depicts Dolores Ibarruri, from the Basque region of Spain, who had been a Communist member of the Cortes (Spanish parliament) in 1936 and part of the Popular Front Government that was ousted by the Fascists. She wrote in the Socialist press as La Pasionaria (the Passion Flower) and broadcast from Madrid during the conflict. Her war cry "*No Pasaran*" (They shall not pass) was adopted as the Republican motto and on the pedestal of the monument is another famous quote. "Better to die on your feet than live forever on your knees." She spent 30 years of her life in exile in Russia but, after Franco's death, returned to her native land and was re-elected to the Cortes at the age of 81. She died in 1989.

At this point, make a short detour into **Jamaica Street** to view a building reminiscent of the techniques used in the construction of London's Crystal Palace. **Gardner's Building** (The Iron Building) ❻ (1855–56) was constructed of a wrought and cast-iron skeleton making it possible to keep the walls very thin and at the same time have large expanses of glass. It has gone through many incarnations, the latest as the Crystal Palace, a large, airy café bar with a large non-smoking area. It's a

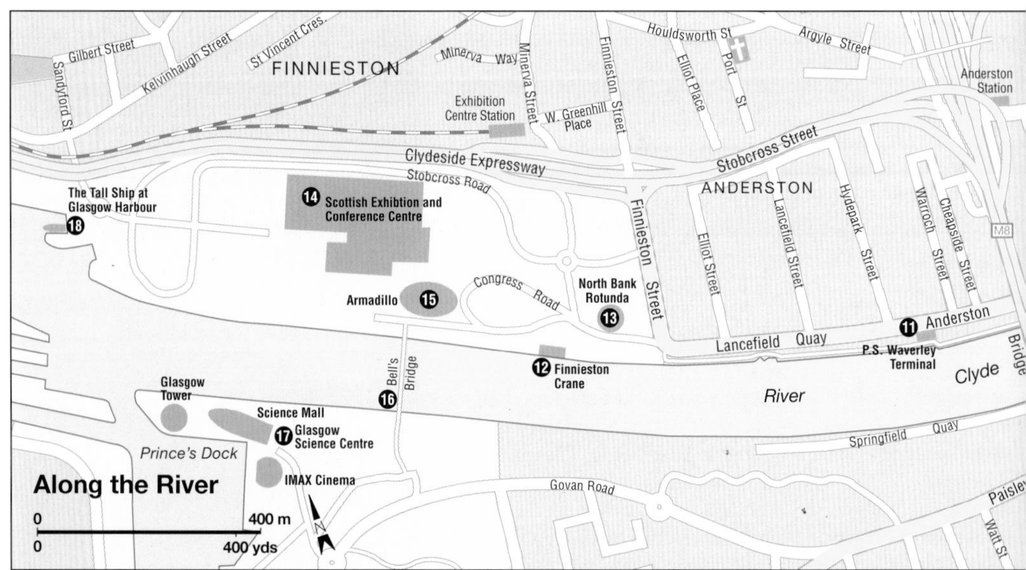

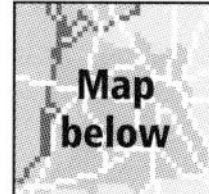

popular spot not least because of its superb all-day menu.

On the opposite corner, look out for **MacSorley's Bar** ❼, opened by Philip of that name in 1899 as an oyster bar. MacSorley had a well-known bar in New York and that's probably why the building was modelled on an American brownstone block. Apparently MacSorley imported a barman from New York to run his new pub. It has been restored to something close to its original condition. The Art Nouveau glazing is the real McCoy. Return to the Clyde Walkway and pass under the railway bridge.

The last ferry

Cross George V Bridge to the **Broomielaw**, in its heyday, the busiest spot on the river. From here, up to 50 passenger steamers would depart each day for Port Glasgow, Greenock, Gourock, Helensburgh and the islands in the Firth. When moorings were not available, steamers would tie up across the river at Bridge Quay, now called **Clyde Place Quay**. The result was often "a regatta of demented chimney pots".

Now, where paddle steamers fought for moorings, all that can be seen these days – and this at Clyde Place Quay – is what appears to be a floating conservatory. This is the last **Renfrew Ferry** ❽ (0141-429 8676, riverbank@btinternet.com), a breed of craft, which was pulled to and fro by cables across the Clyde at Renfrew. Nowadays the ferry is a nightclub and the old car deck has become a dance floor capable of withstanding the pounding feet of some 450 party animals.

On the corner of **Robertson Street**, is the **Clyde Port Authority/Navigation Trust building** ❾ now the base of Clydeport. This is another example of a building constructed to display the wealth generated by shipping. Despite the fact that the finished building is only half the size the trust had planned, it is still one of the finest in the city. The front is Roman in style, its pediment topped by an enormous statue of Poseidon, the corner extension continues the design but becomes more ornate, tending towards Baroque.

The Greek mythology theme recurs throughout the sculptures on the facade. But it is the huge dome at the top of the corner that draws the eye, particularly the sculptures. Poseidon's wife, Amphitrite, trident in one hand, cog wheel in the other, drives a pair of sea horses. Opposite her, the goddess of agriculture, Ceres, leads a massive bull by a fine chain while underneath is St Mungo with the city's coat of arms.

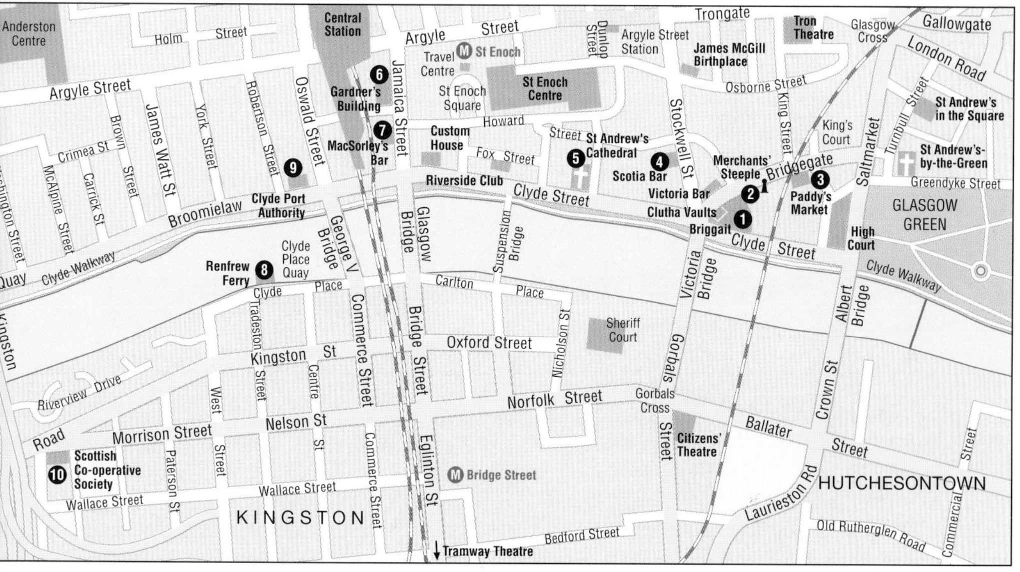

The tea tycoon

A short distance northwest of here is where Thomas Lipton, the son of Northern Irish parents who owned a grocery store in the Gorbals, set up his own "Irish Butter and Ham Market" soon after returning to Glasgow from the United States. In becoming a millionaire, Lipton cut out middlemen, brought produce direct from the Emerald Isle and blended "Lipton's Tea" to suit the different waters in towns where his chain had branches.

Above all, he was a marketing man *par excellence*. Every day two pigs were driven up from the quay wearing a banner which proclaimed "I'm on my way to Lipton's, the best place in town for bacon", and at Christmas 1881 police had to be sent to the Broomielaw to control crowds awaiting the arrival of a giant cheese from the US. Lipton had placed sovereigns in the cheese and the entire 1,375 lbs (625 kg) was sold in less than two hours.

Across the river, on the south bank, even dwarfing the M8, which it stands alongside, is a French renaissance palace, which was actually built as a Victorian warehouse. The former headquarters of the **Scottish Co-operative Society** ❿, it is now converted into apartments. It is reasonable to see in this massive pile echoes of the City Chambers for rumour circulated – and was vehemently denied by the architects – that the plan for this building was their unsuccessful submission for the City Chambers competition. During its existence the Society was not just the working classes' favourite retail store, especially for provisions; it was also a vehicle for political education, a social club with choirs and drama groups, a bank through the medium of the Co-op "share book" and quarterly dividends – in a word, an alternative society.

Best-selling boat trip

Back on the north bank, the world's last ocean-going paddle steamer, the ***P.S. Waverley*** (0141-221 8152, www.btinternet.com/Paddlers/PSWaverley/index.htm), has its

BELOW: the *Waverley*, last of the ocean-going paddle steamers.

Map on page 154

berth at **Anderston Quay** ⓫ beyond the Kingston Bridge. During the summer the *Waverley*, with its two distinctive red raking funnels – the very last of the "doon the watter" ships – still sails to such places as Greenock, Largs, Dunoon and the islands of Bute and Arran. She was built in 1947 and named after the Waverley novels of Sir Walter Scott. She was originally in the service of the LNER Railway and ultimately ended her working life as a Caledonian MacBrayne ferry.

In 1974 she was sold to the Paddle Steamer Preservation Society for £1 but she was in a sorry state and it has taken many years and massive injections of cash to get her back to a condition closely approaching her original. Now she offers a varied programme of cruises some of them traditional "doon the watter" jaunts to Rothesay and Dunoon while others leave from a variety of ports on the Firth of Clyde like Ayr and Girvan for short trips round scenic attractions like Ailsa Craig.

A *Waverley* cruise is much more than experiencing travel in the style of a bygone age. You can lounge or stroll on the decks, enjoy the live entertainment or relax in one of the many refurbished lounges. In essence, everything is as it would have been in 1947 with the exception of the toilet facilities, which have been upgraded. And it's the only vessel in the world where the engine room is open and can be seen working by all passengers without the need to clamber down steep ladders or suffer oppressive heat.

Further along (and seen before it is reached) is the massive **Finnieston Crane** ⓬ (it carries the logo CLYDEPORT), an industrial monument which, on occasions, is still brought into use. Built in 1932, this hammerhead crane was once the largest in Europe and hoisted to new levels of fame not only locomotives but also the Glasgow, which built them. Glasgow was then the most important locomotive city in Europe; steam locomotives built in the Springburn district were brought on loaders to this crane to be placed on ships, which

BELOW: cruising along the Clyde.

steamed off to India, Egypt and Russia.

The round building in the lee of the crane was formerly the entrance to and the exit from the now defunct Harbour Tunnel which opened in 1895 and was closed to vehicular traffic in 1940. However, until 1980, pedestrians could descend the 138 steps and walk, if not *on* water, then at least *under* water. The **North Bank Rotunda** ⓭ is now a restaurant, while its twin on the south bank is empty but enjoyed a brief spell as the Dome of Discovery, a forerunner of the new Science Centre, which stands close to it.

The Armadillo

Another half-a-mile leads to **Stobcross Quay** and the former **Queen's Dock**, which has been filled in and where now stands the **Scottish Exhibition and Conference Centre** ⓮. A wide variety of events, including exhibitions, conferences and pop concerts, are held here in several halls. The silver building, which bears a remarkable similarity to Sydney Opera House, is the **Clyde Centre**, a 3,000-seater conference and concert venue designed by Sir Norman Foster. But in true Glasgow style it was dubbed **"The Armadillo"** ⓯ and that's what it is now called, even by the SECC.

Near here the walkway meets **Bell's Bridge** ⓰, built in 1988 for the Garden Festival. Crossing here will bring you to the **Glasgow Science Centre** ⓱ (0141-420 5000, www.gsc.org.uk), a collection of futuristic looking buildings that together make up Scotland's biggest Millennium project. One building, looking like an astronaut's helmet and visor, contains Scotland's only **IMAX Cinema** with a massive 80-ft (24-metre) wide screen.

Next door is the **Science Mall** itself, the core of the centre where visitors can explore, create and invent as they are immersed in the world of science. Using the very latest in technology, this touchy-feely, hands-on extravaganza is about to emerge as one of Glasgow's and Scotland's top attractions and a great place to

BELOW: the Clyde Centre, popularly known as the Armadillo.

take children. Here they can see glass smashed by sound, liquid nitrogen, dry ice and explosive hydrogen, have a look at the bacteria lurking on their bodies, or build cool things like a lie detector.

The third building in the complex is the **Glasgow Tower** which, at 330 ft (100 metres), is the tallest freestanding structure in Scotland and the only one in the world which will rotate through 360 degrees. It's shaped like a gigantic aeroplane wing, one end in the ground and the other way up in the air with a pod containing the viewing deck. The two-minute lift journey to the top for a selection of uninterrupted views over Glasgow and beyond to the islands of the Firth of Clyde and the hills of Loch Lomond is well worth taking.

Back on the north side of the river and heading west from Bells Bridge the next attraction reached is **The Tall Ship at Glasgow Harbour** ⓲ (0141-339 0631, www.glenlee.co.uk, daily 10am–5pm, Dec–Feb 11am–4pm). This is the *SS Glenlee*, the pride of the Clyde Maritime Trust and one of only five steel hulled Clyde-built sailing ships still afloat. Built in 1896 by Anderson Roger and Co of Port Glasgow, she had a long career as a cargo vessel, circumnavigating the world five times and going round Cape Horn on 15 occasions. She ended her life as a training ship in the Spanish Navy prior to being decommissioned in 1969 and thereafter sinking when her sea cocks were stolen for scrap.

She was purchased by the trust in 1992, brought back to the Clyde and restored to exhibition condition. Visitors can explore the ship and see, and hear, what life was like for sailors at sea in a late 19th-century cargo vessel.

Next to the berth is the Italianate former Pumping Station, which was built to operate the hydraulic machinery on the Queen's Dock, particularly the capstans and the swing bridge. It's now the visitor centre for the *SS Glenlee* and contains exhibition galleries, a souvenir shop and the restaurant/café bar, Pier 17. ❑

BELOW: fun and games at the Scottish Exhibition and Conference Centre.

THE WEST END

Apart from the university, the big attractions in this area are the museums and galleries, including the Kelvingrove, the Hunterian and the Transport Museum

Glasgow's West End is home to Glasgow University and several of the city's best galleries and museums. Here, too, are many of those buildings, which led John Betjeman, who was an architectural enthusiast as well as Britain's Poet Laureate, to describe Glasgow as the "Greatest Victorian city in Europe".

The solid, copper-domed Edwardian Baroque building on North Street at Charing Cross, is the place to visit in order to learn more about Glasgow. The **Mitchell Library** ❶ was founded in 1877 by Stephen Mitchell, a tobacco baron, and moved to its present site in 1911. It's the largest public reference library in Europe and has collections devoted to Glasgow, Robert Burns and rare books.

The **Burns Room** contains the largest collection of first editions of the poet as well as a host of Burnsiana. The first editions, of which there are more than 4,000, are in 32 languages, which range from Bohemian to Welsh and even include English. Pride of joy in the **Rare Book** collection are the four folio volumes of *Audubon's Birds of America* and two Kilmarnock editions of the works of Burns.

The rear of the building, on **Granville Street**, boasts one of the most powerful facades of any Glasgow building and is the entrance to the **Mitchell Theatre**. Observe the eight caryatids at the upper level and, below, inscribed on the cornice, the names of Mozart, Beethoven, Bach, Michelangelo and Raphael. The musicians' names give the clue to the fact that, until a fire in 1962, this was St Andrew's Hall, home of the Royal Scottish National Orchestra.

Name changes

The first buildings of the **Park Conservation Area** ❷ are just north of the Mitchell, on the other side of Sauchiehall Street. All the buildings, which occupy the gentle slopes of Woodlands Hill, are three-storey, yellow, sandstone terraces: mansards have been added to some. All were originally private homes but now nearly all are offices. (Incidentally, those looking for an actual address may well be frustrated: names here change and then re-appear frequently and the same name can describe street, place, terrace, circus and crescent.)

It all began in 1831 with **Woodside Crescent**, which starts at right angles to Sauchiehall Street. Today, this is scarcely a homogeneous terrace with both stone and iron balconies and only some of the entrances fronted by porticoes. However, this soon curves gently into Woodside Terrace, which parallels **Woodside Place** below and from which it is separated by a private green park 50 yards wide.

PRECEDING PAGES: Park Circus. **LEFT:** relaxing at a university degree ceremony, **RIGHT:** the Mitchell Library.

Doric porticoes reached by flights of stairs with metal banisters punctuate **Woodside Terrace** where the windows are supported by consoles. The porticoes at the ends of the terrace form pavilions and are topped by a balcony. The entire facade has a balustrade, raised at each end.

Woodside Terrace is bisected by a short stretch of **Claremont Place**, at the north end of which a broad flights of stairs leads to a massive square Gothic tower to the left and three taller Lombard towers to the right. The former belonged to the **Park Church** ❸ and has now been recycled into offices. The latter were part of the **Trinity College and Church** ❹ and now house delightful apartments. Collectively, from a distance, these towers evoke images of a sun-kissed Italian hill town – San Gimigano, perhaps? – rather than of a mist-shrouded Scottish metropolis.

This leads after a few yards, via **Lynedoch Place** and **Park Circus Place**, to **Park Circus**, which is not quite circular despite its name but rather a flat centre-piece with curving quadrants. This is the highest point of Woodlands Hill. Several of the buildings on Park Circus are University of Glasgow halls of residence.

Not far from here, at the junction of Woodlands Road and Woodlands Gate, is one of the finest equestrian statues anywhere in the city – even if the horse only has two legs. **Lobey Dosser** ❺ (www.netsavvy.co.uk/lobey/author.htm) was "erected by public subscription on 1 May 1992, to the memory of Bud Neil 1911–1970 cartoonist and poet". Neil was responsible for a host of cartoon characters but it was Lobey Dosser (term for a down and out sleeping in a tenement landing) the Sheriff of Calton Creek, arch enemy, Rank Bajin and his horse El Fideldo, that has attracted a cult following in the years since his death. When once asked why the horse had only two legs Neil is reported as having said "It's my *[expletive deleted]* horse and if I want it to have two legs it will have." The Halt Bar across the road is well worth a visit for a

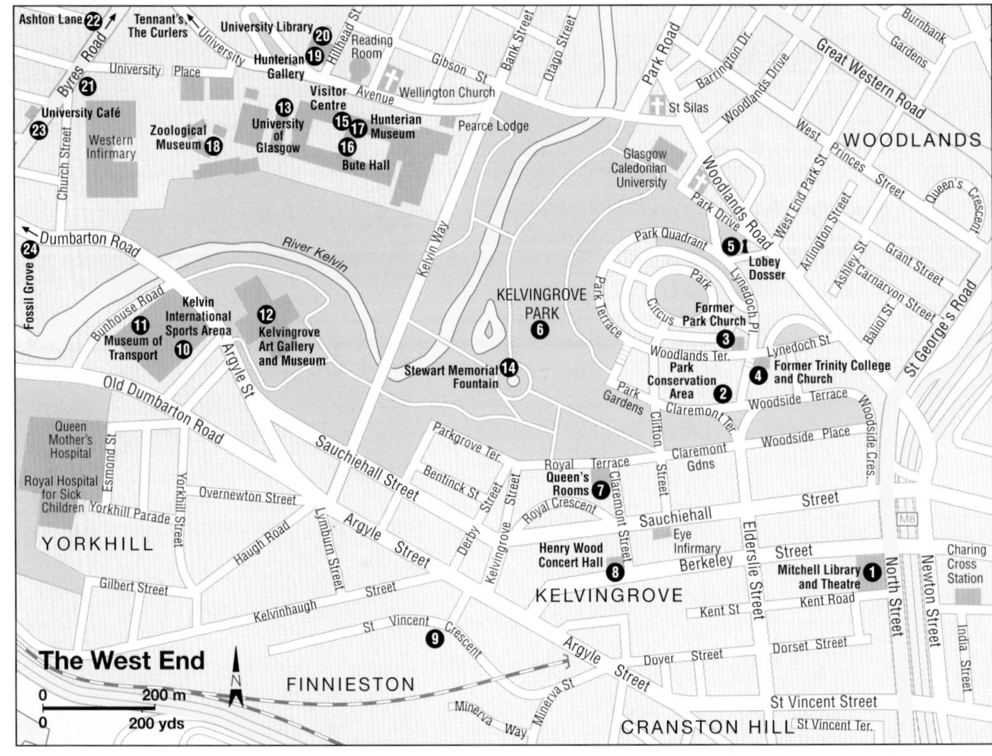

Map on page 164

pint or a dram and, who knows, you might even meet someone who will tell you some Bud Neil stories.

Wonderful vistas

Return to Park Circus to a belvedere above **Kelvingrove Park** ❻ and marvel at the glorious vistas. Immediately ahead, across the valley of the park, stands the university: to the left is the River Clyde with the cranes of those few shipyards which still function; to the right are the northern suburbs of the city and the Campsie Fells. A more traditional bronze equestrian statue, surrounded by weeping willows, which enjoys these vistas every day, is of Field Marshall Lord Roberts of Pretoria and Waterford, the hero of the Crimean War.

The belvedere is backed by **Park Quadrant** to the northeast and **Park Terrace** to the southwest. These are probably the most magnificent of all the terraces in the Park Conservation Area. The architecture of the quadrant and the terrace is more or less identical and the north-facing parts of each, with doors and windows with consoles and carved heads on the facade, resemble French châteaux. Now the visitor can fully appreciate why this part of Glasgow has been called "the grandest town planning exercise in mid-Victorian Britain".

From Park Terrace, descend a flight of steps to **Park Gardens**, one of the most handsome and homogeneous terraces on the hill. This leads to almost as beautiful **Claremont Terrace**, which ends at the junction of **Claremont Gardens** and Woodside Place. Turn right along the former to **Claremont Street**; a left turn then leads back to Sauchiehall Street. Some buildings have bay windows; others have basements protected by wrought-iron rails; still others have wrought-iron rails fronting balconies. All have grandeur and style.

The **Queen's Rooms** ❼, an ashlar, pedimented, temple-like box, solid rather than columned, with a broad, deep frieze, stands at the corner of Claremont Gardens and Claremont Street. The frieze on the east wall illustrates the progress of civilisation

BELOW: Kelvingrove Park in winter.

while that on the north shows Minerva distributing gifts to representatives of the arts and sciences. Minerva, it was claimed, is a "fair portrait" of Mrs Bell, the wife of the original owner of the building: also seen are Mr Bell and Charles Wilson, the architect, holding the building plans.

The medallion carvings between the frieze and the rounded windows on the east side are of Watt (science), Hamilton (architecture), Reynolds (painting), Flaxman (sculpture), Handel (music), Peel (politics) and Burns (poetry). Originally this building was a concert hall: today, it is a **Christian Science Church**.

Architects and builders did not neglect Sauchiehall Street and a series of terraces was built on both sides of this thoroughfare. Lacking the rarified atmosphere of Woodlands Hill, these enclaves are, in the main, not so elegant nor so well maintained as those on the hill. One exception is **Royal Crescent**, which is possibly the most eclectic stretch in this part of the city. Claremont Street, which bisects Sauchiehall Street between Fitzroy and Sandyford Places, leads to the tall spire of the former **Trinity Church**, which is now the Royal Scottish National Orchestra's **Henry Wood Concert Hall** ❽. The building is used as a rehearsal hall for the RSNO and as a concert hall for other groups who perform on a stage backed by pretty stained-glass windows.

From here, head to Argyle Street where **St Vincent Crescent** ❾, on the left down Corunna Street, is the most outstanding late classical terrace to be built in all Scotland. This terrace, unlike those just visited on Woodlands Hill, contains flats rather than three-storey homes. Some of the flats in this imposing 700-yard sweep of three-storey tenements with balustraded eaves and solid Doric porches, had as many as 10 rooms.

Continue along **Argyle Street** for about 1,000 yards, to just past its intersection with Sauchiehall Street (about 300 yards). Handsome red sandstone buildings stand on either side of the road. That on the left

BELOW: Kelvin Hall.

Map on page 164

is the former **Kelvin Hall**, once Glasgow's premier centre for conferences, circuses, concerts and carnivals. When it was superseded by the SECC, the building was converted to a dual-purpose venue. The front is now the **Kelvin International Sports Arena ⑩**, one of Britain's most comprehensive indoor sports complexes. There's a 200-metre indoor running track, and three-court and two-court sports halls.

Museum of Transport

The rear of the building, with its entrance on Bunhouse Road on the banks of the Kelvin, is the **Museum of Transport ⑪**, probably the finest transport museum in the UK. Glasgow and the Clyde built not only ships and steam locomotives but also, at one time or another, aeroplanes and airships, motorcars and motorcyles, and their fleet of tramcars was the envy of the world. On display are examples of many of these forms of transport, as well as bicycles, horse-drawn vehicles, steam rollers and fire engines.

Kelvin Street is the first exhibit on entering the museum. Immediately you are transported back across the years to the late afternoon of Friday 9 December 1938. Kelvin Street never existed but this reproduction is typical of a Glasgow West End side street from the 1930s through the 1950s. On your right is a Post Office with the oldest pillar box in Scotland beside it. You can pop your postcards in here.

Pass Teachers Pub and the Art Deco Continental Café and turn right into the Underground. This is a faithful reproduction of the former Merkland Street Underground and includes the original fittings. Several cars are standing at the platform, including one with the red and cream livery of the 1930s and another in the bright red of the 1950s – the predecessor of the current Clockwork Orange. Elsewhere in the street, other shops include a toy shop, photographer, fishmongers and a cinema. On the cobbled street, a variety of vehicles from the period are parked.

As you exit Kelvin Street, the main

BELOW: queens of the sea in the Museum of Transport.

display area on the ground floor houses the museum's collection of automobiles, with splendid examples of the Scottish automobile companies of the early 20th century, long since gone out of business, such as Argyll, Albion and Arrol-Johnston. From later in the 20th century they have a Hillman Imp car produced at the nearby Linwood factory. Then there are the special cars, including a stately black Rolls-Royce Phantom II, which was a gift to Sir William Burrell from his wife, a blue 1935 Lagonda tourer, and a 1934 green Bentley. There are early cars from the dawn of motoring like the 1898 Benz Comfortable and idiosyncratic wee machines from the mid-20th century, including a superbly refurbished Messerschmitt bubble car.

Tramcars were a familiar sight on Glasgow streets for 90 years and the trams on display range from horse-drawn vehicles to the elegant, green-and-yellow double-decker Coronation trams. In their heyday the Glasgow trams were unequalled for their cheapness, comfort and colour: different coloured panels around the upper deck designated different routes and so were readily identifiable from a distance.

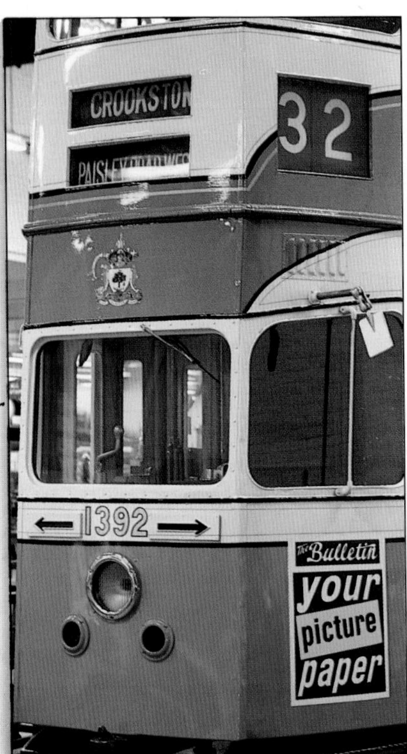

The city's love of these vehicles was strikingly demonstrated on 5 September 1962, a rain-soaked day, when 250,000 people turned out to cheer one last procession of 20 trams from Dalmarnock depot, in the northeast of the city, to Coplaw depot (now the Tramway Theatre) on the southside. Every tenement along the 3-mile (5-km) route was occupied by *hingers'oot.*

Springburn, in the northeast of the city, was once the world's largest centre of locomotive manufacture; four great works built steam locomotives, which were exported to more than 60 countries. Among the engines on display is No. 123-4-2-2 (Scottish locomotives were seldom provided with nameplates), which exceeded speeds of 70 miles (110 km) an hour in a famous London to Edinburgh race in 1888.

Elsewhere in the museum, look out amongst the display of two-wheeled vehicles for the world's oldest bicycle, a contemporary copy of Kirkpatrick MacMillan's machine made in 1842; superb early motorcycles including an AA Patrol bike and sidecar and the Rolls-Royce of motorbikes, the Brough Superior SS80. There are old fire engines, horse-drawn vehicles and a display of caravans ranging from the traditional Gypsy wagon to a relic from the Faslane Peace Camp.

Maritime history

It's the **Clyde Room** on the first floor that is the true Glasgow heart of this collection with more than 200 model ships (this represents only about one-third of the total collection), which can be enjoyed not only for their historical value but also for the skill and artistry that have gone into their construction. And, just to show that Glasgow is not parochial, a few models are of ships, which were not built on Clydeside. Most models are built to the traditional 0.25 inch = 1 ft scale, being 1:48 (or approximately one-fiftieth full-size). Some models are 18 ft (more than 5 metres) long and in all instances enormous attention has been paid to detail.

The large case containing three of the

LEFT: going nowhere at the Museum of Transport.

Map on page 164

great Cunarders, the *Queen Mary, Queen Elizabeth* and the *Queen Elizabeth 2* epitomises the great traditions of Clyde-built quality, the craftsmanship, skills and pride that went into making Glasgow the shipbuilding capital of the world in the 19th and 20th centuries. The hulls of both the *Queen Mary* and the *Queen Elizabeth* are the builder's models, while the 6-metre model of the QE2 was the test-tank hull, which was worked up to a fully detailed reproduction by the museum's technicians.

Other models (and all mentioned here are Clyde-built) range from the tiny *Comet*, the first steam-driven passenger vessel in Europe, to the giant battleship *Hood,* which was sunk in World War II. Look out for the *Sirius*, a wooden paddle steamer which was the first ship to cross the Atlantic under continuous steam power (1838); the *Cutty Sark,* which broke the China Clippers' record in the 1870s; the *Livadia*, a fantastic, almost circular yacht built for the Tsar (1880); Glasgow's own Clyde paddle-steamers, including the *Columba*, "the most perfect of all the Clyde steamers", which gave immense pleasure to millions of Glaswegians for almost 60 years; and, of course, the royal yacht *Britannia,* now berthed permanently in Edinburgh but built by John Brown Ltd in 1954.

Then there is *Le Stanley*, built for the journalist and explorer of the same name to use on his Central African explorations, and the *Nepaul,* a paddle steamer built for the Irrawadday Flotilla in Burma. Both craft, although launched about 100 years ago, were prefabricated – constructed in sections to be re-assembled later.

Kelvingrove's treasures

Cross the road to the imposing **Kelvingrove Art Gallery and Museum ⓬**, which is topped by a veritable forest of spires, turrets and towers. Visitors might wonder why they enter from the rear rather from the front: they do not. During the construction of the building the location of the main road was altered so that it now passes the rear of the building. It's

BELOW: Kelvingrove Art Gallery.

Glasgow's most enduring urban myth that the architect who designed the building got the drawings the wrong way round and committed suicide as a result.

A bronze statue of St Mungo, who is depicted as protector of art and music, guards the entrance to a soaring atrium with a black, white and straw-coloured marble floor, red sandstone arches and an organ. (Evening concerts are not infrequently given in the Gallery.) The names of various Incorporated Trades of the city – barbers and bonnetmakers, masons and maltmen, wrights and weavers and the like – are carved in the spandrels of the first-floor arches and on a frieze above these are the names of famous composers including Wagner, Mendelssohn, Listz, Gluck and lesser luminaries. (The Wallace mentioned is not the fiery national hero but rather a 19th/20th-century Greenock composer.)

Kelvingrove will be closed to the public from January 2003 and re-open January 2005 (provisional dates) as part of a £30 million refit and alteration programme. Prior to the closure visitors will find the ground floor devoted mainly to natural history and archaeology (Egyptian as well as local) and to an outstanding collection of armour. Scottish weapons and militaria form an intriguing background for this collection but the most valuable items are the Gothic Milanese field armour (1450), probably the earliest and most complete plate armour in Britain, and the "richly graven and gilded" Greenwich field armour for man and horse (*circa* 1550–58). Children delight in the latest exhibit in this collection, which really never existed. It's a set of Imperial Stormtroopers armour from *Star Wars*.

The galleries situated on the upper floor are devoted mainly to paintings and sculpture and include works by Flemish, Italian, British and Dutch artists and range from the great masters of Italian Art to modern classics, the Pre-Raphaelites and the Impressionists. After a visit to Kelvingrove, visitors will not leave Glasgow in the belief that Sir William Burrell was the

BELOW: lost for words at Kelvingrove Art Gallery.

Map on page 164

only Glasgow shipowner to leave his art collection to the city. William McInnes (1868–1944) was another Glasgow ship owner who bequested his paintings, prints, drawings, silver, ceramics and glass to the city. This gift included 33 French works by such artists as Monet, Degas, Renoir, van Gogh, Cézanne and Picasso, while British works included canvasses of the Glasgow Boys and the Scottish Colourists, of whom McInnes was a regular patron.

The Glasgow Boys

Charles Rennie Mackintosh and his wife Margaret are well represented, as are their contemporaries, the Glasgow Boys, who spent their summers painting the Scottish countryside. A charming example to look for is *The Last Turning* by James Paterson, painted in the tiny Dumfriesshire village of Moniaive where he took up residence when he married. Other Glasgow Boys exhibited here include John Lavery, James Guthrie, George Henry and of course E.A.Hornel, perhaps the most famous of "The Boys". They joined together, not so much to promote a style of painting, but to fight the Royal Academy in London and the Scottish Royal Academy in Edinburgh, both of whom ostracised them.

Paintings by Scottish artists predominate in the British collections. However, especially in the period before 1850, sufficient characteristic works by their English contemporaries permit the viewer to study the development of Scottish painting within the British school. Many consider that the most important British painting on display – albeit the work of an American – is Whistler's *Arrangment in Grey and Black no. 2: Portrait of Thomas Carlyle*, the first Whistler to be hung in a British gallery. (Whistler was proud of his Scottish background, announced by his name: James A. McNeil.)

Also on view are the works of the Scottish Colourists – Peploe, Cadell, Hunter and Fergusson. The term Colourist was first coined in 1948 when three of them were already dead and simply announced

BELOW: Rembrandt's *The Man in Armour.*

their love of colour – nothing more. One hundred years after the first Scottish School, a second, which includes Steven Campbell, Peter Howson and Ken Currie, all graduates of the Glasgow School of Art, appeared and has gained a reputation far beyond Glasgow.

The Print collection, which is frequently changed, is mainly of British artists, with Scots such as Strang, McBey, Cameron and Muirhead Bone featuring strongly. In addition, there are European prints from the 18th century to the present and a few old masters. Most of the watercolours and drawings are 19th and 20th-century British.

The sculpture collection covers the period from the late 18th century to the present and is predominantly of the British school with works of Flaxman, Benno Schotz (a Glasgow man and Scotland's most prominent 20th-century sculptor), Caro and Paolozzi. The Continent is represented by, among others, Degas, Renoir and Rodin.

Memories of Wounded Knee

In another gallery there is a video about the Native American Ghost Dance religion and the infamous massacre at Wounded Knee Creek in 1890. The main exhibit here is the replica of a Ghost Dance Shirt, which had been taken from one of the dead at Wounded Knee. The shirt was supposed to have made the wearer impervious to bullets but it didn't work. It came to Glasgow with Buffalo Bill's Wild West Show and was donated to Kelvingrove. In the closing years of the 20th century members of the Wounded Knee Survivors Association appealed to Glasgow council for the return of what they considered a sacred relic. The Council agreed and it was returned in 1998. The replica was made by Marcella Le Beau, a Two Kettle Lakota Indian who presented it to the gallery.

The balconies on this floor house Decorative Art, including glass (especially strong in items from Spain), silver (much of it donated by Victor J. Cumming, not a ship owner but one of the managers of a shipping line), metalwork and ceramics. Here, too, are the yachting trophies of Sir Thomas Lipton, including the cup that the Americans awarded to him as "Gamest Loser in the World of Sport".

A unique permanent exhibition is the Seton Murray Thomson collection, devoted entirely to horses. On display are more than 400 quadrupeds from 19 different countries, spanning three-and-a-half millennia and made of more than 30 materials ranging from amber to wax by way of mother-of-pearl, papier-mâché and ivory. Back downstairs is a real horse's skeleton with a fascinating story. The Baron of Buchlyvie became the most expensive horse of its age after a dispute over ownership led to a court case where the judge ruled that the horse be sold. One of the parties to the dispute then paid £9,500 for him, an absolute fortune at the time. It was a bad investment, for two years later the Baron broke his leg and was destroyed. His skeleton was later disinterred and donated to Kelvingrove and the break can still be seen.

For the estimated two years when this building is closed, the core of the art col-

BELOW: Peploe's *Still Life, White Roses* in the Kelvingrove Gallery.

Map on page 164

lection – about 100 of the most important paintings – will be on permanent display in the McLellan Galleries in Sauchiehall Street, their original home. When Kelvingrove re-opens, it will have been restored to its original Victorian colour scheme but the displays will be very different.

The idea is to present a 21st-century museum within a Victorian building. The basement will have been converted from storage and offices to provide 35 percent more display space, allowing a 50 percent increase in the number of objects that can be displayed. There will be a new café in a conservatory overlooking the park and the River Kelvin, and there will be a major change in the way the collections are organised. No longer will the big collections like Armour be grouped together but instead will be shown in their proper contexts. Italian Armour will be found with the Renaissance paintings, and the Earl of Pembroke and his armour will be part of the display on Scottish Battles. As Mark O'Neill, Head of Glasgow's Museums, explains: "He was a mad young fighting fellow and we know a lot about him and will now be able to tell that story in much more detail."

The new themes will include *Looking at Art, Scottish Art, Looking at Design, Mackintosh and Glasgow Style* and an *Art Discovery Centre* occupying one wing on the ground floor along with *Words and Music*. The opposite wing will look at *Glasgow and its World, Scottish Wildlife, Prehistoric Life, the Earth* and *Flight* and will have an *Environment Discovery Centre*. Upstairs will feature paintings in one wing, from Old Masters to Scottish Art, while the opposite wing will include *History and Technology, Scottish Battles, Armed and Dangerous, Culture under Threat* and *Early Settlers of Western Scotland*.

Seat of learning

From the gallery's rear entrance, a massive Victorian building can be seen on a ridge on top of a tree-covered slope. This is the main building of the **University of Glasgow ⓭**, its design an eclectic but

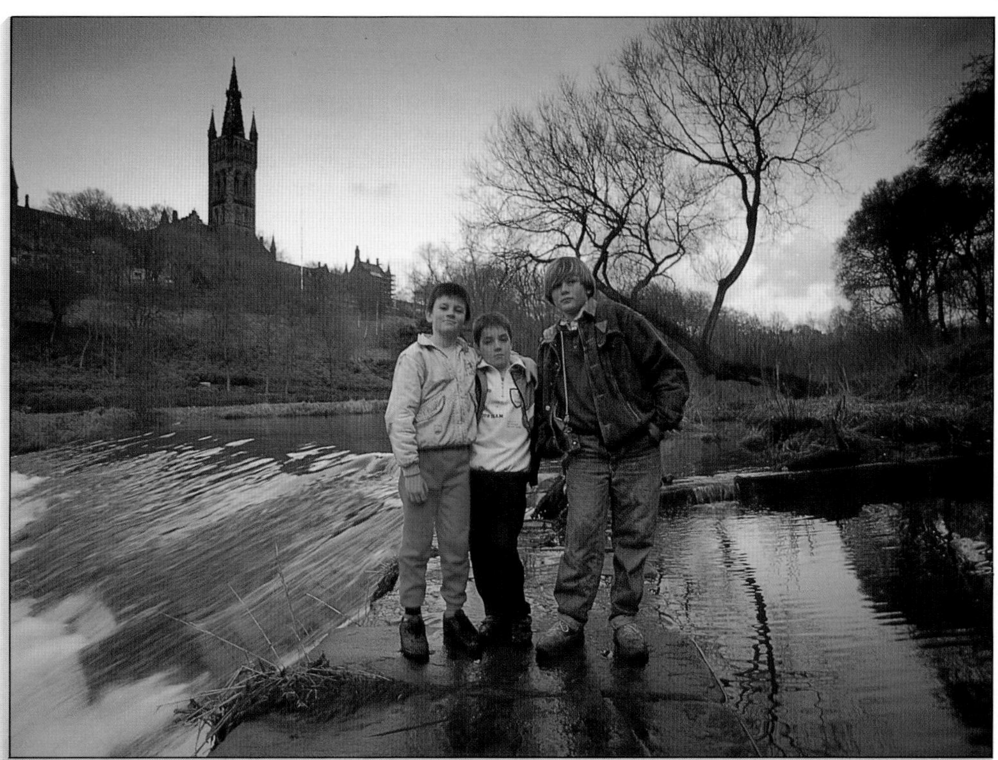

BELOW: the River Kelvin by the university.

successful mixture of Gothic and Scottish baronial, dominated by its soaring Flemish style tower. It can be reached by strolling through **Kelvingrove Park**, through which the River Kelvin flows, by Kelvin Way to **University Avenue**.

Just after the bridge, turn right for a short detour into the park and a glance at the richly sculptured **Stewart Memorial Fountain** ⓮. The bronze figure of *The Lady of the Lake* atop the fountain is the clue to the fact that this structure honours a former Lord Provost (= mayor) of Glasgow during whose term of office Loch Katrine's water was first piped to the city. Note the birds, one of them with a fish in its mouth, on the fountain's rim.

Great physicist

Back on the main road, an even shorter detour to the left leads to the statues of Lord Lister and then Lord Kelvin, two of the most distinguished figures associated with the University of Glasgow. William Thomson, Lord Kelvin, was probably the Victorian era's greatest applied scientist and certainly the greatest physicist. He was professor of natural philosophy at Glasgow for 50 years and thrice declined the prestigious Cavendish Chair at Cambridge. He was also one of those most responsible, in 1871, for the University being moved from High Street to its present site.

Pearce Lodge at the foot of University Avenue is one of the oldest parts of the university, having been transferred in 1870 to its present location from the Old College on High Street. It now houses computing services.

Rather than entering through the gates at Pearce Lodge, proceed to the crest of **University Avenue**. The university is all around: some of the buildings are old, some are modern; some are former terrace houses, some are purpose-built. The whole is an outdoor architectural museum, which illustrates building in Glasgow over the past 150 years.

Enter the university through the gates, at the top of University Avenue, which bear the names of 28 distinguished alumni or former faculty, including Lister, Kelvin, Watt and Adam Smith. The gates were erected in 1951 to commemorate the founding of the University by a Papal Bull issued in 1451. The University of Glasgow is the fourth oldest university in Britain. Enter through these gates and facing, on the ground floor of the main building, is a **Visitor Centre** ⓯.

From here, ascend the stairway and visit the east and west quadrangles and, between them, the **Cloisters** (or Undercroft) which support the **Bute Hall** ⓰, possibly Britain's most glorious Victorian Gothic hall. The columns are of wrought iron, the arches are severely pointed, fleur-de-lys and rosettes are common themes, and four sets of handsome stained-glass windows pay tribute to 32 world figures. Behind the wooden screen at the back of the hall is the smaller Randolph Hall, which has portraits of William Hunter by Reynolds and of Joseph Black by Raeburn. On occasions, both rooms may be visited.

Next, make for the flag-pole vista point in front of the 300-ft (90-metre) tower whose spire is not that designed by G.G. Scott, the original architect but that of his

LEFT: the Stewart Memorial Fountain in Kelvingrove Park.

Map on page 164

son, John Oldrid Scott. Scott senior's spire design was top-heavy and the present delicate tracery is much to be preferred. Excellent as are the views from the base of the flag-pole, they are nothing compared to those obtained from the Tower which can be ascended (tel: 041-339 8855, ext. 4271, for current opening hours).

Back on *terra firma*, visit the adjacent **Professors' Square**, where the Principal still lives (No. 12). The lamps around the square are original and a VR (Victoria Regina) mailbox is still in use. The **Memorial Chapel** (1926) on the left (open to the public) is entered by the **Lion and Unicorn Stairway** constructed in 1690, which was brought here in 1872 from the Old College.

About half of the university's 10,000 or so undergraduates are locals who commute from home. On the other hand, half of the graduate students are from overseas: they come from countries ranging from Austria to Zimbabwe, with the largest numbers being from Algeria, Iraq, Malaysia, Hong Kong, Singapore and Norway. Most Asian students are in the engineering faculty, which is the oldest engineering faculty in the world. Largest of the seven faculties is arts, and the medical faculty is, in terms of undergraduates, the largest in Europe. Other faculties are social sciences, law and financial studies, veterinary medicine, divinity and science.

The Hunterian Museum

Few of these students – they are too busy studying – will be found in the **Hunterian Museum** ⓱, which is adjacent to the Bute Hall. The museum's extravagant wrought-iron supports are extremely attractive and, if the university tower is closed, then excellent panoramas of the north of Glasgow can be enjoyed from the museum's mezzanine floor. When opened in 1807, it was Scotland's first public museum and the basis of its contents – and of that of the Hunterian Gallery which occupies another part of the campus – are private collections of William Hunter, a

BELOW: scrolls of success on graduation day.

magpie of a collector and one with the most catholic of tastes. Hunter was a student at Glasgow in the 18th century. He subsequently achieved fame and fortune in London, first as an anatomist and pathologist, then as a medical teacher and finally as an obstetrician – he delivered Queen Charlotte of her children. Yet, for all this, he remained true to his *alma mater*, to which he bequeathed his enormous and varied collection.

The emphasis in the museum is on geology, ethnography and archaeology and there is also an outstanding numismatic collection with more than 30,000 coins, most of which belonged to Hunter. If you've ever wondered what a Scottish bawbee was or what a groat looked like then you'll find them here alongside Spanish doubloons and pieces of eight for this section tells the history of money from the time of its invention. Elsewhere in a plastic box is £1 million in shredded £10 notes. Look for the earliest collection of Scottish fossils from the Rev David Ure (1749–98) and the Bearsden Shark, a late 20th-century discovery by the legendary Stan Wood. In the Egyptology section is a replica of the famous Rosetta Stone made close to the time the original was discovered.

Elsewhere on the campus is the little visited **Zoological Museum ⓲**. It's usually full of students but it is open to the public. It's compact and delightful containing a mixture of live specimens and others, which have benefited from the art of the taxidermist. Chipmunks, rats, snakes and an incredible Trinidad Leaf Frog are in glass tanks, the frog having been imported from its native habitat as a tadpole. A bank of cabinets with many sliding trays holds one of the most comprehensive insect collections in the country.

The Hunterian Gallery

The **Hunterian Gallery ⓳** on the other side of University Avenue is entered through handsome cast-aluminium doors by Eduardo Paolozzi. It houses a splendid collection of European paintings, including canvasses of Rembrandt, Ramsay

LEFT: exhibit in the Hunterian Museum. **BELOW:** a Mackintosh bedroom in the Hunterian.

Map on page 164

and Reynolds. Fergusson, Guthrie, Peploe, Earley and McTaggart. Some of Scotland's best 19th and 20th-century painters are also represented and should not be missed.

But most visitors come here to see the paintings of Whistler, a collection rivalled only by that in the Freer Museum in Washington. Not only are the artist's paintings displayed but one can also see his painting equipment and the furniture, silver and porcelain he collected. This was essentially the contents of Whistler's studio when he died and was left to Glasgow probably because this was where his first public sale was made, although perhaps it was because his mother was Scottish. In any case, his mother is to visit Scotland in 2003, the centenary of his death. As part of a special exhibition planned for the summer of that year *Whistler's Mother* will be at the Hunterian on loan from the Musée d'Orsay in Paris.

The Gallery's print collection, the largest in Scotland, includes works of Dürer, Picasso and Hockney as well as Whistler and Mackintosh. Exhibitions are mounted in the Print Gallery and the entire collection can be viewed, on request, by serious scholars.

A longitudinal mail box in a white door on the outside of the Gallery suggests Mackintosh and indeed that door is part of a reconstruction of three levels of the nearby home in which the Mackintoshes lived for eight years. The interior decoration, where cool colours predominate, duplicates the original and contains more than 60 pieces of Mackintosh furniture.

On the ground floor, the dining room, though obviously Mackintosh, is dark in colour reminiscent of the fashion of the day. But climb the stairs and emerge into the blindingly white living room and you could be forgiven for thinking that you had stumbled into the future rather than the past. This studio drawing room was made from two existing rooms and that, together with the addition of a window, gives it a light, airy feel. White carpet, white furniture and muslin curtains combine to startling effect.

BELOW: the Mackintosh House in the Hunterian Gallery.

Hunter's contributions to his *alma mater* did not stop with those items seen in the Museum and the Gallery. The **University Library** ⑳, adjacent to the Gallery, contains Hunter's library of more than 10,000 books, one-quarter of which are from the 16th century, plus 650 beautifully and intricately decorated manuscripts, including the York psalter dating from 1170.

Next to the reading room is the **Wellington Church**, which, with its splendid Corinthian portico atop an enormous stylobate, looks as if it could have come from the drawing board of "Greek" Thomson – but it is by Thomas Watson of a later generation. It is most unusual in that the Corinthian colonnades on the north and south side are not tetrastyle nor hexastyle but consist of five columns.

From here, a stroll down University Avenue leads to **Byres Road** ㉑, with its pubs, restaurants and bookshops. For students this is the centre of the known universe and, although the pubs and shops may change frequently with the fashions, there are a number of old favourites that remain constant. **The Curlers** at 256 was originally beside an ice rink, hence the name. Nowadays it has a basic snack menu, great deals for students and lots of music. **Tennant's** at 191 has been on the go since 1884 and the clientele is a mixture of old timers, gents in suits and celebrities. *The List*, the Glasgow Bible of things entertaining and gastronomic described it as the "Cheers of the West End". Just off Byres Road is the cobbled **Ashton Lane** ㉒, an eclectic mix of individual cafés, bars, restaurants and a small cinema. **Blur**, much favoured by locals and visitors alike, is a rustic conversion of a former stable block, serving excellent food accompanied by Belgian beer. Nearby, the **Ubiquitous Chip** may well be as good as eating gets in Glasgow. It's certainly a contender.

Map on page 164

Before leaving Byres Road, consider a visit to the **University Café** ㉓, an unreconstructed Art Deco establishment which has provided sustenance to the student population since Noah beached his Ark. Nothing fancy or fusion here; expect greasy bacon rolls and frothy coffee served in classic thick white cups.

Finding out about fossils

Join **Dumbarton Road** at the south of Byres Road and travel westwards for 1½ miles (2 km) to **Victoria Park**. The **Fossil Grove** ㉔ (0141-287 2000, www.clyde-valley.com/glasgow/fossil.htm, 1 Apr–30 Sept, noon–5pm, free), at the western end of this park, is Glasgow's oldest tourist attraction; it was uncovered during road construction in 1887.

Fossilised tree stumps from the Carboniferous Period, which started some 363 million years ago, were discovered and carefully excavated to remove the sandstone and shale surrounding the fossils. The tree stumps and root systems you will see in the grove are not petrified wood but casts formed by mud which penetrated into the trees and set while the bark retained its shape. Nowadays the grove is enclosed in an interpretation centre so that in all weathers it is possible to see the trees in the spot where they grew in Glasgow's prehistoric rain forest. ❑

LEFT: Guthrie Hall in the university library.

Glasgow Chic

If Edinburgh has poise, Glasgow has swagger. Edinburgh was born easily out of quiet, unassailed prosperity; Glasgow was a love-child, the impudent offspring of a shotgun marriage between stubbornness and deprivation.

Men in the rag trade always used to claim that girls in Glasgow had bigger breasts than elsewhere in Britain – shorter legs but bigger breasts, giving them a look that was simultaneously wholesome and sexy. Today the felicitous bosom is still the life and soul of Glasgow's party, but the legs are longer than those of a generation ago, thanks to a better diet and a keep-fit culture.

Part of Glasgow's physical swank, of course, is derived from its large Italian and Irish communities which have rarely been burdened by any puritan guilt about dressing up. "Glaswegians love to put on the style," says a leading chain-store director. "In fact, in terms of fashion and hairdressing, I would say this is the most alert city outside London."

That said, Glasgow still thinks like an individual in matters of fashion. Determined to break free of the straitjacket imposed by multiple deprivation, the city, well before its present renaissance, has always been willing to give anything a whirl. Out of the city's defiant vitality, a new aspect of Glasgow style has emerged as a generation of home-grown young artists, designers and craftsmen learn the hard, commercial lessons of how to sell innovation and élan. At the heart of such activities there usually lies a training gained at Glasgow School of Art, internationally regarded for the vigorous and original quality of its design education. Stretching from graphics to ceramics, from furniture to jewellery, textiles and industrial products, exhibitions of students' work are seen regularly at the School and annually in London.

Certainly, Glasgow believes that it is the most vital and vibrating city in Britain, but is it chic? It is too full of jagged energy for that. What many outsiders appreciate is, indeed, its lack of overwhelming middle-class gentility. The resilience that underpins its folk memory of hardship has also taught how to get by on outrageous friendliness and laughs. One visiting American claims that it has the same sort of vibrancy as parts of New York and Chicago.

"This town shakes with activity," says John Mauceri, stylish New Yorker and Scottish Opera's former musical director. When he was away from his brownstone on West 20th Street, he regarded Glasgow as being as close as he can get to the pace and disputatious cheek of Manhattan. "The reason I feel so comfortable here is because Glasgow in temperament is so much more like New York than London, Paris or Rome. It has a grit to it and an ethnic exhibitionism which makes the place buzz."

The people's innate irreverence means they are always ready to prick the bubble of pomposity. Glasgow, therefore, seeks no shrine status, like Edinburgh, Venice, London or Paris. It is – and always has been – essentially its people, equipped with merry anarchy and enterprise, heroic forbearance, quick-on-the-uptake daftness, and a grand, effusive ability to dress up, hit the town, and have a great time. ❑

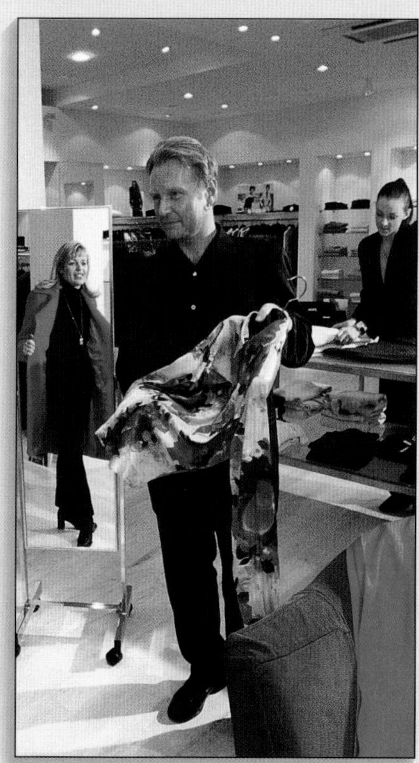

RIGHT: shopping at the Italian Centre.

TO THE NORTHWEST

Here is Victorian Glasgow at its finest, from Alexander "Greek" Thomson's terraces and Charles Rennie Mackintosh's churches to John Kibble's Crystal Art Palace and the Forth and Clyde Canal

St George's Cross, ❶ at the northwest of the city centre, is now nothing but a memory and has been replaced by a spaghetti junction dominated by the motorway. **Great Western Road**, which begins here, is probably the longest absolutely straight road in Glasgow and, were it not for a couple of drumlins, then Anniesland Cross, 2½ miles (4 km) to the northwest, would be visible.

This road was projected in the 1830s to provide a grand new approach to the city, thus avoiding the squalor which had accompanied the rise of Glasgow as a manufacturing and trading centre.

Victorian planning

Decimus Burton, the most eminent English suburban planner of the day, was commissioned to mastermind the project and prepared a plan of crescents and terraces which would line the thoroughfare. Behind these would be detached houses. It is fortunate that the glorious result still stands for when, in the late 1960s, the city fathers were determined to make Glasgow "the most modern city in Europe", ring roads and radial motorways were all the rage. Great Western Road was to become one of the latter; but, in the nick of time, sanity prevailed, and the road remains, little changed after a century.

Here, when the sun shines the flowers bloom and the birds twitter, one can imagine being on a continental boulevard – alas, without the sidewalk cafés. And, indeed, during Victorian times this was the place for the *passeggiaro*. Today's visitors can be excused for doubting this panegyric as they set off along the road but very soon the soaring spires of two churches beckon and the plaudits for this great avenue begin to be justified.

St Mary's Episcopal Cathedral ❷ and **Landsdowne Church** ❸ both stand on the north side of the road about half-a-mile from St George's Cross. The architecture of both is Early English. The steeple of the cathedral, which is the first of the two edifices but almost 50 years younger than the church, is not quite as tall as that of its neighbour; this difference is accentuated by the slimness of the latter, one of the city's most attractive Gothic Revival churches. In the church the well-to-do have individual pews with private doors: the hoi-polloi know their place upstairs.

Just after this comes **Great Western Bridge** ❹, opened on 29 September 1891 and the third bridge on this site. For the best view of the bridge, head down the steps on the downstream side and on to the river walkway. The next building of note on Great Western Road is Caledonian

PRECEDING PAGES: wedding group in the Botanic Gardens.
LEFT: inside the Botanic Gardens.
RIGHT: Kirklee Terrace.

Mansions, on the left just after the bridge. Built in 1895 for the Caledonian Railway Company, this Arts and Crafts style building is decorated on all sides and even the back is worth the walk round to have a look. **Ruskin Terrace** ❺, from 1858, is the first of the great terraces you'll encounter. They are separated from the street by a raised driveway but each is to a different design. Even in this terrace you will note the gradually changing style of the houses as the terrace marched west during the four-year period of its construction.

Kibble Palace

One mile past St George's Cross is the busy intersection with **Byres Road** to the south and **Queen Margaret Drive** to the north. The enormous spread of glass visible just beyond the entrance to the **Botanic Gardens** ❻ (0141-334 2422, daily 7am–dusk, free), which occupies the northwest corner of this intersection, is **Kibble Palace** ❼ (open 10am–4.45pm summer, 4.15pm winter, free), one of the largest and most spectacular glasshouses in Britain.

The Kibble Crystal Art Palace and Royal Conservatory, as it used to be called, did not always occupy this site. Rather it graced the estate on Loch Long of John Kibble, an eccentric engineer for whom it was built in 1865. Kibble moved it to its present site in 1873, bringing it up the River Clyde on a raft towed by a puffer (a small, locally built tramp-steamer). It became the immediate focus for life in the West End hosting concerts, the first of which was advertised as having the capacity to accommodate 6,000 people.

In 1876 the British Association visited Glasgow and held its inaugural meeting in the Palace. The heat must have been more intense than usual on those occasions when Disraeli (1871) and later Gladstone (1877) gave their rectorial addresses here. Unfortunately, enthusiastic revelers destroyed both the peace of the neighbourhood and the plants of the gardens and John Kibble was forced to turn over

LEFT: the Botanic Gardens.

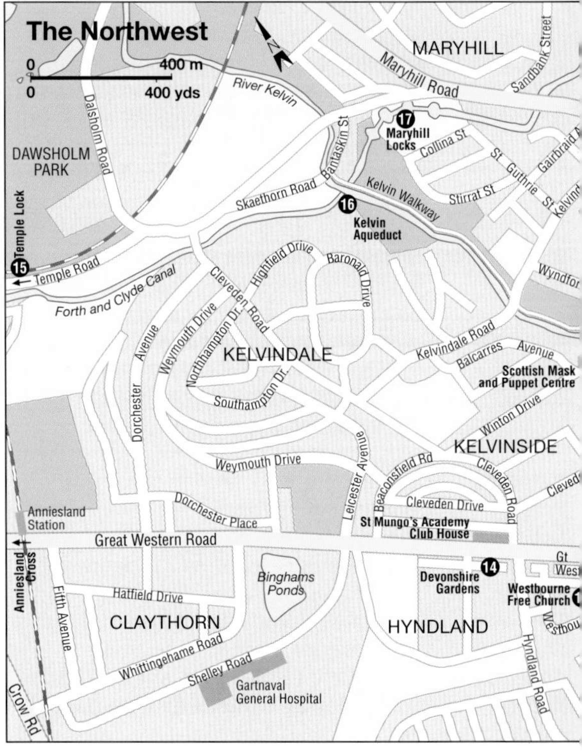

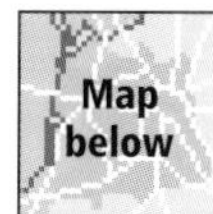

his palace to the directors of the latter. (Rector is an office peculiar to Scottish universities. Different student factions, usually mischievously, nominate candidates who are, in one way or another, famous or infamous. A notable contest a few years ago was that between Winnie Mandela and Yasser Arafat in which Winnie Mandela prevailed.)

In 1881 the Kibble Palace became the plant house for the Botanic Garden and now houses a wide selection of ferns from temperate lands, mainly Australasia. Nothing can be more pleasant on a grey day than to sit here nudged by ferns through which peeps one of the statues that grace the conservatory. The British National collection of begonias and a gorgeous array of orchids can be enjoyed in the neighbouring and more conventional range of glasshouses, each of which houses a particular speciality.

Around, and stretching away from, the glasshouses are a constantly changing kaleidoscopic variety of blooms in the rock garden, the herb garden and the systematic garden.

The long march

Those still in search of nature will make for the **River Kelvin** at the northern side of the park and stroll along the **Kelvin Walkways** ❽. Citywards, it proceeds in a rather circuitous manner to Great Western Bridge: westwards, it ultimately joins the West Highland Way, which stretches to Fort William and beyond.

Urban ramblers will exit from the Botanic Gardens immediately to the north of where they entered and find themselves on **Queen Margaret Drive**. Facing is an architectural hotch-potch, which is home to the **British Broadcasting Corporation** ❾ in Scotland. The core building, which is now a tiny part of the entire complex, is Northrop House, built in 1869 to house the art collection of the Bell brothers, who owned the Glasgow Pottery at Port Dundas, Scotland's largest pottery.

One of the two brothers was an avowed

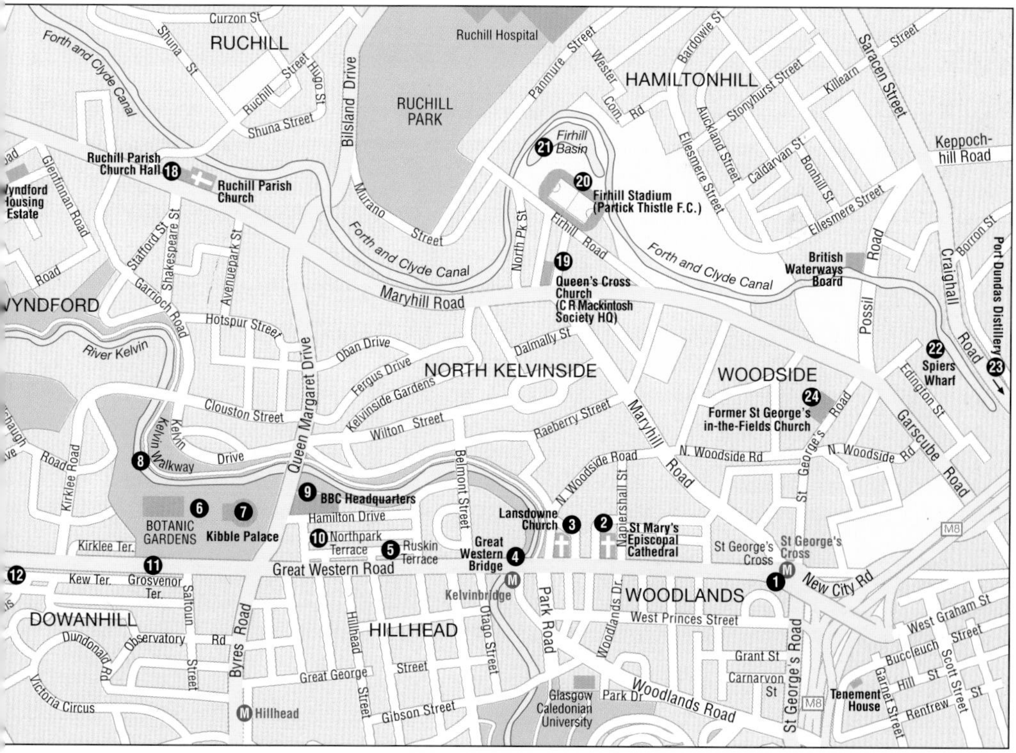

recluse and misogynist. How he must have turned in his grave when, in 1883, the building was sold and, in honour of King Malcolm Canmore's wife, was named Queen Margaret College and became a centre of higher education for women. Before this, professors from the university had given "Occasional Lectures for Women". By 1892 the University admitted women to its classes on equal terms with men, one of the first in Britain to do so.

From Queen Margaret Drive it's worth heading along past the BBC on Hamilton Drive to look for **Northpark Terrace**, ❿ a subtly detailed three-storey terrace from the drawing board of "Greek" Thomson.

Back on Great Western Road, the first terrace to be encountered is on the south side. **Grosvenor Terrace** ⓫ (1855), which faces the Botanic Gardens, is reminiscent of a Venetian renaissance palazzo. Repetitiveness is the theme and individuality absent from this glorious 200-yard stretch of three equal storeys, each with round-headed windows which are separated by the slivers of classical mullions. In 1978 a fire gutted the Grosvenor Hotel at the east end. It has subsequently been rebuilt and is now a Hilton Hotel with the facade recreated in concrete.

Grosvenor Terrace is followed by unremarkable **Kew Terrace** (1849), which possesses a discreet, dignified air and then, across the road, immediately beyond the Gardens, is **Kirklee Terrace**, another grand Italianate palace with each house having a projecting porch. This, somewhat raised above the level of the main road, was the first of the glorious Great Western Road terraces to be built (1845).

Back across the road, and also somewhat raised, stands the great *oeuvre* of "Greek" Thomson which is simply called **Great Western Terrace** ⓬ (1869). Two three-storey pavilions interrupt the long two-storey facade and the balanced ensemble announces a splendid dignity. This, possibly the greatest of Thomson's terraces, bears his unmistakable Greek imprint. Sir William Burrell, of the acclaimed Burrell

BELOW: West End antiques store.

Map on page 184

Collection, lived in the terrace at number 8.

Immediately to the rear of Great Western Terrace is **Westbourne Gardens** whose architecture is not as distinguished as that seen in some of the Great Western Road terraces and yet which forms a unified triangle with a pretty park in the centre and which has, at its northwest extremity, the most unusual – at least for Glasgow – **Westbourne Free Church** ⓭. This classical two-storey Italian Renaissance style building, the lower windows being enclosed by Ionic columns, the upper by Corinthian columns, would surely appear perfectly at home in Italy.

Nearby Westbourne Terrace is another "Greek" Thomson terrace, notable for the incorporation of the fashionable bay window into the classical design.

Devonshire Gardens ⓮ is the next noteworthy terrace along the road. At its western end, number 5 is Glasgow's finest five-star hotel, The Devonshire. while numbers 1 to 4 are simply One Devonshire Gardens, an exceedingly fine upmarket hotel beloved by celebrities and rock stars. Its restaurant has been taken over by the chef Gordon Ramsay.

Anniesland Cross is reached 2½ miles (4 km) after leaving St. George's Cross. Great Western Road does not stop here but continues, albeit not so straight, for several more miles, passing diminutive boxes rather than elegant terraces until it disappears beyond the city boundary towards the Kilpatrick Hills. Rather than following this, turn right before Anniesland Cross into Crow Road and eventually arrive at the **Forth and Clyde Canal** at **Temple Lock** ⓯.

From sea to sea

This somewhat inconspicuous ribbon of water is part of what was dubbed Scotland's Grand Canal when it opened in 1790. This was Britain's first sea-to-sea waterway and linked the Firth of Clyde on the west coast with the Firth of Forth on the east. The west terminal was at Bowling and the east at Grangemouth, a

BELOW: Great Western Terrace in winter.

distance of 35 miles (56 km). In addition, there was a 4-mile (6-km) Glasgow branch. The absence of fixed bridges enabled masted vessels to voyage between the Atlantic and the North Sea. In 1963 in an act of bureaucratic vandalism, the canal was closed for navigation. However, in 1999, work started on a £78 million two-year project, Millennium Link, British Waterways' biggest engineering undertaking in Scotland; it was designed to restore the Forth and Clyde Canal connection between Glasgow and Edinburgh.

Stroll eastwards along the canal for about half-a-mile and arrive at the impressive aqueduct, which carries the canal across the River Kelvin. When the **Kelvin Aqueduct** ⓰ was opened in 1790 it was the largest structure of its kind in Britain. It is 70 ft (21 metres) high and its four 50-ft (15-metre) arches with arched spandrels supported by massive buttressed piers carry the canal for 135 yards (122 metres).

To appreciate better the glory of this massive structure, which so impressed the populace that odes were written in its honour, stroll down to the Kelvin Walkway (five minutes). Unfortunately, even from here, the grandeur of the aqueduct is partially masked by trees.

Return to the canal and the **Maryhill Locks** ⓱, which are linked by oval basins, are immediately reached. Locally, this group of five locks is known as "The Botany Locks", possibly reminiscent of the stark choices people faced – either work on the canal or emigrate to Botany Bay in Australia. These locks and the Kelvin Aqueduct are now listed as scheduled ancient monuments.

Difficult to believe that puffers – including the world's first – were built in the Kelvin Dock Boatyard, between Locks 22 and 23, until 1949. Puffers were cargo boats, which derived their name from the fact that the exhaust of the early puffers was turned up through the funnel and produced a puffing noise. On average, they were about 60 ft (18 metres) long and 15 ft (4.5 metres) wide and had a 6-ft (2-metre) draught. Puffers were celebrated in the writings of Neil Munro and their TV adaptations. *Para Handy* was the inimitable captain of the *Vital Spark*, a puffer which, like most of these craft, plied the Clyde and its estuary rather than the canal.

More Mackintosh

Leave the canal at this point and enter **Maryhill**, a blend of 19th- and 20th-century tenements which survived the wholesale demolition of the 1950s. Proceed towards the city on **Maryhill Road** passing on the right **Wyndford Housing Estate**, one of the city's earliest and most successful post-World War II public housing schemes. After about three-quarters of a mile (1 km) turn left into **Ruchill Street** and immediately observe the red sandstone Ruchill Parish Church.

Much more renowned, although less conspicuous, is the adjacent white sandstone Art Nouveau **Ruchill Parish Church Hall** ⓲ which was built in 1898 and which is from the drawing board of Charles Rennie Mackintosh.

It has been suggested that Mackintosh was not chosen as church architect

LEFT: a handy lamp-post in Maryhill.

because of his extravagant style, although little of this is evident in this hall. Still, seven years elapsed between the building of the hall and the church, a period during which his idiosyncratic style evolved.

About 1,000 yards further down Maryhill Road, which then becomes Garscube Road, at the junction with Firhill Road stands Mackintosh's only church. **Queen's Cross Church** ⓳ (0141-946 6600 www.crmsociety.com Mon–Fri 10am–5pm, Sat 10am–2pm, Sun 2pm–5pm, donation) is contemporary with the Ruchill church hall and is Art Nouveau Late Gothic in style. Built in 1897–99, it has several influences in its design, notably the tower inspired by the Merriot Church in Somerset, a medieval church which Mackintosh examined in 1895. Mackintosh's innovative ideas are exemplified by the use of giant steel ties, which cross the nave. The spaciousness is enhanced by a high arched wooden ceiling, which is identical, even to the extent of caulking, with the inverted hull of a wooden boat.

The church, vacated in 1976, is now the HQ of the **Charles Rennie Mackintosh Society**, and houses a Mackintosh reference library and a small exhibition.

Behind the church is **Firhill Stadium** ⓴, home of Partick Thistle, another of Glasgow's major soccer clubs, frequent butt of the standing Glasgow joke that the number on the field exceeds the number of spectators. A flight of stairs at the city side of the stadium ascends to the Glasgow Branch of the **Forth and Clyde Canal**. This branch was described by the *Edinburgh Courant* in 1797 as "a ditch, a gutter, a mere puddle". At the top of the steps, turn left and stroll a short distance to the **Firhill Basin** ㉑ in which timber was once seasoned. A right, rather than a left, turn leads towards the city on a towpath bordering water where mallards and moorhens, heron and swans, enjoy their leisure. Some ditch! Some gutter! Some puddle!

After about half-a-mile a bascule bridge (such bridges work on the see-saw principle) crosses the canal and leads to the new

BELOW: the church that Mackintosh designed. **RIGHT:** detail from a Maryhill tenement.

Scottish headquarters of the **British Waterways Board**. Near here, Sir William Burrell had a small shipyard. Continue past the bridge for a few hundred yards, admiring the superb vistas of the city.

The canal now makes an acute right turn. Dominating the opposite bank is **Speirs Wharf** ㉒, a magnificent range of five- and six-storey Victorian buildings, among the best surviving buildings from old industrial Glasgow. Originally, these were grain mills and then were used as a whisky bond. They have been lovingly recycled to become luxury apartments.

The handsome two-storey Georgian building at the city end was where, formerly, the business of the canal was conducted. From this building passenger boats, the *Swifts*, which could carry 60 people, left for Falkirk and, later, for Edinburgh. These boats offered a comfort which the stagecoaches couldn't equal.

From here, too, would leave cargo vessels preferring these non-tidal waters to the as yet undredged River Clyde. Between 1893 and 1939 pleasure steamers, the *Queens* – the *Fairy*, the *May* and the *Gipsy* – which could carry 200 passengers, departed from here for trips on the canal.

A wee dram

This marks the end of the Glasgow branch of the canal. The heady aroma is from the neighbouring **Port Dundas Distillery** ㉓, which produces 8½ million gallons (40 million litres) of whisky a year. Some is matured *in situ* while most is sent to other distilleries to be used in popular blends.

The motorway passes here, and below, a short distance to the south, is **St George's Road**, which leads to St George's Cross. En route, spare a glance for the building of **St-George's-in-the-Fields** ㉔, the flowering of classical revival in Glasgow. Standing in splendid isolation, this classical basilica, which is now apartments, has a raised Ionic portico carrying a carving of Christ feeding the multitude in the tympanum of the pediment. ❑

Right: from Maryhill – and proud of it.

EAST OF THE CROSS

The legendary Barras market, one of the city's oldest pubs and Celtic Football Club are the highlights of this latest area to be targeted for gentrification

Immediately east of Glasgow Cross and occupying an area between the **Gallowgate** and **London Road** is the **Barras** ❶, Glasgow's – and probably Scotland's – best known market. As in the great Paris flea market, everything can be found here from snake oil to the latest bootleg CD. Despite the anglified cast-iron gateways bearing the title "Barrowland" the name may not be a simple corruption of the barrows from which goods were sold but from the name of the gate at the foot of the Saltmarket, Barras Port.

Whatever the origin, there is no doubt about the foundation of the market. It was started by a woman called Maggie McIver, who was the first to rent out market carts. Then she rented various premises in this locality and her stock of barrows increased to more than 300. She first rented and then bought the land that the present market stands on, had it covered and was operating during the economic depression of the early 1930s on a site covering half a mile.

In 1934 she opened the **Barrowland Ballroom**, which immediately attracted Eastenders and others who loved to tango, to Charleston and to foxtrot, and which is still going strong as a concert venue. By the time she died at the age of 78 Maggie McIver had become a millionairess several times over.

Selling with style

A visit to the Barras is not just a shopping expedition. It's a day of pure entertainment, exploring the rabbit warrens of tenements, sheds and warehouses, emerging occasionally to enter one of the colorful pubs, then diving back in to laugh at the wit and style of the stallholders, Glasgow patter merchants who are first-class comedians.

The time to visit the Barras, where you can buy everything from second-hand furniture and used clothing to fresh fruit and vegetables, is at weekends.

Exhausted by shopping and laughing at the Barras, stop for a "refreshment" at the **Saracen's Head** on the Gallowgate for a slice of the real old Glasgow.

This was Glasgow's first hotel and there has been a pub of the same name on this spot since 1754 when the original was constructed of stone cannibalised from the nearby castle. It has been frequented by such notables as James Boswell and Dr Samuel Johnson who lodged here when they were on their Highland Tour in 1769.

Later Robert Burns popped in, and more recently it became the scene of the Last Supper in Billy Connolly's parody of the Crucifixion. The current incarnation dates from 1905. Before you order your drink, you should be aware of the fact that the

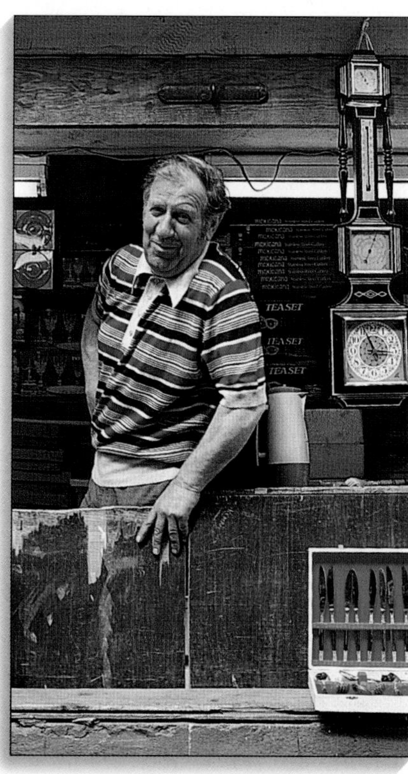

LEFT AND RIGHT: Barras traders.

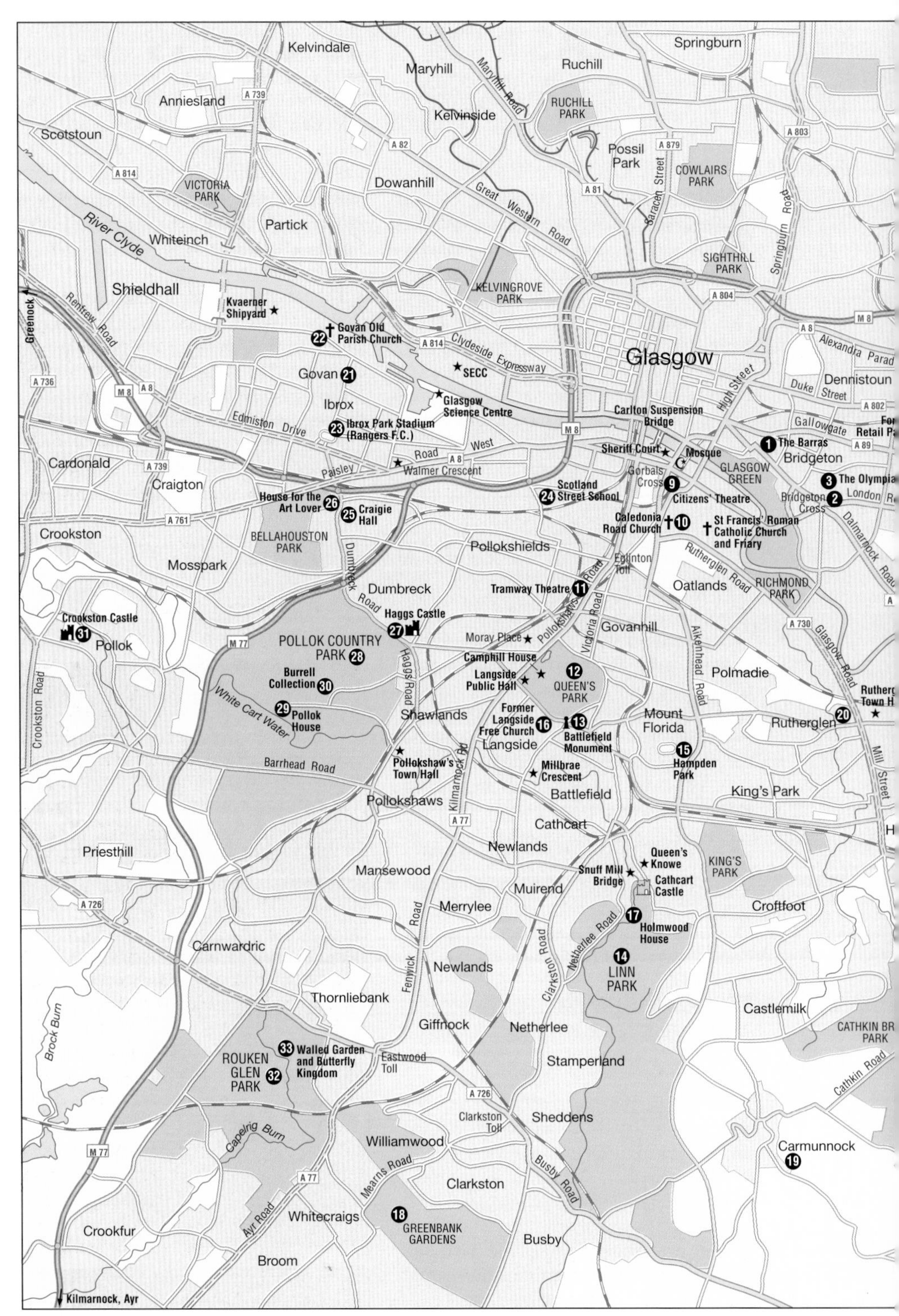
Kelvindale
Springburn
Maryhill
Ruchill
Anniesland
Maryhill Road
RUCHILL PARK
Kelvinside
Scotstoun
Possil Park
COWLAIRS PARK
Saracen Street
Springburn Road
VICTORIA PARK
Dowanhill
Great Western Road
River Clyde
Whiteinch
Partick
SIGHTHILL PARK
Shieldhall
KELVINGROVE PARK
Kvaerner Shipyard
Greenock
Renfrew Road
Govan Old Parish Church
Clydeside Expressway
Glasgow
Alexandra Parade
High Street
Govan
SECC
Dennistoun
Duke Street
Ibrox
Glasgow Science Centre
Carlton Suspension Bridge
Edmiston Drive
Ibrox Park Stadium (Rangers F.C.)
Gallowgate
Forge Retail Park
The Barras
Paisley Road West
Sheriff Court
Mosque
Bridgeton
Cardonald
Walmer Crescent
Gorbals Cross
GLASGOW GREEN
The Olympia
Craigton
Scotland Street School
Citizens' Theatre
Bridgeton Cross
London Road
House for the Art Lover
Craigie Hall
Caledonia Road Church
St Francis' Roman Catholic Church and Friary
Dalmarnock Road
Crookston
BELLAHOUSTON PARK
Pollokshields
Eglinton Toll
Mosspark
Dumbreck Road
Rutherglen Road
Oatlands
RICHMOND PARK
Dumbreck
Tramway Theatre
Crookston Castle
Haggs Castle
Pollokshaws Road
Victoria Road
Govanhill
Glasgow Road
Pollok
POLLOK COUNTRY PARK
Moray Place
Camphill House
Langside Public Hall
QUEEN'S PARK
Polmadie
Aikenhead Road
Burrell Collection
Haggs Road
Rutherglen Town Hall
White Cart Water
Pollok House
Crookston Road
Shawlands
Former Langside Free Church
Battlefield Monument
Mount Florida
Rutherglen
Langside
Hampden Park
Mill Street
Barrhead Road
Pollokshaw's Town Hall
Millbrae Crescent
Kilmarnock Rd
Battlefield
King's Park
Pollokshaws
Cathcart
Priesthill
Newlands
Queen's Knowe
Mansewood
Snuff Mill Bridge
KING'S PARK
Cathcart Castle
Muirend
Merrylee
Croftfoot
Holmwood House
Fenwick Road
Netherlee Road
Carnwardric
Clarkston Road
Newlands
LINN PARK
Thornliebank
Castlemilk
Brock Burn
Giffnock
Netherlee
CATHKIN BRAES PARK
Walled Garden and Butterfly Kingdom
Eastwood Toll
ROUKEN GLEN PARK
Stamperland
Cathkin Road
Clarkston Toll
Sheddens
Capelrig Burn
Williamwood
Carmunnock
Mearns Road
Busby Road
Clarkston
Ayr Road
Whitecraigs
GREENBANK GARDENS
Crookfur
Busby
Broom
Kilmarnock, Ayr

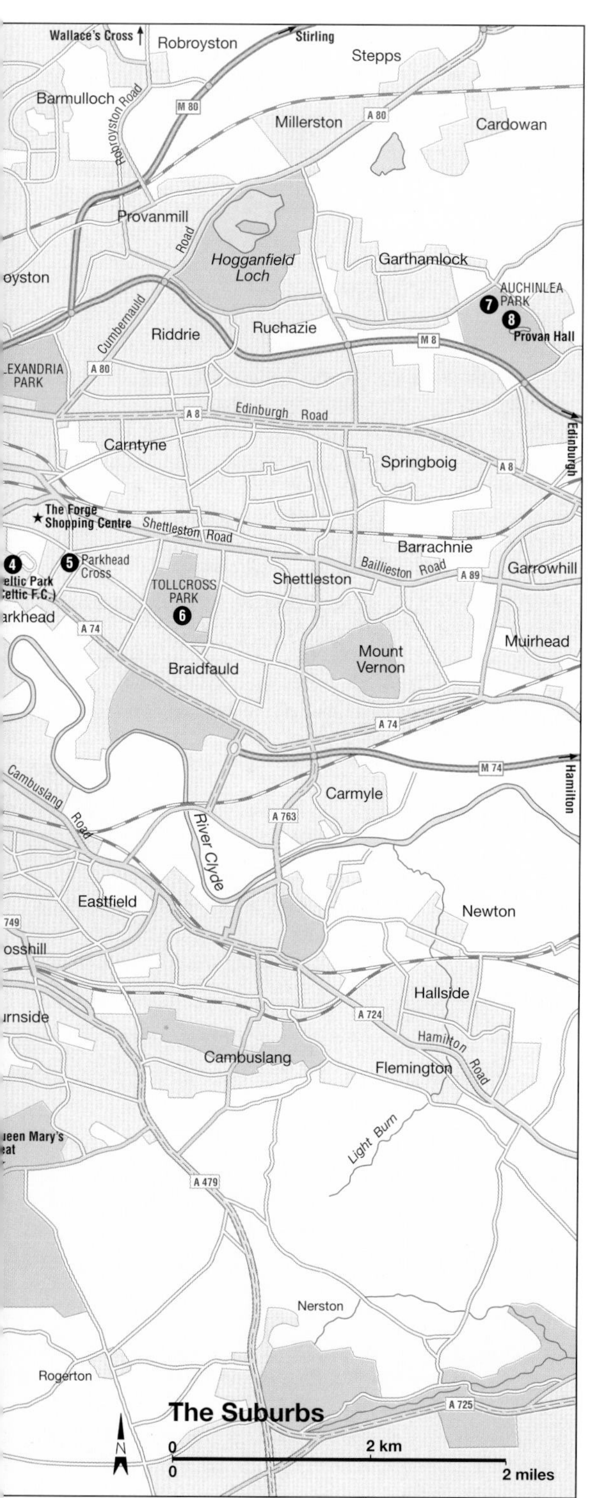

reputation of the "Sarry Heid" rests on the lethal qualities of its cider. Further along the Gallowgate, flanking the junction with Claythorne Street are a pair of 18th century buildings which have been well restored. They were originally built as houses and inns with wallhead gables, quoins and turnpike stairs. One is now a sheltered housing development, while the other is **Hielan Jessie's**, a rare old pub.

Head back to "Ra Barras" and through then south onto London Road, then proceed eastward for about three-quarters of a mile (1 km) to **Bridgeton Cross** ❷ where an apparently infinite number of roads intersect and form a veritable maze. Standing in splendid isolation in the midst of this confusion is the 115-year-old "Umbrella", an elegant cast-iron gazebo whose roof is supported by 10 slender columns. Above the roof is a clock-tower with four faces, below which are four Glasgow coats of arms.

Echoes of the past

The **Olympia** ❸, a large red building at the corner of **Orr Street**, is now a bingo hall; it was formerly a cinema and, before that, a music hall. However, its claim to fame is that here, after World War I, charismatic Jimmy Maxton, a "Red Clydesider" if ever there was one, made his fiery speeches which led to his being elected to parliament in 1922 and to Bridgeton having the strongest branch of the Independent Labour Party (ILP) in Scotland. (The ILP was a party well to the left of mainstream Labour.) Sir Winston Churchill, who often crossed words with Maxton, said that he "was the greatest gentleman in the House of Commons".

The word gentlemen could scarcely be used to describe the Billy Boys, a gang who frequented Bridgeton Cross in the 1930s and who were allegedly the prototype for the main gang in *No Mean City,* that infamous novel about the Glasgow Razor Gangs *(see page 92)*. They could be heard singing their theme song "Hello, hello, we are the Billy Boys" to the tune of *Marching through Georgia* even before they could be seen.

From Bridgeton Cross, proceed along

London Road. After about a mile, "Paradise" for many Glaswegians – and for others – comes into view. **Celtic Park ❹**, with its modern red brick frontage, is the home of the green and white, the **Celtic Football Club** (0141 551 4308 website: www.celticfc.co.uk/)**,** one of Glasgow's two great rival soccer teams.

Tours of the stadium include a visit to the pitch, trophy room and the museum, which includes lots of memorabilia including a cup which they won from arch rival, Rangers, in 1901. Rangers had won the cup as part of a competition in 1888 held during the International Exhibition. In 1901 there was a disaster at Ibrox (Rangers' ground) and a competition was arranged to raise money for the victims. Rangers put the cup up as the prize and Celtic won.

Soon after this, turn left into **Springfield Road** and observe, on the left, the large, undistinguished modern red factory. This is the home of Barr's, Britain's largest soft drinks manufacturers and, much more importantly, the makers of Scotland's "other national drink", Irn Bru, the drink "made from girders". This drink now making inroads into the international market is said to possess remarkable medicinal properties, particularly when it comes to curing of hangovers. However, new trendy uses are now being found for it as a mixer for alcoholic drinks (Irn Bru and vodka) and there's even an alcopop version.

Glass pyramids

It is apt that the drink "made from girders" should have its home here for, just to the north, on **Duke Street**, stood the Parkhead Forge, a huge ironworks "which by day enshrouded the city in clouds of smoke, by night in shafts of fire". Now, where Hector, Priam and Achilles, and Samson and Goliath (the names given to steam-hammers) once rocked Parkhead to its core, stand elegant glass pyramids which enclose a large shopping complex.

Parkhead Cross ❺, other than Glasgow Cross, the best survivor of the impact

BELOW: Irn Bru, "made from girders".

Map on page 194

of ring roads, stands between the Parkhead Forge and Barr's at the intersection of five roads. Here are spectacular century-old red sandstone buildings with turrets, towers and battlements. Unfortunately, because the buildings are crammed together, the parts are greater than the whole. Bas-reliefs are carved on the exterior walls of some buildings.

During the summer months, enthusiastic horticulturists should proceed from Parkhead Cross along **Tollcross Road** for about 1,000 yards (1 km) to the entrance to **Tollcross Park** ❻. The hillside to the right of the entrance is ablaze with roses in a recently constructed rose garden which, each summer, wins major British awards.

From here, it is about 2 miles (3 km) through the districts of Shettleston and Springboig to pleasantly landscaped **Auchinlea Park** ❼ at the eastern extremity of the city. The entrance on Auchinlea Road immediately leads to pretty **Provan Hall** ❽, possibly the most perfect example in all Scotland of a pre-Reformation house. The small, round tower and delicate crow-stepped gable of this two-storey, 15th-century house, which was the country abode of the prebend (canon), are especially attractive.

Return to the motorway, head back towards the city, exit at interchange 11 and travel northwards through fairly open countryside to the northeastern limits of the city. Here, alongside a farm at the side of the northern and narrow part of **Robroyston Road**, a 20-ft (6-metre) granite cross marks the spot where William Wallace was captured by the English in 1305 and taken to London where he was accused of treason and done to death.

The cross, which incorporates the double-handed sword always associated with Wallace, was restored in 1986 with the aid of donations from members of the Clan Wallace in the United States. The donors were unimpressed by historians who believe that such swords were not known to have been used by knights until the late 15th century. ❑

BELOW: eating out.

PAW
THE SALVATION ARMY

THE GORBALS AND THE SOUTHEAST

Once notorious but now rejuvenated, the Gorbals is home to the famous Citizens' Theatre. Further south is Hampden Park, the national stadium and home to the Scottish Football Museum

A good place to start an exploration of the southeast of the city is **Carlton Place**, situated on the south bank of the river, linked to the city by the elegant Carlton Suspension Bridge. Carlton Place is backed by a 400-yard-long stately Georgian terrace, built at the beginning of the 19th century at the behest of the Laurie brothers, David and James, who took up residence in the house with the rounded portico at the eastern end of the terrace. The interior of this house boasts exquisite plasterwork which is believed to have been executed by Italian artists employed by George IV to decorate Windsor Castle.

Carlton Place is neatly bisected by broad South Portland Street, which was intended as a continuation of Buchanan Street, albeit interrupted by St Enoch Square and the Carlton Suspension Bridge, and which would reflect the elegance of that street. It was intended as the linchpin of the distinguished district of Laurieston whose showpiece would be a great academy which would provide education for all men – sons of the middle-class during the day and craftsmen and apprentices in the evening.

End of the dream

The Laurie dream was never realised and Carlton Place turned out to be little more than an architectural folly, although it and other Gorbals streets still carry the names of aristocracy and royalty such as Carlton and Cumberland, Cavendish and Oxford, Bedford and Norfolk. The absence of civic control permitted ironworks and railways to destroy the dreams and Laurieston ended as "a slum annexe to the Gorbals; a useful overflow district with large homes capable of subdivisions into warrens housing 150 people under one roof".

PRECEDING PAGES: time for reflection in the Gorbals. **LEFT:** the reborn Gorbals. **RIGHT:** the Central Mosque.

The Gorbals was torn apart after World War II in order to improve living conditions, although those who occupy the high-rise blocks in the district do not believe this was achieved. As a result, South Portland Street was truncated to just 150 yards and the late, lamented Gorbals Cross, whose centrepiece was a gentleman's public lavatory, disappeared from the face of the earth. Yet a few handsome buildings, often ecclesiastical, have survived and some new interesting, if scarcely handsome, buildings have appeared.

Among the latter, immediately east of Carlton Place, is the forbidding, heavy, totalitarian **Sheriff Court**, the second

The Citizens' Theatre

The window was flung open and the housewife shouted: "Poofter, what's playing tonight?" The man so addressed looked up and said "*Hamlet*", to which the response was: "Ah dinny think al come: that's nae for me". The place was the Gorbals: the man was an actor in the Citizens' Theatre Company and the interlocuter a working woman exhibiting that Glasgow characteristic of affectionate name-calling. She probably would have thoroughly enjoyed the *Hamlet* for the three co-directors of the Citizens' (the Cits, as it is colloquially known) believe that theatre should be fun and lively and any Cits production is dazzling, even outrageous.

The first production of Giles Havergal, Philip Prowse and Robert David MacDonald when they took control in 1970 was an outré *Hamlet* that terrified the then conservative Labour District Council, which threatened to withdraw its grant to the company. Since then, the Cits has developed an idiosyncratic non-naturalistic style, a part of which is that the actors remember at all times that they are acting. The directors – and the presence of three directors makes it difficult for outside directors to get a look-in – are involved in everything from the cost of a seat to the price of a bottle of beer at the bar.

This is all a far cry from the original Citizens' Theatre which was founded in the middle of World War II, in 1943, by James Bridie and Tom Honeyman. Their avowed aim was the development of a Scottish theatre, but by the late 1950s the works of foreigners were being performed.

However, Scottish actors including international names such as Molly Urquhart, Alastair Sim and Duncan Macrae still trod the boards. All agree that it was the inspiration of Bridie and Honeyman and the Cits which led to the Scottish political and working-class theatre now so popular in Glasgow.

When the present directors arrived on the scene in 1970, all this changed. What was of concern was quality and equality and since then the theatre has staged the works of Balzac and Brecht, Genet and Goethe, Albee and Arrabal. Their productions are stylish, visual and full of blood and thunder.

Equality is enforced on both sides of the proscenium arch. All the actors, many of whom have been with the company since the triumvirate took over, receive the same pay and all seats are the same low price. Pensioners and the jobless are admitted free. Formerly, The Close, a small experimental Club theatre, was part of the Citizens' but when it burned down in 1973 the present directors refused to be involved with its resurrection: because it was a club, it smacked of elitism.

Havergal believes that classical drama must always be popular drama. He is fascinated by the Elizabethan idea of a theatre to which everybody came: not just a specific audience pre-selected by class or income or occupation. The location of the Citizens' is perfect for this ideal: it is enclosed within the Gorbals and 400 yards to the north is the Merchant City with its young and affluent population. If Havergal had his way, all seats at the Cits' would be free: his is a utopian world. ❑

LEFT: a performance at the Citizens'.

Map on page 194

largest such building in Europe and one of the most expensive structures ever erected in Glasgow. Prettier by far is the salmon-coloured **Strathclyde Police Training Centre**, crowned by a gigantic white coat-of-arms, just to the southwest.

The **Citizens' Theatre** ❾, to the east of this Kremlin-Pentagon, is another relatively modern Gorbals landmark. and is pleasant, in spite of its exterior of bathroom-like tiles – is it attempting to commemorate the lost gentlemen's lavatory? Enter the foyer under statues of the Four Muses and be greeted by larger than life-size statues of Robert Burns and William Shakespeare, and then pass into the auditorium through doors flanked by gilded elephants. All these figures are part of Glasgow's theatrical heritage and were rescued from city theatres now destroyed.

The **Glasgow Central Mosque and Islamic Centre**, immediately to the north of the theatre, is instantly recognisable because of its minaret and relatively unpretentious multi-faceted glass dome. The Gorbals has always been the magnet for new immigrant groups. The Irish made it their Erin and then the Jews found that it was the Promised Land. They, in turn, were followed by the Pakistanis who had found Paradise.

Nothing remains of the Great Synagogue or of the many other Jewish buildings but the **St Francis' Roman Catholic Church and Friary** still stand on that part of Cumberland Street which is about 400 yards southeast of the mosque. This 1880 building, incorporating stones from the first Franciscan complex in Glasgow which was dedicated in 1477, is a delightful example of early decorated style. The interior, whose beauty matches that of the exterior, has excellent acoustics.

Whisky distillery

Spirit of a different kind is distilled a couple of hundred yards to the north at the **Strathclyde Distillery** (look for its distinctive tall chimney). Regrettably, this building, in which 7 million gallons (32 million litres)

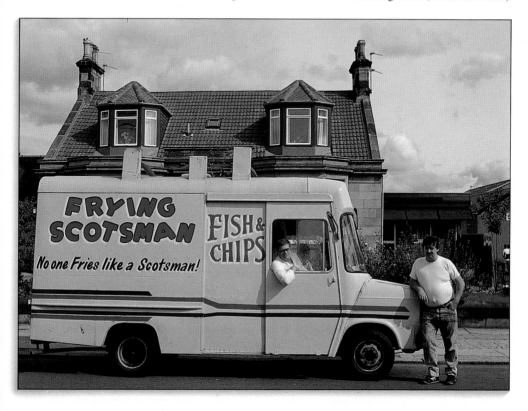

BELOW: the original fast food.

of the guid stuff is distilled each year, is not open to the public.

From here, travel west for about a mile along Caledonia Road, towards a beacon-like square tower which rises from alongside a raised Ionic colonnade and clearly bearing the imprint of "Greek" Thomson. The **Caledonia Road Church** ⑩ dates from 1856–57 and, when functional, had – in sharp contrast to most of its contemporaries – a bright and colourful interior. This, Thomson's first church and one of the great 19th-century Scottish buildings, was burnt to a shell in 1965 and its future is in doubt. Possibly it is best left, as has been suggested, as it is: a work in picturesque decay like the Acropolis from which Thomson sought his inspiration.

Turn south along Pollokshaws Road and in half-a-mile St Andrew's Cross (invariably referred to as **Eglinton Toll**) and the exit to the Gorbals is reached. Eglinton Toll, a major intersection of five roads, was, in years gone by, bathed in the hellish orange glow of the open-top blast furnaces of Dixon's Blazes – or, to give them their more correct name, the Govan Colliery and Iron Works – which were a major source of employment for inhabitants of the Gorbals. It is said of the great blast furnaces that "the bright glare cheers the long winter night, and at the same time does the work of a score of policemen, by scaring away the rogues and vagabonds who so plentifully infest other and darker parts of the city." Nothing remains.

From Eglinton Toll, a wide, straight-as-a-die, mile-long, handsome, suburban thoroughfare runs south to the gates of Queen's Park, the first of the city's green lungs south of the river. However, before proceeding along Victoria Road, make a short detour from Eglinton Toll to Pollokshaws Road, the other southbound artery. Here, at the corner of Albert Drive, stands the **Tramway** ⑪; it owes its name to the fact that its home is the former tramway sheds which, when opened in 1893, housed 385 tramcars and 4,000 horses. The cavernous Tramway is ideal for experimental, imaginative and inventive theatre and the first production mounted here was the première of Peter Brook's spectacular epic *The Mahabharata*.

Magnificent views

A broad flight of granite steps stretches from the Art Nouveau gates at the main entrance to **Queen's Park** ⑫ to the summit where stands a 209-ft (64-metre) flagpole. Magnificent views can be enjoyed to the north, across the city to the Campsie Fells and, on a clear day, beyond to Ben Lomond, somewhat to the west.

Within the park are **Camphill House** and, at the northwest corner, **Langside Public Hall**. The former is a pleasant two-storey building with an Ionic porch, which was built in 1815 and which housed a small Museum of Costumes from 1894 but has now been converted to flats. The latter, built about 30 years later, is a strikingly handsome renaissance building with keystone heads over the lower openings representing the rivers Clyde, Thames, Shannon and Wye. Atop the cornice stand the royal coat-of-arms flanked by Britannia and Plenty; the base of the building is

LEFT: a game of bowls at Queen's Park.

marred by ghastly green wooden doors. This edifice started life as the National Bank when it stood in Queen Street in the very heart of the city. It was uprooted and transported to its present site at the beginning of the 20th century.

Mary's defeat

The reason for the park's name can be found just outside its southern extremity which is about the same altitude as the flagpole. Here stands the **Langside (or Battlefield) Monument ⓭**, a 60-ft (18-metre) column with four eagles perched at the base and topped by a couchant lion. This marks the site of the Battle of Langside where Mary Queen of Scots was defeated. Eleven days before the battle, Mary had escaped from imprisonment on Loch Leven and had made her way to Hamilton. Here, she attracted an army of 6,000 under the leadership of the Earl of Argyll and planned to make her way to the River Clyde at Renfrew, ford the river and then make for the security of Dumbarton Castle.

The enemy, which was led by the Regent Moray, Mary's half-brother, learnt of these plans and took up position at Langside. Mary's troops, who were superior in numbers and who had the support of powerful families including the Maxwells of Pollok and of Haggs, gained ascendancy during the first part of the one-hour battle but then – some claim because of internal strife, others say because of the incompetence or illness of Argyll – were soundly defeated. Mary fled to England in such terror that she did not stop or dismount until she reached Sanquhar, 60 miles (100 km) to the south. She was never to return to Scotland.

Mary is believed to have watched the defeat of her troops and, at one point, even to have ridden forward in a vain attempt to encourage their flagging spirits, from Queen's Knowe which is about 2 miles (3 km) to the southeast of where the battle was enacted. The spot, reached via Battlefield and in the northeast corner of **Linn Park ⓮**, is marked by a plaque, the

BELOW: memorial to the Battle of Langside.

original of which is in the People's Palace.

Old Castle Road cuts through the park, whose attractive mixture of woodlands and riverside (the White Cart Water flows through here) attracts many birds.On the other side of Old Castle Road are the sparse, ivy-covered ruins of 15th-century **Cathcart Castle**. The paucity of these ruins prompted an indignant and proud Glaswegian to exclaim: "If it had been somewhere in Edinburgh, they would have protected and floodlit it".

Immediately to the northwest of these vestigial remains is the charming **Snuff Mill Bridge**. Alongside this stands a former snuff-mill now converted into luxury apartments. The date 1624 is inscribed on the eastern outer wall of the bridge and Burns is said to have crossed these very stones. Justification for the claim is that, at the time of Burns, this was the main stagecoach route between Ayr and Glasgow.

Don't be surprised if you hear a most enormous roar while you're travelling between the Monument and Linn Park: Scotland must have scored a goal at soccer. The route passes close to **Hampden Park** ⓯, Scotland's national stadium and home of Queen's Park, the only amateur club in a major British soccer league.

Hampden is also home of the new **Scottish National Museum of Football** (www.scottishfa.co.uk/museum/). Glasgow was the site of the world's first international football match in 1872 so it is fitting that the museum is based here. The exhibits presents a social history of the game and included amongst the exhibits is the home changing room rescued from the recent refurbishment. There's something for everybody, with highlights including the football signed by the Lisbon Lions in 1967, George Best's Hibs strip, Kenny Dalgliesh's 100th cap , the world's biggest football, 8 ft (2.4 metres) high, and Celtic legend Jimmy McGrory's boots and the ball from a game in 1928 when he scored 8 goals in one match against Dunfermline.

LEFT: "Greek" Thomson's distinctive double villa.

The Thomson touch

The vandalised two-storey **Langside Free Church** ⓰ with its imposing Ionic facade suggests the drawing board of Alexander "Greek" Thomson. However, both it and the Monument are the work of Alexander Skirving, for many years his chief draughtsman. The tympanum of the church pediment was intended to hold a sculpture of John Knox exhorting Queen Mary, with the Regent Moray as onlooker. However, the congregants were too canny to spend the money. For many years this lay vandalised and empty but has now found new life as the Church on the Hill, a rather fine Glasgow pub.

Continue along Algie Street past the pub, turn left into Langside Place, then right into Millbrae Road, and then left into **Millbrae Crescent**, a long curving terrace of low two-storey houses from the drawing board of "Greek" Thomson and possibly, after he died, completed by his partner.

Return along Millbrae Road, turning left into Camphill Avenue and right into **Mansionhouse Road**. The double villa at number 25 was designed by "Greek" Thomson and built in 1856–7. It is typical of his style and was supposed to be the

Map on page 194

first of many such buildings on this site but none of the others were built. This design combined two smallish houses in a larger, asymmetrical composition.

A short walk back through Queen's Park from the Langside monument to the exit on Pollokshaws Road is close to another of Thomson's terraces. Cross Pollockshaws Road, continue along Queen Square and at the end of it turn right or left into Moray Place, the finest of the Grecian Terraces. It's a row of 10 two-storey houses. Many of his favourite motifs are included on the carved facade and even the chimney pots are in the style of Egyptian lotus flowers. Thomson moved into number 1 on its completion and stayed there until his death.

Because all of those buildings are private homes, only the outside can be viewed, but for a rare view of a Thomson interior head for **Holmwood House** ⓱ (61–63 Netherlee Road, Cathcart, www.nts.org.uk/holmwood.html, 0141-332 7133. 1 Apr–31 Oct, daily 1.30–5.30pm). This is near Linn Park and is reached from Netherlee Road. Thomson built this villa for the wealthy paper manufacturer James Couper who gave him a free rein with the design. Thomson rewarded him with an aysymetrical villa with on one side what appears to be a Greek temple rammed into the front of the living room. Inside the house, investigation has uncovered some of Thomson's original designs based on classical themes. Painstaking work by conservators continues to uncover more of his great stencil work.

Greenbank Gardens

Back on Clarkston Road, go south for about 2 miles (3 km) to Clarkston Toll and then travel along the Mearns Road for a similar distance to Greenbank Gardens which are set in pleasant farmland. (The estate is also reached from Eastwood Toll, close to the southeast corner of Rouken Glen.) **Greenbank Gardens** ⓲ has a handsome two-storey, modest-sized home dated 1763. The style immediately suggests the Adam family, but it is too soon for Robert and too light for William.

BELOW: Holmwood House – again clearly the work of "Greek" Thomson.

Map on page 194

The house is not open to the public (the interior decor is simple) but the grounds are most attractive; they include woodlands and a splendid walled garden (this serves as a demonstration and advice centre) with more than 2,000 perennials. Several highland cattle from the prize-winning City of Glasgow herd adorn the landscape.

Return to Clarkston Toll, take the Busby Road and, immediately after passing under the Busby railway bridge, turn left for the attractive village of **Carmunnock** ⓳ (2 miles/3 km); here, some 18th-century houses still stand in the lee of the church.

After Carmunnock, continue for a further mile on the B759 to the crest of the hill atop which stands a television tower. This is **Queen Mary's Seat**, the highest point (600 ft/180 metres) of Cathkin Braes Park. With its immense vistas, it must be the best view point in Glasgow.

The inevitable game of golf is being played immediately below. Beyond that are all those places which have already been visited and all those still to be visited. Then, from west to east, are Paisley and Gleniffer Braes, the Campsies, Arthur's Seat and the Pentland Hills. Beyond this are Ben Lomond, Ben Ledi and the Cobbler and even Goatfell on the island of Arran.

LEFT: tossing the caber at Carmunnock Games.

Rutherglen

Continue on the B759 and then turn left and travel north for about 3 miles (5 km) following the "Rutherglen" signposts. Small but busy **Rutherglen** ⓴ is Scotland's oldest burgh, having gained that honour half-a-millennium before Glasgow, and resents now being a part of the City of Glasgow. (Its status as a burgh gave a town or a community rights and privileges of administration and trading within a defined area.) Parliament sat in Rutherglen in 1300 and tradition suggests that here Sir John Menteith agreed to betray William Wallace to the English.

Both events are believed to have occurred in the Parish Church; it is entered from Main Street by the Kirk Port, which was built in 1663 with fines paid by those who profaned the sabbath. Within, and on either side of, the Port stand stone alcoves where church elders collected offerings from the congregants before services. These sentry boxes were also used, it is believed, by church officers on the lookout for body-snatchers whose target was the graves in the cemetery surrounding the church.

The church windows, even the upper ones, are protected with mesh against vandalism by today's violent youth. Yet, already in the 17th century, the town council had passed legislation which stated "considering the brakeing of the glass windowes in the kirk. Under the payne of fyve pounds money and the parents to be lyable and answerable for their children". *Plus ça change, plus c'est la même chose*. The free-standing steeple in the cemetery dates from about 1500 and was a bell tower for both the church and town.

Situated next to the church is the striking baronial Town Hall (1862) with its sun-seeking tower and turreted frontage. The centre of Glasgow is about 4 miles (6 km) north of here. ❑

The Legacy of "Greek" Thomson

More than any other architect, Alexander Thomson is responsible for the way Glasgow looks today. Born in Balfron, Stirlingshire, in 1817, the seventeenth child of a bookkeeper, he went to live with his elder brother, William, near Glasgow while still quite young. By 1834 he was apprenticed to the architect Robert Foote, where he received his training in classical architecture, which was the touchstone for all his later work. This gained him the nickname "Greek" Thomson, although he never visited Greece. The range of his work in Glasgow was extraordinary, from churches, public buildings and warehouses to private villas.

Much has been destroyed, either by World War II bombs or by town planners in the 1960s and '70s. His one remaining church in St Vincent Street in the city centre is a massive construction of pillars and a tower on its own acropolis dominating the hill. Queen's Park church, a masterpiece of colour and light with strong Egyptian influences, was destroyed in the war, while the Caledonia Road church stands ruined, its great tower overseeing successive regenerations of the Gorbals.

Around the city centre, many of Thomson's warehouse buildings still stand. In Union Street, the Egyptian Halls were built on a cast-iron frame with a brick facade. The decoration rises in tiers of pillars and pediments to an elaborate cornice carried on strange squat pillars. Similar squat columns adorn the Grecian Chambers on Sauchiehall Street, the elegant classical lines contrasting with the Scottish baronial mass of Mackintosh's School of Art looming above.

In the West End, Great Western Terrace combines simplicity and grace, with lovely Ionic pillars and windows undecorated in any way, but perfectly placed. In Moray Place in Strathbungo, the two end houses project, linked by an unbroken colonnade of 52 square columns running the length of the first storey of the eight houses in between. Thomson was so pleased with Moray Place that he moved in to number 1 and remained there until he died.

Holmwood is perhaps the greatest of Thomson's private houses, built for a wealthy paper manufacturer, James Couper. It is asymmetrical, with a circular bay window, fronted by free-standing pillars on one side, while the other side is flat with three large windows. Couper gave Thomson a totally free hand in the design of the house. None of the furniture has been found, but about 85 percent of Thomson's original wall stencilling has survived under layers of paint and wallpaper. Friezes depicting scenes from the Trojan war adorn the wall of the dining while the ceiling of the drawing room is the deep blue of the night sky, dotted with stars.

Thomson was so well regarded at his death in 1875 that a memorial fund was created which provided the Alexander Thomson Travelling Studentship. Charles Rennie Mackintosh was the second student to benefit from it. A bust of Thomson, commissioned by the fund and carved by his friend John Mossman, is in Kelvingrove Art Gallery, along with the mahogany sideboard he designed for his own home at 1 Moray Place. ❑

RIGHT: "Greek" Thomson detail at St Vincent Street church.

STATE

Map on page 194

FROM GOVAN TO THE BURRELL

Once an ancient religious site, this area became one of the world's great shipbuilding centres and is today the home of a quirky international art collection

Govan, ㉑ on the south side of the river, is one of Glasgow's oldest suburbs and was once one of the most famous. Today, however, its economic importance has largely disappeared but urban renewal has been less drastic here than in other parts of the city.

This might be the place to enjoy Glasgow's "Clockwork Orange", the affectionate sobriquet bestowed upon the subway or, as it is now called, the Underground. This charming and extremely efficient system – dare it, because of its size, be called "toy"? – consists of two 6½-mile (10.5-km) circular tracks, one within the other, on 4-ft (1-metre) gauge. One line runs clockwise, the other counter-clockwise, through separate 11-ft (3-metre) diameter tunnels and both serve the same 15 stations. An entire circuit takes just 25 minutes.

The system opened in 1896 and was originally cable-driven. It was electrified in 1935 and modernised in 1979. Be warned: at most stations only one platform, which is about 10 ft (3 metres) wide, serves both lines. During the rush hour it can get quite crowded.

Ancient stones

The **Govan Old Parish Church** ㉒, the site of which has been in ecclesiastical use longer than any other in Scotland, stands next to Pierce Hall and hides one of Glasgow's best-kept secrets. Within the church, which is usually locked but whose keys – and many are required to gain entry – can be obtained in the Pierce Hall, is the most remarkable and the largest collection of Celtic crosses in the country. These 26 stones represent the best of 46 stones which were uncovered in the churchyard in the 19th century.

It is believed that the stones originally formed a Druid Circle and that, when Christianity came, they were inscribed with Celtic crosses. However, the initials on them are of a much later date and some were used by Govanites as tombstones. The most unusual stones are five hog-backed ones; they resemble sea animals and were possibly originally erected above the graves of Viking chiefs. Within the chancel church is a delicately decorated sarcophagus which contained the relics of St Constantine, the 6th-century founder of this very handsome church.

Greatest-ever liners

A few towering cranes stand on the riverside just beyond the churchyard. They are part of the **Kvaerner Shipyard**, the last great yard on the Clyde. In years gone by, it boasted 40 yards and, at one time, launched nearly two out of every three

PRECEDING PAGES: Pollok House. **LEFT:** art isn't confined to the galleries. **RIGHT:** cranes at Clydebank.

ships built in the world. Some of the greatest-ever liners were launched from this site, which was known first as the Govan Shipyard, then as Fairfields, and is now Norwegian-owned. When the Grand Duke Alexis of Russia came to this yard in 1880 for the launch of his turbot-shaped yacht *Livadia*, he spoke of Glasgow as "the centre of intelligence of England". Few dared to dissent.

Board the Underground at Govan station and alight at the next stop, Cessnock. Immediately next to the station is **Walmer Crescent**, one of the more monumental works and the only surviving tenement building by Alexander "Greek" Thomson. Stark simplicity is the theme here, although it is slightly relieved by the grouping together of projecting bow windows. It was probably the first of many tenement blocks designed by Thomson and was built here in the 1860s in what were once open fields. The blocks, when they were built, were large, spacious apartments, intended for prosperous merchants.

Soccer with style

A few hundred metres to the west is **Ibrox Park Stadium** ㉓, the home of Glasgow Rangers, one of the city's two famous soccer clubs (www.ibrox.dircon.co.uk/ ibrox.html). It is one of only 12 grounds awarded five star status by UEFA. None, not even followers of Celtic, their traditional rivals, will deny that this is Glasgow's most luxurious soccer stadium. Tours are possible.

Travel two further stops on the Underground to Shields Road. Across the road from this station stands the **Scotland Street School** ㉔ (225 Scotland Street, 0141-429 1202, Mon–Sat 10am–5pm, Sun 2–5pm, free), now a Museum of Education. It is the work of Charles Rennie Mackintosh – not, as some might suppose, an early oeuvre but one from the beginning of the 20th century.

The north facade is dominated by stairway bays, constructed almost entirely of glass, while the rear of the building displays some pretty art deco touches with, in parts, the rich red sandstone offset by

BELOW: Walmer Crescent.

Map on page 194

delicate green tiles. Inside are displays of Scottish school life through the ages, incuding classrooms from Victorian, pre-war and the 1950s, some with local children dressed in period costume getting a taste of what schooldays were like long ago and wondering why their mild-mannered teacher has suddenly become a fire-breathing dragon.

Craigie Hall

Return to the Govan Underground station. From here, a drive of about a mile on Broomloan Road leads to Dumbreck Avenue (immediately after the Ring Road) where, on a slight incline on the left, stands a sign to **Craigie Hall ㉕**. This glorious villa, surrounded by other equally beautiful villas in what was (and still is to some extent) Glasgow's most elegant residential district, is now a business centre.

Neglect and vandalism had brought the villa to the verge of extinction when a Glasgow engineer and businessman, Graham Roxburgh, purchased and refurbished it, following the original schemes as much as possible. The house had been built in 1873 according to the plans of John Honeyman and, 20 years later, his junior partner, assisted by recently recruited Rennie Mackintosh, extended it and made internal improvements. Mackintosh's imprint is seen in the hall and the library fittings and in the organ, which is said to be the only extant Mackintosh musical design.

House for the Art Lover

Quintessential Mackintosh can be enjoyed in **Bellahouston Park**, across the road from Craigie Hall. **The House for the Art Lover ㉖** (www.houseforanartlover.co.uk/, 0141-353 4770) was built in 1990 from plans Mackintosh had submitted in 1901 for a competition sponsored by *Zeitschrift fur Innen-Dekoration*, a German magazine. He failed to win the prize – one reason given is that he submitted fewer than the required number of plans – but he received a special award. The judges commented that "the design especially stands out because of its pronounced personal quality, its novel and austere form, and the unified configuration of interior and exterior".

The plans sat gathering dust until Mr Roxburgh (of Craigie Hall) decided to build a genuine Mackintosh, almost a century after it was designed and 62 years after the architect's death. In an act of generosity, the city fathers agreed to sacrifice a tiny part of their beloved parks for the building of this house which is quintessential in that it was not built to satisfy a client but to satisfy the architect.

It is one of only three domestic buildings designed by Mackintosh. Touring the rooms, it is possible to look at Mackintosh's original drawings and see how they have been interpreted.

To appreciate the building at its best, visit, if possible, on one of the occasions when a musical ensemble is playing in the music room. From here, a practically uninterrupted green belt of both parks and golf courses – of which only the last, Deaconsbank, is public – stretches for 5 miles (8 km) to the south. Continue along Dumbreck Road and, after about 2 miles (3 km), a roundabout is

RIGHT: Mackintosh's House for the Art Lover.

reached where there is a non-vehicular entrance to Pollok Estate and a road to St Andrew's Drive.

The former is a delightful way to enter the Estate for those who wish to enjoy nature; those whose interests are man-made rather than natural and who are driving rather than walking should enter Pollok from Pollokshaws Road.

Haggs Castle ㉗, at 100 St Andrew's Drive, is an imposing baronial edifice rather than a fortified castle. It was built in 1685 and occupied, as was nearly all of this part of Glasgow, by the Maxwell family. Covenanters met here in the 17th century, after which the castle fell into disuse. It was restored during the 19th century when the north wing and spiral staircase were added.

In 1972 Glasgow Corporation purchased the property and carried out substantial renovations. Thereafter it was the Museum of Childhood until 1997 when the Corporation sold it and it reverted once again to a private residence.

Pollok Country Park

Return to the roundabout and follow Haggs Road to the Pollokshaws entrance to **Pollok Country Park** ㉘ (about 1 mile) which is immediately opposite the charming Pollokshaws Town Hall with its crow-stepped gables (1897). Those without their own transport can board buses into the park at this entrance.

Pollok Estate is something of a rarity: a country park complete with rangers in the heart of the city. Enter through its gates and the city, which is just a few yards away, has vanished. Yet rurality does not exclude urbanity. Pollok Country Park offers Italian earthenware as well as earthworms; tapestries as well as playing fields; glorious autumn paintings (Sisley's The Bell Tower at Noisy-le-Roi) as well as glorious autumn days. Here at Pollok there is something for everyone.

Violent game

There is fishing in the **White Cart Water** and, when the weather is clement, swim-

BELOW: Pollok House.

Map on page 194

ming in the waters below the weir. One can watch shinty, a violent Scottish field game which is a cross between mayhem and murder and a near relative of the Irish game of hurling, or applaud as Fruin and Fraz, Czar and Haig go through their paces. They are among the 70 German shepherds, golden labradors and English springer spaniels at the Strathclyde Police Dog Training Centre. (Demonstrations are often held on Tuesday mornings between 10 and 11am.)

Then there are nature walks and garden walks and the opportunity to gaze at shy roe deer and at brilliant kingfishers, at dragon-flies over the pond and at culture vultures in and around Pollok House and the Burrell Collection. For Pollok Country Park is the home of two magnificent art collections.

Pollok House ㉙, which was designed in the middle of the 18th century by William Adam and completed by his more famous son John, houses a superb art collection, assembled around 1850 by Sir William Stirling Maxwell, an authority on Spanish art. The collection includes works by Goya, El Greco, Murillo and outstanding prints by William Blake, as well as a collection of exquisite oriental furniture, silver, porcelain and Spanish glass. Some will wish to visit the basement kitchens to see how, not that long ago, the oh-so-rich were taken care of.

Always competing for the visitor's attention are the magnificent vistas which can be seen through the tall glass windows. How splendid to look past an El Greco to the fields where Caitin and Unadubh, Magaidh and Maili graze, their ruminations disturbed only by a hooked golf ball from the nearby golf course. Caitin and friends belong to the Pollok Fold, a herd of about 70 prize-winning Highland beasts which belong to the city of Glasgow. Aye, and beasts they are, with their long, shaggy, brown hair covering their eyes. Yet, despite that ferocious look (the result of their long horns), they are the most gentle of all cattle.

BELOW: pristine collection at Pollok House.

The formal gardens at the rear of the house, which is more attractive than the front, are at their glorious best in summer. Immediately east of this is the Woodland Garden which is planted mainly with shrubs and rare trees. Rhododendrons are a special attraction. Many of the cultivars, including Jock, Glasgow Glow and Scarlet Lady, were originally produced by Sir John and his head gardener, "Jock" McTavish. Just south of this is the demonstration garden and the gardeners' bothy (a landworker's cottage) in what was originally the estate's Walled Garden. The bothy shows just how life was for a gardener working here 100 years ago.

The Burrell Collection

And so to the **Burrell Collection** ㉚, which for many is the *pièce de résistance* not only of the Park but of Glasgow and even of Scotland. Sir William Burrell, a Glasgow shipowner, was a compulsive collector. When other youngsters were buying cricket balls with their pocket money, he was buying prints. And so, for 80 years, with good sense and, in most cases, good taste, he built up a remarkable art collection which rivals those of such great American collectors as Frick, Mellon or Rockefeller. On one occasion, Burrell bought from William Randolph Hearst, another compulsive collector, a 12th-century stone archway. Hearst had shipped it from France to California, and Burrell was able to buy it for one-tenth of what Hearst had paid.

LEFT: Sir William Burrell assembled an exotic collection of objects.

On his death in 1958, Burrell left his collection to the city of Glasgow. However, there were provisos which could not be fulfilled: Burrell wanted the collection to be housed at least 6 miles (10 km) from Glasgow so that it would be protected from urban pollution, and demanded that certain items of medieval stonework which he had collected should be incorporated into the collection's permanent home. As a result, the collection lay in storage – small sections were occasionally exhibited – for many years.

Then, in 1966, Mrs Anne Maxwell Macdonald gifted the 360-acre (145-hectare) Pollok Estate to the city. A custom-built prize-winning museum to house the impressive collection was added in 1983, and instantly became one of Scotland's top visitor draws. The red sandstone building incorporates a covered courtyard, and the *rus in urbe* location is for many visitors as much of an attraction as the exhibits.

The collection consists of more than 8,000 objects from Egypt, Greece, the Near East and the Orient and tapestries and stained glass from medieval Europe. Chinese ceramics and Japanese prints mingle with Turkish carpets and European glassware. The massive Warwick Vase has been reconstructed from pieces found at the site of the Emperor Hadrian's villa near Rome. The collection – regarded by fans as eclectic and idiosyncratic and by some critics as the work of an undisciplined magpie – also includes exhibits of entire rooms from Sir William's home at Hutton Castle in Berwickshire.

Favourites with Glasgow visitors are the Degas collection, a superb Cézanne, *A rainy landscape at Arles*, Rodin's *Thinker* (one of

14 casts made from the original) and the Warwick Vase, an 8-ton marble which dominates the courtyard.

The pot-pourri nature of the collection attracts some and irritates others, but most visitors agree that a major attraction is the exhibit's pleasant surroundings. The building itself, with its deceptively simple lines, has drawn as much admiration as the contents. Medieval archways from the collection are blended with new red sandstone and some halls have glass walls to the floor, giving the impression that the exhibits are being viewed in the open air. Others are completely enclosed and provide a warmly lit backdrop for some of the world's most exquisite tapestries.

Honeymooners' retreat

Back on Pollokshaws Road, turn right and travel for about half-a-mile to a large roundabout. Turn right onto the Barrhead Road and journey between golf courses for 2½ miles (3 km), after which a right turn on to Crookston Road leads, after another mile, to **Crookston Castle** ㉛. The castle, the first property in Scotland to come under the aegis of the National Trust (1931), stands amongst trees on top of a mound in the middle of a low-rise housing estate. The black-stone castle, which stands three storeys high in parts, owes its fame to the fact that Mary Queen of Scots and her cousin Henry Stuart (Lord Darnley) spent a few days here in 1565 after their marriage.

From here **Rouken Glen Park** ㉜ lies about 5 miles (8 km) to the southeast. The principal formal attractions in this glorious estate, much of which has been left in its natural state and through which tumbles a waterfall, are the **Walled Garden** and the **Butterfly Kingdom** ㉝. In the hothouses of the latter, the visitor can enthuse over Common Jezebels and Red Admirals which spread their wings among orange trees, bougainvillea and passion flowers. Somewhat less colourful and more deadly are the scorpions and tarantulas and myriad other insects in the Insectarium. ❑

BELOW: the Burrell Collection.

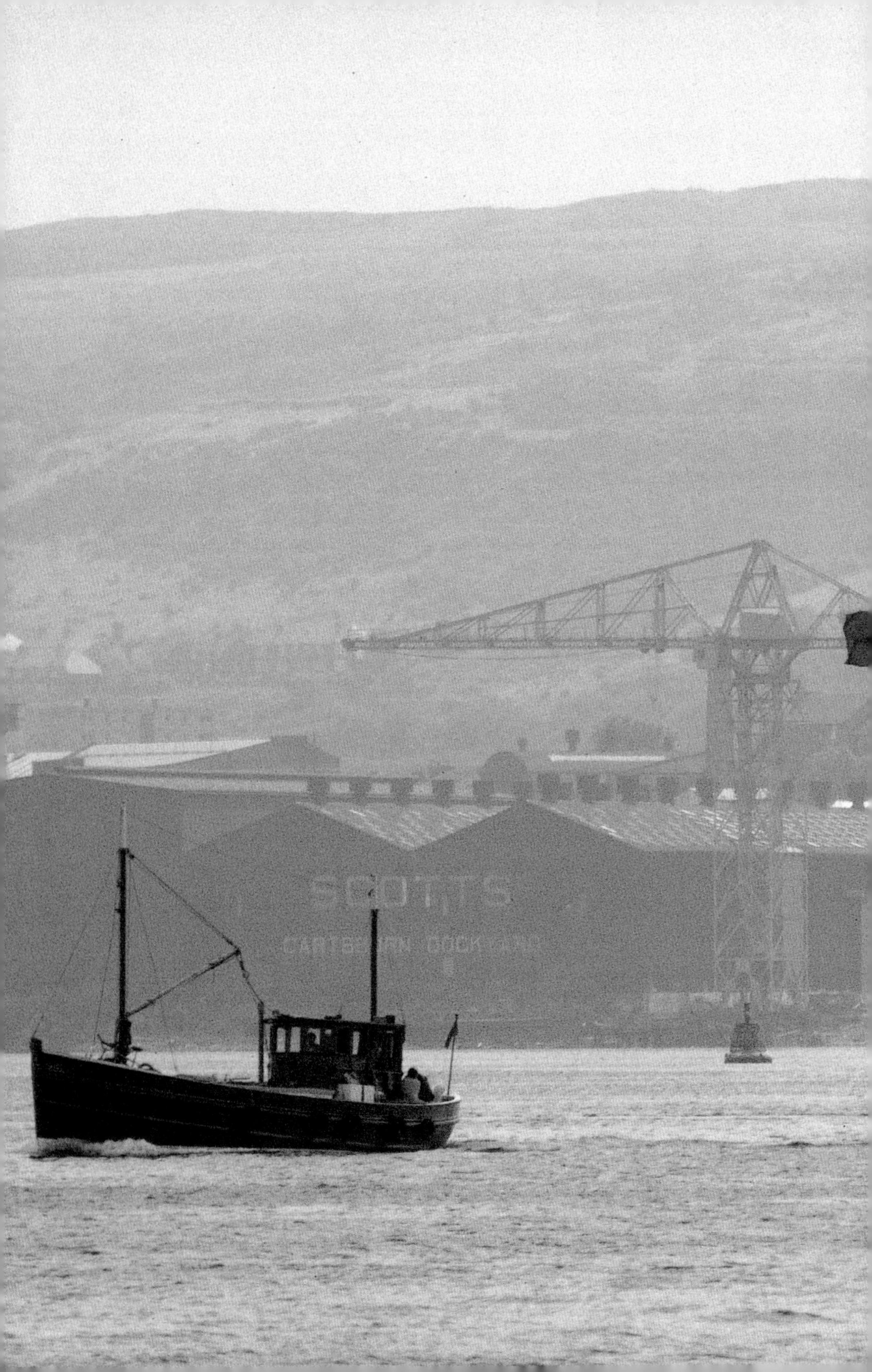
SCOTTS

TS
K23
SLOW

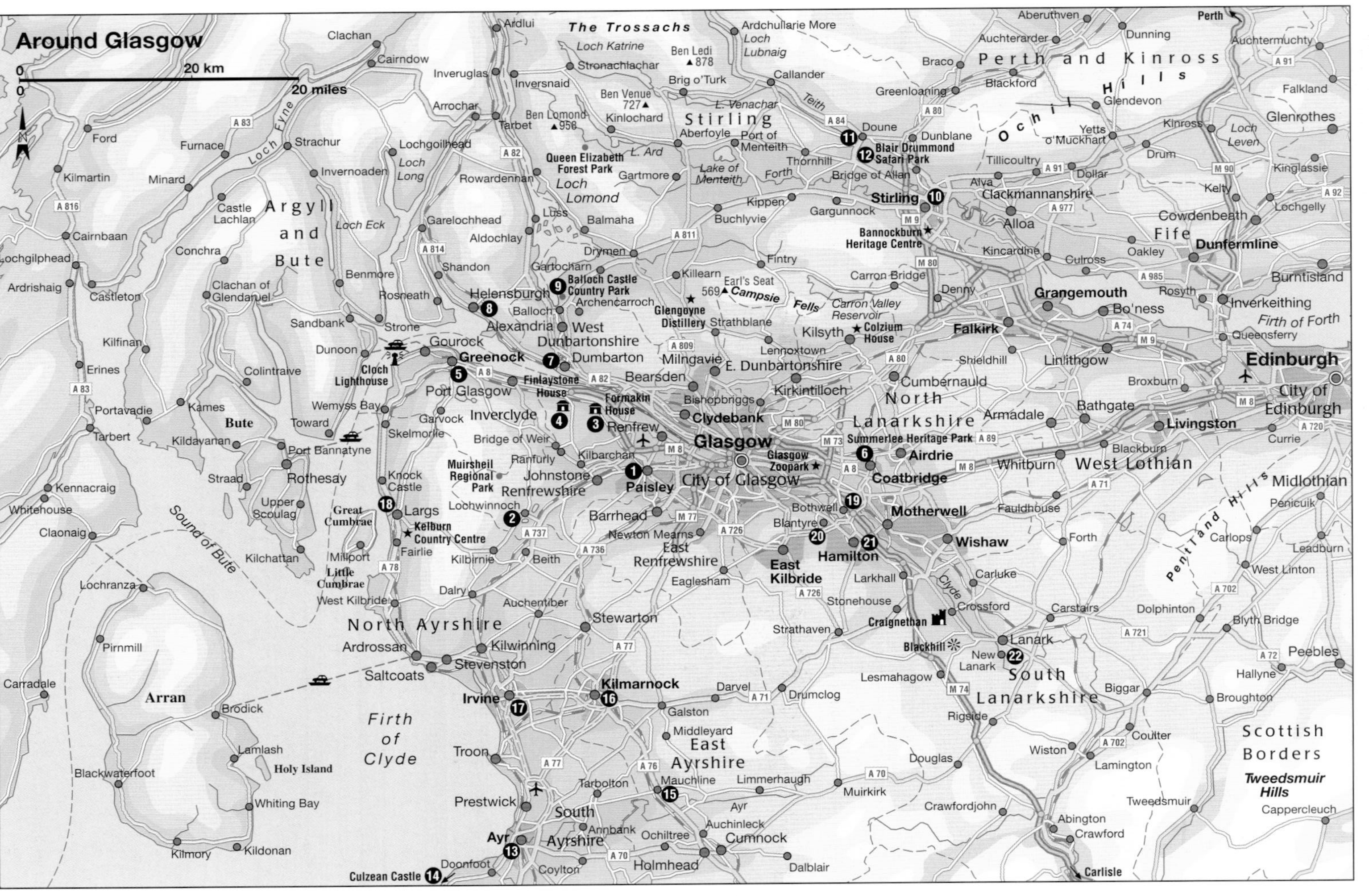
Around Glasgow
0 20 km
0 20 miles
Perth
Auchtermuchty
Falkland
Glenrothes
Kinglassie
Lochgelly
Loch Leven
Kinross
Kelty
Cowdenbeath
Dunfermline
Fife
Burntisland
Inverkeithing
Firth of Forth
Queensferry
Rosyth
Edinburgh
City of Edinburgh
Currie
Penicuik
Leadburn
Midlothian
West Linton
Carlops
Pentland Hills
Peebles
Blyth Bridge
Hallyne
Broughton
Scottish Borders
Tweedsmuir Hills
Cappercleuch
Tweedsmuir
Dolphinton
Coulter
Biggar
Lamington
Carlisle
Crawford
Abington
Wiston
Dunning
Perth and Kinross
Ochil Hills
Glendevon
Drum
Oakley
Bo'ness
Grangemouth
Culross
Kincardine
Alloa
Clackmannanshire
Dollar
Yetts o'Muckhart
Tillicoultry
Alva
Aberuthven
Auchterarder
Blackford
Braco
Greenloaning
Dunblane
Doune
Blair Drummond Safari Park
Bridge of Allan
Stirling
Bannockburn Heritage Centre
Denny
Falkirk
Linlithgow
Broxburn
Livingston
Blackburn
Bathgate
West Lothian
Whitburn
Armadale
Shieldhill
Cumbernauld
North Lanarkshire
Summerlee Heritage Park
Airdrie
Coatbridge
Motherwell
Wishaw
Fauldhouse
Forth
Carstairs
Lanark
New Lanark
South Lanarkshire
Carluke
Crossford
Clyde
Craignethan
Blackhill
Lesmahagow
Rigside
Douglas
Crawfordjohn
Muirkirk
Larkhall
Stonehouse
Hamilton
Bothwell
Blantyre
East Kilbride
Strathaven
Drumclog
Dalblair
Carron Bridge
Carron Valley Reservoir
Colzium House
Kilsyth
Fells
Campsie
Earl's Seat 569
Kirkintilloch
Lennoxtown
E. Dunbartonshire
Strathblane
Glasgow Zoopark
Glasgow
City of Glasgow
Clydebank
Bishopbriggs
Milngavie
Bearsden
Glengoyne Distillery
Killearn
Fintry
Kippen
Buchlyvie
Gargunnock
Thornhill
Port of Menteith
Lake of Menteith
Forth
Teith
Callander
Ardchullarie More
Loch Lubnaig
L. Venachar
Stirling
Aberfoyle
Brig o'Turk
Ben Ledi 878
The Trossachs
Loch Katrine
Stronachlachar
Ben Venue 727
Kinlochard
L. Ard
Gartmore
Balmaha
Drymen
Queen Elizabeth Forest Park
Loch Lomond
Ben Lomond 958
Inversnaid
Ardlui
Inveruglas
Tarbet
Arrochar
Luss
Gartocharn
Balloch Castle Country Park
Archencarroch
Balloch
Alexandria
West Dunbartonshire
Dumbarton
Formakin House
Renfrew
Paisley
Finlaystone House
Greenock
Port Glasgow
Inverclyde
Gourock
Bridge of Weir
Kilbarchan
Johnstone
Renfrewshire
Barrhead
Newton Mearns
East Renfrewshire
Eaglesham
Ranfurly
Muirshiel Regional Park
Lochwinnoch
Beith
Kilbirnie
Dalry
Auchentiber
Stewarton
Kilmarnock
Galston
Darvel
Middleyard
East Ayrshire
Mauchline
Limmerhaugh
Ayr
Auchinleck
Cumnock
Ochiltree
Holmhead
Annbank
Tarbolton
South Ayrshire
Coylton
Ayr
Prestwick
Troon
Irvine
Kilwinning
Stevenston
Saltcoats
Ardrossan
North Ayrshire
West Kilbride
Doonfoot
Culzean Castle
Firth of Clyde
Largs
Kelburn Country Centre
Fairlie
Knock Castle
Skelmorlie
Wemyss Bay
Garvock
Great Cumbrae
Little Cumbrae
Millport
Cloch Lighthouse
Dunoon
Strone
Rosneath
Shandon
Garelochhead
Rowardennan
Aldochlay
Helensburgh
Lochgoilhead
Loch Long
Cairndow
Clachan
Invernoaden
Loch Eck
Benmore
Sandbank
Strachur
Loch Fyne
Argyll and Bute
Colintraive
Toward
Port Bannatyne
Rothesay
Upper Scoulag
Kilchattan
Bute
Straad
Kildavanan
Kames
Clachan of Glendaruel
Castle Lachlan
Conchra
Furnace
Minard
Sound of Bute
Arran
Brodick
Lamlash
Holy Island
Whiting Bay
Kildonan
Kilmory
Blackwaterfoot
Pirnmill
Lochranza
Portavadie
Kilfinan
Tarbert
Erines
Kennacraig
Claonaig
Whitehouse
Carradale
Castleton
Ardrishaig
Lochgilphead
Cairnbaan
Kilmartin
Ford
A 91
A 92
M 90
A 985
M 9
A 74
A 720
M 8
A 702
A 72
A 721
A 71
A 977
A 80
M 80
A 89
A 84
M 73
A 8
M 74
A 726
A 70
A 811
A 809
A 82
M 77
A 736
A 737
A 77
A 76
A 78
A 814
A 83
A 816

Map on facing page

GREATER GLASGOW

Within easy driving distance of the city can be found Paisley, Lochwinnoch Nature Reserve, Greenock, Wemyss Bay, Gourock and the Campsies

The realignment of boundaries in 1973 resulted in Glasgow simultaneously shrinking and expanding. This apparent anomaly was the result of the boundaries of the actual city being drawn back while new outlying districts were included. In 1993 a further local government reorganisation changed the administrative map yet again.

However, for the purpose of this guide, Greater Glasgow is taken as including all the territory stretching north to Lennoxtown and as far south as Lochwinnoch and to Wemyss Bay in the west and Airdrie/Coatbridge in the east. The east-west axis is 40 miles (64 km) long and the north-south axis about half that.

Paisley's appeal

Visitors to solid, sensible **Paisley** ❶, in Renfrewshire, can be excused if confused about the exhortation "Keep your eye on Paisley". When Benjamin Disraeli gave this advice, which was to become a catchphrase to politicians who had enquired how they might gauge the tide of national opinon, Paisley was a craft-based (mainly weaving), money-making burgh eager to mind its own business. Paisley has fallen on lean times since these halcyon days and it is only lately that urban renewal has begun to gain momentum.

To reach Paisley, with a population of 75,500, either travel west on the M8 and leave at exit 27, a total distance of about 7 miles (11 km) or take the A737 from Glasgow city centre. Alternatively, there are frequent trains from Central Station: the journey takes about 15 minutes.

Smack in the heart of town, on the banks of the tiny White Cart Water is **Paisley Abbey** (0141-889 7654, Mon–Sat 10am–3.30pm). Nearby in Abbey Close is the **Town Hall** (0141-887 1007), a classical Victorian building with hexastyle colonnades – Corinthian to the east and Ionic to the west – on top of a high piano nobile. Two dissimilar towers – the taller, to the north, more slender and with clock faces – complete the picture.

This is a popular venue for conferences, concerts and shows. The abbey was founded in 1163 as a monastery of the Cluniac order by Walter Fitz Alan, who was the first hereditary high steward of Scotland and a founder of the Royal House of Stewart. It was largely destroyed by Edward I in 1307 in response to its monks assisting William Wallace but was rebuilt during the 14th and 15th centuries.

The exterior of the abbey belies a much more attractive interior. Worth observing are the choir with its stone vaulted roof and stained-glass windows and St Mirin's

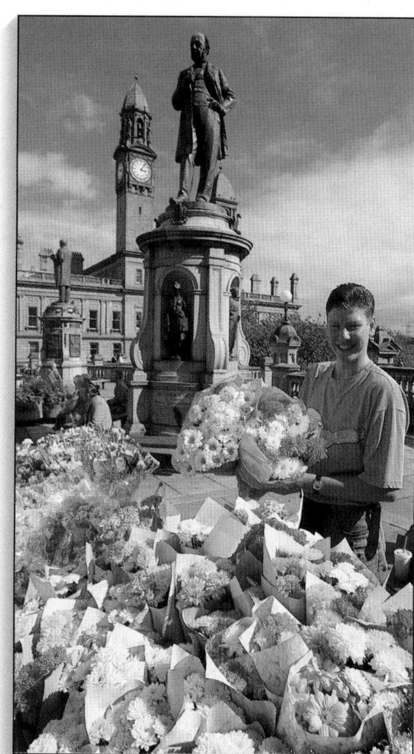

PRECEDING PAGES: a tall ship on the Clyde at Greenock. **RIGHT:** petals at Paisley.

chapel which occupies the place of the south transept and where a series of 12th-century panels depict episodes, of doubtful authenticity, from the life of Mirin, the town's patron saint.

Also in this chapel is a recumbent effigy of Marjory Bruce, daughter of the Scottish hero Robert Bruce. Standing at the eastern end of the north aisle is the 11-ft (3.4-metre) weathered, 10th-century Celtic Cross of St Barochan. Attached to the south of the abbey is the Place of Paisley, which was converted to secular use in the 16th century.

A stroll to the west and to the hilly north of the abbey along New and Shuttle streets and then across High Street and up Church Hill to Oakshaw Street – the entire distance is only about 1,000 yards (1 km) – reveals a surprising number of churches and several statues and buildings bearing the name Coats. The Coats family were the pre-eminent merchants of Paisley and generous in their gifts to the town in which they made their fortunes. Statues of Thomas and Sir Peter, the two principal benefactors, stand just to the west of the Town Hall, across the river.

LEFT: Paisley Abbey.

Acrobatic angels

The large number of churches reflects the fact that the weavers, who formed the main corpus of Paisley's workers, had much time to contemplate, not so much the number of angels who could stand on one of their pins, but rather about the relationship between church and state.

Secession was very much the in-word, followed by excommunication and, by the 18th century, the town had its Burgher and anti-Burgher churches, the East Relief and the West Relief churches, Primitive, United and Congregational Methodist churches. As if all these were not enough, one group of weavers, the Pen Folk, founded their own church.

Some churches are now secular and so, at the corner of Shuttle and New Streets stand the unprepossessing Laigh Kirk (Low Parish Church) which is now an **Arts Centre** (0141-887 1010) and, opposite it, the even less prepossessing Free Gaelic Church which is now part of the University of Paisley. Here, too, are the Sma' Shot Cottages, (11–17 George Place, 0141-889 1708 , www.smashot.com, Apr–Sept, Wed & Sat 1–5pm, free), restored artisans' houses from the Victorian era with various photographs and artefacts of local interest. (The "small shot" was a hidden linking thread in cloth which was being woven.)

Much more impressive is the **High Church** whose steeple, which rises in five stages to support an obelisk spire, dominates the Paisley skyline. It is reached by a long flight of stairs: in this respect, and in no other, it recalls Rome's Trinita dei Monti and the Spanish steps. A much wider and more elegant flight of steps leads to the majestic, cruciform, red sandstone **Thomas Coats Memorial Church** (0141-889 9980, May–Sept, Mon, Wed & Fri 2–4pm, free), more a cathedral than a mere kirk. The marble and alabaster interior of this Baptist church, one of the most splendid in the land, is just as handsome as the exterior.

Immediately east of this church is the **Paisley Museum and Art Gallery** (0141-

889 3151, Tue–Sat 10am–5pm, Sun 2–5pm, free), Scotland's first municipal museum, the gift of Peter Coats. It has sections devoted to local history, natural history, art and, most importantly, the world's largest collection of Paisley shawls. These shawls and their accompanying patterns were introduced to Britain in the early 1700s by members of the East India Company who had visited Kashmir. Although several motifs existed, it was the tear drop (or tadpole, or comma or pine cone) which caught the imagination. These were originally filled with an abstract mosaic of colours but were later replaced by buds, stalks and leaves.

Paisley pattern

It says much for Paisley that it was able to imprint its name on these colourful designs, for they were executed not only in Paisley but in other weaving centres such as Edinburgh and Norwich, Paris and Lyons and Vienna. Both Edinburgh and Norwich were making "Paisley" pattern shawls 20 years before they were produced in Paisley. Yet shoppers invariably asked to be shown "Paisleys".

This marketing success was made possible by a combination of hard work and low costs; by pirating Norwich designs (the government introduced patenting of designs only in 1842); and by using the mechanical French Jacquard loom which was able to produce a smooth curved line and which required only one, rather than the two, operators needed for the traditional and slower drawloom. By the middle of the 19th century, Paisley shawls were booming; but by the end of the century interest had waned. However, by then Paisley had become the world's premier centre for the production of cotton thread.

Behind and above the Museum and open to members of the public is the **Coats Observatory** (49 Oakshaw Street West, 0141-889 2013, Sun 2–5pm, Tue–Sat 10am–5pm). The benefactor was Thomas Coats. It is readily recognisable because of its observation drum, below

BELOW: punks at Paisley Abbey.

which runs a lovely Doric frieze and cornice supporting a baslustrade. Astronomical and meteorological data have been recorded in this, one of the best equipped observatories in the country, since the late 19th century. There are displays of astronomy, astronautics, seismology and meteorology and on Thursdays, 7.30–9.30pm Oct–Mar, an opportunity to view the night sky through the massive telescope.

On the way back to the town centre the visitor might stop for a refreshment at the **Bull Inn** on New Street where art nouveau glass and woodwork from the 1920s is joined by juke boxes and slot machines. Then, back in the centre of town observe the former glory of Paisley by looking at the **Terrace Buildings**, a glorious three-storey Italianate confection with pedimented windows held up by brackets and a corbel table supporting a balustrade on top of which are festooned urns.

Leave Paisley for the southwest on the A737 and, after 3 miles (5 km), at the far end of the village of **Elderslie**, a monument marks the birthplace of William Wallace – despite the fact that Scotland's hero was in fact born at Ellerslie, in Ayrshire, a considerable distance away.

Turn right on the B789 and after a mile turn left on the A761 for a further mile to reach the former weaving village of **Kilbarchan**. Weaving demonstrations are given in a small 1723 cottage which houses the last of the village's 800 looms (Shuttle Street, at the Cross, 01505-705588. www.nts.org.uk/weaver.html, 1 Apr–30 Sept, daily 1.30–5.30pm; weekends in Oct, 1.30–5.30pm; last admission 5pm, charge).

Water sports

Backtrack to the A737 and, passing through delightful rolling country, turn right after 5 miles (8 km) on to the A760 and enter a landscape which shelters several lakes and which provides enormous pleasure for ornithologists and water sports enthusiasts and which has some interesting sights for antiquarians and historians.

After about 800 yards, a Norwegian

BELOW: a cooper at Lochwinnoch makes barrels for a distillery.

Map on page 222

spruce building with a tower is the headquarters of the Royal Society for the Protection of Birds' **Lochwinnoch Nature Reserve** (Largs Road, Lochwinnoch, 01505-842663), a habitat for more than 150 species of birds and extremely popular with winter migrant wildfowl. (Lochwinnoch Railway Station is just opposite the reserve: one train an hour from Glasgow makes the journey in 15 minutes.)

Soon after this, a right turn at the garage leads through the main street (B786) of the village of **Lochwinnoch** ❷ to **Castle Semple Loch**, where sailing, fishing and rowing are available.

A 2-mile (3-km) stroll along the loch leads to an early 16th-century Collegiate Church while beyond that – and better reached from the village of Howarth – is The Temple, a folly, from where crippled Lady Semple could watch the hunt. Besotted antiquarians will also visit The Peel and Barr Castle, scanty remains of which are located near Lochwinnoch.

About a mile north of Lochwinnoch, a single-track takes off to the left and leads to **Muirshiel**, at an altitude of more than 1,000 ft (330 metres), in the heart of **Muirshiel Regional Park** (01505-614791 www.scottishpark.com/), offering a variety of activities ranging from archery, to orienteering, boating and birdwatching. Over a distance of 4 miles (6 km) the scenery has changed from a neat domestic landscape to a grand valley leading into open moor. (The park covers a superb stretch of countryside and extends for 16 miles/26 km to the northwest.)

Lochwinnoch is almost at the southwest extremity of Greater Glasgow. From here one can return directly on the A737 to Glasgow (17 miles/25 km) or travel further to the southwest on the A737 (19 miles/30 kms) to Irvine *(see page 249)* or on the A760 (15 miles/24 km) via Kilbirnie to Largs.

To visit Inverclyde, travel west on the M8 from Glasgow. Pass Glasgow Airport and 16 miles (26 km) after leaving the city centre take an acute left turn. This leads

BELOW: Fenwick Church, a centre for militant 17th-century Covenanters.

on to the A8 and, after about a mile, turn right onto the B789 on which, after about another mile, stands **Formakin House** ❸ in the estate of that name in Bishopton. The design of the house – which was never completed, although all the ancillary buildings were – is pure Scottish baronial. The house is called the Monkey House because of stone monkeys which clamber all over the exterior and the interior – on the eaves, on mantlepieces. Another whimsical touch are the initials D.L. (Damned Lie) above the entrance to the stable courtyard.

This was to be not only a home but a museum to house the not inconsiderable collection of John Holms which included Chinese porcelain, oriental rugs, English silver plate and furniture. The entire collection was sold at auction in 1936 and some pieces were purchased by Sir William Burrell and are now exhibits in the Burrell collection in Glasgow *(see page 218)*. The house stands in 160 acres (64 hectares) of extremely attractive grounds which are home to an excellent collection of rare farm animals.

Travel westwards along the A8, which parallels the River Clyde, for less than 2 miles (3 km) to **Langbank** and, just within the Renfrew-Inverclyde boundary, observe the entry to **Finlaystone House** ❹. This large, somewhat rambling building, the oldest parts of which date from the 14th century, is the home of MacMillan, chief of the clan of that name. He and his wife make visitors very welcome; they will point out the yew tree under which John Knox is said to have sat and the exact spot where Robert Burns scratched his name on a window-pane.

Burns considered the then Laird of Finlayson as his only true patron, but a problem exists. The date etched on the window pane below the signature is 1772, at which time Burns would have been a mere stripling and patronage would scarcely have entered his head. The matter is resolved by suggesting that the date represents the year of the bottle of wine which Burns quaffed when he

BELOW: a quiet afternoon at Greenock.

visited Finlayson.The grounds are delightful. One of the rooms contains an extensive doll collection.

Continue for about 4 miles (6 km) along the A8 until the Port Glasgow roundabout is reached. To the right, on the shores of the river, in stark contrast to the neighbouring shipyard stands, the solid, symmetrical 16th and 17th-century **Newark Castle** (not to be confused with the 18th-century castle of the same name at Selkirk in the Borders), yet another mansion of the Maxwells. With crow steps and gabled windows, turrets and 15th-century tower, this is a good example of Scottish baronial.

Greenock

There is little to attract the visitor to **Port Glasgow** other than an excellent replica of the *Comet*, the first commercial steamship in Europe. **Greenock** ❺, which today has a population of 55,013, was an important shipbuilding and industrial town in the 18th and 19th centuries. The oldest dock on the Clyde was built here in 1711 and in 1859 the last great wooden ship was launched. Down on the waterfront stands the massive, classically correct, renovated Customs House Building, considered to be the most splendid such building in Britain.

The focal point for the visitor is Cathcart Square with the impressive Municipal Buildings and the soaring 245-ft (74-metre) Victoria Tower, which is from a previous building. When built, it was said of the municipal buildings that they "had every beauty but the beauty of economy". The elevation is incomplete at the east end because the owner of the property refused to sell. Opposite is the Mid Kirk, built in 1761, with a pedimented Ionic portico.

James Watt, inventor of the steam engine, was born in Greenock in 1736 and the **McLean Museum and Art Gallery** (15 Kelly Street, 0147-572 3741, Mon–Sat 10am–5pm), houses items relating to his career as well as an art collection which features the works of several Scottish artists alongside canvasses of Boudin and

BELOW: the McLean Museum.

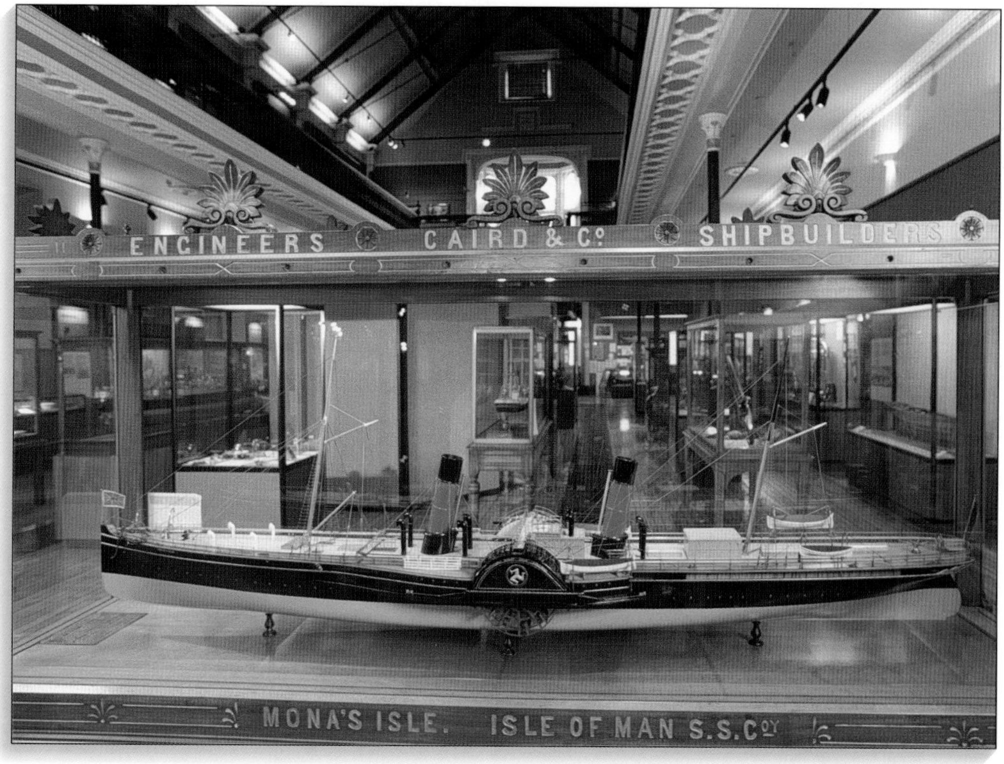

Corbin. The tombstone of Robert Burns's beloved Highland Mary, who died in 1798, can be seen in the local churchyard.

Most interesting of the city's several churches is the **Old West Kirk** (www.greenockoldwestkirk.freeserve.co.uk/). In 1920, it was removed to the east end of the esplanade which runs west from town. This was the first church built after the Reformation (1591) and the first Presbyterian church confirmed by Parliament. Its windows have stained glass by the pre-Raphaelites, Morris, Rossetti and Burne Jones.

On the way out of Greenock, turn left on Lyle Road and ascend to Lyle Hill where a large granite Cross of Lorraine commemorates the Free French who were based here in World War II. This is the great viewpoint of the region, and the views of the Clyde and its estuary and the lochs and mountains of the Highlands are breathtaking. Rather than retracing the same route to the main road, continue along Lyle Hill to join the A78 which, after 2 miles (3 km) arrives at Inverkip, with possibly the best marina on the Clyde.

LEFT: James Watt remembered at Greenock.

Continue for a further 5 miles (8 km) to **Wemyss Bay** from where the ferry leaves for the Isle of Bute and Rothesay. The main attraction in Wemyss Bay is its magnificent railway station, light and airy and featuring wrought iron and with the reputation of being Scotland's most beautiful railway station. To arrive at Wemyss Bay is to know that one is on vacation.

On the return trip from Wemyss Bay to Glasgow, a distance of 31 miles (50 km), take the coast road after Inverkip, the A770, and drive past the grassy shore of **Lunderston Bay** (this is the western extremity of the Muirshiel Country Park) and stop at the **Cloch Lighthouse**. From here, there are delightful views of the Firth of Clyde.

Proceed onwards to the rather peaceful seaside resort of **Gourock**, from where car ferries leave frequently for Dunoon and passenger ferries for Kilcreggan, near Helensburgh *(see page 238)*. In Gourock visit Granny Kempcock: seven times round this ancient monolith weathered to almost human shape is said to bring good fortune to sailors and fishermen, brides and grooms. Continue to Glasgow on the A770, which becomes the A8, which in turn joins with the M8.

Walks and views

The main attractions in the Strathkelvin District, which is to the north of the city, are the **Campsies** and restored sections of the **Forth and Clyde Canal**. The former offers superb hill-walking and splendid views of Glasgow. Leave the city by the A803 and, after about 5 miles (8 km) cross the canal. A little beyond this take the left arm of a Y-junction (the A807) for a mile and then turn right on the B822 which, after 3 miles (5 km) reachs Lennoxtown. After a further 2 miles (3 km), a large parking lot tells the visitor that this is the place to enjoy magnificent views and to start walking.

One or two pleasure craft (including cruising restaurants) are based on the Forth and Clyde Canal at Bishopbriggs, Kirkintilloch and Kilsyth, which are

respectively 3, 5 and 10 miles (5, 8 and 16 km) northeast of Glasgow. **Colzium House** (Colzium Lennox Estate, 01236-735077), in Kilsyth, is a splendid Victorian mansion housing an art gallery and local museum. Near Kilsyth are two Antonine Wall sites: **Bar Hill** has a fort, rampart and ditch, and **Croy Hill**, a ditch and beacon platforms. The Wall was built by the Romans around AD 143 to keep back marauding Scots *(see panel below)*.

The focus to the northeast of the city is Glasgow's satellite town of **Cumbernauld**, one of Britain's most successful new towns. (Leave the M8 at exit 12 and drive for 11 miles/18 km on the A80.) Cumbernauld, after nearly five decades scarcely "new", had its original headquarters at Cumbernauld House, built by William Adam in 1731. The huge clock in the town shopping centre was retrieved from St Enoch Station in Glasgow when it was demolished. Contemporary art and sculpture are dotted about the town centre.

Due east of the city, the **Summerlee Heritage Park** ❻ (Heritage Way,Coatbridge, 01236-431261, open 10am–5pm 7 days a week, admission charge), shows how Glasgow and Scotland earned the title the "Workshop of the World". This living industrial museum reverberates to the sound of steam and also has reconstructed Victorian buildings. A tramcar runs round the 25-acre (10-hectare) site and a branch of James Watt's 18th-century Monklands Canal has been reopened.

The Park is near **Coatbridge**, formerly the iron and steel capital of Scotland, and can be reached by driving to the end of the M8, then joining the A89 for 3 miles (5 km) and then turning south for a mile on the B804.

The eastern end of the M8 also links with the A74 where, after about a mile, is the rather modest **Glasgow Zoopark** (Calderpark, Uddingston, 0141-771 1185, www.members.tripod.co.uk/GlasgowZoopark/, opens daily at 9.30am). It has elephants, camels, monkeys, deer, big cats, and a reptile house. ❑

THE ANTONINE WALL

In AD 80 the Emperor Vespasian decided to conquer southeast Scotland, probably as a defensive measure to protect the Roman settlement in England since the poor land and damp climate had little else to offer.

The natives remained troublesome and the Emperor Hadrian, arriving in Britain in AD 122, built a series of fortresses across the north of England (Hadrian's Wall), intending that the Romans should stay south of it. But in 142 the Emperor Antoninus elected to have one more go at subduing the Scots. He reinforced and linked a series of forts between the rivers Forth and Clyde.

This "Antonine Wall" was 39 miles (63 km) long, 10 ft (3 metres) high and 6 ft (1.8 metres) wide. But it was less sturdy than Hadrian's defences, being built simply of earth, and, although traces of it can still be seen, most of it was either tramped down by the soldiers who patrolled it, keeping watch for enemy action, or eroded over the centuries by the unyielding elements.

Its practical life was short in any case, since the Scots began to attack it again in 155. This time the Romans concluded that there was little point in risking lives and enduring harsh winters trying to keep such savages at bay, and they retreated for good behind Hadrian's Wall.

RIGHT: a mother and child sculpture, Cumbernauld.

DAY TRIPS

Places worth seeing in this part of Scotland include Loch Lomond, Dumbarton, Helensburgh, Bannockburn, Stirling, Doune, Loch Katrine, Ayr, Kilmarnock and New Lanark

Glasgow may have destroyed much of its heritage in its headlong rush to build Europe's best urban ring-road system but at least it's easy to get out of. The historian's loss is the country lover's gain, because the Campsies, Loch Lomond, the Trossachs, Burns country, and the Clyde Valley are all on the city's doorstep.

Then there is the traditional "Doon the Watter" trip – a visit by paddle steamer to the seaside resorts of the west coast and some of the islands, such as Arran and Bute, in the Firth of Clyde. Even Edinburgh can be reached in 50 minutes by road or rail: trains depart every 15 minutes. (Bus companies run half- and full-day tours to all the places mentioned here, and many more.) The country around the city is well served by theme and day parks, innumerable golf courses, waters which can be fished for brown trout, pike and perch, and racetracks at Ayr and Hamilton which hold flat and hurdle programmes at irregular intervals.

Roman remains

Those who cannot bear to tear themselves away from Glasgow even for a half a day may be able to spare a couple of hours for a visit to the **Campsie Fells**, the hills immediately north of the city. A bonus is the opportunity to visit a distillery. Exit from the city on the A809 at Anniesland Cross and Milngavie (pronounced *Mull Guy*) is reached after 3 miles (5 km). Turn left on the A810 for Bearsden which is reached after about 2 miles (3 kms).

A right turn at Bearsden Cross on to Roman Road leads to Roman Court, a superior housing development whose residents can boast of the ruins in their front yard of a Roman Bath House, built in the 1st century. This bath house, used by soldiers stationed in the adjacent Antonine Wall fort, is Scotland's best surviving visible Roman building. A further mile east and, in the New Kilpatrick Cemetery, are two not very upstanding, yet very important, sections of the Roman Wall which was built to keep out the wild Scots.

Return to Bearsden Cross and travel north on the A809 for 7 miles (11 km) to **Queen's View** (Auchineden Hill, 1,711 ft/ 351 metres) where today's visitor can still enjoy, as did Queen Victoria in 1869, a first glimpse of Loch Lomond and the mountains to the north. Turn south on the A809 for 2 miles (3 km) and then left for 3 miles (5 km) for the village of **Strathblane**; it sits in the lee of Earl's Seat which, at 1,896 ft (569 metres), is the highest point of the Campsies.

Head north on the A81 for 4 miles (6 km) to **Glengoyne Distillery** (01360-

PRECEDING PAGES: Loch Lomond with Ben Lomond in the background.
LEFT: Port of Menteith.
RIGHT: delivering the mail by boat to the islands in Loch Lomond.

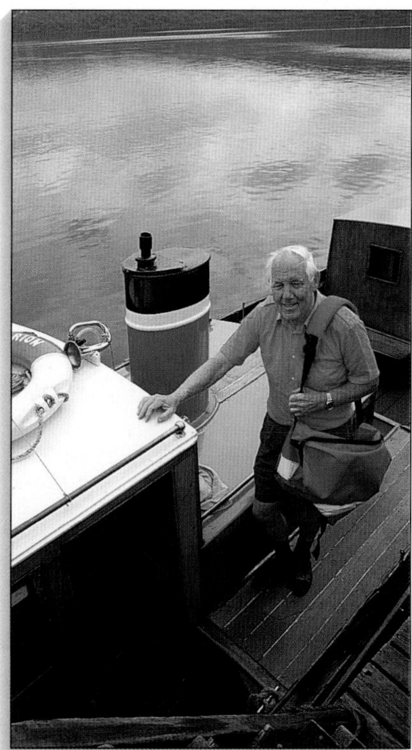

Scotch Whisky

The variety of malt whiskies on sale in Glasgow astounds visitors familiar with only a few heavily marketed brands such as Glenfiddich and The Macallan. But is the diversity an illusion fostered by advertising? Don't they taste much the same?

Certainly not, the experienced Scotch drinker will argue. The practised tongue can easily differentiate between Highland malts, Lowland malts, Campbeltown malts and Islay malts, and there's no mistaking the bouquet of a drink such as Laphroaig, often described as tasting of iodine or seaweed. The sheer variety of Scotch, in fact, far surpasses that of brandy. But which brand is best?

It's a matter of taste, but the one point of agreement is that a whisky made from a good single malt (the product of one distillery) should not be drunk with a mixer such as soda or lemonade, which would destroy the subtle flavour – though ice and water *can* be added. After dinner, malts are best drunk neat, as a liqueur. The well-known brands of blends (such as Bell's, Teacher's, Dewar's and Johnnie Walker) contain tiny amounts of as many as 30 or 40 malts mixed with grain whisky containing unmalted barley and maize. A typical blend for a popular brand is 60 percent grain whisky to 40 percent malt.

In contrast with the upmarket images conferred on Scotch today, the drink's origins were lowly. In the 18th century, a spoonful was given to new-born babies in the Highlands, and even respectable gentlewomen might start the day with "a wee dram". The poorest crofter could offer his guest a drink, thanks to the ubiquity of home-made stills.

Today two grain whiskies are produced in Glasgow itself (Strathclyde and Port Dundas) and several Lowland malts (such as Auchentoshan and Inverleven) are distilled within easy reach. However, so automated have Scotland's 100 or so distilleries become that visitors to establishments such as Glengoyne which run guided tours are left with only the haziest idea of what goes on inside the beautifully proportioned onion-shaped copper stills.

What happens is this. To make malt whisky, plump and dry barley (which, unlike the water, doesn't have to be local) is soaked in large tanks of water for two or three days. It is then spread out on a concrete floor or placed in large cylindrical drums and allowed to germinate for between eight and 12 days. Next it is dried in a kiln, preferably heated by a peat fire. The dried malt is ground and mixed with hot water in a huge circular vat called a mash tun. A sugary liquid, "wort", is drawn off from the porridge-like result, leaving the solids to be sold as cattle food. The wort is fed into massive vessels containing up to 45,000 litres of liquid, where living yeast is stirred into the mix to convert the sugar in the wort into crude alcohol. It's a bit like mixing cement.

After 48 hours, the "wash" (a clear liquid containing weak alcohol) is transferred to the copper stills and heated to the point where alcohol turns to vapour. The vapour rises up the still, to be condensed by a cooling plant into distilled alcohol, which is then passed through a second still. The trick is to know precisely when the whisky has distilled sufficiently. It is then poured into porous oak casks and left to mellow for at least three years – and sometimes for 10 or 15. ❑

LEFT: a whisky still.

Map on page 222

550254, Mon-Sat 10am-4pm, tours start on the hour, every hour, admission charge), where visitors are graciously (on payment of a fee) received, given a tour of the distillery and fortified with a dram or two of the Highland malt which is distilled here.

Proceed for a further 4 miles (6 km) on the A81 to Killearn. From here it is 6 miles (10 km) on the A875 and then the B818 to the village of Fintry, the northernmost point of this outing.

One mile from Fintry on the B818 leads to the B822 which ascends and descends across the moors of Campsie Fells to **Lennoxtown** (7 miles/11 km). Stop at the summit (1,000 ft/300 metres) which is on the Greater Glasgow boundary for spectacular views of the Clyde Valley. Glasgow can be seen to the west.

At Lennoxtown join the A891 and immediately turn right on the B822 for Torrance, from where it is a further 5 miles (8 km) to the city centre.

An outing to the Campsies can be combined with a visit to Loch Lomond or a trip to Stirling. In either case, travel northwards from Fintry on the B822 and journey for 7 miles (11 km) to the pleasant village of **Kippen** with its attractive relatively modern church and a splendid old dovecot. Much more remarkable, considering the weather, was a vine which grew here until 1964 when it was removed in the name of progress. It produced 2,000 bunches of grapes annually and was said to be the largest in the world.

Immediately beyond Kippen the B822 joins the A811. Turn right and, after 9 miles (14 km), Stirling Castle looms in front *(see page 240)*. A left turn at the junction leads after 15 miles (24 km) to Drymen, from where it is a further 7 miles (11 km), still on the A8ll, to Balloch *(see page 239)*.

Loch Lomond and Dumbarton

Few will wish to leave Glasgow without having visited the "bonnie, bonnie banks" and visitors are fortunate in that **Balloch**, at the south end of Loch Lomond, is just 19 miles (30 km) from the city. Drive past

BELOW: Loch Lomond.

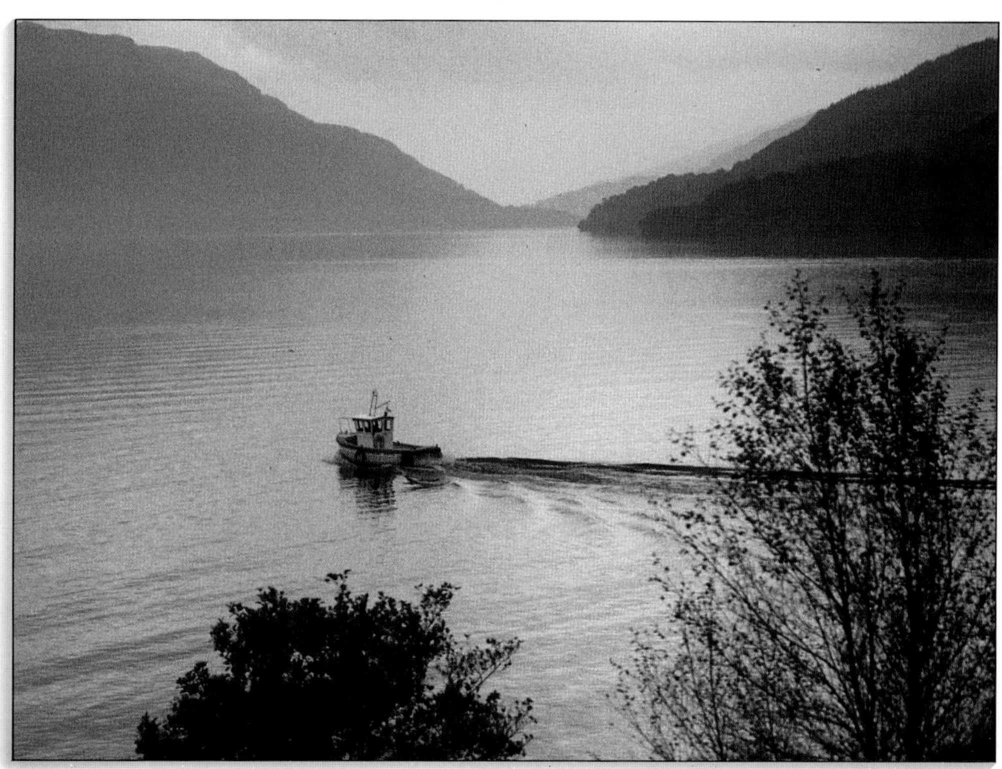

the handsome Erskine Bridge, the last bridge on the River Clyde and the only toll bridge, and then Bowling, the starting point of the now re-opened Forth and Clyde Canal which is readily recognised by its locks and the boats moored in the basin.

Soon, **Dumbarton** ❼ (14 miles/22 km from Glasgow) is reached and the road forks, with the A82, continuing directly to Balloch (for Loch Lomond) and the A814 proceeding to Dumbarton and Helensburgh from where **Loch Lomond** can be reached. Take the latter and soon, on the left, a short road leads to Dumbarton Rock, a massive 240-ft (75-metre) twin-peaked volcanic outcrop which rises sheer from the river.

It was from the castle that stood here that, in 1548, the five-year old Mary, already Queen of Scots, set sail for France, and it was this castle which she was attempting to reach when she was defeated in 1568 at the Battle of Langside. It is also believed that William Wallace, after being captured, was brought here before being sent to his execution in London. The stiff climb to the summit of the Rock, past a sundial which was presented by Mary and then through a portcullis, is well worthwhile and is rewarded by superb views not only of the Clyde estuary but of the mountains to the north.

Also worth visiting in Dumbarton is the **Denny Ship Model Experiment Tank**, (Castle Street, Dumbarton, 01389 763444, www.scottishmaritimemuseum.org/dumbart.htm, Monday to Saturday 10am – 4pm), which was the world's first ship model tank testing establishment and where such famous craft as the Queen Mary were tested. Now restored as part of the **Scottish Maritime Museum**, this massive tank the size of a football park is still occasionally used to test new ship designs.

Helensburgh

From Dumbarton it is a further 8 miles (13 km) to Helensburgh. En route, Cardross, where Robert Bruce died, is passed.

BELOW: Dumbarton Rock and Castle.

Map on page 222

Helensburgh ❽, immediately beyond which is Rhu, with the best marina on this shore of the Clyde, is the birthplace of John Logie Baird, the television, radar and fibre optics pioneer, and of Henry Bell, who launched the *Comet*, Europe's first practical steamship to brave open waters.

A right turn from the main road into steep Colquhoun Street leads, after about a mile, to the **Hill House** (01436 673900, www.nts.org.uk/hillhouse.html, 1 Apr to 31 Oct, daily 1.30-5.30pm, last admission 5pm), generally considered the best extant example of a Rennie Mackintosh domestic commission. When the house was built in 1902 for Walter W. Blackie, the publisher, Helensburgh was not served by two electric trains an hour; today, these make the Glasgow–Helensburgh journey in 50 minutes.

Back on Colquhoun Street, continue eastwards from the main road on the B832 through Glen Fruin where an infamous bloody battle between the MacGregors and the Colquhouns was fought in 1603. Innocent onlookers were also killed.

After 5 miles (8 km) this road joins the A82. Turn left for 3 miles (5 km) to the picturebook village of **Luss** on the west shore of Loch Lomond. From here the visitor can proceed northwards along the loch or turn back to Balloch at the south of the loch (7 miles/11 km from Luss). In **Balloch Castle Country Park** ❾ (01389-758 216), the castle, built in 1808, serves as the Visitor Centre, and sweeping picnic lawns offer lovely views of Loch Lomond and the mountains.

A colourful walled garden is half-hidden in the grounds and unusual specimen trees flourish in the ornamental woodlands. Loch Lomond and the Trossachs (www.lochlomond-trossachs.org/, 01360-870470) will be Scotland's first national park. During the period leading to full national park status, the Interim Committee has visitor centres situated throughout the area at Balloch Castle, Luss and Balmaha.

Stop at Balloch to visit the *Maid of the Loch*, the last paddle steamer and the largest

BELOW: Helensburgh. **RIGHT:** Hill House.

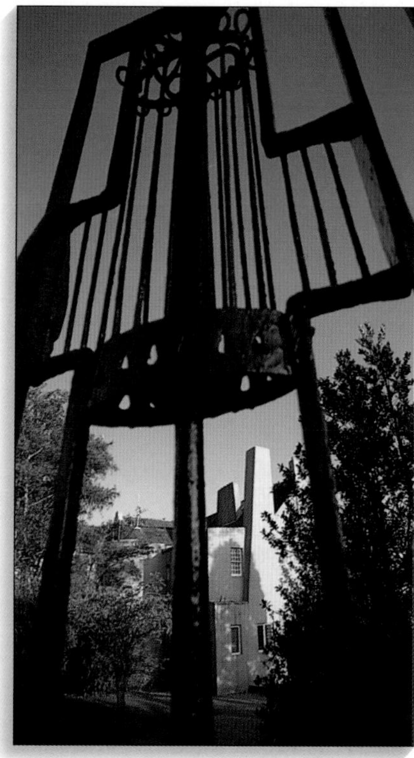

inland waterway passenger vessel built in Britain. She has recently been restored.

You can drive from here up to the picturesque village of **Luss** where the popular Scottish soap opera *High Road* is filmed. As an alternative to the heavy traffic and hordes of tourists, drive along the other side of the loch via Balmaha to Rowardennan. From here you can walk the 5 miles (8 kms) along the eastern shore of Loch Lomond to **Inversnaid**. Rob Roy MacGregor had land here and there is a cave about a mile to the north where he hid while on the run from Government forces. The Snaid Burn with its rock pools and waterfalls provided poetic insiration to Wordsworth and Gerard Manley Hopkins. Sir Walter Scott visited in 1792 and 1828.

The path here is part of a long-distance footpath, the **West Highland Way**, which runs from Glasgow to Fort William.

Rowardennan is also the nearest access for the mighty **Ben Lomond**, 3,192-ft (958-metre), worth climbing for the breathtaking views back over the loch and surrounding countryside. From Loch Lomond, it is a short drive through the scenic Trossachs to Stirling.

LEFT: country house cooking.

Alternatively, to reach Stirling from Glasgow, take the ring road (M8), then the M73 followed by the A80, which becomes the M80, a total distance of 27 miles (43 km). The route is well marked. (Express trains depart from Queen Street station about every two hours, and take 40 minutes.)

Bannockburn

Three miles (5 km) south of Stirling is the **Bannockburn Heritage Centre** (Glasgow Road, Stirling, 01786-812664, www.nts.org.uk/bannockburn.html, site open all year, Centre from 1 to 31 Mar and 1 Nov–23 Dec, daily 10.30am-4pm; 1 Apr–31 Oct, daily 10am– 5.30pm, admission charge). This marks the site of the one battle against the English known to every schoolchild in Scotland.

At the Battle of Bannockburn, fought in 1314, Robert the Bruce defeated vastly superior English forces and won freedom for Scotland. All of this, and much more, can be seen in the Heritage Centre. Outside, a bronze equestrian statue of Bruce overlooks a rotunda which surrounds the Borestone in which the shaft of the hero's standard is said to have been set.

Stirling

The royal burgh of **Stirling** ⑩, standing on a bend of the River Forth was, for centuries, the most strategic spot in Scotland, controlling routes from the south to the north as well as from the east to the west and dominating much of Scotland's history. From the town, steep Spittal Street leads to the forecourt of **Stirling Castle** (01786-450000, open seven days a week, Apr–Sept 9.30am–6pm. Oct–Mar 9.30 am–5pm, admission charge), which occupies a commanding position on top of a 250-ft (75-metre) rocky outcrop.

Most of the castle, which is entered through an impressive gateway, is from the 14th to 16th centuries when it was a residence of the Stuart kings. This is where James II and V were born and both Mary, Queen of Scots and James VI spent several years here. Even before the Stuarts, a

Map on page 222

castle occupied this ground and frequently changed hands in the constant wars fought between the Scots and the English.

Admire the palace which James V had built around a central courtyard and which is one of Scotland's renaissance glories. Today, the most striking feature of this building, with ornate stonework largely cut by French, is the exterior facade. The castle's chapel was built on the instructions of James VI while the 125-ft (40-metre) Great Hall or Parliament House, with its exquisite carving and tracery, dates from James IV. It is being painstakingly reconstructed.

The castle also contains the **Museum of the Argyll and Sutherland Highlanders Regiment** (www.argylls.co.uk, Easter to Sept Mon–Sat: 10am–5.45pm Sun: 11am–4.45pm Oct to Easter 7 days: 10am–4.15pm, free), which, in eight rooms, covers the history of the regiment from its founding in 1794 to the present day, using displays of regimental silver, uniforms and medals.

Superb views can be enjoyed from the spot where, at the northwest corner of the castle ramparts, Queen Victoria gazed across a balustrade which bears her initials. To the west, behind a broad lush plain, are the Campsie Fells and then, from west to north, Ben Lomond, Ben Venue, Ben Ledi and Ben Vorlich. To the northeast are the Ochils, and, much closer, the Wallace Monument and Cambuskenneth Abbey. A statue of Robert Bruce stands on the Esplanade and Queen Mary's lookout carries the inscription MR 1561.

Youth hostellers can expect someting unusual in Stirling. Their destination is **Argyle's Lodging** (St John Street, 01786-473442, www.syha.org.uk); it is Scotland's choicest renaissance mansion and stands just before the castle esplanade. It dates from 1630 and was built by the Earl of Stirling, the founder of Nova Scotia. Further down the hill is Mar's Wark, an unfinished renaissance palace which was started about half a century before the Argyle Lodging. Some say that the Earl

STIRLING CASTLE

The impressive bulk of Stirling Castle was a formidable challenge to any invaders. It had its most active moments during Scotland's Wars of Independence: surrendered to the English in 1296, it was recaptured by the warrior-patriot William Wallace after the Battle of Stirling Bridge (not today's stone bridge, built around 1400, but a wooden structure). It became the last stronghold in Scotland to hold out against Edward I, the "Hammer of the Scots". Eventually, it went back to the English for 10 years, until Robert the Bruce retook it in 1314 after the Battle of Bannockburn, which decisively secured Scotland's independence.

The Stewarts favoured Stirling Castle as a Royal residence, James II and V were born in it, Mary Queen of Scots was crowned there at the age of nine months, and its splendid collection of buildings reflects its history as palace and fortress. Perhaps the most striking feature is the exterior façade, with ornate stonework which was largely cut by French craftsmen. The Great Hall, or Parliament House (so-called because before 1707 this was one of the seats of the Scottish Parliament), also has exquisite carving and tracery, which has recently been carefully reconstructed. A programme of major restoration has also included the kitchens of the Castle, which now re-create the preparations for a sumptuous Renaissance banquet given by Mary, Queen of Scots for the baptism of her son, the future James VI.

RIGHT Robert the Bruce stands guard at Stirling Castle.

of Mar reduced nearby Cambuskenneth Abbey to ruins in order to obtain building stones for this palace which was to have been his town house.

Note the Royal Arms and several curious inscriptions above the entrance. Behind this is the **Church of the Holy Rude** (www.stir.ac.uk/town/facilities/holyrude/), where Mary Queen of Scots and James VI were crowned when babies. The oak roof over the nave is from the early 15th century and the 90-ft (27-metre) square battlement bears scars of a siege held in 1651. Observe, too, the five-sided apse from early in the 16th century.

Broad Street, known as the "Top of the Town", has many buildings of architectural and historic interest. The **Smith Institute** has a collection of Scottish folk material and contains Scotland's earliest curling relic, the Stirling Stone, dating from 1511 – proof positive that this game of "bowls on ice" originated in Scotland rather than the Low Countries. The handsome early 18th-century Tolbooth, capped with a Dutch-like roof, opened in 2001 as a new arts venue.

A footbridge across the River Forth, about a mile due east from the town centre, immediately leads to the remains of **Cambuskenneth Abbey**, from where superb views across the Forth Valley can be enjoyed. (Alternatively, follow the A9 out of town to Causewayhead and then the signposts on the A91.)

This, one of Scotland's most important abbeys, was founded, probably by David I in 1147 and colonised by the Augustinians. Only the west doorway and the freestanding belfry survive. The latter, an extremely impressive three-storey structure, is one of Scotland's greatest Gothic campaniles. James III and his Queen were buried in front of the abbey's high altar. A monument to their memory was unveiled by Queen Victoria in 1864.

The route to Cambuskenneth Abbey also leads, after about 2 miles (3 km) to the beckoning Wallace Monument which commemorates the Battle of Stirling. En

BELOW: Stirling Castle.

Map on page 222

route, on the left, is the Old Bridge from about 1400 which was blown up in 1745 to prevent the Highlanders reaching the south. The **Wallace Monument** (seven days, Jan–Feb and Nov–Dec 10.30am–4pm, Mar–May and October 10am–5pm, June and Sept 10am–6pm and July and Aug 9.30am–6.30pm, admission charge) rises from a courtyard, in wooded country, on 362-ft (109-metre) Abbey Craig. A statue of Wallace surmounts the door and inside are marble busts of famous Scots, including Bruce, Burns, Adam Smith and Sir Walter Scott.

Also on view is Wallace's two-handed sword: the only snag is that experts claim that such swords were not used until the late 15th century. The vistas which reward those who climb the 246 steps of the square 220-ft (66-metre) tower are immense and include seven battlefields.

Below the monument, around Airthrey Loch, spreads the **University of Stirling**, (01786-473171), the youngest of Scotland's universities. Part of this beautiful campus, which occupies grounds landscaped by a pupil of Capability Brown, is Airthrey Castle, designed by Robert Adam. The University's **MacRobert Arts Centre** offers a variety of programmes ranging from opera to folk and jazz throughout the year and is also home of the Stirling Film Theatre.

The **Trossachs**, to the west of Stirling, is an area of remarkable Highland beauty which inspired such literary giants as William and Dorothy Wordsworth, Samuel Taylor Coleridge and, above all, Sir Walter Scott. It was Scott's colourful descriptions which attracted the very first tourists, including Queen Victoria, into Highland Scotland and those who are familiar with *The Lady of the Lake*, *Rob Roy* and *Waverley* will feel very much at home here. The glorious landscape is cut by deep glens filled either by foaming rivers or by sparkling clear lochs, each with its own distinctive characteristics.

Gothic masterpiece

For a half- or full-day of magic in the Trossachs, leave Stirling on the M9 and travel for 7 miles (11 km) to **Dunblane** with its small 13th-century Gothic Cathedral, whose west front, with central doorway and lancet windows, was considered by John Ruskin to be a masterpiece of Scottish church architecture. The Cathedral also has an active society of change ringers who can be heard each Sunday morning and an award-winning team of handbell ringers.

Leave Dunblane on the A820 and, after 5 miles (8 km), cross the bridge over the River Teith and enter **Doune** ⓫. The bridge was built in 1535 by the former tailor to James IV, reputedly to spite the local ferryman who had refused him passage.

The main attraction is **Doune Castle** (01786-841742, Apr–Sept: Mon–Sat 9.30am–6.30pm and Sun 2–6.30pm; Oct–Mar: Mon–Sat 9.30am–4.30pm but closed Thurs afternoon and all day Fri, and Sun 2–4.30pm, admission charge). The castle occupies a triangular site, protected on two sides by the rivers Teith and Ardoch and on the third by a deep moat, and is one of Scotland's most magnificent

RIGHT: the Wallace Monument, Stirling.

examples of medieval architecture and was extensively restored in the 1880s. The massive keep gatehouse soars upwards for 95 ft (29 metres) and the main block rises four storeys high.

Bonnie Prince Charlie imprisoned captives here and Mary Queen of Scots dined and slept here. Magnificent views can be enjoyed from the castle walls.

Visit also the **Doune Park Gardens** and the **Doune Motor Museum** (01786 841203, daily 10am to 5pm Easter until 30 Nov, admission charge). The museum has an outstanding collection of vintage cars, including Hispano Suiza, Frazer Nash and the world's second oldest Rolls-Royce. Some are in running order and compete in the Doune Hill Climb (some weekends in April, June and September).

Continue due west from Doune on the A84 past Drumvaich to reach **Callander**, where the rivers Teith and Leny meet in the lee of Ben Ledi. The streets of this prosperous Highland gateway, which as early as 1818 Keats found "vexatiously full of visitors", are lined by shops, hotels and bed-and-breakfast establishments.

It would be a shame, time permitting, not to make a short detour on the A84 which climbs northwards from Callander through the Pass of Leny, where falls tumble and salmon leap to the south end of **Loch Lubnaig**. (The round trip is 12 miles/19 km.)

From Callander, the shapely peak of Ben Venue acts as a beacon as the A84, which becomes the A821, winds and curves for 6 miles (10 km) along the north bank of Loch Vennachar to **Brig o' Turk**, a lovely village which has long attracted artists. Three miles (5 km) further on, turn right at the Y-junction, at the western end of Loch Achray. Drive between Ben An, to the north, and Ben Venue, to the south, through a short, narrow gorge of rocks and mounds covered with heather and deciduous trees, bog myrtle and foxgloves to Loch Katrine. This mile-long stretch is the heart of the Trossachs which Scott described so evocatively.

BELOW: Killin, near Callander.

Loch Katrine is 9 miles (14 km) long and 1 mile at its broadest and since 1859 has been one of the chief sources of the water supply of Glasgow. It is best enjoyed during the summer months by a cruise aboard the restored Victorian steamer *Sir Walter Scott*, the only surviving screw steamer still offering a regular passenger service in Scotland, although those with energy and/or those who are true aficionados of Scott will wish to stroll for a mile to the site of the Silver Strand whose view is described in *The Lady of the Lake*. Opposite this point is **Ellen's Isle**, named for Ellen Douglas, the heroine of the book.

Splendid views

Return to the Y-junction and take the Duke's Road (A821) south. This spectacular route climbs and twists through the Achray Forest for 6 miles (10 km) to Aberfoyle. Just before the summit, from where there are outstanding views, the **Achray Forest Drive**, 7 miles (11 km) of gravel road open from Easter to September, takes off to the left and touches on four lochans. Immediately before Aberfoyle, situated off to the left, is the David Marshall Lodge, another splendid viewpoint and the visitor centre of the **Queen Elizabeth Forest Park** (www.aberfoyle.co.uk/dmlindex.htm).

Aberfoyle can justly claim to be a major gateway to the Highlands and it was the starting point for the first horse-drawn "coach tours" to the Trossachs which became fashionable after the publication of *The Lady of the Lake*. Here occurred the confrontation between Bailie Nicol Jarvie and Rob Roy and here, at the end of the 17th century, the Reverend Kirk, an authority on the supernatural, was spirited away by the fairies.

Those with time will thoroughly enjoy the scenic side-trip to the immediate west on the B829 along the northern shore of Loch Ard, the eastern shore of Loch Chon and so to a T-junction, 10 miles (16 km) from Aberfoyle. Here, a drive of just a few

BELOW: Loch Katrine.

hundred yards to the north leads to the south shore of Loch Katrine and one of the best viewpoints in the Trossachs, while a steep downhill drive of 4 miles (6 km) ends at Inversnaid on the eastern shore of Loch Lomond. Those pushed for time can return from Aberfoyle to Glasgow on the A81.

To proceed onwards with the Trossachs tour, take the A81 for 5 miles (8 km) to **Port of Menteith** which stands on the northern shore of the lake of that name. The historically minded will wish to board the ferry (regular service, April to September) for the short voyage to the island of **Inchmahome** (www.aberfoyle.co.uk/inchmahome.htm),and a visit to its priory. Here Robert the Bruce prayed before his epic victory at Bannockburn and the young Mary Queen of Scots played beneath the great walls of the priory.

Continue east on what is now the A873 through the hamlets of Blairhoyle and Ruskie and the pleasant village of **Thornhill** which lies just to the north of **Flanders Moss**. This is a National Nature Reserve which has the largest raised bog in the UK that is still in a predominantly near-natural state – a remarkable remnant of the ancient peat bog which once covered much of the Forth Valley.

Next, 8 miles/13 km from Port of Menteith, comes **Blair Drummond** ⓬, which has Scotland's only safari park (01786-841456, www.safari-park.co.uk/, daily Apr–Sept, admission charge). Here, lions and tigers roam, sea lions perform, monkeys amuse, and a boat ride to Chimp Island excites. A safari bus is available for those without transport.

Stirling is just 6 miles (9 km) away, but to visit Blair Drummond at the beginning rather than at the end of a Trossachs safari might prove fatal.

Burns Country

Best start an exploration of Burns Country by visiting Ayr, which is 36 miles (58 km) from Glasgow on the A77 or 50 minutes by train from Central Station (two trains an hour). There's quite a spectacular view from the road, a few miles before reaching Ayr, of the Heads of Ayr and the wide bay of which it forms the southern extremity.

Ayr ⓭, the largest of the Firth of Clyde resorts, has a long beach, many amenities and several places of interest to Burns devotees. The great man's statue stands outside the railway station and in nearby High Street is the Tam o' Shanter Inn (230 High Street), immortalised in the poem of the same name. Then there is the still functional Auld Kirk (1654–56) where Burns was baptised and the 13th-century Auld Brig, a "poor narrow footpath of a street Where twa wheelbarrows tremble when they meet".

Two miles (3 km) beyond Ayr is Alloway with the **Robert Burns National Heritage Park** (01292-441 215, www.robertburns.org/heritagepark/). (To begin a Burns tour here, do not enter Ayr at the roundabout immediately before the town but rather take the road marked Alloway.) The whitewashed, thatched cottage in which Burns was born is at the very core of the park and is immaculately maintained and furnished in the style of an 18th-century cottage.

LEFT: a Burns Museum exhibit of Tam o' Shanter.

Map on page 222

Adjacent to it is a museum of relics of the poet's life and works. But start your tour at The Tam O' Shanter Experience with a background video on the life and work of the Bard and a state of the art presentation of his most famous poem, *Tam O' Shanter*. Then leaving the building you can follow the hapless Tam's route as he stumbled upon the witches and warlocks partying with "Auld Nick" in Alloway Kirk to the picturesque Brig o' Doon, where he escaped by crossing running water. But not before a witch had torn the tail from his horse. There's a great view back from the bridge to the Burns monument, designed as a Grecian temple, and housing a museum.

Kirkoswald, 13 miles (21 km) south of Ayr on the A77, is where Burns was sent to study when he was 16. The schoolroom where he attended lessons is now part of the Shanter Hotel. That summer he fell in love for the first time, an event that inspired his first song, *Now Westlin Winds*. Many years later he remembered some of the colourful characters he met in Kirkoswald and imortalised them in *Tam o' Shanter*. The thatched cottage of Souter Johnnie (01655-760603, 1 Apr–30 Sep, daily and weekends in Oct, 11.30am–5pm, admission charge), the village shoemaker and Tam's faithful drinking companion, is now a museum of Burnsiana and can be visited. In the garden at the rear the cobbler, Tam, the innkeeper and his wife are frozen in stone. Across the road round the ruined church are the graves of John Davidson, the Souter, and Thomas Graham of Shanter Farm.

Those who can tear themselves away from their pursuit of Burns will make for magnificent **Culzean Castle** ⓮ (01655-884455, 1 Apr–31 Oct, daily 11am–5.30pm, last admission 4.30, weekends in Mar, Nov and Dec; park open all year, admission charge) and the country park of that name. The castle – whose Oval Staircase with its two-storeyed colonnaded gallery and the Round Drawing Room are breathtaking – is just a couple

BELOW: Burns Cottage at Alloway.

of miles north of Kirkoswald but can be reached only by a slightly circuitous route of about 10 miles (16 km) which involves travelling either to the northeast or to the southwest. There's no doubt which route enthusiast golfers will choose: that to the southwest goes through Turnberry.

Culzean Castle, Robert Adam's masterpiece, is mainly 18th-century and occupies a commanding position above the Firth of Clyde. Clearly visible is Paddy's Milestone, the tiny island of Ailsa Craig, which owes its sobriquet to the fact that it was the first sight of Scotland seen by Irish immigrants. The extensive grounds at Culzean became Scotland's first countryside park in 1970 and offers many attractions to nature lovers.

From Culzean, start the return trip to Glasgow on either the A7129 or the A77. Five miles (8 km) past Ayr, branch right on the A719 and follow the signs to **Tarbolton** (3 miles/5 km) and the 17th-century **Bachelors' Club** (1 Apr–30 Sept, daily 1.30–5.30pm; weekends in Oct, 1.30–5.30pm, admission charge), a building where Burns and a few friends formed a debating club and where he was initiated as a freemason. It was also in Tarbolton in 1779 that Burns, "to give my manners a brush went to a country dancing school" against his father's wishes. Now make south for 1 mile on the B730 and turn left for 5 miles (8 km) on the B743 for Mauchline. En route, stop at the statue of "Highland Mary" which marks the spot where Mary Campbell of Auchnamore and Burns parted with an exchange of vows. (Highland Mary returned to Greenock, where she died.)

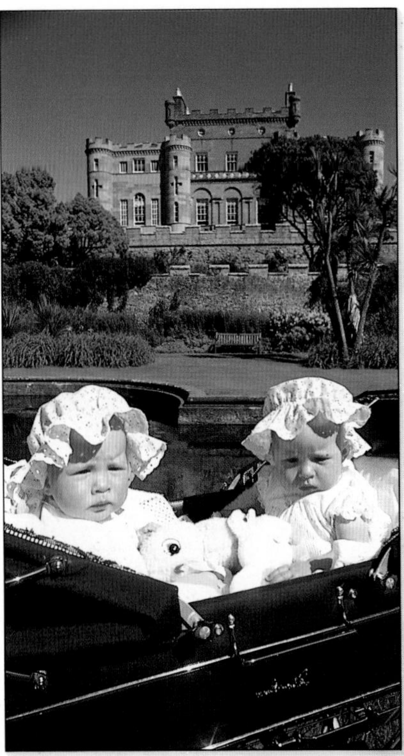

It was at **Mauchline** ⓯ that Burns is said to have met and to have married Jean Armour after she bore him twins. They lived for a while in Burns House (open Easter to October, Tues–Sat, 10.30am-5pm; Sunday 2–5pm, admission fee), now a museum. Mauchline Churchyard contains the graves of four of Burns's children and some of his friends.

Opposite the Church is Poosie Nansie's Tavern, where Burns saw the revels which resulted in his cantata *The Jolly Beggars*. On the outskirts of the town, at the junction of A76 and B744, the National Burns Tower stands above Cottage Homes and houses a small museum.

Before turning north to Kilmarnock, some might wish to make a 6-mile (10-km) detour south on the A76 to **Auchinleck**, where the diarist James Boswell was born and from where, in 1773, he and Dr Samuel Johnson set off on their tour of the Hebrides. Part of the local church is now a **Boswell Museum**, adjacent to which is the Boswell Mausoleum where James is buried. The museum also commemorates another son of Auchinleck: William Murdoch, the 18th-century pioneer of gas lighting.

Kilmarnock

From here it is 13 miles (21 km) north on the A76 to **Kilmarnock** ⓰ where the first edition (known as the Kilmarnock edition) of Burns's poems was published. The Burns Monument in Kay Park is a red-sandstone structure surmounted by a

LEFT: seeing double at Culzean Castle.

Map on page 222

tower and contains a museum of Burnsiana. Also worth a visit is **Dean Castle** (castle open Apr–Oct every day 12–5pm; Nov–Mar weekends only 12–4pm, grounds all year round, admission free). It houses a collection of armour, musical instruments and tapestries. The surrounding Country Park has a riding centre, childrens's corner and rare breeds centre.

From Kilmarnock, travel on the A71 for 8 miles (13 km) to **Irvine** ⓱, the last of Scotland's New Towns and a seaside resort. Here, Burns enthusiasts will make for the Glasgow Vennel, where, in 1781, Burns lodged and learned the trade of dressing flax. The house is now a museum (01294-275059, open all year, Mon, Tues, Thurs, Fri, Sat,10am–1pm & 2–5pm). The Irvine Burns Club, founded in 1826, claims to be the world's oldest Burns Club.

Museum of the sea

Irvine is also the home of the inchoate **Scottish Maritime Museum** (Harbourside, Irvine, 01294-278 283, daily 10am–5pm) which, in addition to shore exhibits, has a number of craft moored alongside, including a Scottish puffer, a former Irvine Harbour tug, and the ongoing restoration of the *S.V.Carrick*, the world's oldest "colonial" clipper ship.

The **Magnum Centre** (01294 278381, Mon & Fri 9am–10pm, Tues–Thurs 10am –10pm, Sat & Sun 9am–6pm) claims to be Scotland's largest leisure centre. It offers opportunities for indoor curling and lawn bowls as well as more mundane ice-skating and swimming.

Immediately to the north of Irvine, just to the west of the A737, is **Eglinton Park** with its late 18th-century ruined castle. In 1839 an historic jousting tournament was held here in an attempt to revive the ceremony of ancient chivalry; since the late 1980s this has been revived and is now held annually.

Another unusual traditional competition is held on the first Saturday of July in **Kilwinning**, a mile to the north on the A737. Then, the Ancient Society of Archers holds

Below: a satirical portrait of James Boswell, who is celebrated in a museum at Auchinleck.

a shoot re-enacting the ancient tradition of "shooting the papingo" which is set on top of the town steeple. Kilwinning claims to be the home of freemasonry in Scotland, the brotherhood having been introduced by European masons who built the 12th-century priory, the fairly extensive remains of which can be seen in the town centre.

Seaside resorts

From Irvine, one can drive south back to Ayr, a distance of 11 miles (18 km) on the A78 passing en route Prestwick International Airport. The land between the road and the sea is devoted to golf and is home to some of the finest links in the world. However, rather than taking this route, proceed northwards for 15 miles (24 km) on the A78 to Largs, passing the seaside resorts of Ardrossan (ferry for the island of Arran) and Saltcoats.

In **Largs** ⓲, visit the Skelmorlie Aisle and the Pencil Monument. The former, situated in the Old Burial Ground, is a magnificent renaissance jewel-box mausoleum with a ceiling painted with decorative local views and abstract scenes. The latter commemorates the Battle of Largs (1263) at which King Haakon of Norway was defeated and subsequently had to secede to Scotland the Isle of Man and the Hebrides which the Norsemen had held for 400 years. Vikingar, Barrfields, (Greenock Road, 01475-689777, admission charge) comprehensively covers the saga of the Vikings in Scotland from their arrival to defeat at the Battle of Largs in 1263.

In the **Kelburn Country Centre** (01475-568685), about 3 miles (5 km) south of Largs, the oldest castle in Scotland to have remained in the hands of the same family stands among extensive wooded slopes. The castle, parts of which date from the 12th century, is the home of the Earl of Glasgow. The 18th-century farm buildings form a village square and the grounds offer a wide variety of amusements, including pony trekking and a commando assault course. The glorious gardens have an extraordinary weeping larch, two

BELOW: eating out at Largs.

Map on page 222

yew trees more than 1,000 years old and Scotland's largest Monterey pine. (Those with a yen to stay in a baronial castle with a genuine Earl and Countess as hosts can have this wish fulfilled at Kelburne; note that the rates are steep and the hosts prefer parties of between 8 and 16 people.)

Immediately facing Largs are the islands of **Great** and **Little Cumbrae**. On the former is the resort of **Millport**, which has the Cathedral of the Isles, the smallest in Europe. The highest point on the island, at 417 ft (125 metres), is Glaidstaine, from where there are outstanding and exhaustive views.

From Largs to Glasgow there is a choice between the A78, which hugs the coast until becoming the A8 at Greenock, or the inland A760, then the A737 to Paisley. The former route is 31 miles (50 km) while the latter is 41 miles (66 km).

Lanarkshire

For a trip to the fertile **Clyde Valley**, lined by garden centres, leave Glasgow by the M8 and at Junction 8 join the A73 which immediately becomes the M74. Leave this at Junction 5 for East Kilbride and drive to the handsome small town of **Bothwell** ⓳ with its bridge dating to the 14th century. A monument here marks the Battle of Bothwell Brig which was fought in 1679 and resulted in the defeat of the Covenanters and five-month imprisonment for 1,200 of them. Near the bridge the magnificent red sandstone ruins of Bothwell Castle loom beside the River Clyde. This, the best preserved 13th-century castle in the land, was repeatedly fought over by the Scots and the English; after Robert Bruce's followers captured it, they knocked part of the impressive east tower into the River Clyde.

From Bothwell, travel to the home of the explorer and missionary David Livingstone in nearby **Blantyre** ⓴. He was born in 1813 in a one-room tenement in Shuttle Row, a block of flats built in 1780. The entire block has been beautifully restored and is now the **Livingstone**

BELOW: Bothwell Castle.

National Memorial and Museum (165 Station Road, 01698-823140, 8 Jan–31 Mar and 1 Nov–23 Dec, Mon–Sat 10.30am–4.30pm, Sun 12.30–4.30pm; 1 Apr–31 Oct, Mon–Sat 10am–5.30pm, Sun 12.30–5.30pm, admission charge), which vividly traces the life of this remarkable man. An adjacent African Pavilion illustrates modern Africa and a social history museum houses agricultural, cotton spinning and mining exhibits from the district at the time of Livingstone. The great man's statue stands on the tower of the Livingstone Memorial Church.

Hamilton

From Blantyre, drive southeast on the A724 through industrial yet historically important **Hamilton** ㉑. Mary Queen of Scots rested here after escaping from Loch Leven Castle and in 1651 Oliver Cromwell made the town his headquarters. Visit the octagonal Parish Church designed by William Adam in front of which stands the pre-Norman Netherton Cross, an ancient Christian relic. On the east wall of the churchyard is the famous Heads Memorial commemorating four local Covenanters beheaded after a 1666 rising. Of interest are two museums, one military, the other local history, emphasising transport.

The **Hamilton Mausoleum** was built in the middle of the 18th century as a crypt for the 10th Duke of Hamilton but its echo, said to be the longest in the world, prevented it ever being used. The original bronze doors, removed and placed inside, have mouldings illustrating Bible stories and are facsimiles of the renowned panels on Ghiberti's doors at the Baptistry in Florence. The Mausoleum now stands in the Strathclyde Country Park which has something for everyone and whose man-made lake is used for international rowing regattas.

Look south from the mausoleum to see, at the end of a tree-lined avenue, the **Chatelherault Hunting Lodge** (Carlisle Road, Ferniegar, 01698-426 213, open

LEFT: David Livingstone effigy at Blantyre.
BELOW: Lammermuir Day parade at Lanark.

Map on page 222

Jan–Dec, admission charge), erected in the 1730s at the command of the 5th Duke of Hamilton. Until the late 1980s this building was a ruin but was then lovingly restored. The lodge, which resembles a small French château, was designed by William Adam. The rooms are few but the decoration is quite superb.

The lodge is now the centre of a Country Park where one of the attractions is the Cadzow herd of white cattle, believed to be descended from animals introduced by the Romans. Only two herds of these animals exist: the other is in Northumberland. Another attraction is a stand of magnificent oak trees dating from about 1450. The grand avenue of trees which stretched southwards for 2 miles (3 km) to Hamilton Palace has been replanted with yews and will soon grow again. Not the case, however, with grandiose Hamilton Palace, which was destroyed in 1927.

Continue south on the A72 for 8 miles (13 km) to the village of Crossford. Turn right on a minor road which, after about 2 miles (3 km) comes to the tiny village of Tillietudlem. A further 1,000 yards on, a negotiable track leads to 15th-century **Craignethan Castle**, a defensive gem from medieval times which is protected on three sides by cliffs and on the fourth by a moat. This is assumed to be the castle about which Scott wrote in *Old Mortality*, although he said: "I did not think on Craignethan in writing about Tillietudlem [Old Mortality], but there can be no objection in adopting it as that which public taste has adopted as coming nearest to the ideal of the place". Nowhere, in all her travels, did Mary Queen of Scots remain longer than at Craignethan, which she visited after her escape from Lochleven and before her defeat at the Battle of Langside in1568; her ghost, it is said, puts in an occasional appearance.

Lanark

Back on the A72, continue for 6 miles (10 km) on a delightful road which parallels the River Clyde, which has excellent fish-

BELOW: grand designs at Chatelherault.

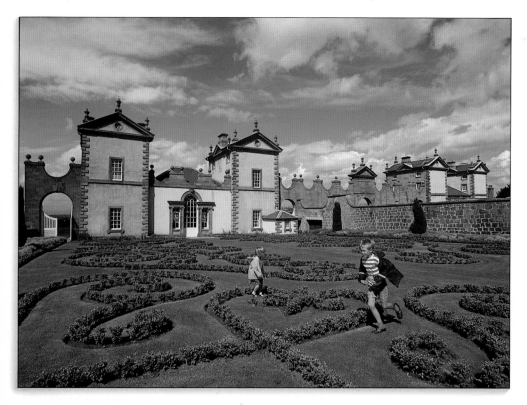

ing, to **Lanark**, 25 miles (40 kms) from Glasgow. Other than on its market day each Monday, Lanark, attractive as it is, has little to offer. However, travel from here for about a mile on a clearly signposted, twisting and steeply descending road and, at one's feet, in a wooded gorge through which flows the Clyde, is a handsome, virtually intact 18th-century village.

New Lanark

New Lanark ㉒ (01555-661345, www.newlanark.org, open all year, 11am–5pm, admission charge), is no ordinary village: it was the cradle of Scotland's Industrial Revolution. Once the largest cotton-spinning complex in Britain, it has an urban rather than a rural feel; the solid stone, Georgian-style buildings are three and four storeys high and stretch, in some instances, for hundreds of yards. The mills closed in 1968.

It all began in 1785 when David Dale, utilising the power of the nearby falls of the River Clyde, built cotton spinning mills here. Robert Owen, his son-in-law, became the manager of the mills and village in 1800 and commenced what he asserted, with some justification, was "the most important experiment for the happiness of the human race that has yet been instituted at any time in any part of the world". Owen set up Britain's first infant school, dormitory accommodation for the apprentices, an adult education and social club with the high-falutin' title of "New Institution for the Formation of Character", and a workers' co-operative.

Map on page 222

Although the mill closed in 1968, successful efforts to restore and revitalise it have been made by the New Lanark Association, one of whose founders was Kenneth Dale Owen, a great-great-grandson of Robert. Many of the old mill buildings have been restored as modern houses, shops and craft workshops. One is the Visitor Centre, where those interested can learn how Robert Owen's mills, in the days of satanic workshops, were able to marry better working conditions and improved output.

Well worth seeing is the state-of-the-art Millennium Experience where visitors are taken back and forwards through time, learning about the founding of New Lanark and exploring historical topics such as the use of child labour.

The village dyeworks is now home to a **Scottish Wildlife Centre**, which tells the story of the Falls of Clyde and its natural heritage.

From here, it is a delightful 30-minute walk along the Clyde to the Cora Linn Falls with their 90-ft (27-metre) fall and a viewing platform. A further 30 minutes lead to the Bonnington Linn Falls.

For an overview of the route travelled – and, on a clear day, for views as far north as Ben Lomond and the island of Arran in the Firth of Clyde – drive west of Lanark on the A72 for 5 miles (8 km) and then turn left on the B7018 for about 2 miles (3 km). A secondary road to the right soon climbs to the viewpoint of Blackhill (951 ft/285 metres). Weary of the vistas? Then all around are the well-preserved remains of an Iron Age Fort and a Bronze Age Cairn. ❑

Left: New Lanark, cradle of Scotland's Industrial Revolution.

The Golfing Capital of the World

Fifty courses lie within the city limits and 90 are within 20 miles (32 km) of its centre. Spread the net wider and within 32 miles (48 km) there are about 150 courses. These range from pleasant, straightforward nine-hole affairs (about 30 courses, which will appeal to the perpetual hacker) to ferocious 18-hole tigers.

Although golf was played in and around Edinburgh before the madness struck Glasgow, the first eye-witness account of the game is a 1721 poem about golf on Glasgow Green by James Arbuckle, a Glasgow University student. Later, those Glasgow Green players founded the **Glasgow Golf Club** whose Tennant Cup, played for on their course at **Killermont**, 16 miles (24 km) north of the city, is the world's oldest open amateur tournament.

The simplest way for the visitor to Glasgow to play golf is to make for one or other of the city's eight municipal courses, four of which are 9-hole. **Linn Park** and **Littlehill** are the best public courses. At the other end of the scale is **Turnberry**, one of three locations within an hour's drive of Glasgow which has hosted the Open. Turnberry's two courses are quintessential links courses – and it is links courses which the avid golfer must experience on a visit to Glasgow.

Sixteen miles (25 km) north of Turnberry is **Ayr**, with three parkland courses open to the public. **Belleisle**, from the drawing board of the great James Baird, is considered by many to be the best parkland course in Scotland. Coalescing with Ayr, to the north, is **Prestwick** whose **Prestwick Club (Old Prestwick)** advertised in 1860 as "A General Golf Tournament for Scotland". And so began The Open. (A stone cairn commemorates the first tee of the original Championship course.) **Prestwick's St Nicholas** is just as challenging while its flat **St Cuthbert**, a parkland rather than a links course, is that wee bit easier.

From Prestwick 13 miles (21 km) northwards to **Irvine**, there are a dozen superb links courses interrupted by only the occasional field or habitation. An attraction of these Ayrshire courses is that they usually remain playable throughout winter at times when the inland courses are closed because of frost or snow. **Troon**, a short drive (with a wood, not in a car) from Prestwick, is home of the Royal Troon Club Old course, which possesses both the longest and shortest holes on any Open course. Its **Portland** course is somewhat easier. **Lochgreen** is the most challenging of Troon's three municipal courses.

Nearer Glasgow – only a couple of miles west of Glasgow Airport – is the **Langbank** public course, which offers magnificent views of the Vale of Leven and Ben Lomond. It is part of the **Gleddoch House Golf and Country Club**,which has an 20-room hotel.

Within, or on the fringe of Glasgow, are the excellent courses of **Haggs Castle**, **Pollok** and **Whitecraigs** to the south of the city, **Sandyhills** to the north and **Bridge of Weir** to the west. Twelve miles (19 km) south of the city is the windy, moorland **Bonnyton Moor** course, a **Glasgow Jewish Golf Club** which is open to those who are not of the faith. All these are private clubs whose greens are open to *bona fide* members of other clubs. ❑

RIGHT: the famous course at Turnberry.

RADIO CLYDE
261

INSIGHT GUIDES

TRAVEL TIPS

AT&T Direct® Service

The easy way to call home from anywhere.

AT&T Access Numbers

Argentina .0800-555-4288	Czech Rep.▲ .00-42-000-101
Australia ...1-800-881-011	Denmark........8001-0010
Austria● 0800-200-288	Egypt●(Cairo) ...510-0200
Bahamas..1-800-USA-ATT1	France.....0800-99-00-11
Belgium● ..0-800-100-10	Germany..0800-2255-288
Bermuda✚ 1-800-USA-ATT1	Greece● 00-800-1311
Brazil 000-8010	Guam 1-800-2255-288
Canada...1 800 CALL ATT	Guyana○ 165
Chile 800-225-288	Hong Kong ..800-96-1111
China, PRC▲ 10811	India▲ 000-117
Costa Rica .0-800-0-114-114	Ireland 1-800-550-000

Global connection with the AT&T Network | **AT&T direct service**

The best way to keep in touch when you're traveling overseas is with **AT&T Direct® Service**. It's the easy way to call your loved ones back home from just about anywhere in the world. Just cut out the wallet card below and use it wherever your travels take you.

For a list of AT&T Access Numbers, cut out the attached wallet guide.

Israel	**1-800-94-94-949**	**Portugal ▲**	**800-800-128**
Italy ●	**172-1011**	**Saudi Arabia ▲**	**1-800-10**
Jamaica ●	1-800-USA-ATT1	Singapore	800-0111-111
Japan ● ▲	**005-39-111**	**South Africa**	**0800-99-0123**
Korea, Republic ●	**0072-911**	**Spain**	**900-99-00-11**
Mexico ▽ ●	**01-800-288-2872**	**Sweden**	**020-799-111**
Netherlands ●	**0800-022-9111**	**Switzerland ●**	**0800-89-0011**
Neth. Ant. ▲ ❂	**001-800-USA-ATT1**	**Taiwan**	**0080-10288-0**
New Zealand ●	**000-911**	Thailand ❮	001-999-111-11
Norway	**800-190-11**	**Turkey ●**	**00-800-12277**
Panama	00-800-001-0109	U.A. Emirates ●	800-121
Philippines ●	**105-11**	**U.K.**	**0800-89-0011**
Poland ● ▲	**00-800-111-1111**	**Venezuela**	**800-11-120**

FOR EASY CALLING WORLDWIDE

1. Just dial the AT&T Access Number for the country you are calling from. *2.* Dial the phone number you're calling. *3.* Dial your card number.*

For access numbers not listed ask any operator for **AT&T Direct®** Service.
In the U.S. call 1-800-222-0300 for **AT&T Direct** Service information.
Visit our Web site at: **www.att.com/traveler**

Bold-faced countries permit country-to-country calling outside the U.S.

- ● Public phones require coin or card deposit to place call.
- ✚ Public phones and select hotels.
- ▲ May not be available from every phone/payphone.
- ○ Collect calling only.
- ▽ Includes "Ladatel" public phones; if call does not complete, use 001-800-462-4240.
- ❂ From St. Maarten or phones at Bobby's Marina, use 1-800-USA-ATT1.
- ❮ When calling from public phones, use phones marked Lenso.
- * AT&T Calling Card, AT&T Corporate, AT&T Universal, MasterCard®, Diners Club®, American Express®, or Discover® cards accepted.

When placing an international call ***from*** the U.S., dial 1-800-CALL ATT.

WW ©6/00 AT&T

Israel	**1-800-94-94-949**	**Portugal ▲**	**800-800-128**
Italy ●	**172-1011**	**Saudi Arabia ▲**	**1-800-10**
Jamaica ●	1-800-USA-ATT1	Singapore	800-0111-111
Japan ● ▲	**005-39-111**	**South Africa**	**0800-99-0123**
Korea, Republic ●	**0072-911**	**Spain**	**900-99-00-11**
Mexico ▽ ●	**01-800-288-2872**	**Sweden**	**020-799-111**
Netherlands ●	**0800-022-9111**	**Switzerland ●**	**0800-89-0011**
Neth. Ant. ▲ ❂	**001-800-USA-ATT1**	**Taiwan**	**0080-10288-0**
New Zealand ●	**000-911**	Thailand ❮	001-999-111-11
Norway	**800-190-11**	**Turkey ●**	**00-800-12277**
Panama	00-800-001-0109	U.A. Emirates ●	800-121
Philippines ●	**105-11**	**U.K.**	**0800-89-0011**
Poland ● ▲	**00-800-111-1111**	**Venezuela**	**800-11-120**

FOR EASY CALLING WORLDWIDE

1. Just dial the AT&T Access Number for the country you are calling from. *2.* Dial the phone number you're calling. *3.* Dial your card number.*

For access numbers not listed ask any operator for **AT&T Direct®** Service.
In the U.S. call 1-800-222-0300 for **AT&T Direct** Service information.
Visit our Web site at: **www.att.com/traveler**

Bold-faced countries permit country-to-country calling outside the U.S.

- ● Public phones require coin or card deposit to place call.
- ✚ Public phones and select hotels.
- ▲ May not be available from every phone/payphone.
- ○ Collect calling only.
- ▽ Includes "Ladatel" public phones; if call does not complete, use 001-800-462-4240.
- ❂ From St. Maarten or phones at Bobby's Marina, use 1-800-USA-ATT1.
- ❮ When calling from public phones, use phones marked Lenso.
- * AT&T Calling Card, AT&T Corporate, AT&T Universal, MasterCard®, Diners Club®, American Express®, or Discover® cards accepted.

When placing an international call ***from*** the U.S., dial 1-800-CALL ATT.

WW ©6/00 AT&T

CONTENTS

Getting Acquainted

NOTE: Unless a separate exchange code is shown, all telephone numbers are for Glasgow (UK dialling code 0141, international 44-141).

The Place

Glasgow straddles the River Clyde, 14 miles (22 km) upstream from its estuary at Dumbarton (Strathclyde's ancient capital) and is at 55 degrees 51 minutes north, 4 degrees 17 minutes west. Glasgow proper covers an area of roughly 76 sq. miles (197 sq. km). Its population, like that of most UK cities, has been declining gradually since the 1930s; between 1978 and 1988 it plummeted from 815,000 to 703,000 as people moved out to surrounding areas. The decline has slowed to around 5,000 people a year and the current population is around 611,440.

It is generally believed that the siting of the city was due to the shallows of the Clyde creating a ford with good pastureland on both banks suitable for grazing animals. Walking along the Clyde today, one can see that south of the river it is very flat and that this flatness continues for a short distance onto the north bank. Looking further north and to the northwest, the horizon changes and is broken by a multitude of irregular oval-shaped hills known as drumlins. These small hills rise quite sharply to a height of 100 to 250 ft (30 to 75 metres). The Necropolis, at 225 ft (68 metres), is one of the highest.

The steeper slopes of these whalebacked hillocks face northwest and gentler banks point southeast, indicating the direction of the glacial advance through the valley. The Victorians tailored many of their handsome terraces around these slopes: an impressive example is the Park Conservation Area on Woodlands Hill.

By the late 19th century, Glasgow had become the second city of the British Empire, with a population of over 1 million. This burgeoning population was in part the result of the Irish potato famines of the 1840s and the rapid depopulation of Scotland's highlands and islands. The city fathers fought hard to overcome the deprivations within the town but it is only within the past decade that inner city renewal has begun in earnest.

As recently as 1985, one-third of Glasgow's occupied housing stock was found to be unsatisfactory, many dwellings lacking baths or wash-basins, and there is still a shortage of good-quality council houses. Dampness is the most persistent problem. Around 52 percent of the city's dwellings are owned by the local authority and another 33 percent are owner-occupied; the remainder are rented privately or from housing associations.

As manufacturing has declined, service industries now form the core of the city's economy (74 percent of employment). However, there is still a lot of leeway to make up: in January 1998, some 26,896 people were registered as unemployed. This represents 10.3 percent of the economically active in the city and a reduction of registered unemployment from 31,638, or 15 percent in the previous 12 months.

Government & Economy

Scotland became part of the United Kingdom after the Act of Union with England in 1707. It retains its own legal system, educational system and national church.

Scotland's Parliament, dissolved in 1707 by the Act of Union, was recreated in 1999 and deals with devolved domestic government while the UK Parliament at Westminster continues to be responsible for UK-wide issues.

Local government in Glasgow is run by Glasgow City Council (www.glasgow.gov.uk), which has its headquarters at the City Chambers in George Square.

Throughout the centuries, Glasgow's economy has had a strong mercantile base. In the 18th century the city traded in tobacco, sugar and cotton and continued to do so into the 1800s. As the Clyde was widened and deepened, heavier industries such as shipbuilding became established. But they began to falter shortly before World War II and never really recovered. Light industry continues and the city is a burgeoning commercial centre. Tourism is a major growth area.

The resurgence of energy and wealth within the city is most visible in some of those areas which suffered from neglect and decay. Parts of the docks and the Merchant City are prime examples of this phenomenon and now provide scores of luxury dwellings for young urban professionals.

Time Zones

Scotland, like the rest of the UK, follows Greenwich Mean Time (GMT). In late March the clocks go forward one hour for British Summer Time and in late October are moved back to GMT.

Climate

George Square and the City Chambers lie closer to the Arctic Circle than Red Square and the Kremlin in Moscow. Fortunately, Glasgow has a milder climate than that experienced in Russia because of the city's proximity to the Atlantic with its warm currents.

There are no extreme temperature changes. Winters are generally mild (the mercury seldom falls much below zero) and summers cool with the mercury hovering in the mid-60s (F) or around 20°C. The city usually has less than 40 inches

(100 cm) of rain a year. The most pleasant time to visit is May through September. In the summer the days are long with sunrise being as early as 3.30am and night not falling until after 10pm.

Culture & Customs

Glasgow has a history steeped in culture and learning and is the home of the second-oldest university in Scotland. Even during its most impoverished times it continued to open magnificent galleries and concert halls, often finding funds from private individuals. There has always been a tremendous driving force behind theatre, music and art, which has continued throughout this century.

Playwright and physician, James Bridie (Dr Osborne Henry Mavor), was determined that Scottish writing and acting should have a venue of its own and was a driving force behind the creation of the Citizens' Theatre. Today, its directors and actors have established its international reputation on the basis of a wide selection of works ranging from Shakespeare to Pinter.

Music is well represented with the National Symphony Orchestra (www.rsno.org.uk), the BBC Scottish Symphony Orchestra (www.bbc.co.uk/bbcsso), Scottish Opera (www.scottishopera.org.uk), several chamber music groups and choirs. In addition, the city is the home of the Scottish Ballet (www.scottishballet.co.uk). Contemporary visual arts are strengthening as the city continues to produce and to attract talented young people.

LANGUAGE

A book could be written about the Glasgow vernacular – and indeed, an excellent one exists, written by Michael Munro *(see Further Reading)*. Glaswegian is an infectious dialect which gives an excellent insight to the Glaswegian personality with its warmth tempered by aggression and black humour.

Planning the Trip

What To Wear

Unfortunately, not infrequent rain calls for raincoats and umbrellas. It is always a good idea to carry some warm clothing – just in case. Glaswegians appear to be impervious to the vagaries of the weather, preferring to look fashionable, come what may. Formal dress is a rarity, even in the smartest places.

Entry Regulations

VISAS & PASSPORTS

An integral part of the UK, Scotland has the same passport and visa requirements as the rest of Britain. There is no border check of any kind for visitors travelling between England and Scotland. Enquiries should be made to the relevant embassy.

CUSTOMS

There are no restrictions on the amount of British or foreign currency you can bring into the country.

Following the introduction of the European Union's Single Market in 1993 there are no longer any official restrictions on the movement of goods within the community, provided those goods were purchased within the EU. However, British Customs have set the following 'guide levels' on the following: 800 cigarettes or 400 cigarillos or 200 cigars or 1kg tobacco; 10 litres spirits or 20 litres fortified wines etc or 90 litres wine or 110 litres beer. EU nationals no longer need to exit through a red or green channel.

Travellers from further afield are subject to the following allowances: 1 litre of spirits, or 2 litres of fortified or sparkling wine, or 2 litres of table wine (an additional 2 litres of still wine if no spirits are purchased); plus 200 cigarettes or 100 cigarillos, or 30 cigars, or 250g of tobacco; plus 60cc perfume, 250cc toilet water.

Any queries should be made to Customs and Excise at 21 India Street, Glasgow (tel: 221 3828).

ANIMAL QUARANTINE

Since February 2000 pet cats and dogs from certain countries are allowed into the UK, without quarantine, provided they meet certain conditions. Birds and mammals not covered by the scheme will normally be quarantined for six months, during which time regular visits to pets can be arranged. For full details of regulations and kennels in the UK, contact Ministry of Agriculture, Fisheries and Food, 1a Page Street, London SW1P 4PQ, tel: 0207 904 6222, email: quarantine@ahvg.maff.gsi.gov.uk, www.maff.gov.uk/animalh/quarantine/

Health

European Union nationals qualify for free medical care; for others, medical insurance is advisable. Everyone is entitled to free emergency treatment at a hospital casualty department.

Money

Scotland shares a common currency with the UK. Each Scottish bank issues its own notes, but English banknotes are perfectly acceptable. The £1 note has been retained in Scotland and is in use alongside the English £1 coin. City centre banks have bureaux de change, and all banks cash travellers cheques.

Banks are open Monday–Friday 9.30am–12.30pm and 1.30–4pm,

with city centre banks staying open at lunchtime. Thomas Cook at Glasgow Airport (tel: 887 7220) offers a limited banking service seven days a week 8am–8pm.

For those wishing to change money outside banking hours, the following are open on Saturday: Thomas Cook, Central Station, tel: 207 3400, 9am–4.30pm; American Express, 115 Hope Street, G2, tel: 222 1401, 9am–noon; Glasgow Tourist Information Centre, 11 George Square, G1, tel: 204 4400.

A number of foreign banks, other than English, have offices in Glasgow. These include:
Bank of China, 450 Sauchiehall Street, G2. tel: 332 3354.
Bank of Ireland, 65 St. Vincent Street, G1. tel: 221 9353.
Habib Bank, A.G. Zurich, 52 Oswald Street, Gl. tel: 204 2197.
Habib Bank Ltd., 141 Norfolk Street, G15. tel: 420 1319.

Electrical Supply

240 volts is standard. Hotels will usually have dual 110/240 volt sockets for razors. Sockets take a standard UK three-pin plug and visitors from overseas will need an adaptor.

Public Holidays

Local, public and bank holidays can be frustrating for visitors, but generally there will usually be a small shop open somewhere during the major public holidays such as 25 and 26 December and 1 and 2 January. Glasgow's annual holiday, known as the Glasgow Fair, starts on the Saturday after the second Monday in July and lasts for two weeks. This is an excellent time to visit the city because it empties as quickly as an uncorked whisky bottle, making parking almost enjoyable.

Getting There

BY AIR

Glasgow International Airport (GLA), www.baa.co.uk/main/airports/glasgow/, is situated 8 miles (13 km) west of the city centre alongside the M8 motorway at Junction 28. It was designed in the early 1960s by Sir Basil Spence, who is perhaps better known for his less successful apartments in the Gorbals. It is Scotland's busiest airport and the fourth busiest in the UK.
British Airways, tel: 0845 773 3377, www.british-airways.com, runs a regular shuttle service to London (Heathrow and Gatwick).
British Midland, tel: 0870 607 0555, www.iflybritishmidland.com, also run a fairly regular service to London (Heathrow).
Three low-cost airlines,
Easyjet, tel: 0870 600 0000, www.easyjet.com
Go, tel: 0845 605 4321, and
Scotairways, tel: 0870 606 0707, www.scotairways.co.uk, fly to London (Luton), London (Stansted) and London (City).

Other UK destinations are well served, with BA flying to the Scottish Islands, Aberdeen, Inverness, Plymouth, Southampton, Birmingham, Bristol and Manchester. British Midland fly to East Midlands, Leeds and Manchester. Smaller carriers like **Eastern Airways**, tel: 01652 680600, www.easternairways.com, cover Norwich and Humberside, **Manx Airlines**, tel: 0345 256256, www.manx-airlines.com, the Isle of Man, **Jersey Airlines** serve the Channel Islands, Birmingham and Exeter. The low fares airline **Ryanair** www.ryanair.com, has nine flights a day to London Stansted, two to Paris, three to Dublin, one to Frankfurt and one to Brussels.

Direct flights to and from the USA are provided by:
American Airways, tel: 0345 789 789, www.aa.com, to Chicago, and **Continental**; tel: 0800 776 464, www.continental.com, to New York.
Air Canada, tel: 0990 247226, www.aircanada.ca, have a direct link with Toronto.
Icelandair, tel: 020 7388 5599, www.icelandair.net, fly to New York, Boston and Baltimore via their hub in Reykyavik.
KLM UK, tel: 0870 5074 074, www.klmuk.com, cover many international destinations via Amsterdam. Flights to Amsterdam are also provided by low-cost airline Easyjet. Brussels, Copenhagen and Malta are served by **Sabena**, tel: 0345 581 291, www.sabena.com, British Midlands and **Air Malta**, tel: 020 8785 3177, www.airmalta.com; while charter airline, **Air 2000**, tel: 01293 596620, www.air2000.co.uk, offers direct flights to most of the popular holiday destinations in Spain.
Scottish Citylink, tel: 08705 505050, www.citylink.co.uk, run a regular shuttle service from Glasgow Airport and Buchanan Street Bus Station with drop-off points at Glasgow Central and Queen Street railway stations. The service runs 630am–midnight Mon–Fri and Sun and from 6am–midnight on Saturday. During peak times there are eight buses an hour. The journey time is approximately 20 minutes. All services operate from the front of the terminal building. A 24-hour taxi service (Cab Fly, tel: 0141 848 4588) also operates from the front of the terminal, journey time is 20 minutes and costs approximately £17 to the city centre.

Glasgow Prestwick International Airport, tel: 01292 511000, www.glasgow.pwk.com, is a 30-minute drive south from Glasgow City Centre and 44 minutes by train. It is the only airport in Scotland with its own railway station, 80 metres from the check-in desks and accessed by an enclosed skywalk. Trains run every 30 minutes to Glasgow. Passengers in possession fo a valid flight ticket or Ryanair Official Itinerary can obtain a 50 percent discount on the standard rail fare to and from any Scotrail station.

Stagecoach Airbus operate a half-hourly service to Glasgow Buchanan Street Bus Station from the front of the concourse. A special one-way price of 50p is available to all passengers producing a valid airline ticket. Otherwise the charge is £3.50.

BY RAIL

Glasgow, one of the main cities within British Rail's network, has two busy stations: Central, for trains heading for destinations to the south (including London) and Queen Street, for the northern towns, the Highlands and Edinburgh. (The West Highland Line is a route of renowned beauty, passing through some of the country's finest scenery.)

Trains from Glasgow Central arrive at London Euston after 5½ hours. The first train for Euston leaves Glasgow Monday–Saturday 6.33am, the last at 11.55pm. Euston to Glasgow service: Monday–Friday starts at 6.25am, ending 11.40pm. This service is considerably reduced on Sundays, with the journey taking seven hours or even longer.

24-hour passenger enquiries, tel: 0345 484950.

Sleeper Reservations (Monday–Saturday 7am–10pm, Sunday 8am–10pm), tel: 08457 550033

BY ROAD

During the early 1960s, as part of a fiercely criticised communications policy, Glasgow pushed an inner ring road through the heart of the city, destroying many splendid buildings. Charing Cross, once an imposing area of almost Continental elegance, now stands as a testament to 20th-century road engineering. This "channel of noise and smell", as the new road was described by many, is more often acknowledged today as a excellent piece of planning and a necessary evil.

Glasgow would never claim that mistakes have not been made during its long and chequered history – it has frequently learned the hard way – but it is in part thanks to these past errors that its inner city renewal programme is the envy of many other cities.

From the south, Glasgow is approached by the M74, which is the continuation of the M6. Edinburgh and Glasgow are linked by the M8, and the A82 carries traffic to and from the west coast.

BY BUS

Scottish Citylink, tel: 08705 505050, www.citylink.co.uk, runs daily coaches between London's Victoria Coach Station and Glasgow's Buchanan Street Bus Station.

Stagecoach, tel: 333 1100, www.stagecoach-westernbuses.co.uk/, also runs frequent coaches between Buchanan Street and London's King's Cross. The journey takes between 7½ and 8½ hours depending on the number of stops made en route (check express services at time of booking).

Porter Services

Porters are like gold dust at Central and Queen Street Railway Stations, but they do exist. For disabled or infirm travellers, to be certain of assistance, telephone the Station Assistant beforehand at Central (tel: 335 4352) or Queen Street (tel: 332 9811).

At Glasgow Airport ask at the Information Desk on the first floor. People with special needs should contact the airport in advance on 887 1111. Neither airport nor railway porters charge, but tipping, though not mandatory, is customary.

Useful Addresses

TOURIST INFORMATION

Glasgow and Clyde Valley, 11 George Square,G2 1DY. tel: 204 4480.

Strathclyde Transport Travel Centre, St Enoch Square. tel: 226 4826.

Tourist Information Desk, Glasgow Airport. tel: 848 4440.

CONSULATES

Danish Consulate, Eadie House 74, Kirkintilloch Rd, Bishopbriggs G64 2AH, tel: 333 0618

German Consulate, Pentagon Centre 36, Washington Street G3 8AZ, tel: 226 8443.

Greek Consulate, 1 Kirklee Quadrant, tel: 334 0360.

Icelandic Consulate, 389 Argyle Street G2, tel: 221 6943.

Italian Vice-Consulate, 24 St Enoch Square, tel: 226 3000.

Netherlands Consulate, 3 Annandale Terrace, Old Kilpatrick G60 5DJ, tel: 01389 875744

Norwegian Consulate, 18 Woodside Crecsent G3 7UL, tel: 333 0618

Pakistan Vice-Consulate, 137 Norfolk Street G5, tel: 429 5335.

Spanish Consulate, 389 Argyle Street, tel: 221 6943.

Thai Consulate, 4 Woodside Place, tel: 353 5090.

The following countries have consulates in Edinburgh:

American Consulate General, 3 Regent Terrace EH7, tel: 0131-556 8315.

Canadian Consulate, Standard Life House, 30 Lothian Road, Edinburgh Midlothian EH1 2DH, tel: 0131 220 4333.

Practical Tips

Emergencies

SECURITY & CRIME

In emergencies, dial 999. No money is required to make a 999 call from a phone box; dial, and ask for either the Fire, Police or Ambulance service. For non-urgent enquiries contact the nearest Police Station: Cranstonhill Police Station, 945 Argyle Street, tel: 532 3200; St Enoch Centre, 55 St Enoch Square, tel: 532 3278; *North:* Baird Street, tel: 532 4100; *East:* London Road, tel: 532 4600; *South*: Craigie Street, tel: 423 1113.

MEDICAL SERVICES

There are several 24-hour Accident and Emergency hospitals in the city: Glasgow Royal Infirmary, 82–84 Castle Street, tel: 211 4000; Royal Hospital for Sick Children, Yorkhill (close to the Kelvin Hall), tel: 201 0000; Western Infirmary, Dumbarton Road, tel: 211 2000. At the emergency clinic at the Dental Hospital, 378 Sauchiehall Street, tel: 211 9600, hours are Mon–Fri 9–10.30am and 2–3.30 pm, Sunday 10.30–noon; there is a charge for treatment on Sundays.

Useful Numbers

- Directory enquiries **192**
- International directory enquiries **153**
- Assistance in making UK calls **100**
- Assistance in making international calls **155**
- Emergencies – police, fire and ambulance **999**

Media

NEWSPAPERS

The *Herald*, www.theherald.co.uk/, published in Glasgow since 1783, provides sound coverage of national, international and financial news, while the *Evening Times*, www.eveningtimes.co.uk/, the *Herald*'s sister paper, covers local news. The *Sunday Herald*, www.sundayherald.com/, another sister paper of the *Herald*, is a quality broadsheet covering national and international news.

The Glasgow-based *Daily Record*, www.dailyrecord.co.uk, is the most widely read tabloid in Scotland, which with its sister paper, the *Sunday Mail*, www.record-mail.co.uk, provide comprehensive coverage of local, national and international news.

But the top-selling Sunday paper in Scotland is the renowned *Sunday Post*, www.dcthomson.co.uk/mags/post/, which boasts a readership of 1.6 million and has quirky coverage.

Most of the London-based national newspapers now have a specifically Scottish edition and are widely available.

Scotland also produces a variety of business and literary magazines, along with a fair number of glossy freesheets that can be found in the smaller, upmarket shops throughout the city.

Specifically Scottish topics are covered by glossy monthlies like the *Scottish Field*, the *Scots Magazine*, www.scotsmagazine.com/ and *Caledonian*. The *List*, www.list.co.uk/, an Edinburgh-based listings magazine, provides comprehensive coverage of Glasgow events.

RADIO & TV

BBC Radio Scotland (FM 92.5-94.6 MW 810kHz/370m), www.bbc.co.uk/scotland/, is a national network with news and talk programmes. Scot FM (100.3 FM in), www.scot-fm.com/, broadcasts throughout central Scotland, and Radio Clyde (FM 102.5 MW 1152kHz/261m), www.radioclyde.co.uk, is the local commercial station. BBC Scotland and Scottish Television (STV), www.scottishtv.co.uk, are the two television stations based in the city. Most of their output is a relay of the national BBC1 and ITV networks, but they substitute a few hours each day of Scottish news, features and drama.

Postal Services

There are several post offices in the city centre including Cowcaddens, 5 Buccleugh Street, Anderston, 76 St Vincent Terrace and Charing Cross, 53 Sauchiehall Street. In the West End the most centrally situated is Hillhead sub-post office at 494 Byers Road.

Post offices open Monday–Friday 9am–5.30pm and Saturday 9am–12.30pm. Some post offices are housed within newsagents and supermarkets and open at slightly different times, with some closing for lunch and remaining closed on Wednesday afternoons. For information on services, tel: 0345 223344.

Telecoms

The traditional red telephone box has been replaced by modern glass booths, although a few of the older style still remain. There are two types, one operated by coins (£1, 50p, 20p and 10p) and the other by phonecards, which can be purchased from newsagents and post offices. Phone boxes are scattered throughout the city, and there are several inside the post office building in George Square. To enquire about BT services call 0800-190190. To call the operator, dial 100; Directory Enquiries, 192; Telephone Repair Service, 151; Talking Clock, 123.

Internet/Fax

All the major hotels have a fax service available to residents. In addition, faxes can be sent from city centre copying shops. For internet access, Easyeverything, two blocks from George Square, at

57/61 St Vincent Street, has 375 computers.

Tipping

Most restaurants do not add a service charge to the bill. In this case, it is normal (but not compulsory) to give a 10–15 percent tip. Check the bill carefully; if a charge for service is included, there is no need to pay extra unless you wish to reward exceptional service. If the service has been very poor, the service charge can be subtracted from the bill.

A similar percentage tip should be paid to hairdressers and taxi drivers. A tip of about £1 minimum is appropriate for porters at transport terminals or in your hotel. It is not necessary to tip in self-service establishments or pubs.

Contacts for Gays

The Gay and Lesbian Centre at 11 Dixon Street, just off St Enoch Square, tel: 221 7203, has a café, meeting rooms and information. Or call the Lesbian and Gay switchboard 7pm–10pm, tel: 332 8372, www.scotsgay.co.uk/

Religious Services

The main Sunday church services are at 11am. Many churches also hold a Sunday evening service.
Church of Scotland, St George's Tron Church, 165 Buchanan Street, G1, tel: 221 2141.
Episcopal Church of Scotland, Diocese of Glasgow, 5 St Vincent Place, G1, tel: 221 5720.
Catholic Church, Archdiocesian Office, 196 Clyde Street G1, tel: 226 5898.
Church of Jesus Christ of Latter Day Saints, Julian Avenue G12, tel: 357 1024.
Jewish Orthodox Synagogue, Garnethill, 29 Garnet Street G3, tel: 332 4151.
The Central Mosque, 1 Mosque Avenue, tel: 429 3132.
First Church of Christ Scientist, 87 Berkeley Street G3, tel: 248 1698.

Getting Around

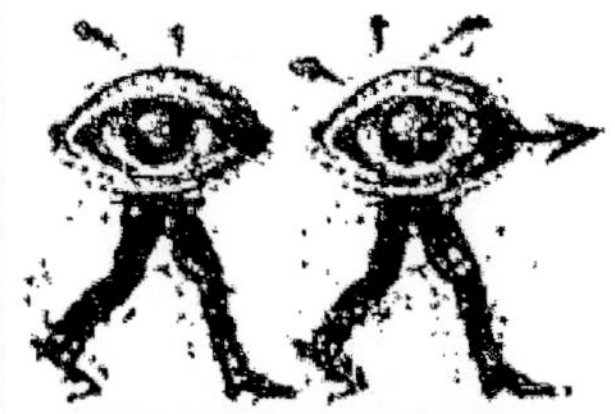

Orientation

Because Glasgow is built on so many hills, it is sometimes difficult to appreciate its area and wealth of architecture on foot. Yet walking is the best (if the most tiring) method of exploring. Do remember to lift your eyes occasionally from the hazards of the street to glance upwards at the wide range of Victorian building design and craftsmanship. Alternatively, for £2.50, unlimited travel for a day can be purchased on the city's underground railway.

Left Luggage

Glasgow Central Station has a bank of left luggage lockers located on platform 10.

Public Transport

BY BUS

A number of competing bus companies operate throughout Glasgow and tend to use the same bus stops and cover most of the city with frequent services (running every 10–15 minutes until about 11pm when the much-reduced Night Service operates). For information on these services, visit the Travel Centre at St Enoch Square, open Monday–Saturday 9.30am–7.30pm or telephone 226 4826 Monday–Saturday 7am–9pm; Sunday 9am–7.30pm.

BY UNDERGROUND

Glasgow has a small, 15-stop underground, known locally as the Clockwork Orange (its coaches are the same lurid colour as the Strathclyde buses). It is an excellent way to get around the city on a wet day, costing 90p regardless of the number of stops. It operates Monday–Saturday from 6.30am–10/10.30pm and on Sunday between 11am and 6pm. Trains run every 4–6 minutes at busy times, with 8-minute intervals during evenings and on Sundays.

A Discovery ticket permits one day's unlimited travel on the system.

The original cable-operated Subway was first opened on 14 December 1896, though it closed again the same day after a collision under the River Clyde; it re-opened five weeks later. The loss-making company was bought by Glasgow Corporation in 1922. The last train was hauled by cable in 1935, when a full electric service began. In 1977 the dilapidated system was shut down for modernisation; the new Underground was inaugurated by the Queen on 1 November 1979.

The total length of the system is 6½ miles (10.4 km) and the track gauge is an exceptionally narrow 4 ft (1.22 metres). Around 14 million passenger journeys are made each year. The deepest station is Buchanan Street and the shallowest Cessnock. The maximum speed of the cars is 34 mph (54 kph).

BY TAXI

Glasgow is well equipped with taxis. Unless it is pouring with rain, when demand exceeds supply, the black taxi cab is fairly easy to flag down. They run 24 hours a day and can be picked up from the taxi ranks outside Central Station, Queen Street Station and the two bus stations, at Anderston Cross and Buchanan Street. They may also be found on the following roads: Cambridge Street, Holland Street and Queen Margaret Drive (Great Western Road end).

The fare is displayed on the metre next to the driver. There is an extra late-night charge and normally a surcharge if the taxi is to travel to a destination beyond the city boundary. If travelling beyond the city limits it is prudent to obtain an estimate before setting off.

TOA Radio Taxis, tel: 556 3232; Glasgow Private Hire, tel: 400 5050; Glasgow Wide Taxis, tel: 429 7070.

Private Transport

BY CAR

Car Hire

There is a wide variety of self-drive car hire companies: **Connect Car** (nationwide), tel: 0807 282828; **Hertz**, 106 Waterloo Street, tel: 0141 248 7736; **Mitchells Hire Drive**, 260 Glasgow Road Rutherglen, tel: 647 3939; **Avis**, 161 North Street G3, tel: 221 2827; **Arnold Clark**, 10 Vinicombe Street G12, tel: 334 9501; **Europcar**, 38 Anderston Quay, tel: 248 8788; **Budget**, 101 Waterloo Street G2, tel: 243 2047. Most of the major companies also have a presence at Glasgow International Airport.

The following chauffeur-driven car hire companies also offer experienced guides: **American Limousines** UK, Boghall Street, tel: 774 0510; **Little's Chauffeur Drive**, 1282 Paisley Road West G52. tel: 883 2111.

Parking

Parking meters are used extensively throughout the city centre and take 20p coins. There are 24-hour multi-storey car parks at Anderston Cross, Cambridge Street, George Street, Mitchell Street, Oswald Street and Waterloo Street.

Where to Stay

Hotels

A wide variety of accommodation is available in Glasgow from simple bed and breakfast to hotels of an international standard. As Glasgow has grown in popularity as a major tourist destination, the number of hotel rooms has increased to provide extra capacity. A number of new budget hotels have been built in and around the city centre providing visitors with good-quality accommodation at an affordable price. Prices quoted are usually per person with a supplement payable for single occupation of a room and the price normally includes breakfast. However, in the newer and budget hotels prices are being quoted per room irrespective of the number of occupants, so check which applies when making a reservation.

Most of the larger hotels and guest houses will accept major credit and debit cards, but this may not be the case in small guest houses and it is not unusual to find some proprietors who expect to be paid in cash.

When enquiring about accommodation it is acceptable to ask to see the room before committing yourself. During the peak season it is advisable to book rooms well in advance.

Good-value accommodation can also be found in the student residences of the universities during the holiday period and other budget options include youth and backpacker hostels. Glasgow and Clyde Valley Tourist Board publish an annual accommodation guide containing over 300 entries.

Angus Hotel
970 Sauchiehall Street
Tel: 0141 357 5155
Private hotel in Georgian terrace by Kelvingrove Park and a few minutes walk from the art galleries, university and transport museum. 18 Rooms. **££**

Babbity Bowster
16–18 Blackfriars Street
Tel: 0141 552 5055
Named after a traditional Scottish dance, this place is better known for its food and atmosphere and its great folk music sessions. But it's a handy base in the Merchant City and close to the shopping and nightlife. 6 rooms. **££**

Bewleys Hotel
Bath Street
Tel: 353 0800
Bewley's Oriental Cafés were part of Dublin life since Joshua Bewley opened his first one in 1840. Having diversified into hotels, they opened their first Scottish one in Glasgow's Golden Z shopping area providing an excellent quality of comfort at a very low price. 103 rooms. **£**

Price Guide

Approximate guides to prices per person per night for two people sharing a double room are:

£ = below £30
££ = £30–£60
£££ = £60–£100
££££ = over £100.

The Brunswick Hotel
106–108 Brunswick Street
Tel: 552 0001
Situated in the Primevera building in the heart of the Merchant City, this small, modern hotel has air-conditioned rooms a café-bar and bistro. 22 rooms plus a two-level penthouse suite complete with sauna and kitchen. **££**

Carlton George Hotel
44 West George Street
Tel: 353 6373
A class establishment in the city centre near George Square and Queen Street Station. The rooftop restaurant has some of the finest

dining views of Glasgow and food to match. 65 rooms. **£££**

Cathedral House
28–32 Cathedral Street
Tel: 552 3519
Another of those superb eateries with rooms that have sprung up all over the city with some great views of the Necropolis and the Cathedral. 8 rooms. **££**

The Devonshire
5 Devonshire Gardens
Tel: 339 7878
Small friendly five-star hotel tucked away on the corner of a tree-lined Victorian terrace in the West End. Luxury from a bygone age combined with the latest in high-tech and modern conveniences. From the Victorian entrance hall, a majestic staircase sweeps upstairs past a conservatory with original stained glass on the half landing. This is as good as hotels get. 14 rooms. **££££**

One Devonshire Gardens
1 Devonshire Gardens
Tel: 339 2001
At the other end of the terrace from the Devonshire is Ken McCulloch's conversion of three town houses much loved by visiting celebrities. Opened in one building in 1986, it won the Egon Ronay Hotel of the Year award in 1994. Celebrity chef, Gordon Ramsay took over the restaurant in 2001. 27 rooms. **££££**

Ewington Hotel
Balmoral Terrace, 132 Queens Drive
Tel: 0141 423 1152
South-side town house with some interesting international cuisine. A mere six minutes to the city centre by train and very close to the Burrell Collection. 45 rooms. **££**

Glasgow Hilton
1 William Street, G3
Tel: 0141 204 5555
Sheer unashamed luxury in one of the city's five-star hotels. Every conceivable luxury including two restaurants, a pool, gymnasium and sauna. Twenty floors with five of them non-smoking. 319 rooms. **££££**

The Glasgow Thistle
36 Cambridge Street
Tel: 0870 333 9154
Tony Blair, the Prime Minister, stayed here, so it has to be good. Situated behind Sauchiehall Street, is is well placed for exploring the city centre and in particular the School of Art and the Willow Tea Room. Facilities include the Otium Health & Leisure Club with swimming pool, steam room and fitness equipment, and the on-site car parking. 300 Rooms. **££££**

Jurys Glasgow Hotel
Great Western Road
Tel: 334 8161
Budget hotel in the West End complete with pool, fitness suite, jacuzzi and sunbed. 136 rooms. **££**

The Inn on The Green
25 Greenhead Street
Tel: 554 0165
Boutique-style hotel in a B-listed building on the edge of Glasgow Green five minutes from the city centre. Each of the rooms has an individual style of décor and furnishing; satellite TV, electronic safe and a trouser press. The restaurant is as famous for its live jazz as for the quality of its food. 18 rooms. **££**

Langs Hotel
2 Port Dundas Place
Tel: 332 0330
Just across the road from the Royal Concert hall and Buchanan Galleries and adjacent to Buchanan Street bus station, this is one of the finest and newest of Glasgow's hotels. Las Brisas, the restaurant, serves excellent Californian cuisine. 100 rooms. **££–£££**

The Merchant Lodge
52 Virginia Street
Tel: 0141 552 2424
Tucked away in a street behind the Corinthian in the Merchant City, this is a hidden gem and doesn't even look like a hotel from the outside. This former tobacco lord's home is one of the oldest buildings in the city and features a cobbled courtyard and an old stone turnpike stair. 40 rooms. **£**

The Millennium Hotel
50 George Square
Tel: 0141 332 6711
The latest incarnation of one of Glasgow's grand old hotels in a splendid Victorian building on the edge of George Square. Fully refurbished in 2000, it is now the premier deluxe hotel in the city centre. The glass veranda fronting the hotel is one of the most atmospheric places to sit with a drink and watch Glasgow go by. 117 rooms. **£££**

The Pipers Tryst
30–34 McPhater Street
Tel: 353 0220
This very small hotel is part of the Glasgow Piping Centre and is very close to the Royal Concert Hall and the city centre – and no, the sound of bagpipes will neither keep you awake nor wake you early in the morning. 8 rooms. **££**

Greek Thomson Hotel
140 Elderslie Street
Tel: 332 6556
Budget option near Charing Cross. Little or no connection to "Greek" Thomson other than the use of his name. Nevertheless it's a small friendly hotel that will provide a very comfortable base and an awesome breakfast. 17 rooms. **£**

Groucho St Judes
190 Bath Street
Tel: 352 8800
Yet another superb small hotel attached to a smashing restaurant in the fashionable Merchant City. 6 rooms. **££**

Hillhead Hotel
32 Cecil Street
Tel: 0141 339 7733
Close to Byers Road and the busy West End, this small, warm and friendly hotel also offers free car parking. 10 Rooms. **£**

Kelvin Hotel
15 Buckingham Terrace
Tel: 0141 339 7143
Private, family-run hotel in one of the Victorian terraces just off Great Western Road and very close to the Botanic Gardens and Byers Road. 9 rooms. **£**

Kirklee Hotel
11 Kensington Gate
Tel: 0141 334 5555
An Edwardian town house in an almost original condition in the West End conservation area. The extensive collection of paintings and drawings add to the atmosphere of a bygone age. One

Price Guide

Approximate guides to prices per person per night for two people sharing a double room are:

£ = below £30
££ = £30–£60
£££ = £60–£100
££££ = over £100.

of the hidden gems of Glasgow. 9 rooms. **££**

Malmaison
278 West George Street
Tel: 572 1000
Upmarket city-centre hotel with gym and brasserie bar. 72 Rooms. **£££**

Manor Park Hotel
28 Balshagray Road
Tel: 339 2143
Privately run, top-quality wee hotel in the West End where Gaelic is spoken and promoted throughout by the proprietors Catherine and Angus. 10 rooms. **£–££**

Rennie Mackintosh
59 Union Street
Tel: 221 0050
Mackintosh décor provides a rather tenuous link with the architect but nevertheless this is a grand hotel on the doorstep of Central Station and just across the street from Greek Thomson's Egyptian Halls. Cheap and cheerful and with a breakfast that will keep you going all day. 40 rooms. **£**

Strathclyde Graduate Business School Hotel and Conference Centre
199 Cathedral Street
Tel: 553 6000
Modern building near the oldest part of the city and well situated for exploring the area round the cathedral and the Merchant city. 107 rooms. **££**

Theatre Hotel
25–27 Elmbank Street
Tel: 227 2772
Traditional Scottish hospitality is a speciality in this tastefully converted listed building close to the city centre. 55 rooms. **££**

The Townhouse Hotel
21 Royal Crescent
Tel: 0141 332 9009
Set back from Sauchiehall Street and overlooking private gardens in a tree-lined terrace of handsome Victorian town houses, this hotel is close to the city centre, Kelvingrove and the university. 17 rooms. **£**

The Travel Inn
187 George Street
Tel: 553 2700
Another newly built budget hotel in the Merchant City just two blocks behind the city chambers and probably the best value-for-money deal in the city centre. 254 rooms. **£**

Wickets
52 Fortrose Street
Tel: 334 9334
Small, friendly West End hotel situated next to a cricket ground and close to Kelvingrove Art Gallery and Museum and the Transport Museum. 11 rooms. **££**

Bed and Breakfast

Alamo Guest House
46 Gray Street
Tel: 339 2395
Beautifully furnished guesthouse on a quiet road alongside Kelvingrove Park. **£**

Chez Nous
33 Hillhead Street
Tel: 334 2977
Close to Glasgow University and Hillhead underground. **£**

The Flower House Bed & Breakfast
33 St Vincent Crescent
Tel: 204 2846
The flowers crowding round the front of the building explain the name. A warm, friendly guest house. 3 rooms. **££**

Iona Guest House
39 Hillhead Street
Tel: 334 2346
Well-established and comfortable: close to the Botanic Gardens. **£**

McLays Guest House
268 Renfrew Street
Tel: 332 4796
Well-appointed, comfortable guest house only a few minutes from the city centre. **£**

Kirkland House
42 St Vincent Crescent
Tel: 248 3458
Open all year. In the quieter part of this beautiful crescent. **££**

The Town House
4 Hughenden Terrace
Tel: 357 0862
Situated to the west of the city. Well-established and comfortable guest house in a listed Victorian building. **£££**

University of Glasgow
Cairncross House,
20 Kelvinhaugh Place
Tel: 330 5385
July–Sep vacation accommodation in student rooms. 153 units. **£**

University of Strathclyde
Baird Hall, 460 Sauchiehall Street
Tel: 553 4148
Campus accommodation based in an Art Deco building that was the Beresford Hotel in a previous life. Rooms available throughout the year. **£**

B & B Price Guide

£ = under £25
££ = £25–£35
£££ = over £35

Self-Catering

The Serviced Apartment Company
53 Cochrane Street
Tel: 204 4610
Luxury serviced apartments in the Merchant City overlooking George Square. The interior-designed apartments include washing machine, dishwasher, satellite TV and telephone. From £420 per week.

University of Glasgow
Kelvinhaugh Gate
115–119 Kelvinhaugh Street
Tel: 330 5385
Student flats available only during July–Sept. Sleeps 1–5 people. From £210 per week per person.

West End Apartments
401 North Woodside Road
Tel: 342 4060
Near Kelvinbridge Underground station, these apartments are self contained with all the usual facilities including a cooker, refrigerator and microwave. From £259 per week.

Campgrounds

There is a lack of large campsites in and around Glasgow; many are mainly residential with only a few plots to rent, so telephone in advance to check.

Craigendmuir Caravan Park
Campsie View, Stepps
Tel: 779 4159
Accommodation suitable for all self-catering holidays, plus amenities for camper vans and tents. From £8 per night. Open all year round. Take the M80 out of town and follow the signs for Stepps.

Lomond Woods Caravan Park
Tullichewan Old Luss Road
Balloch
Tel: 01389 755000
www.holiday-parks.co.uk/
This is one of the largest sites close to Glasgow; take the turning for Balloch off the A82.

Youth Hostels

Bunkum Backpackers
26 Hillhead Street
Tel: 581 4481
Dormitory accommodation in the West End from £9 per night. Open all year.

Euro Hostel
318 Clyde Street
Tel: 222 2828
This is hostelling 21st century-style. In a former hotel building on the banks of the Clyde, all rooms are en suite and there is a choice of sharing or single. Cycle storage, Internet access, games room, laundry and fresh bed linen. Within a five-minute walk of Central Station. Breakfast is included in the price. Open all year. 115 rooms. **£**

Glasgow Backpackers Hostel
Maclay Hall, 17 Park Terrace
Tel: 332 9099
Twin, triple or dormitory rooms from £10 per person. Open Jul–Sep only.

Glasgow Youth Hostel
8 Park Terrace
Tel: 332 3004
The original Glasgow hostel, part of the Scottish Youth Hostels network. All rooms are en suite. Open all year. From £10 per person.

Where to Eat

Eating Out

Eating in Glasgow has improved beyond measure in the past few years with new restaurants opening on an almost weekly basis. You'll find everything here and at a price to suit most pockets, from the trendy and expensive restaurants of the celebrity chefs to cheap and cheerful café-bars. For up-to-the-minute details of the latest 'in' places, check the weekly listings magazine *The List*, or get a copy of their latest *Eating and Drinking Guide to Edinburgh and Glasgow*, or go to www.list.co.uk/eat.htm.

It is still possible to eat well, without wine, for under £10.

Price Guide

Approximate guide to prices for a three-course evening meal excluding wine:

£ = under £10
££ = £10–£20
£££ = over £20.

Scottish

(These restaurants do not serve *only* Scottish food.)

Babbity Bowster
16 Blackfriars Street
Tel: 552 5055
Friendly upstairs restaurant serving Scottish food. Renowned for its Burn's Night supper. **££**

Nairn's
13 Woodside Crescent
Tel: 353 0707
www.nairns.co.uk
Nick Nairn has built a solid reputation for modern high-quality Scottish cooking at an affordable price and his new lunchtime set menus will set you back less than £10. **£–£££**

Rab Ha's
83 Hutcheson Street
Tel: 553 1545
The Rab in question was a famous Glasgow glutton who has survived as a children's street rhyme. Interesting dishes with fresh fish and game. **££**

International

City Merchant
97 Candleriggs
Tel: 553 1577
www.citymerchant.co.uk
West Coast seafood a speciality. **££**

Two Fat Ladies
88 Dumbarton Road
Tel: 339 1944
Bingo addicts will know how this restaurant got its name. Small and gets very busy so book in advance if you want to sample the fishy treats like Cullen Skink, Loch Fyne oyster gratin or the steamed seabass with green pepper. **££**

The Buttery
652 Argyle Street
Tel: 221 8188
It looks on the outside like an ancient Glasgow corner pub that has somehow escaped demolition. Inside is a traditional Victorian pub and restaurant with all the ambience of a bygone age. The food is nothing short of superb and the deserts sinful. Try them all as a selection on one plate. **£££**

The Belfry
652 Argyle Street
Tel: 221 0630
Very comfortable and restful restaurant below The Buttery offering a reasonably priced menu. **££**

Amarylis
1 Devonshire Gardens
Great Western Road
Tel: 339 2001
Holder of one Michelin star and although the former chef, Andrew Fairlie, has departed to Gleneagles, the restaurant has been taken over by the triple Michelin-starred celebrity chef, Gordon Ramsay, a native Glaswegian. Booking is now essential. **£££**

Groucho Saint Jude's
190 Bath Street
Tel: 352 8800
www.grouchosaintjudes.com
A "see and be seen" place much frequented by media types. Chargrilling is a speciality as are the puddings and the superb selection of wines to accompany them. **££**

The Ubiquitous Chip
12 Ashton Lane
Tel: 334 5007
The Chip is much more than a Glasgow institution. For over 30 years Ronnie Clydesdale has ensured that it is a legend in many people's lunchbreaks, not to mention in the evening. Beloved by the people at the BBC up the road, it also attracts more than its fair share of international and local celebrities. It's the ambience and the food that brings them and scores of others. **£££**

Stravaigin
28–30 Gibson Street
Tel: 334 2665
www.stravaigin.com
Fresh Scottish ingredients with an international twist. Fast becoming one of Glasgow's favourite restaurants. The prime fillet served medium rare on a bed of pesto mashed potatoes is outstanding. Great wine list. **££**

The Inn On the Green
23 Greenhead Street
Tel: 554 0165
www.theinnonthegreen.co.uk
While international, the emphasis is on good Scottish ingredients and traditions. The beef with haggis and whisky is particularly good, as is the traditional stew from the North East, Cullen Skink. Live piano every night with occasional bands. **££**

Yes
22 West Nile Street
Tel: 221 8044
A class establishment with an ever-changing innovative menu serving everything from fillet of Sea Bream with ravioli to pan-fried chicken with savoury bread and butter pudding. Not cheap but worth the money.
£££

78 St Vincent
78 St Vincent Street
Tel: 248 7878
www.78stvincent.com
This should be the fate of all banks. Following the collapse of the BCCI Bank, this early 20th-century building was converted into a restaurant with a particularly Parisian atmosphere. The two-course pre-theatre deal at £10 is one of the many bargains to be had in the city centre. **££**

Price Guide

Approximate guide to prices for a three-course evening meal excluding wine:
£ = under £10
££ = £10–£20
£££ = over £20.

Fish

Mussel Inn
157 Hope Street
Tel: 572 1405
www.mussel-inn.co.uk
Mussels, scallops and oysters are the stars of this restaurant opened by a collective of West Coast shellfish producers. **££**

Harry Ramsden's
251 Paisley Road
Tel: 429 3700
Ten years on the south bank of the Clyde and still the best fish and chips in town. **£**

The Rogano
11 Exchange Place
Tel: 248 4055
One of the city's oldest restaurants, decorated in 1930s Art Deco, giving a slightly austere feel. When the fish is good (other food also served) it is excellent but tends to rest a wee bit on its laurels. **£££**

Italian

The Battlefield Rest
55 Battlefield Road
Tel: 636 6955
This was a former tram stop complete with waiting room and ticket office. Now it is one of the most popular eating spots on the south side. The lunchtime menu is incredibly cheap with two courses for under £6, and other special deals are available in the early evening as a pre-theatre menu.
£–££

Bon Gusto
30 Bothwell Street
Tel: 204 5442
Another bank put to better use. Crisp salads, freshly cooked pizzas and huge helpings of pasta combine to make this new kid on the block a perfect choice for a night out. **££**

Fazzi's
65–67 Cambridge Street
Tel: 332 0941
Exceedingly cheap but excellent two-course lunches can be had in this establishment that is a cross between a delicatessen and a café bar. Delicious home-made pizzas, imported cheeses and hams and plenty of pasta. And you can buy most of the ingredients to take home and try it yourself. **£**

L'Ariosto
92–94 Mitchell Street
Tel: 221 0971
This place looks tiny from the front, but inside it opens out on to a traditional Italian courtyard, although this one is indoors. This is Tuscan cuisine at its very best, and by the middle of the main course, after a glass or three of the excellent house red you'll forget you're in Glasgow.
££

La Parmigiana
447 Great Western Road
Tel: 334 0686
Small restaurant with an excellent lunch menu. Particularly good is the roasted Gressingham duck in a delicious grape and red wine sauce.
££

Ristorante la Fiorentina
2 Paisley Road West,
Paisley Road Toll
Tel: 420 1585
Upmarket Italian restaurant south of the river but pretty near the city. Classic Tuscan cooking meets modern Mediterranean with a classy wine list and great seafood.
£££

La Lanterna
35 Hope Street
Tel: 221 9160
Basement restaurant opposite Central Station much frequented by Glasgow's Italian population. **££**

The Fire Station
33 Ingram Street
Tel: 552 2929
Friendly staff in large old fire station – pasta a speciality. **£**

Di Maggio's
21 Royal Exchange Square
Tel: 248 2111
61 Ruthven Lane
Tel: 334 6000
1038 Pollokshaws Road
Tel: 632 4194
Straightforward, no-nonsense Italian cooking at an affordable price. A favourite with students. **£**

Indian

Café India
171 North Street
Tel: 248 4074
Large restaurant with a pleasant ambience. Extensive wine list. **££**

Koh-i-Noor
235 North Street
Tel: 221 1555
Long-established favourite which established the fantastic mid-week buffet of 10 starters, 11 main courses and a host of sweets. As much as you can eat and all for less than £10. **£**

Ashoka
108 Elderslie Street
Tel: 221 1761
www.ashokaflame.co.uk
This is the original Ashoka, located near the Mitchell Library and the best of several Indian restaurants in the vincinity. There is an excellent buffet and good *à la carte* but try also the Ashoka Flame in the basement for a touch of something different. **££**

Ashoka Ashton Lane
19 Ashton Lane
Tel: 0141 337 1115
www.harleguingroup.net
No connection with the original Ashoka but part of a chain of similar restaurants found throughout the city. Right in the heart of the West End and student country. It's usually packed, so booking is advisable. **££**

Shish Mahal
60–68 Park Road
Tel: 0800 072 5771
www.shishmahal.co.uk
Established in 1964 as one of the original curry houses and still run by the same family. Hundreds of Glaswegians were first introduced to Indian food here and countless more had their first stab at cooking curries at home using the Shish Mahal Cookbook. **££**

Chinese

Amber Regent
50 West Regent Street
Tel: 331 1655
Up-market with a wide selection of Cantonese dishes and a good selection of dim sum. Main courses are half price before 7pm during the week. Booking essential, particularly at the weekend. **££**

Peking Inn
191 Hope Street
Tel: 332 7120
Delightful Cantonese/Pekinese restaurant serving tasty seafood. Booking essential, particularly at the weekend, when long queues are likely. **££**

Ho Wong
82 York Street
Tel: 221 3550
Off the beaten track a bit, but a more upmarket restaurant serving excellent Cantonese dishes and a superb selection of seafood. **££**

Miscellaneous

Air Organic
36 Kelvingrove Street
Tel: 0141 564 5200
Pacific rim-influenced cuisine with a wide selection of dishes from Thai fishcakes to Miso broth, and the salads are unbeatable, particularly the spinach in a dressing of crème fraîche and balsamic vinegar served on top of a cold lightly poached egg and with optional anchovies. **££**

The Arches Café Bar
253 Argyle Street
Tel: 0901 022 0300
www.thearches.co.uk
The arches is an arts venue under the main railway bridge at Central Station. This café-bar is in the cellar underneath and it has been set up like a minimalist jazz bar. The menu is limited but what they have is superb and very cheap. Spicy chicken strips with bread and salad and a beer makes a good pre-theatre dinner or a filling lunch. **£**

Brel
39–43 Ashton Lane
Tel: 342 4966
Belgian food and drink served in a former mews stable block. Wooden tables with brown paper covers match the simplicity of the original bare-brick and white-tile décor and the food is awesome, particularly the Belgian *moules*, which come with a variety of sauces.

Café Gandolfi
64 Albion Street
Tel: 552 6813
Fresh Scottish ingredients with a slight Mediterranean twist is the staple of this Merchant City eaterie. Unlike most of the rest of the trendy places in the Merchant City, the Café Gandolfi has been here for 20 years, way back when this was a less than fashionable part of town. **£–££**

Corinthian
191 Ingram Street
Tel: 552 1101
www.corinthian.uk.com
This fine Victorian building was once a bank and after that a courthouse. Now restored to its original grandeur, it is enjoying a new lease of life as a gathering spot for the smart and trendy. It has several bars and a nightclub as well as a restaurant, making it a bit of a one-stop shop for a night out, but despite that the food is very, very good. A fine selection of wines are stored in the bank's former safes. **£££**

Eurasia
150 St Vincent Street
Tel: 0141 204 1150
Ferrier Richardson's latest gift to the people of Glasgow. From the man who gave us Yes comes the latest word in fusion cooking and a constantly changing set-price menu. If you like top quality, adventurous

cooking at a reasonable price and have time for just one meal in Glasgow, have it here.

Fusion Sushi Bar
41 Byres Road
Tel: 0141 339 3666
Authentic Japanese food, Glasgow-style, in a small, intimate restaurant with a difference and a set-price lunch for under a fiver. **£**

Nardini's
24 Cambridge Street
Tel: 333 1374
Famed for generations in the seaside town of Largs, this famous ice-cream family recently exported their Art Deco-style of café and legendary ice cream to Glasgow. **£**

Pancho Villas
26 Bell Street
Tel: 552 7737
Owned and run by a Mexican, this is about as good as Mexican eating gets in the UK. With the quality of its food and its Merchant City location it attracts a wide mix of people and can get busy. **£–££**

Sloans
Argyll Arcade
Tel: 221 8917
An old, pleasant, traditional pub-restaurant serving steak pies, mince, chips and custard. **£**

Thai Fountain
2 Woodside Crescent
Tel: 332 1599
Classic and innovative Thai cuisine produced from fresh ingredients make this the top spot in Glasgow. Main courses can be had for half price before 6.30pm weekdays and 6pm on a Saturday. **£–££**

Tron Theatre
Chisholm Street
Tel: 552 8587
Café-bar serving a wide range of foods from sandwiches and soup to Scottish favourites like herring in oatmeal. **£**

University Café
87 Byres Road
Tel: 339 5217
It seems to have been here forever with its Art Deco façade, traditional booths and real Italian ice cream. The Verrecchia family have been feeding west-enders and students formore than 70 years. Ideologically sound it is not, but if you crave a wee taste of the stuff that puts Glasgow at the top of the world's heart-attack league then this is the place. Try the macaroni cheese, the fish and chips or the full Scottish, coronary-on-a-plate, breakfast then this is the place. And remember anything in moderation won't kill you. **£**

Whistler's Mother
116 Byres Road
Tel: 334 2666
Dutch bistro with cosmopolitan foods including tasty, tangy salads. **£**

Willow Tea Rooms
217 Sauchiehall Street
Tel: 332 0521
Most tourist attractions have a tearoom. In this case it's the tearoom that is the attraction. Charles Rennie Mackintosh designed the interior of this for tearoom baroness Kate Cranston, and it's still possible to take lunch here or enjoy afternoon tea. **£**

Price Guide

Approximate guide to prices for a three-course evening meal excluding wine:

£ = under £10
££ = £10–£20
£££ = over £20.

Vegetarian

Many of the bistros/brasseries offer at least one vegetarian dish. Most of the larger restaurants will cater for vegetarians but it is wise to phone beforehand to forewarn them. The following are strictly vegetarian.

The Bay Tree Café
403 Great Western Road
Tel: 334 5898
Middle Eastern cuisine predominately from Egypt, Turkey and the Arabian countries is what to expect in this friendly little place with a café atmosphere. **£**

The 13th Note
50–60 King Street
Tel: 553 1638
Strictly vegetarian and vegan-based mainly on Greek dishes, particularly *mezzes*, but with other influences as wide-ranging as Italy and the Far East. **£**

Grassroots Café
97 St Georges Road
Tel: 333 0534
Cosy sofas, curtained booths and modern décor create a unique atmosphere in this Charing Cross establishment. As well as being vegetarian, they also cater for vegans and people on gluten- and wheat-free diets. Superb sandwiches, crispy salads and a wide variety of main dishes. **£**

The Granary
82 Howard Street
Tel: 226 3770
Comfortable and friendly atmosphere in the city centre. Excellent baking. **£**

Drinking Notes

PUBS

The Glasgow pub still exists, even though the visitor or the returning Glaswegian is much more likely to notice the slick new brasseries with their highly polished facades and gleaming tables.

Most pubs sell a selection of real ale of varying strengths known as 60 shilling, 70 shilling and 80 shilling. Imported bottled beers are *de rigueur* in brasseries, with real ale putting in a rare appearance. Most city pubs now also serve basic food.

The majority of city pubs are open from 11am until 11pm on Sunday through Thursday and from 11am until midnight on Friday and Saturday. During festivals some pubs remain open until 2am.

A few traditional favourites where entertainment is often provided unconsciously by Glaswegians are:

Bon Accord, 151 North Street.
Corn Exchange, 88 Gordon Street.
Exchequer Bar, 59 Dumbarton Road; also has a beer garden.
Fixx II, 86 Miller Street.
Griffin, 226 Bath Street. This watering hole has three bars: serious drinkers make for the Griffin; the Griffiny has a lounge;

and the Griffinette is just that wee bit more classy.
Halt Bar, 160 Woodlands Road: popular with artists, journalists and film makers; regular live music.
Heraghty's Free House, 708 Pollokshaws Road: traditional south-side pub much frequented and written about by journalist Jack McLean.
Horseshoe Bar, 17–21 Drury Street: the longest continuous bar in Europe.
Ingram, 138 Queen Street.
Scotch Corner Bar, 221 Buchanan Street: stocks more than 150 different whiskies.
The Saracen Head, 209 Gallowgate. One of the oldest pubs in town and previously a very wild place. Considerably tamer these days, it still retains much of the atmosphere of a traditional Glasgow boozers.

WINE BARS

Bull and Bear, 158 Buchanan Street. In the Stock Exchange building.
Smiths, 47 West Nile Street.

Attractions

Places of Interest

HISTORIC BUILDINGS

City Chambers, George Square, tel: 287 4018, www.glasgow.gov.uk. Tours Monday–Friday at 10.30am and 2.30pm. Lavishly decorated inside with marble pillars, delicate plasterwork and mosaic floors. An excellent example of the wealth in the city in the late 1800s.
Glasgow Cathedral, Castle Street, tel: 552 6891. April–September Monday–Saturday 9.30am–7pm; Sunday 2–5pm. October–March Monday–Saturday 9.30am–4pm; Sunday 2–4pm. Outstanding example of pre-Reformation Gothic architecture from the 12th century.
Glasgow School of Art, 167 Renfrew Street, tel: 353 4500. Monday–Friday 10am–noon and 2–4pm (fee for tour). One of the best examples of Charles Rennie Mackintosh's work to be found in the city. Started in 1896, it is built on the steep incline of a drumlin. Look out for the fabulous oriels on the western section (built 1907) rising to a height of 65 ft (21 metres).
Headquarters of Charles Rennie Mackintosh Society, 780 Garscube Road, tel: 946 6600. Tuesday, Thursday, Friday noon–5.30pm; Saturday 10.30–1pm; at other times by arrangement. These are in the former and recently renovated Queen's Cross church, which is from the Mackintosh drawing board. Library, small Mackintosh exhibition and refreshments.
Hutchesons' Hall, 158 Ingram Street, tel: 552 8391. Monday–Friday 9am–5pm. This 1802 building has an impressive hall.
Merchants' House, 7 West George Street, tel: 221 8272. May–September: Mon–Thurs, 9am–12.30pm. Home of the Glasgow Chamber of Commerce with two superb halls.
Mitchell Library, North Street, tel: 305 2999. Monday–Friday 9.30am–9pm; Saturday 9.30am–5pm. The largest public reference library in Europe is housed in an impressive building. The west section contains a theatre, café and conference rooms, which may be entered via Granville Street. For those interested in learning more about Glasgow, a visit to the Glasgow Room on the third floor is obligatory.
Stock Exchange, 69 Buchanan Street, tel: 221 7060. Monday–Friday 10am–4.30pm. Modern interior within exceptional example of Venetian Gothic architecture.
Trades House, 85 Glassford Street, tel: 552 5071. Open by appointment only. Designed by Robert Adam with magnificent interior.
Templeton Carpet Factory. On the northern edge of Glasgow Green. An extraordinary building, based on the Doge's Palace in Venice, with a brightly coloured facade belonging to a warmer climate. Now a business centre.

CHURCHES & GRAVEYARDS

Glasgow Cathedral as it stands today was begun in the middle of the 12th century by Bishop William de Bondington. St Mungo, Glasgow's patron saint, was buried here in AD 603. Observe the excellent collection of post-war stained-glass windows.

Several old churches of note are scattered throughout the city. One of the more central is St George's Tron in Buchanan Street. Modern churches of note are rare within the city, but St Charles Roman Catholic Church in Kelvinside Gardens has a wonderful, calming atmosphere, with Benno Schotz's "Stations of the Cross" as an added bonus.

The Necropolis by Glasgow Cathedral was modelled on the Père Lachaise Cemetery in Paris and is filled with temples, pillars and obelisks erected by the then wealthy of the city. More than 250,000 graves lie in the South Necropolis, off Caledonia Road. Both paupers and millionaires were buried here.

PUBLIC GALLERIES & MUSEUMS

Admission, unless stated to the contrary, is free.

Burrell Collection, Pollok Country Park, tel: 287 2550. Monday–Saturday 10am–5pm; Sunday 2–5pm. Enormous, catholic collection including Daumier cartoons, ivories, glass and tapestries. Several rooms of William Burrell's home, Hutton Castle, have been recreated as requested by Burrell when donating the collection to Glasgow.

Collins Gallery, University of Strathclyde, Richmond Street, tel: 552 4400. Monday–Friday l0am–5pm; Saturday noon–4pm. Contemporary exhibitions of photography, sculpture and paintings.

Hunterian Art Gallery, University of Glasgow, tel: 330 5431. Monday–Saturday 9.30am–5pm. Excellent collection of 19th- and 20th-century French and Scottish works plus substantial print collection including many Whistlers. Superb re-creation of the house once occupied by Mackintosh situated in the gallery's tower. Open same hours as museum but closes for an hour at 12.30pm. (Admission charge to Mackintosh house.)

Hunterian Museum, University of Glasgow, tel: 330 4221. Monday–Saturday 9.30am–5pm. Includes extensive coin and medal collection dating back to ancient Greece.

Kelvingrove Art Gallery and Museum, Kelvingrove Park, tel: 287 2700. Daily 10am–5pm except Friday and Sunday 11am–5pm. The UK's best civic collection of British and European paintings. Also displays of arms and armour, the Glasgow style, porcelain, silver, pottery and natural history, archaeology, history and ethnography. Will close some time in 2002 for two years as part of a major refurbishment. The core of the picture collection will be temporarily housed in the McLellan galleries while other selected paintings embark on a world tour.

McLellan Galleries, 270 Sauchiehall Street. Hours vary. Major venue for temporary local and touring exhibitions of paintings and sculpture.

Museum of Transport, Kelvin Hall, tel: 287 2700. Daily 10am–5pm except Friday and Sunday 11am–5pm. Fascinating exhibits with a fine collection of tramcars and railway locomotives. The Clyde Room has an outstanding collection of model ships.

People's Palace, Glasgow Green, tel: 554 0223. Daily 10am–5pm except Friday and Sunday 11am–5pm. The social history of Glasgow is explained through its exhibits.

Pollok House, Pollok Country Park, tel: 632 0274. Daily 10am–5pm except Friday and Sunday 11am–5pm. A beautiful 18th-century Robert Adam house with superb collection of Spanish paintings and works of others, including William Blake.

Provand's Lordship, 3 Castle Street, tel: 553 2557, www.glasgow.gov.uk. Daily 10am–5pm except Friday and Sunday 11am–5pm. Only surviving medieval house in the city. One room has been left as it would have been when the hospital chaplain was resident.

Regimental Museum of the Royal Highland Fusiliers, 518 Sauchiehall Street, tel: 332 0961. Daily 9am–4.30; closes 4pm Friday. Uniforms and other militaria relating to the regiment's fascinating 300-year history.

The Tenement House, 145 Buccleuch Street, tel: 333 0183. March–October, daily 2–5pm Between 1911 and 1965 one lady lived in this house, changing none of its features. Today it remains as it was, with gas lighting, lace curtains and old newspaper cuttings. (Admission charge.)

PRIVATE GALLERIES

Glasgow has a host of small privately run galleries which supplement the large civic collections with frequently changing exhibitions. Entry is normally free.

T & R Annan, 164 Woodlands Road, tel: 332 0028. www.annangaleries.co.uk Monday–Friday 10am–5pm; Saturday 10am–12.30pm. This gallery has been owned by the same family since 1855, selling original paintings and prints mainly in traditional style. Also home of the Annan collection of old photographs.

Compass Gallery, 178 West Regent Street, tel: 221 6370. Monday–Saturday 10am–5.30pm. A gallery renowned for helping young artists launch their work.

Cyril Gerber Fine Art, 148 West Regent Street, tel: 204 0276/221 3095. Regularly changing exhibitions concentrating on Scottish artists. Monday–Friday 9.30am–5.30pm; Saturday 9.30am–5.30pm.

Gallery of Modern Art, Queen Street, tel: 229 1996. Glasgow's newest art gallery, featuring the work of local artists on four floors. Daily 10am–5pm except Friday and Sunday 11am–5pm.

Mackintosh & Company, situated in the Glasgow Style Gallery, 1 Bothwell Lane, tel: 357 3601. Monday–Friday 9.30am–5.30pm; Saturday 10am–5.30pm. Art Nouveau glass, metalwork, Glasgow-Style furniture and quality copies of Rennie Mackintosh furniture, mirrors and fabrics.

Glasgow Centre for Contemporary Arts (CCA), 350 Sauchiehall Street, tel: 332 7521. www.cca.com. Sun–Thurs 11am–11pm, Fri–Sat 11am–midnight. Frequently changing contemporary exhibitions in spacious rooms. Also recherche bookshop and café.

CITY PARKS

Several of Glasgow's more than 70 public parks have interesting features.

Victoria Park lies to the west of the city and has a remarkable covered Fossil Grove (330 million-year-old tree stumps), which was discovered accidently in 1880 when a new path was under construction.

Rouken Glen Park is a magnificent country estate with a waterfall. Walk through the tropical **Butterfly Kingdom** and be surrounded by exotic butterflies and moths. Open daily at 10am from the end of March until the beginning of November (tel: 620 2084).

Botanic Gardens on Great Western Road opposite the Grosvenor Hotel. Open daily from 7am–dusk, tel: 334 2422. The glasshouses open around lunchtime and close 4.15pm in winter and 4.45pm in summer. The large glasshouse known as the Kibble Palace is the gardens' main attraction. It is well over 100 years old and contains a fine display of plants from temperate regions, interspersed with sculptures.

COUNTRY PARKS

Glasgow is fortunate in that not only is there a Country Park within the city boundaries but it is surrounded by a further 16 such parks. Some of these are:

Pollok Country Park (2060 Pollokshaws Road, Glasgow G43 1AT, tel: 632 9299) is home to the Burrell Collection, Pollok House with its art collection, a herd of Highland cattle and a police-dog training school. It has many attractive woodland and parkland walks, picnic areas and a "Walk about a bit" trail.

Balloch Castle Country Park (leave the B854 in Balloch at the southern tip of Loch Lomond, has beautifully landscaped grounds which offer excellent views of Loch Lomond. A history trail and a tree trail will appeal to those who require further stimulation.

Castle Semple Country Park (10 miles/16 km southwest of Paisley with access from the A760, tel: 01505 842882) has, as its main feature, a large shallow loch that is open throughout the whole year for sailing, windsurfing, rowing and canoeing. There is a bird observation centre and woodland walks. Fishing permits are available.

Chatelherault Country Park (1 mile southeast of Hamilton on the A72, tel: 01698 426213) surrounds a William Adam lodge and includes the wooded gorge of the River Avon, a site of Special Scientific Interest. The ancient Cadzow oak trees and the Cadzow herd of white cattle are both intriguing.

Culzean Country Park (12 miles/20 km southwest of Ayr) has as its main feature a magnificent Adam's Castle. In the grounds are a treetop walkway, an adventure playground, swan ponds, a deer park and formal gardens and woodlands. Superb views. Caravan/camping park available.

Eglinton Country Park (southeast of Kilwinning off the A78 and A737), has the ruined Eglinton Castle as its hub and offers formal gardens, woodland, river and loch walks.

Kelburn Country Centre on the A78 between Largs and Fairlie, tel: 01475 568685 www.kelburncoutrycentre.com. Open mid-Easter to mid-October daily 10am–6pm; remainder of year only the grounds are open from 11am–5pm. The castle is open only in May: tours commence at noon, with last tour at 4pm.

Muirshield Country Park (3 miles/5 km northwest of Lochwinnoch and reached from the B786, tel: 01505 842803) is a high valley with woodlands, rhododendrons and rough moorland. Features are a nature trail and scenic walks.

Strathclyde Country Park (between Hamilton and Motherwell with access from either the A725/M74 or the A723/M74 intersection: tel: 01698 266155) has a nature reserve. It is also a great place for sports enthusiasts, having an international rowing course, water sports centre, golf course, pitch and putt and a jogging trail. In addition, there is Strathclyde loch, woodlands and a nature trail and the Hamilton Mausoleum. Caravan/camping park available.

GREATER GLASGOW & BEYOND

Bachelors' Club, Sandgate, Tarbolton, tel: 01292 541424. Easter–October daily 10am–6pm, other times by appointment. Robert Burns helped found this club, which is now filled with Burns memorabilia while the lower rooms are set up as a typical cottage interior of his time.

Bannockburn Heritage Centre, off M80, 2 miles (3 km) south of Stirling, tel: 01786 812664. March–October 10am–6pm. Audio-visual presentation of events leading up to Battle of Bannockburn.

Bothwell Castle, situated near Uddingston Cross, tel: 01698 816894. April–September weekdays 9.30am–6.30. October–March daily (except Sunday) 9.30am–4.30pm; Sunday 2–4.30pm (closed Thursday afternoon and Friday in winter). Imposing red sandstone castle on the banks of Clyde, considered to be the best surviving 13th-century castle in Scotland.

Robert Burns National Heritage Park, Alloway, Ayr, tel: 01292 443700. June–August 9am–7pm; April–October 9am–6pm; November–March 9am–5pm. Birthplace of Robert Burns and leading museum of Burnsiana. Start of the Burns Heritage Trail.

Burns House Museum, Castle Street, Mauchline. Easter–October Monday–Saturday 11am–12.30pm and 2–5.30pm; Sunday 1.30–5.30pm. At other times enquire next door. Burns and family lived here. Also fascinating collection of Mauchline ware, for which the town was famous in the 19th century, and a display of curling memorabilia.

Cambuskenneth Abbey, Stirling. April–September, Monday–Saturday 9.30am–7pm; Sunday 2–7pm. This abbey was founded in the 12th century and used on occasions for meetings of the Scottish Parliament.

Cameronians Regimental Museum, Mote Hill, of Muir Street, Hamilton, tel: 01698 283981. Daily 10am–noon and 1–5pm except Wednesday pm. Memorabilia relating to the history of the regiment from 1689 to the present.

Coats Observatory, 49 Oakshaw Street West, Paisley, tel: 889 3151. Tuesday–Saturday 2–5pm; closed from 1–2pm; Sunday 2–5pm. Public viewing, October–March, Thursday 7–9.30pm. Two large working astronomical telescopes along with seismic and meteorological equipment. Access suitable for disabled.

Craignethan Castle, 5 miles (8 km) northwest of Lanark. A 15th-century castle with later additions illustrating outstanding examples of military fortification.

David Livingstone Centre, Blantyre, tel: 01698 823140. Approached by the M74 or A724 and about 8 miles (13 km) south of Glasgow. The home of Scotland's most celebrated explorer and missionary. Museum and visitor centre open Monday–Saturday 10am–6pm; Sunday open from 12.30pm.

David Marshall Lodge, off A81, one mile north of Aberfoyle. Mid-March–mid-October daily 10am–6pm. Visitor centre with magnificent views.

Denny's Ship Model Experimental Tank, Castle Street, Dumbarton, Monday–Friday 10am–4pm. The world's first commercial experimental tank.

Doune Castle, Doune, April–September, Monday–Saturday 9.30am–7pm, Sunday 2–7pm; October–March, Monday–Saturday 9.30am–4pm; Sunday 2–4pm. Splendid ruins of one of the best preserved medieval castles in Scotland.

Dumbarton Castle, Dumbarton,. April–September, Monday–Saturday 9.30am–7pm, Sunday 2–7pm; October–March, Monday–Saturday 9.30am–4pm, Sunday 2–4pm. It was from here that Queen Mary left for France in 1548, aged five years.

Dunblane Cathedral, Dunblane. April–September, Monday–Saturday 9.30am–7pm, Sunday 2–5pm; October–March, Monday–Saturday 9.30am–4pm, Sunday 2–4pm. 13th-century masterpiece of Scottish architecture.

Finlaystone Estate and Country Park, Langbank, tel: 01475 540505. Daily 9am–5pm. Country park with woodland walks and views of the River Clyde. House has doll collection.

Glasgow Zoo Park, Calderpark, Uddingston, tel: 771 1185. September–June 10am–5pm, July–August 10am–6pm. Wide range of animals and reptiles; paths suitable for wheelchairs.

Glengoyne Distillery, on the A81, beyond Strathblane, tel: 01360 550254. April–November 10.30am–3.15pm. Guided tours about every 30 minutes and the opportunity to sample a Highland malt.

Greenbank Gardens, south of city off the B767, tel: 639 3281. Attractive gardens open all year 9.30am–sunset.

Low Parks Museum, 19 Muir Street, Hamilton, tel: 01698 328232. Monday–Saturday 10am–5pm; Sunday 12–5pm. This museum in a 17th-century coaching inn is rich in local material.

Hamilton Mausoleum, 18th-century chapel renowned for its echo.

Hill House, Upper Colquhoun Street, Helensburgh. Originally a private house designed by Charles Rennie Mackintosh for the publisher Walter Blackie. Open all year, daily 1–5pm (last tour 4.30).

Inchmahome Priory, situated on the island in Lake of Menteith, 4 miles (6 km) east of Aberfoyle. Access from Port of Menteith. April–September, Monday–Saturday 9.30am–7pm; Sunday 2–7pm. Ruined priory where the infant Mary Queen of Scots sent for refuge in 1547.

Irvine Burns Club Museum, Wellwood Eglinton Street, Irvine, tel: 01294 2745. Daily 11. 2.30–5pm. Burnsiana, including letters from Tennyson, Dickens and Garibaldi.

McLean Museum & Art Gallery, 9 Union Street, Greenock, tel: 01457 715624 . Monday–Saturday 10am–noon and 1–5pm. Material relating to social, industrial and maritime history of Inverclyde District. Important collection of Scottish paintings.

New Lanark and the Falls of Clyde. Well signposted off the A74. Nature reserve is open all year. Village is open seven days a week 11am–5pm.

Newark Castle, Port Glasgow. April–September, Monday–Saturday 9.30am–7pm, Sunday 2–7pm; October–March, Monday–Saturday 9.30–4pm, Sunday 2–4pm. Standing on the River Clyde, the oldest part of this castle dates to the 15th century. It contains small collections of historical prints of Port Glasgow.

Paisley Abbey and Place of Paisley, tel: 889 7654. Monday–Friday 10am–12.30pm and 1.30–3pm, Saturday 10am–noon and 1.30–3pm. Birthplace of the Stewart dynasty.

Paisley Museum & Art Galleries, High Street, tel: 889 3151. Tuesday–Saturday 2–5pm; Closed from 1–2pm; Sunday 2–5pm. Superb collection of Paisley shawls.

Scottish Maritime Museum, Laird Forge, Gottries Road, Irvine, tel: 01294 2778283. March–mid-October 10am–4pm. Several local craft moored at pontoon may be visited

Skelmorlie Aisle, Largs. April–September Monday–Saturday 9.30am–7pm; Sunday 2–7pm. Magnificent renaissance mausoleum.

Sma' Shot Cottages, 11/17 George Place, Paisley. tel: 889 0530. May–September Wednesday & Saturday 12–4pm. Restored and furnished artisan's house of the Victorian era.

Smith Art Gallery and Museum, 40 Albert Place, Dumbarton Road, Stirling, tel: 01786 471917.

Wednesday, Thursday, Friday & Sunday 2–5pm; Saturday 10.30am–5pm. The story of Stirling from William Wallace to the present.
Souter Johnnie's Cottage, Main Street, Kirkoswald, tel: 01655 760603. Easter–September noon–5pm; other times by appointment. This thatched cottage displays Burns relics and life-size figures of Burns characters.
Stirling Castle, Visitor Centre, tel: 01786 450000. Open April–September, Monday–Saturday 9.30am–5.15pm, Sunday 10.30am–4.45pm. Castle and palace built on volcanic rock. The public can visit most of the buildings, lawns and gardens; the views are spectacular. The visitor centre is situated in the esplanade.
Summerlee Heritage Trust, West Canal Street, Coatbridge, tel: 01236 431261. Open daily 10am–5pm. Possibly the world's noisiest museum, with working steam cranes and locomotives and an operational tramway.
Thomas Coats Memorial Church, High Street, Paisley, tel: 889 9980. May–September, Monday, Wednesday, Friday 2–4pm. Other times by arrangement. One of Europe's most magnificent Baptist churches.
Wallace Monument, Causewayhead, nr. Stirling, tel: 01786 472140. February, March and October 10am–5pm; April and September 10am–6pm; May through August 10am–7pm. A monument to one of Scotland's national heroes; superb views.
Weaver's Cottage, Shuttle Street, Kilbarchan, tel: 01505 705588. April, May, September and October Tuesday, Thursday, Saturday, Sunday 2–5pm. June–August daily 2–5pm. A typical 18th-century weaver's home with working looms. Attractive garden.

Excursions

Scotguide Tourist Services, 153 Queen Street, tel: 204 0444. Tours of surrounding areas including Loch Lomond, Stirling, Ayr, etc.
Clyde Marine Motoring Company Ltd, Princes Pier, Greenock, tel: 01475 721281, www.clyde-marine.co.uk Pleasant cruises to various Clyde Coast resorts and islands during the summer season.
Waverley Excursions, Anderston Quay, tel: 221 8152. Cruises down the river and around the islands of the Firth of Clyde on "the last sea-going paddle steamer in the world".

Culture

CONCERTS

During the winter the Royal Scottish National Orchestra (RSNO) presents regular Saturday evening concerts and the BBC Scottish Symphony Orchestra presents Friday evening concerts. In the summer months the RSNO has a short Promenade season. For other concerts by numerous chamber music and choral groups see the daily press.

January kicks off the year with the annual Celtic Connections extravaganza. Jazz musicians flock to Glasgow in June for the annual Jazz Festival and August is the big blow when Glasgow hosts the World Pipe Band championships.
City Hall, Candleriggs, tel: 287 5024. A wide variety of entertainment is presented in this hall which has excellent acoustics.
Glasgow Royal Concert Hall, 2 Sauchiehall Street, tel: 353 8000, www.grch.com. The city's premier concert venue with seats for 2,500 people.
Henry Wood Hall, 73 Claremont Street, tel: 225 3555. Home of the RSNO.
Scottish Exhibition and Conference Centre, tel: 248 3000 (Information), 287 5024. The rather soulless SECC is injected with life when it hosts concerts by visiting rock bands.
Stevenson Hall, Royal Scottish Academy of Music and Drama, 100 Renfrew Street, tel: 332 5057. Venue for Friday night concerts by the BBC Scottish Symphony Orchestra and for many other delightful classical offerings.

DANCE

Scottish Ballet, 261 West Princes Street, tel: 331 2931, www.scottishballet.co.uk. A Glasgow-based touring company which performs regularly at the Theatre Royal and at their Robin Anderson auditorium in West Princes Street.

OPERA

Scottish Opera, 39 Elmbank Crescent, tel: 248 4567, www.scottishopera.org.uk. For performance information, contact the Theatre Royal box office, tel: 332 9000. Scottish Opera is in residence at the Theatre Royal from September to June. Strong company with magnificent stage sets and a large and varied repertoire.

THEATRES

Atheneum Theatre, 100 Renfrew Street, tel: 332 5057. Beautiful theatre in the Royal Scottish Academy of Music and Drama.
Citizens' Theatre, 119 Gorbals Street, tel: 429 0022 (box office), www.citz.co.uk (online booking). Repertory company internationally renowned for its adventurous productions.
King's Theatre, Bath Street, tel: 227 5511 (box office) , www.kings-glasgow.co.uk. Light drama, music events and amateur shows are shown in this comfortable old theatre.
Mitchell Theatre, Granville Street, tel: 227 5511. This well-designed theatre, a part of the Mitchell Library, mounts concerts and amateur shows.
Pavilion Theatre, Renfield Street, tel: 332 1846 (box office), www.paviliontheatre.co.uk (online booking facility). Somewhat old-fashioned commercial theatre favoured by comedians. Variety shows and the occasional concert.
Theatre Royal, Hope Street, tel: 332 9000 (box office). This beautifully furnished theatre is the

home of Scottish Opera and is used by major visiting theatre and ballet companies.

Glasgow Centre for Contemporary Arts (CCA), 350 Sauchiehall Street, tel: 332 0522 (box office), www.cca-glasgow.com. Small studio theatre which can be slightly claustrophobic. Enjoyable productions by touring companies.

Tramway Theatre, Albert Drive, tel: 227 5511 (box office), www.tramway.org. A cavernous theatre suitable for epic productions.

Tron Theatre, 63 Trongate, tel: 552 4267 (box office), www.tron.co.uk. The place to see new Scottish works; very lively atmosphere and popular bar.

CINEMAS

MGM Filmcentre, Sauchiehall Street, tel: 332 1592. Five screens showing the latest commercial releases.

Glasgow Film Theatre, 12 Rose Street, tel: 332 8128, www.gft.org.uk. Two screens. This specialises in foreign language and minority films but does not turn up its nose at quality new releases.

Grosvenor, Ashton Lane, tel: 339 4298, www.caledoniancinemas.co.uk/cinemas/glasgow.phtml. Two screens in West End. Late-night screenings.

Odeon, Renfield Street, tel: 332 3413. Recent popular releases on six screens.

Nightlife

Musical Venues

MUSICAL PUBS & BARS

Certain pubs have a tradition of live music, often at the weekends.

Blackfriars, 36 Bell Street, tel: 552 5924. Regular venue for jazz, blues and folk with a Comedy Club on Sunday night.

Curlers, 256 Byres Road, tel: 338 6511. Emphasis on pub fun in this student haunt. DJs on Wednesday, Friday and Saturday and live bands on a Tuesday.

Grand Ole Opry, 2 Govan Road, nr. Paisley Road Toll, tel: 429 5396. Live country music nightly and the drinks are cheap. Suitable for the whole family, but to get a table be there by 7.30pm.

Halt Bar, 160 Woodlands Road, tel: 332 1210. Horseshoe-shaped bar with traditional pub feel. Rock, folk or jazz most nights.

Jinty McGuinty's, 23–29 Asgton lane, tel: 339 0747. Irish groups such as the Pogues played here.

Solid Rock Café, 19 Hope Street, Tel: 221 1105. Hard rock and heavy metal all played at the regulation maximum volume.

Nice 'N' Sleazy, 421 Sauchiehall Street, tel: 333 9637. A popular night spot, regularly playing host to many up-and-coming bands.

King Tuts Wah Wah Hut, 272 St Vincent Street, tel: 221 5279. Renowned establishment, which puts on performances most nights of the week.

Nightclubs

Glasgow has always enjoyed a thriving club scene. Over the years there have been many hotspots, some of which have achieved truly legendary status amongst a ceaseless throng of club enthusiasts who have many a night danced away their cares in a crowded, sweaty environment.

The scene in Glasgow caters for almost every taste from dance music to indie. For up-to-date information, check *The List*, which has a comprehensive guide to club life in both Glasgow and Edinburgh.

Bennets, 90 Glassford Street, tel: 552 5761. Mainly gay. The Shimmy Club on Tuesdays is its straight night, which has an enthusiastic following.

Fury Murrys, 96 Maxwell Street, tel: 221 6511. Wide range of music but favours rock.

The Tunnel, 84 Mitchell Street, tel: 204 1000. Considered to be one of the top 10 clubs in the country, this stylish spot caters for the young, trendy and energetic. Favours dance music.

The Garage, 490 Sauchiehall Street, tel: 332 1120. Inexpensive popular student hang out, live gigs and dancing in three areas including the Attic and G2.

The Arches, Midland Street (off Jamaica Street), tel: 221 9736. A serious nightspot for the committed club goer, this huge converted warehouse provides hypnotic dance beats till the early hours of the morning.

The Shack, 193 Pitt Street, tel: 332 7322. Cheapest nightclub in Glasgow, big comfortable sofas and popular with students.

Gambling

The law requires that you become a member of a casino about 48 hours before you play. Membership is free. Men are expected to wear a jacket and tie.

Stanley Casino Club, 508 Sauchiehall Street, tel: 332 0992.

Ladbroke Casino, 95 Hope Street, tel: 226 3856.

Ladbroke Riverboat Casino, 61 Broomielaw, tel: 226 6000.

Princes Casino, 528 Sauchiehall Street, tel: 332 8171.

Shopping

Where to Shop

Start in the Golden Z, Glasgow's main shopping area comprising of Sauchiehall Street, Buchanan Street and Argyll Street. The latest shopping mall is the huge Buchanan Galleries on the junction of Sauchiehall Street and Buchanan Street. However, for those more interested in fleamarket than upmarket, continue along Argyll Street and then Gallowgate or London Road from the Cross to Glasgow's famous Barras, crammed full of bargains and counterfeits.

The Italian Centre, behind the City Chambers on George Square, has the latest in designer fashion, while Princess Square in Buchanan Street is a small, compact, mall with a grand diversity of shops. Great Western Road, from St George's Cross to the Botanic Gardens is full of quirky shops selling crafts, ethnic goods and food, and just off it, in Otago Lane, are two of the best second-hand bookshops in Glasgow.

As in any other city, the shopping scene is fluid, with new stores opening and old ones closing on an almost daily basis. Those listed below were in existence as we went to press but that's no guarantee that they're still there today. If your plan is just to wander, that's no problem, but if you intend making a special visit to any of these shops, a phone call beforehand, just to make sure that they still exist, may save a wasted journey. However, this being Glasgow, even if the shop you seek has gone you'll more than likely find something equally interesting in its place or nearby.

SCOTCH WHISKY SHOPS

The Whisky Shop, Unit 12, Princes Square Buchanan Street, tel: 226 8446.
The Whisky Shop, Buchanan Galleries, 220 Buchanan Street, tel: 331 0022.

HIGHLAND DRESS AND TARTAN

Douglas Alexander Tailoring Ltd, 60 St. Enoch Square, tel: 204 0038.
Kintail Bagpipes, 113 Barrack Street, tel: 553 0902.
Gilt Edged Highlandwear, 67–73 Saltmarket, tel: 552 1534.
Discount Highland Supplies Ltd, 18 Glebe Street, tel: 552 1252.
Keogh & Savage Kilt Makers, 984 Shettleston Road, tel: 778 2308.
Geoffrey (Tailor) Highland Crafts Ltd, 309 Sauchiehall Street, tel: 331 2388.
Gaelic Themes, 14 Park Circus, tel: 332 0407.
Highland Exchange, 60 St. Enoch Square, tel: 204 0039.
Macgregor & Macduff, 41 Bath Street, tel: 332 0299.

OUTDOOR PURSUITS

Sports Warehouse, Unit 1 66 New City Road, tel: 353 7455.
Blacks Outdoor Leisure Ltd, 28–40 Union Street, tel: 221 2295.
Camping & Hiking, 1016 Argyle Street, tel: 564 1326.
Graham Tiso Glasgow Outdoor Experience, Couper Street, tel: 559 5450.
Graham Tiso, 129 Buchanan Street, tel: 248 4877.
Rohan Designs, 118 Union Street, tel: 204 0775.

SCOTTISH KNITWEAR

Thistle Knitwear, Unit 79/80 Savoy Centre, Sauchiehall Street, tel: 332 1456.
TR Hand Knitters, 6 Armadale Place, tel: 575 4888.
James Pringle Weavers of Inverness, 130 Buchanan Street, tel: 221 3434.
The Edinburgh Woollen Mill, 52–54 Busby Road Clarkston, tel: 638 6699.
Jumper, Unit 32 Princes Square, Buchanan Street, tel: 248 5775.

JEWELLERY

Cairn Celtic & Charles Rennie Mackintosh Watches & Clocks, PO Box 985 Newton Mearns, tel: 639 7090.
James Porter & Son, 31 Argyll Arcade, tel: 221 7385.
Diamond Design, 11 Argyll Arcade, tel: 248 3555.
Harold Barclay Ltd, 3 Argyll Arcade, tel: 248 4087.
Goldsmiths, Buchanan Galleries, Buchanan Street, tel: 332 3033.
Fraser Hart, 60 Argyll Arcade, tel: 221 7537.
Ethos, 107 Essex Drive, tel: 954 9000.
S & S Jewellery, De Courcey's Arcade, Cresswell Lane, tel: 337 1717.
Harkins Thomas, 11 Byres Road, tel: 339 0409.
Laing The Jeweller Ltd, 46–48 Argyll Arcade, tel: 221 7199.
Orro Contemporary Jewellery, 49 Bank Street, tel: 357 6999.

ANTIQUES

Antichita, 5 Abbot Street, tel: 632 5665.
Finnie Antiques, 103 Niddrie Road, tel: 423 8515.
Yester-Year, 14 Kildrostan Street, tel: 423 0099.
Stuart Myler, 93 West Regent Street, tel: 353 2013.
Victoria Antiques, 350 Pollokshaws Road, tel: 423 7216.
Saratoga Trunk, Top Floor 93, West Regent Street, tel: 331 2707.
Circa, 37 Ruthven Lane, tel: 581 3307.
Antique City, 2b Fernleigh Road, tel: 637 1836.
Kittoch Antiques, 336 Crow Road Partick, tel: 339 7318.

Antiques Centre, 188 Woodlands Road, tel: 332 5757.
R Rutherford, Victorian Village, 93 West Regent Street, tel: 332 9808.
All Our Yesterdays, 6 Park Road.
Butlers Furniture Galleries, 191 Scotland Street, tel: 429 8808.
The Antiques Warehouse, Unit 3b Yorkhill Quay Estate, tel: 334 4924.
Mr Ben Vintage Clothing, Unit 6 Kings Court, Kings Street, tel: 553 1936.

GIFT AND CRAFT SHOPS

Spirito, 195 Crow Road, Broomhill, tel: 337 3307.
Alba Dhearg, 1148 Argyle Street, tel: 400 5439.
Truly Gifted, 74 Glasgow Road, tel: 01360 770551.
Orientique, 106a Byres Road, tel: 357 5375.
Mumbo Jumbo Designs, 8 Cresswell Lane, tel: 334 8002.
Knots & Crosses, 171 Hyndland Road, tel: 339 6575.
Inscape Ltd, 141 Great Western Road, Street. Georges Cross, tel: 332 6125.
Eurasia Crafts, 528 Great Western Road, tel: 339 3933.
Highland Trading, Unit 55 St Enoch Centre, St Enoch Square, tel: 248 1506.
Little Niceties, 998 Pollokshaws Road, tel: 636 6663.
Lucky White Heather, 90 Dumbarton Road, Partick, tel: 342 4411.
Gumps, 181 Byres Road, tel: 576 0025.
Rococo, 399 Great Western Road, tel: 339 3437.
The Scottish Craft Centre, 3 The Courtyard, Princes Square, Buchanan Street, tel: 248 2885.

BOOK SHOPS

Waterstone's Booksellers, 153–157 Sauchiehall Street, tel: 332 9105, and 174–176 Argyle Street, tel: 248 4814.
Borders Books & Music, 98 Buchanan Street, tel: 222 7700.
Bookworld, St Enoch Centre, St Enoch Square, tel: 204 2301.
John Smith & Son, 50 Couper Street, tel: 559 5450.
Ottakar's, Buchanan Galleries, 220 Buchanan Street, tel: 353 1500.
Bargain Books, 74 Sauchiehall Street, tel: 332 7170.
W. H. Smith, 53–55 Argyle Street, tel: 204 0636, and 177 Sauchiehall Street, tel: 331 2833.

Secondhand and Antiquarian Books

Voltaire & Rousseau, 18 Otago Lane, tel: 339 1811.
Cooper Hay Rare Books, 182 Bath Street, tel: 333 1992.
Caledonia Books, 483 Great Western Road, tel: 334 9663.
Oxfam Secondhand Bookshop, 171 Byres Road, tel: 334 7669.
Gilmorehill Books, 43 Bank Street, tel: 339 7504.
Thistle Books, 61 Otago Street, tel: 334 8777.

Shopping Hours

High street shops are open 9am–5.30pm Monday to Saturday and until 7 or 8pm on a Thursday. Smaller shops may not open until 10am, closing at 6pm or later. Some of the bigger bookshops will stay open until 10pm during the week and are open on Sunday afternoons. There is a growing trend for shops in the centre to open on Sundays and most of the large out-of-town shopping centres are open seven days. Several small general stores, particularly in the West End, are open on a Sunday and there are a few that open 24 hours.

The majority of off-licences in the city are open and will sell alcohol on a Sunday.

Complaints

Contact the Consumer Advice Centre at Nye Bevan House, 20 India Street, tel: 287 6681, or the Citizens Advice Bureau at 5 Dalrymple Court, Townhead, tel: 578 0160.

Sport

Participant Sports

FACILITIES

Glasgow and its surrounding towns have many council-run sports facilities. These include swimming pools, tennis courts, bowling greens, croquet courts, boating ponds, putting greens, pitch and putt courses and golf courses, all of which are open to the public at very reasonable rates. These, apart from swimming pools, are found in public parks, which are open from 8am–dusk. Best of these parks, in terms of facilities, are:
Alexandra Park, 10 Sannox Gardens G31 3JE, tel: 554 4887
Bellahouston Park, 16 Dumbreck Road G41 5BW, tel: 427 0558
Botanic Gardens, 730 Great Western Road G12 0UE, tel: 334 2422
Carscadden Knightswood Park, 81A Chaplet Avenue G13 3XW, tel: 959 3514
Glasgow Green, Greendyke Street G1 5DB, tel: 552 1142
Househill Park, Barrhead Road G53 7DA, tel: 881 2547
Mugdock Country Park, Mugdock Country Park G62 8EL, tel: 956 610
Pollok Country Park, 2060 Pollokshaws Road G43 1AT, tel: 632 9299
Queens Park 520, Langside Road G42 9QL, tel: 649 0331

SPORTS CENTRES & COMPLEXES

Allander Sports Complex, Milngavie Road Bearsden G61 3DF, tel: 942 2233. Swimming pool, squash, badminton and snooker.

Bellahouston Sports Centre, Bellahouston Drive G52 1HH, tel: 287 5454. Squash, gymnasium, indoor tennis and badminton. Non-members cannot book in advance.
Kelvin Hall International Sports Arena, Argyle Street, G3 8AW, tel: 357 2525. Badminton, tennis, athletics and weights.
Pollok Leisure Centre, Pollok Leisure Centre G53 6EW, tel: 881 3313. Family leisure pool.
Scotstoun Leisure Centre, 72 Danes Drive G14 9HD, tel: 959 4000. Magnificent sports multiplex with indoor and outdoor pitches and a ten-lane pool.

GOLF COURSES

There are no shortage of golf courses in Glasgow and the surrounding countryside, ranging in price and standard from small municipal clubs to the exclusive championship courses.
Alexandra Golf Club, Alexandra Parade, G31, tel: 556 1294
Bearsden Golf Club, Thorn Road, G61, tel: 942 2351
Bonnyton Golf Club, Kirktonmoor Road, Eaglesham G76 0QA, tel: 01355 302781.
Cathkin Braes Golf Club, Cathkin Road, Rutherglen G73 4SE, tel: 634 4007. Non members Monday to Friday only.
Glasgow Golf Club, Killermont, G61, tel: 942 2011
Haggs Castle Golf Club, 70 Dumbreck Road G41 4SN, tel: 427 0480. Part of Pollock Park and close to the Burrell.
Linn Park Golf Club, Simshill Road G44 5EP, tel: 633 0377
Littlehill Golf Club, Auchinairn Road, G64, tel: 772 1916
Pollok Golf Club, 90 Barrhead Road G43 1BG, tel: 632 4351. Wooded parkland course near the Burrel Collection still operating a sexist men-only policy.
Sandyhills Golf Club, 223 Sandyhills Road, G32, tel: 763 1099. The top out-of-town courses are:
Prestwick Golf Club, 2 Links Road, Prestwick KA9 1QG, tel: 01292 477404. www.prestwickgc.co.uk. The birthplace of the Open Championship in 1860 and a must-play for visiting enthusiasts.
Royal Troon, Craigend Road, Troon, South Ayrshire KA10 6EP, tel: 01292 311555. No visitors on Wednesdays, Fridays or at the weekend. Only those with a letter of introduction, a handicap certificate of under 20 and who have booked in advance have a chance of playing on this Open Championship course.
Turnberry Hotel Golf Courses, Turnberry Hotel, Ayrshire, tel: 01655 331000, www.turnberry.co.uk. The world's first hotel and golf complex boasting two of the finest courses in Scotland.

Other Sports

Dumbreck Riding School, 82 Dumbreck Road G41 4SN, tel: 427 0660
Linn Park Equestrian Centre, Linn Park, Simshill Road G44 5EN, tel: 637 3096
Easterton Riding School & Livery, Easterton Stables, Mugdock Milngavie G62 8LG, tel: 956 1518
Busby Equitation Centre, Wester Farm, Westerton Avenue, Clarkston G76 8JU, tel: 644 1347
The East Kilbride Ice Rink, The Olympia Shopping Centre, Town Centre, East Kilbride G74 1PG, tel: 01355 244065
Kenmure Riding School, Kenmure farm, Kenmure Road, Bishopbriggs, tel: 772 3041

Spectator Sports

FOOTBALL

Glasgow is the Brazil of the north, being absolutely "fitba' mad". Celtic and Rangers are undoubtedly Scotland's most famous teams and both have their grounds within Glasgow. **Celtic FC**, www.celticfc.co.uk/, Celtic Park, 95 Kerrydale Street (tel: 551 4362). **Rangers FC**, www.rangers.co.uk, Ibrox Stadium, Edmiston Drive (tel: 427 8500).

Hampden Park, G42 9AY, is the national stadium and home to the Scottish Football Association, www.scottishfa.co.uk/, tel: 616 6100 and the Scottish Football Museum can be reached at www.scottishfootballmuseum.org.uk, or 616 6000

ATHLETICS

Kelvin Hall International Sports Arena, Argyle Street, G3 8AW, tel: 357 2525. Occasional track meets.

GREYHOUND RACING

Shawfield Stadium, Rutherglen Road, G73 1SZ, tel: 647 4121. Racing every Monday, Tuesday, Thursday, Friday and Saturday at 7.45pm.

RUGBY

Several local teams have grounds around the city: Balgray (Kelvinside Academicals), Great Western Road G12; Old Anniesland (Glasgow High School), Crow Road G11; and Garscadden (Glasgow University), Garscadden Road South G15.

Further Reading

Non-Fiction

Berry & White *Glasgow Observed* (John Donald 1981).
Blair, Anna *Tea at Miss Cranston's: A Century of Glasgow memories.*
Burrow, A *Shipbuilding History 1750–1932* (Alexander Stephen 1932).
Corrance & Boyd *Glasgow* (Collins 1981).
Cunnison, J & Gilfillan, J.B.S. (eds.) *The Third Statistical Account of Scotland: Glasgow* (Collins 1958).
Daiches, David *Glasgow* (Granada 1982).
Gallaghar, Tom *Glasgow, The Uneasy Peace* (Manchester University Press 1987).
Gibb, Andrew *The Making of a City* (Croom Helm 1983).
Glasgow Herald Book of Glasgow (Mainstream Publishing, 1990).
Gomme, Andor & Walker, David *Architecture of Glasgow* (Lund Humphries 1987).
House, Jack *Heart of Glasgow* (Richard Drew 1987).
Lindsay, Maurice *Portrait of Glasgow* (Robert Hale 1972).
McDowall, John *The People's History of Glasgow* (S.R.Publishers 1970).
McLellan, Duncan *Glasgow Public Parks* (John Smith 1894).
Muir, Edwin *Scottish Journey* (Mainstream 1975).
Munro, Michael *The Patter* (Glasgow District Libraries 1985).
Worsdall, Frank *The City that Disappeared: Glasgow's Demolished Architecture* (Richard Drew 1981).
Stamp, Gavin *Alexander "Greek" Thomson* (Laurence King Publishing 1999)
Worsdall, Frank *The Tenement: A Way of Life* (Chambers 1979).
Worsdall, Frank *Victorian City* (Richard Drew 1982).

Fiction

Anderson, Freddy *Oiney Hoy* (1987)
Banks, Ian *Espedair Street* (Fortuna 1988).
Barke, James *The Land of the Leal* (1939, 1987 Canongate).
Bell, J.J. *Wee McGreegor* (1902, 1978 Panther paperback).
Berman, Chaim Ickyk *The Second Mrs Whitberg* (Allen and Unwin 1976).
Blake, George *The Shipbuilders* (1935, 1986 Magna Print).
Bridie, James (Osborne, Henry Mavor) *The Anatomist* (1930 Constable).
Byrne, John *The Slab Boys* (1978, 1987 Penguin).
Byrne, John *Tutti Frutti* (1987 BBC).
Carswell, Catherine *Open the Door* (1920, 1986 Virago).
Davis, Margaret Thomson *The Breadmakers Trilogy* (Allison and Busby 1972).
Gray, Alasdair *Lanark* (Edinburgh: Canongate 1981, 2000).
Hanley, Clifford *Dancing in the Streets* (Mainstream 1983).
Hanley, Clifford *Glasgow: A Celebration* (Mainstream 1984).
Hind, Archie *The Dear Green Place* (Polygon 1984).
Kelman, James *the Bus Conductor Hines* (1984 Polygon).
Kelman, James *A Disaffection* (Secker and Warburg 1989).
McCrone, Guy Fulton *Wax Fruit Trilogy* (Constable 1947).
McGinn, Matt *Fry the Little Fishes* (1975 J Calder).
McIlvanney, William *Laidlaw* (Hodder and Stoughton, 1977).
Munro, Hugh *The Clydesiders* (1961).
Munro, Neil *Para Handy and other Tales* (Wm. Blackwood, 1980).
Osborne, Brian D. and Armstrong, Ronald (eds) *Mungo's City, A Glasgow Anthology* (Birlinn 1999)
Pryde, Helen W. *The first book of the McFlannels* (1947).
Sharp, Alan *A Green Tree in Geddie* (1965 Richard Drew).

Poetry

Anderson, Freddy *At Glasgow Cross* (1987).
Cocker, W.D. *Poems, Scots and English* (1932, 1980 Browns, Son and Ferguson).
Leonard, Tom *Six Glasgow Poems* (1969).
Lochhead, Liz *Dreaming Frankenstein* (1984 Polygon).
McGinn, Matt *Scottish Songs of Today* (1964).
Morgan, Edwin *From Glasgow to Saturn* (1973).
Mulrine, Stephen *Poems* (1971).
Whyte, Hamish (Ed) *Noise and Smoky Breath, An illustrated Anthology of Glasgow Poems 1900–1983* (Third Eye Centre 1983).

Other Insight Guides

Among the 190 **Insight Guides**, the following cover the British Isles: *Great Britain, England, Wales, Scotland, Edinburgh, London, Oxford, Ireland and Dublin.*

Insight Compact Guides

A companion series of 130 titles provides encyclopaedic information in a highly portable form, with text, pictures and maps all carefully cross-referenced for easy on-the-spot use. More than two dozen titles cover every major tourist destination in the UK. Titles include: *Scotland, Scottish Highlands, Edinburgh*, and *Glasgow.*

Insight Pocket Guides

These provide carefully timed itineraries and personal recommendations from a local host to help you make the best use of limited time in a destination. Each contains a full-size, fold-out map. Destinations include *Scotland, London, Southeast England* and *Ireland.*

Insight Fleximaps

These combine clear, detailed cartography with essential information about a destination, and a laminated finish makes the maps durable and easy to fold.

ART & PHOTO CREDITS

Annan Collection 45, 49
Matthew Ashton/Empics 72
British Museum 28
Marcus Brooke front flap bottom, spine centre, back cover right & centre, 2B, 4BL/R, 5BL, 156, 184, 206, 207, 209, 214, 215, 232/233, 234, 235, 236, 237, 238, 239L/R, 240, 242, 244, 245, 246, 247, 248
Douglas Corrance front flap top, back cover top & bottom, back flap top & bottom, 1, 2/3, 4/5, 6/7, 8/9, 10/11, 12/13, 14, 16, 17, 18L/R, 19, 22, 23, 24, 35, 46, 50, 51, 52, 53, 56/57, 58, 60, 62, 63, 64, 65, 66, 68, 70, 76/77, 76, 78, 79, 80, 82, 83, 85, 86, 87, 88, 89, 91, 94/95, 96/97, 98/99, 104, 105, 108, 109L, 110L/R, 111, 113L/R, 114, 115, 116L/R, 118/119, 120, 121, 123, 124, 126, 129, 132/133, 134, 135, 137, 140, 141, 142, 143L/R, 144, 145, 146, 147L/R, 148, 149, 150/151, 152, 153, 157, 159, 160/161, 162, 163, 165, 166, 167, 168, 169, 170, 171, 172, 173, 174, 175, 176R, 177, 178, 179, 180/181, 182, 183, 186, 187, 188, 189L/R, 190/191, 192, 193, 197, 198/199, 200, 202, 203, 204, 205, 208, 208, 210/211, 212, 213, 217, 218, 219, 220/221, 223, 224, 225, 226, 227, 228, 229, 230, 231, 241, 250, 251, 252L/R, 253, 254, 255, 256
Ken Currie/Raab Galleries 81, 84
Adam Daly/Empics 71
Jerry Dennis/APA 61, 67, 69, 109R, 117, 122, 125, 127, 128L/R, 130, 131, 138L/R, 139, 158, 176, 196, 201, 216
Edinburgh University Library 25
Glasgow Libraries 20/21, 42, 43
Glasgow Museums & Art Galleries 36, 41, 48L
Guildhall Art Gallery, London 32
Hulton Archive 90, 92
Hunterian Art Gallery 47
Imperial War Museum 54/55
Michael Jenner spine top, 5BR
Catherine Karnow back cover left
People's Palace Museum 38, 39, 48R
Secker & Warburg, The Random House Group 93
Towneley Hall Art Gallery, Burnley 31
Bill Wassman/APA 100, 243

Map Production Phoenix Mapping

Editorial Director **Brian Bell**
Cartographic Editor **Zoë Goodwin**
Picture Research
Hilary Genin, Britta Jaschinski

Index

Numbers in italics refer to photographs

a

b

c

d

e

f

t

u

v

w–z